MAURICE D. WEIR, an associate professor of mathematics at the Naval Postgraduate School in Monterey, California, is the author of another Spectrum Book titled *Calculator Clout*. He received his Doctor of Arts from Carnegie-Mellon University.

ANTELL, D. W.I., and behaviour aspects of pollination in the ...... and provides critical ... sanitary conditions ... the future ... borer and ... on their ... the TVCTL report ... the ... borer in new ... and ... economic importance.

MAURICE D. WEIR

CALCULUS BY CALCULATOR

Solving Single-Variable Calculus Problems
with the Programmable Calculator

A SPECTRUM BOOK

Prentice-Hall, Inc., Englewood Cliffs, New Jersey 07632

Library of Congress Cataloging in Publication Data

Weir, Maurice D.
  Calculus by calculator.

  (A Spectrum Book)
  Includes index.
    1. Calculus—Data processing. 2. Programmable calcu-
lators. I. Title. II. Series.
QA303.W398   515'.028'54   81-23505
ISBN 0-13-111930-3   AACR2
ISBN 0-13-111922-2 (pbk.)

This Spectrum Book is available to businesses and organizations at a special discount when ordered in large quantities. For information, contact Prentice-Hall, Inc., General Publishing Division, Special Sales, Englewood Cliffs, N. J. 07632.

10 9 8 7 6 5 4 3 2 1

Some of the material and figures in this book have been adapted from *Calculator Clout: Programming Methods for Your Programmable* by Maurice D. Weir. © 1981 by Prentice-Hall, Inc. Published by Prentice-Hall, Inc., Englewood Cliffs, New Jersey 07632.

Editorial/production supervision by Frank Moorman
Cover design by Jeannette Jacobs
Manufacturing buyer: Barbara A. Frick

ISBN 0-13-111930-3

ISBN 0-13-111922-2 {PBK.}

Prentice-Hall International, Inc., *London*
Prentice-Hall of Australia Pty. Limited, *Sydney*
Prentice-Hall Canada, Inc., *Toronto*
Prentice-Hall of India Private Limited, *New Delhi*
Prentice-Hall of Japan, Inc., *Tokyo*
Prentice-Hall of Southeast Asia Pte. Ltd., *Singapore*
Whitehall Books Limited, *Wellington, New Zealand*

Contents

3

Differentiation, 139

4

Integration, 200

5

Differential Equations, 264

6

Infinite Series, 293

Preface

This is a different kind of calculus book. Nevertheless, it presents nearly all the traditional first-year calculus concepts. It also presents a number of ideas and techniques that are not ordinarily covered in a beginning calculus study. What is unique about this book is its use of the handheld programmable calculator and its emphasis on numerical methods to develop the fundamental ideas and methodologies inherent in calculus. Teachers and textbook authors have previously seen that calculators can be used as an aid to solving certain kinds of calculus problems, but what might have been overlooked is the full extent to which a powerful programmable calculator can be employed to do virtually all the computational aspects of the calculus. This book has been written to exploit the calculator as a new tool for developing the methods and ideas of calculus.

Specifically, this book develops and presents the standard methods and problem-solving techniques of single-variable calculus using specially prepared programs that are permanently recorded on magnetic cards for the Texas Instruments TI–59 programmable calculator. The program listings are given in the Appendix and are to be keyed in and then recorded on your own personal calculator. Since all the programs are prewritten, only a very slight familiarity with TI–59 programming is demanded on your part, all of which is thoroughly exemplified in this book. So we do not assume by any means that you are an expert programmer. The only requirement is that you have a very basic keyboard familiarity with your TI–59.

The motivation for writing this book was to make calculus accessible even to individuals who have very limited mathematical experience. The advantage of using a programmable calculator is that it frees you from the burden of carrying out tedious numerical calculations. Now you can explore the results of those calculations, what they mean, and how they can be used to solve practical problems. You are no longer restricted by the necessity to solve problems with involved arithmetic and algebraic requirements. Rather, you can routinely treat realistic problems that might be nontrivial because of their arithmetic or algebraic substance. While mastery of algebraic methods is virtually eliminated as a prerequisite to your learning calculus, you will have the opportunity to improve gradually and master even those skills as you go along.

There is another reason for writing this book. Modern mathematics education requires calculator and computer literacy. Calculators and microcomputers recently have become very inexpensive, and they are beginning to permeate modern American society. You see them everywhere: in business and industry, in government, in the university, and now even in the home. In the real world most practical problems are being solved with the aid of some kind of computing device. You can take advantage of this and prepare yourself mathematically for the demands of a computer-oriented society. The advantage is that a powerful calculator like the TI-59 is affordable and can be used as an instrument to aid greatly in the learning of traditional college level mathematics. The challenge is to make sure you relegate the calculator to its proper role; the goal is not to make a mere "button pusher" out of you. Rather, it is to employ the calculator for what it is designed to do; namely, to carry out tedious calculations and thereby free you to think about how the calculations are applied and what might be inferred from them. Of course, you do not want to neglect the assumptions and methods supporting those calculations.

There are side benefits too. You begin to see that there are both analytic and numeric attacks on the same kind of problem and that each approach may have its advantages or disadvantages. Furthermore, you can make subtle changes in the parameters entered into a problem and discover the effects on the results produced. With pencil-and-paper problem-solving techniques, such experimentation, or tuning, is quite impossible except for trivial problems. On the other hand, tuning is very illuminating when investigating a particular concept or technique.

The book begins with a chapter on elementary analytic geometry and the study of polynomials. These subjects are the natural extensions of your high school algebra and geometry courses; moreover, they contain the seeds for many of the ideas and techniques considered in calculus. The next chapter is a further extension to the general idea of a function and the various types that are commonly encountered in real world applications. The emphasis is on graphing functions so that you begin to understand their behaviour geometrically, by visualizing them. Later you see how certain computations made in calculus reveal various aspects of that behavior. The idea of the limit of a function is then introduced, an idea which most students of calculus find difficult to grasp on their first exposure. You will have the opportunity to explore the limit process numerically, which circumvents the more abstract nature of a formal treatment. Preliminaries aside, subsequent chapters deal with the core of elementary calculus: the derivative, the definite integral, and their numerous applications to science, engineering, and, to a lesser extent, business. The final chapters treat the important topics of differential equations and infinite series.

Finding numerical answers is an important part of applying mathematics, and our emphasis throughout is on problem solving and applications. Our style of presentation is to begin with a discussion of an idea or method of the calculus in an appropriate context and then obtain results supported by that discussion using a prewritten calculator program. Complete instructions on how to use the program are given, followed by numerous examples illustrating its use. Often the numerical examples point the way toward new speculations or considerations that demand attention. So in this text examples are presented as organic parts of calculus, not as appendages or afterthoughts. Each section of the text is accompanied by numerous exercises, some of which are routine to give practice in using the programs, while others stress applications of the numerical methods.

This book is designed to stand by itself in treating the topics discussed. For that reason we do include the important analytical or theoretical ideas that simply cannot be ignored. Even though some ideas do not lend themselves to calculator methods, they support others that do and serve to put the latter into a context that gives substance to the overall point of view. Thus this book can be used as a calculus textbook for engineers, for natural and social scientists, or for persons in the business and management disciplines. It is organized in such a way as to be compatible with many existing popular calculus texts, so it can also be used as a supplementary text in traditional calculus courses to provide insight into the numerical aspects of the calculus. This book is also suitable for high school students interested in mathematics and computers and as a self-study manual in a continuing education course for mathematics teachers, engineers, scientists, social scientists, or persons in more general disciplines, including business and management.

This book is one of several calculator books being published in the Spectrum Books series of Prentice-Hall, Inc. The first book, *Calculator Clout* (written by the author), presents methods and techniques for programming your TI–59 programmable calculator. Two other books, *Probability by Calculator* and *Statistics by Calculator* are written by my colleagues Peter W. Zehna and Donald R. Barr. Those books present the ideas and methods of probability and statistics using the TI–59 in the same way that is exploited here.

I wish to thank my colleagues and students at the Naval Postgraduate School for their encouragement in the preparation of this book. Special thanks go to Joseph M. Barron, Robert E. Gaskell, Richard W. Hamming, and Herbert D. Peckham, who all got me interested in programmable calculators. Finally, I thank John Hunger, Editor of Spectrum Books, for his interest in pursuing this project.

Maurice D. Weir
Monterey, California

To Gale, Maia, and Renée

1

Coordinates, Lines, and Polynomial Functions

Calculus is the study of change and motion. Certain kinds of problems have motivated the development of calculus. For instance, one such concern is finding the velocity and acceleration of a body at any particular moment as it travels along a path in time. Another is finding the tangent to a given curve since the direction of motion of a moving body at any point of its path is the direction of the tangent to the path. A third problem is determining the largest and smallest values of some variable quantity, such as the maximum height a projectile will attain when fired from the ground or the selling price that will maximize a manufacturer's profit. Other problems involve ascertaining such quantities as the length of the path traced out by a moving body during some fixed period of time, the area bounded by plane curves, the volume bounded by surfaces, the force of water pressure on a dam, or the work done in stretching a spring or lifting a weight. All these problems illustrate the many applications of calculus to science, engineering, and business. Calculus is used also to model problems in biology, medicine, and economic and social behavior. Indeed, the methods of calculus are essential to understanding the dynamic forces that change our world.

Much of the nature of the physical world is revealed to us—that is, we seem to experience the world—geometrically. Yet the methods of geometry, as developed by the ancient Greeks and as we still study them today in high school, are diverse and specialized, and they do not yield to general applicability. Rather it is algebra that provides the method and process leading to generalization. By combining geometric ideas with algebraic and quantitative methods, we bring together the intuitive and rational aspects of our thought process, thereby generating a powerful new tool for the study of physical reality. The application of algebra to geometry, called *analytic geometry,* was originally created by Pierre de Fermat and René Descartes in the early seventeenth century. Their contribution and insight in associating algebraic equations with geometric curves and surfaces then paved the way for the new methodology of calculus developed by Sir Isaac Newton and Gottfried Wilhelm Leibniz in the latter half of that century.

In this chapter we cover the elements of analytic geometry that are "musts" for any serious study of calculus. Even as the concepts of analytic geometry are developed, the basic ideas of calculus germinate and become apparent. Moreover, we are incorporating another dimension to aid us in our investigations: the electronic programmable calculator. Through the use of the Texas Instruments TI-59 programmable calculator, with its capability of permanently recording programs on magnetic cards, we avoid the burden of carrying out tedious numerical calculations. Thus we are freed to concentrate our efforts on the methods of calculus and of analytic geometry, as well as on their applications to solving interesting and important problems for which the methodology is intended. This capability is a significant leap forward in learning and applying these new tools. Indeed, the ideas of calculus become more transparent. And calculus problems that used to be difficult, if not impossible, to solve without the aid of a calculator can now be handled with routine ease.

Before you begin your study of this chapter, record the four programs LINES, QUADS, POLYPROBE, and POLYROOT, which are listed in the Appendix A at the back of this book, on separate magnetic cards. (For instructions on recording magnetic cards see the TI-59 owner's manual *Personal Programming* or Section 10.1 of the author's book, *Calculator Clout: Methods of Programmable Calculators* published by Prentice-Hall, 1981.) These programs will be used throughout this chapter, and instructions for their usage will be given as we progress. All the programs use standard 479.59 partitioning.

When you finish recording the magnetic cards, you are ready to commence your study of the material in this chapter.

Section 1.1 Coordinates, Distance, and Line Segments

Remember the standard coordinate system that you studied in beginning algebra? One way to locate points in the plane is to draw a horizontal x-axis intersecting at right angles with a vertical y-axis. The point of intersection is called the *origin* of this *rectangular coordinate system.* A unit of length is selected, and positive directions are assigned to the coordinate axes: A number on the horizontal x-axis is positive if it is to the right of the origin; a number on the vertical y-axis is positive if it is above the origin. The negative directions are then to the left and downward. The units +1 and −1 are marked on the coordinate axes according to the previously selected unit of length and positive/negative directions.

Given a point P in the plane, an ordered pair of numbers can be assigned to P in the following way. Through P first draw a vertical line that perpendicularly intersects the x-axis at the place marked a. Then draw a horizontal line through P perpendicular to the y-axis and intersecting it at b. The ordered number pair (a,b) is then associated with the point P, as shown in Figure 1.1. The number a is called the *x-coordinate* of P, and the number b its *y-coordinate*. Notice that the x-coordinate is listed first, and the y-coordinate second, in writing the pair (a,b). That is what we mean when we say it is an *ordered* pair: The two pairs (a,b) and (b,a) refer to different points unless $a = b$.

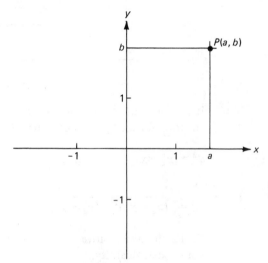

Figure 1.1 The vertical line through $x = a$ and the horizontal line through $y = b$ intersect at the point $P(a,b)$.

EXERCISE 1.
DISTANCE BETWEEN TWO POINTS
IN THE PLANE

Let $P_1(x_1,y_1)$ and $P_2(x_2,y_2)$ denote two points in the plane. To find the distance between P_1 and P_2 we use the point $Q(x_2,y_1)$ so that P_1QP_2 form a right triangle as shown in Figure 1.2. We can apply the Theorem of Pythagoras, which says that *the square of the hypotenuse of a right triangle equals the sum of the squares of the lengths of its other two sides.* For right triangle P_1QP_2, we then have

$$(P_1P_2)^2 = (P_1Q)^2 + (QP_2)^2$$

Since P_1 and Q lie on the same horizontal line,

$$(P_1Q)^2 = (x_2 - x_1)^2 = (x_1 - x_2)^2$$

Similarly, P_2 and Q lie on the same vertical line giving

$$(QP_2)^2 = (y_2 - y_1)^2 = (y_1 - y_2)^2$$

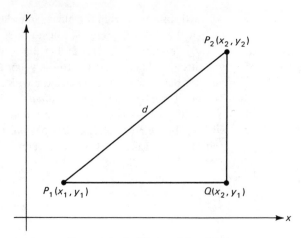

Figure 1.2 P_1QP_2 is a right triangle.

If d represents the distance between P_1 and P_2, then substitution into the equation for the Pythagorean Theorem gives

$$d^2 = (x_2 - x_1)^2 + (y_2 - y_1)^2$$

or

$$d = \sqrt{(x_2 - x_1)^2 + (y_2 - y_1)^2} \qquad (1.1)$$

Notice that the positive square root is taken for d because distance is always a nonnegative quantity.

Equation 1.1 is programmed on the magnetic card called LINES. To use the program to calculate the distance between two specified points in the plane, carry out the following procedures.

Calculating the Distance Between Two Points in the Plane

Step 1: Read side 1 of the magnetic card LINES into your TI-59. LINES uses standard partitioning 479.59.

Step 2: Enter x_1 into the T-register: Enter the value of x_1 and press $\boxed{x \blacktriangleleft t}$.

Step 3: Enter y_1 into the display and press $\boxed{A}$.

Step 4: Enter x_2 into the T-register, and then enter y_2 into the display. Press $\boxed{D}$ and the program will stop with the distance between (x_1, y_1) and (x_2, y_2) showing in the display.

Illustrations 1. Given the points $(3,1)$ and $(-7,4)$ with LINES read into your calculator, perform the following keystroke sequence:

$\boxed{3}\ \boxed{x \blacktriangleleft t}\ \boxed{1}\ \boxed{A}\ \boxed{7}\ \boxed{+/-}\ \boxed{x \blacktriangleleft t}\ \boxed{4}\ \boxed{D}$

4   and $d = 10.4403$ rounded to four decimals shows in the display.

2. Using the points $(-5.7,\pi)$ and $(\sqrt{2},13)$:

$\boxed{5.7}\ \boxed{+/-}\ \boxed{x \updownarrow t}\ \boxed{\pi}\ \boxed{A}\ \boxed{2}\ \boxed{\sqrt{x}}\ \boxed{x \updownarrow t}\ \boxed{13}\ \boxed{D}$

and $d = 12.1573$ rounded to four places is in the display.

EXERCISE 2.
MIDPOINT OF A LINE SEGMENT
IN THE PLANE

Let $P_1(x_1,y_1)$ and $P_2(x_2,y_2)$ denote two points in the plane. Then the mid-point of the line segment joining P_1 and P_2 has coordinates

$$\left(\frac{x_1 + x_2}{2}, \frac{y_1 + y_2}{2} \right) \tag{1.2}$$

The midpoint formula is calculated in LINES.

Calculating the Midpoint on the Line Segment Joining Two Points
Step 1: Enter x_1 into the T-register: Enter the value of x_1 and press $\boxed{x \updownarrow t}$.
Step 2: Enter y_1 into the display and press $\boxed{A}$.
Step 3: Enter x_2 into the T-register, and then enter y_2 into the display. Press $\boxed{C}$ and the program will stop with the x-coordinate of the mid-point in the display.
Step 4: Press $\boxed{x \updownarrow t}$ to display the y-coordinate of the midpoint.

Illustrations 1. Given the points $(3,1)$ and $(-7,4)$ with LINES read into your calculator, perform the following keystroke sequence:

$\boxed{3}\ \boxed{x \updownarrow t}\ \boxed{1}\ \boxed{A}\ \boxed{7}\ \boxed{+/-}\ \boxed{x \updownarrow t}\ \boxed{4}\ \boxed{C}$

The display shows the x-coordinate $= -2$ of the midpoint. Press $\boxed{x \updownarrow t}$ for the y-coordinate $= 2.5$.

2. Using the points $(-\pi,\sqrt{2})$ and $(11.9,\frac{5}{3})$:

$\boxed{\pi}\ \boxed{+/-}\ \boxed{x \updownarrow t}\ \boxed{2}\ \boxed{\sqrt{x}}\ \boxed{A}\ \boxed{11.9}\ \boxed{x \updownarrow t}\ \boxed{5}\ \boxed{\div}\ \boxed{3}\ \boxed{=}\ \boxed{C}$

The x-coordinate $= 4.379$ and the y-coordinate $= 1.540$, rounded to three decimal places.

EXERCISE 3.
SLOPE OF A LINE SEGMENT IN THE PLANE

Let $P_1(x_1,y_1)$ and $P_2(x_2,y_2)$ denote two points in the plane. Suppose you think of a particle starting at the point $P_1(x_1,y_1)$ and traversing the line segment joining this to the point $P_2(x_2,y_2)$. We would like to have some measure of the steepness of the climb (or fall) from P_1 to P_2. When the particle reaches P_2 its coordinates have changed by increments Δx (read *delta x*) and Δy (read *delta y*). That is,

$$\Delta x = x_2 - x_1 \qquad \text{the change in x}$$

and

$$\Delta y = y_2 - y_1 \qquad \text{the change in y}$$

The *slope* of the line segment joining P_1 and P_2 is defined as the vertical change Δy divided by the horizontal change Δx, provided there is a nonzero horizontal change (because division by zero is never permitted). In symbols, if the slope is denoted by m,

$$m = \frac{\text{Rise}}{\text{Run}} = \frac{\Delta y}{\Delta x} = \frac{y_2 - y_1}{x_2 - x_1} \qquad \Delta x = x_2 - x_1 \neq 0 \tag{1.3}$$

The definition of slope is such that the slope of a line segment is positive whenever the segment rises upward and to the right (as in Figure 1.3); the slope is negative whenever the line segment falls downward toward the right (Figure 1.4). A *horizontal* line has slope $m = 0$ because the rise Δy is zero in that case. A *vertical* line segment, where $\Delta x = 0$, is not assigned any slope; that is, m is undefined for vertical lines.

The slope of the line segment joining two specified points $P_1(x_1,y_1)$ and $P_2(x_2,y_2)$ in the plane is calculated in LINES.

Figure 1.3   The slope of the line segment P_1P_2 is the ratio $\Delta y/\Delta x$.

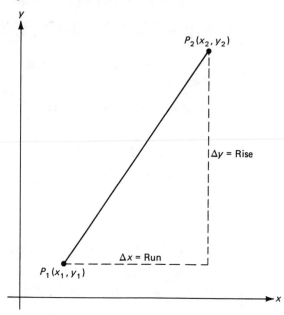

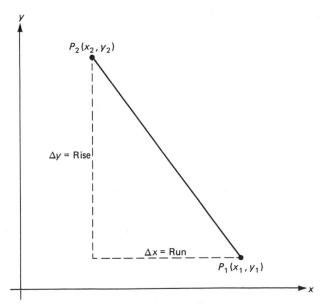

Figure 1.4   A line segment with negative slope.

Calculating the Slope of the Line Segment Joining Two Points

Step 1: Enter x_1 into the T-register.

Step 2: Enter y_1 into the display and press $\boxed{A}$.

Step 3: Enter x_2 into the T-register and y_2 in the display. Press $\boxed{E}$ and
the program will stop with the slope m in the display. If the line segment is vertical, then m is shown in the display as 9.9999999×10^{99}
signifying no slope.

Illustrations   1. Given the points $(-4,6)$ and $(12,-2)$ with LINES read into your calculator,
perform the following keystroke sequence:

The display shows $m = -0.5$ as the slope.

2. Given the points $(-3,1)$ and $(7.5,\pi)$:

$$\boxed{3}\ \boxed{+/-}\ \boxed{x \updownarrow t}\ \boxed{1}\ \boxed{A}\ \boxed{7.5}\ \boxed{x \updownarrow t}\ \boxed{\pi}\ \boxed{E}$$

The display shows $m = 0.204$ rounded to three decimal places.

3. Given the points $(-3,1)$ and $(17,1)$: The display shows $m = 0$, a horizontal
line segment.

4. Given the points $(-3,1)$ and $(-3,-5)$: The display shows $m = 9.9999999$
$\times 10^{99}$, a vertical line segment having no assigned slope.

The idea of slope is a central concept of calculus, and we will return to it
many times during the course of this book.

7

1. Draw a set of coordinate axes and use your calculator to help you plot the following points in the plane. Use one decimal place accuracy.

a. $(\sqrt{3}, \frac{12}{7})$

b. $(-4, \frac{1+\sqrt{5}}{2})$

c. $(\pi^{1/3}, -\sqrt{2})$

d. $(-\frac{1}{\pi}, -\frac{17}{6})$

e. $(1 - \pi^2, \sqrt{\pi - 1})$

f. $(2.27\pi, \frac{-3 - 2\sqrt{5}}{2})$

2. Find the distance between the following pairs of points, correct to three decimal places.

a. $(-3, -5)$ and $(4, -\frac{1}{2})$

b. $(\sqrt{3}, \frac{1}{17})$ and $(-6, \pi^2)$

c. $(-\frac{1}{\pi}, \sqrt[3]{2})$ and $(\frac{13}{5}, 2.78\pi)$

d. $(\frac{1+\sqrt{5}}{2}, -4)$ and $(\sqrt{\pi^2 - 1}, \frac{\sqrt{13}}{2})$

e. $(\frac{2 - 3\sqrt{7}}{\pi}, -5^{1/3})$ and $(\frac{2 + 3\sqrt{7}}{\pi}, 3^{1/5})$

f. $(1 - \pi^{-2}, 2.03^3)$ and $(-\frac{2.6}{0.17\pi}, 0.13^6)$

3. Show that the triangle with vertices $(-1, \sqrt{3}), (\frac{3}{2}, \frac{7\sqrt{3}}{2})$, and $(4, \sqrt{3})$ is equilateral.

4. Find the coordinates of the midpoint of the line segment joining the pairs of points in Problem 2, correct to two decimal places.

5. Find the slope of the line segment joining the following pairs of points, correct to three decimal places.

a. $(2, -1)$ and $(-4, -7)$

b. $(-\frac{1}{2}, \frac{1}{3})$ and $(\frac{3}{5}, -\frac{6}{7})$

c. $(\sqrt{3}, 0.17)$ and $(-2.1, \pi)$

d. $(\frac{3 - 2\sqrt{5}}{7}, -\frac{1}{\pi})$ and $(\sqrt{2}, \pi^4)$

e. $(1 - \frac{\sqrt{2}}{7}, 2 + \frac{\sqrt{7}}{3})$ and $(-\sqrt[3]{5}, \frac{151}{\sqrt{7}})$

f. $(\sqrt{\pi} - 2.6, 1.73)$ and $(-2.79, \frac{1}{7.39 - \sqrt{\pi^2 - 1}})$

6. Use slopes to determine whether the following points lie along a common straight line.

$$A(0,\sqrt{2}), \quad B(\pi\sqrt{2},0), \quad C(\pi,\sqrt{2}-1), \quad D(\sqrt{\pi},\frac{-1+\sqrt{2\pi}}{\sqrt{\pi}})$$

7. The *angle of inclination* of a line that crosses the x-axis is the smallest positive angle that the line makes with the positively directed x-axis (Figure 1.5). The slope of a nonvertical line segment and its associated angle ϕ of inclination are related by the equation

$$\phi = \tan^{-1} m$$

Find the angle of inclination in degrees-minutes-seconds for the line segment joining the following pairs of points.

    a. $(2,-1)$ and $(-4,-7)$
    b. $(1,2)$ and $(3,8)$
    c. $(1-\frac{\sqrt{2}}{7}, 2+\frac{\sqrt{7}}{3})$ and $(-\sqrt[3]{5}, \frac{151}{\sqrt{7}})$

Section 1.2 Straight Lines

A straight line in the plane is characterized by the property that any pair of distinct points on the line will give exactly the same slope, unless the slope is undefined (that is, unless the line is vertical).

    Let us symbolize a line with given slope m by L. We would like to find an equation expressing the relationship between the coordinates x and y whenever the point (x,y) lies on L. Because the line L has a slope, it cannot be vertical and therefore must cross the y-axis at some value $y = b$. We call the number b the y-*intercept* of the line L (Figure 1.6). By the characterization of a straight line, we then know that the slope of L must satisfy

$$m = \frac{y-b}{x-0} \quad \text{or} \quad y = mx + b$$

Figure 1.5   Angle of inclination of a nonvertical line.

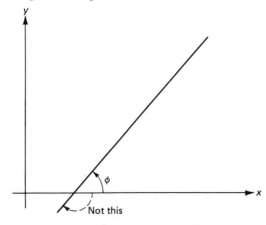

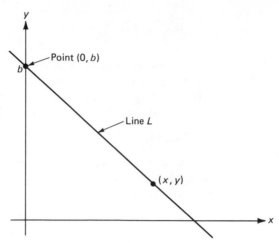

Figure 1.6   Line *L* crosses the *y*-axis with *y*-intercept equal to *b*.

because both points $(0,b)$ and (x,y) lie on *L*. The equation

$$y = mx + b \qquad (1.4)$$

is called the *slope-intercept* form for the equation of a nonvertical straight line. The points in the plane that lie on the line *L* are only the points (x,y) whose coordinates satisfy the Equation 1.4.

If the straight line is vertical, and hence has no assigned slope, it crosses the *x*-axis at some value $x = a$. An equation for this vertical line is

$$x = a \qquad (1.5)$$

Notice that all points of the form (a,y), for any value of *y* whatsoever, satisfy Equation 1.5.

In working with straight lines, the program LINES always uses the slope-intercept form.

EXERCISE 1.
EQUATION OF A LINE
GIVEN TWO OF ITS POINTS

One of the axioms of geometry is that two points uniquely determine a straight line. Suppose the two points are given by (x_1,y_1) and (x_2,y_2). Then the slope of the line is given by

$$m = \frac{y_2 - y_1}{x_2 - x_1} \qquad x_2 \neq x_1$$

(We assume the line is nonvertical.) If (x,y) is any arbitrary point on the line, it is also true that

$$m = \frac{y - y_1}{x - x_1}$$

Equating the right-hand sides of these two equations gives

$$\frac{y - y_1}{x - x_1} = \frac{y_2 - y_1}{x_2 - x_1} \tag{1.6}$$

Equation 1.6 is called the *two-point* form for the equation of a straight line (Figure 1.7). With some algebraic manipulation it can be simplified easily to the slope-intercept form (1.4). The program LINES performs the required calculations.

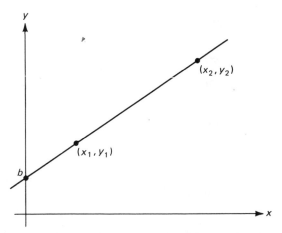

Figure 1.7 A line L is determined by any two points that lie on it.

Calculating the Slope-Intercept Equation Given Two Points on the Line

With LINES read into your TI-59, perform

Step 1: Enter x_1 into the T-register and y_1 into the display; press $\boxed{A}$.

Step 2: Enter x_2 into the T-register and y_2 into the display; press $\boxed{E}$. The program halts with the slope m of the line in the display. If m is undefined, so the line is vertical, the display will read 9.9999999 $\times 10^{99}$.

Step 3: Press $\boxed{x \rlap{\raise1pt{\scriptstyle\blacktriangle}}{} t}$ to display the y-intercept b.

To obtain any other desired point (r,s) lying on the given line carry out

Step 4: Enter the x-coordinate r into the display and press $\boxed{E'}$. The program will halt with the corresponding y-coordinate s in the display. You may repeat this step as often as you like to obtain additional points on the line. It is not necessary to repeat Steps 1–3.

Illustration   Given the points (2,−5) and (−4,19), find the slope m and the y-intercept b for the straight line determined by these points. Using LINES, perform the following keystrokes:

| 2 | $x{\leftrightarrow}t$ | 5 | +/− | A | 4 | +/− | $x{\leftrightarrow}t$ | 19 | E | ($m = -4$)

| $x{\leftrightarrow}t$ | ($b = 3$)

The slope-intercept equation for the line is $y = -4x + 3$. To obtain the value of y when $x = 27.5$,

(enter)   27.5

(press) | E' | The display shows $y = -107$.

To obtain the value of y when $x = -\sqrt{2}$,

(enter) $-\sqrt{2}$

(press) | E' | The display shows $y = 8.66$ rounded to two decimals.

EXERCISE 2.
EQUATION OF A LINE
GIVEN A POINT AND THE SLOPE

If (x_1, y_1) is a point on the nonvertical line L with slope m, then any arbitrary point (x, y) lying on L must satisfy the equation

$$m = \frac{y - y_1}{x - x_1}$$

or, simplifying algebraically,

$$y - y_1 = m(x - x_1) \qquad (1.7)$$

Equation 1.7 is the *point-slope* form equation for a straight line. It can be written in the form $y = mx + b$ by taking $b = y_1 - mx_1$. LINES performs the required calculation.

Calculating the Slope-Intercept Equation Given a Point and the Slope

With LINES read into your TI-59, perform:

Step 1: Enter x_1 into the T-register and y_1 into the display; press | A | .

Step 2: Enter m into the display and press | B | . The program halts with the y-intercept b in the display.

Step 3: To obtain other points (r, s) lying on the line: Enter the x-coordinate r into the display and press | E' | . The program halts with the corresponding y-coordinate s in the display. Repeat this step as often as desired for additional points.

12

Illustration   Given the point $(-9, \frac{1}{2})$ and the slope $m = \frac{3}{2}$, find the y-intercept b for the straight line they determine. Using LINES, perform the following keystrokes:

$\boxed{9}$ $\boxed{+/-}$ $\boxed{x \updownarrow t}$ $\boxed{2}$ $\boxed{1/x}$ $\boxed{A}$ $\boxed{1.5}$ $\boxed{B}$ $(b = 14)$

The slope-intercept equation for the line is $y = 1.5x + 14$. To obtain the y-value when $x = \frac{13}{17}$:

(enter) $\frac{13}{17}$

(press) $\boxed{E'}$ The display shows $y = 15.147$ rounded to three decimals.

EXERCISE 3.
PERPENDICULAR LINES

Two nonvertical lines L_1 and L_2 in the plane are perpendicular to each other if and only if their slopes are negative reciprocals of one another:

L_1 is perpendicular to L_2 if and only if $m_2 = -\dfrac{1}{m_1}$

Let's find the slope-intercept equation of the line L that is perpendicular to the line passing through the two points $(-3,-4.5)$ and $(12,8)$, such that the point $(5,1)$ lies on L. For what value of y is the point $(-\frac{29}{8}, y)$ on L?

Solution. First, using LINES, we determine the slope of the line to which L is perpendicular:

$\boxed{3}$ $\boxed{+/-}$ $\boxed{x \updownarrow t}$ $\boxed{4.5}$ $\boxed{+/-}$ $\boxed{A}$ $\boxed{12}$ $\boxed{x \updownarrow t}$ $\boxed{8}$ $\boxed{E}$ $(m_1 \approx 0.8333)$

We store the negative reciprocal in data register 59:

$\boxed{1/x}$ $\boxed{+/-}$ $\boxed{STO}$ $\boxed{59}$ $(m_2 = -1.2$, the slope of $L)$

Next we find the y-intercept of the line L we seek:

$\boxed{5}$ $\boxed{x \updownarrow t}$ $\boxed{1}$ $\boxed{A}$ $\boxed{RCL}$ $\boxed{59}$ $\boxed{B}$ $(b = 7)$

The slope-intercept equation for L is then $y = -1.2x + 7$, and we can obtain the value of y when $x = -\frac{29}{8}$ as follows:

(enter) $-\frac{29}{8}$

13   (press) $\boxed{E'}$ The display shows $y = 11.35$.

EXERCISE 4.
PARALLEL LINES

Two nonvertical lines L_1 and L_2 in the plane are parallel if and only if their slopes are equal:

L_1 is parallel to L_2 if and only if $m_1 = m_2$

Let us find the slope-intercept equation of the line L that is parallel to the line passing through the two points $(-1,2.7)$ and $(3.87,-4.118)$ and such that the point $(1,-7.01)$ lies on L. For what value of y is the point $(\frac{25}{14},y)$ on L?

Solution. First we find the slope of the line to which L is parallel:

$$\boxed{1}\ \boxed{+/-}\ \boxed{x\text{↨}t}\ \boxed{2.7}\ \boxed{A}\ \boxed{3.87}\ \boxed{x\text{↨}t}\ \boxed{4.118}\ \boxed{+/-}\ \boxed{E}$$

$$(m_1 = -1.4)$$

We store this value in data register 59 since it is the same slope as that of the parallel line L we seek:

$$\boxed{STO}\ \boxed{59}$$

Next, we find the y-intercept of the line L:

$$\boxed{1}\ \boxed{x\text{↨}t}\ \boxed{7.01}\ \boxed{+/-}\ \boxed{A}\ \boxed{RCL}\ \boxed{59}\ \boxed{B}\qquad (b = -5.61)$$

The slope-intercept equation for the parallel line L is $y = -1.4x - 5.61$, and we obtain the value for y when $x = \frac{25}{14}$ as follows:

(enter) $\qquad \frac{25}{14}$

(press) $\qquad\qquad\qquad \boxed{E'}\qquad$ The display shows $y = -8.11$.

PROBLEMS 1.2

In each of the following Problems 1-10, find an equation for the line determined by the given pair of points. Use two decimal place accuracy for the slope m and the y-intercept b.

1. $(-2,1)$, $(2,-2)$
2. $(-2,-3)$, $(4,-1)$
3. $(5.1,7.3)$, $(6.9,-1)$
4. $(\pi,-\sqrt{2})$, $(\frac{1}{2},\frac{2}{7})$
5. $(\frac{3}{8},-\frac{2}{3})$, $(\frac{1}{\pi},\frac{3}{\sqrt{2}})$

6. $(0, \sqrt[3]{2})$, $(-1.3, \sqrt{\pi})$

7. $(\dfrac{3 - 2\sqrt{5}}{7}, -\dfrac{1}{\pi})$, $(\sqrt{2}, \pi^4)$

8. $(1 - \dfrac{\sqrt{2}}{7}, 2 + \dfrac{\sqrt{7}}{3})$, $(\sqrt{\pi^2 - 1}, \dfrac{\sqrt{13}}{2})$

9. $(1 - \pi^{-2}, 2.07^3)$, $(-\dfrac{2.6}{0.17\pi}, 5.91)$

10. $(\dfrac{1 + \sqrt{5}}{2}, \dfrac{1 - \sqrt{5}}{2})$, $(\dfrac{1}{\pi}, -\pi)$

In each of the following Problems 11-14, find the y-intercept for the line with given slope m and passing through the specified point. Use two decimal place accuracy.

11. $m = -1$, $P(2, 5)$

12. $m = \sqrt{2}$, $P(-1, \pi)$

13. $m = -\dfrac{1}{\pi}$, $P(\sqrt{3}, -\dfrac{1}{\sqrt{2}})$

14. $m = \dfrac{2}{7}$, $P(-\dfrac{1}{6}, \dfrac{13}{7})$

In Problems 15-18, solve algebraically the given equations for y in terms of x to find the slope m and the y-intercept b for the lines they represent. Use your TI-59 to do the arithmetic, and carry out your answers to two decimal places.

15. $3x - 5y + 15 = 0$

16. $14y + 1.7x = 21$

17. $9x = 16y - 13$

18. $\sqrt{2}x + \pi y = \dfrac{3}{7}$

19. The endpoints of a line segment are $(-3, 1)$ and $(7, -4)$. Find the slope-intercept equation of the line through the midpoint of the line segment and perpendicular to it. This is the *perpendicular bisector.*

20. Find the slope-intercept equation of the line through the point $(2, 5)$ and parallel to the line $4x - 7y + 12 = 0$. Use two decimal place accuracy.

21. Find the slope-intercept equation representing the altitude of the isosceles triangle with vertices $A(5, \sqrt{5})$, $B(5, \sqrt{5} - 2)$, $C(7, \sqrt{5})$. Use two decimal place accuracy and make a sketch.

22. The *x-intercept* of a nonhorizontal line is the number $x = a$ where the line crosses the x-axis. Find the x-intercept of the following lines correct to two decimal places.

a. $y = -3x + 5$ b. $y = \sqrt{2}x + 1.7$

c. $2x - 3y = \sqrt{3}$ d. $y = -4.61x + 30.82$

e. $x - y = 0$ f. $14x = -\sqrt{3}y$

23. Show that the points $A(-4, -3)$, $B(8, 2)$, $C(11, 6)$, and $D(-1, 1)$ are the vertices of a parallelogram.

Section 1.3 Intersections of Lines and Least Squares Approximation

In this section we will use LINES to solve two different problems. The first problem is to find the coordinates of the point of intersection of two given lines, if it exists. The second problem is to determine the line that best approximates a given collection of points $P_1, P_2, \ldots, P_n$ in the plane.

EXERCISE 1.
INTERSECTION OF TWO NONVERTICAL LINES

Suppose that L_1 and L_2 are two nonvertical lines. Then each can be represented in slope-intercept form:

Line L_1: $y = m_1 x + b_1$ (1.7)

Line L_2: $y = m_2 x + b_2$ (1.8)

If the two lines are not parallel or coincident, then they intersect at a unique point in the plane (Figure 1.8). The program LINES calculates the coordinates of this point of intersection.

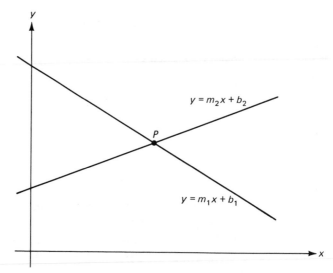

Figure 1.8   Distinct nonparallel lines intersect in a unique point P in the plane.

Calculating the Point of Intersection

Step 1: Enter m_1 into the T-register and b_1 into the display; press $\boxed{A}$.

Step 2: Enter m_2 into the T-register and b_2 into the display; press $\boxed{C'}$.
The program halts with the x-coordinate of the point of intersection in the display.

Step 3: Press $\boxed{x \updownarrow t}$ to display the y-coordinate of the point of intersection.

If the two lines are parallel or coincident, there is no unique point of intersection: The display will read 9.9999999×10^{99} for the x-coordinate, and the T-register will contain 0 for the y-coordinate.

Illustrations   1. To find the point of intersection of the two lines

$$y = 4x + 8.5 \quad \text{and} \quad y = -7x - 4.7$$

perform the following keystrokes using LINES:

| 4 | $x \leftrightarrow t$ | 8.5 | A | 7 | +/− | $x \leftrightarrow t$ | 4.7 | +/− | C′ | $(x = -1.2)$
| $x \leftrightarrow t$ | $(y = 3.7)$

Thus the point of intersection is $(-1.2, 3.7)$.

2. Find the point of intersection of the line L_1 passing through the two points $(5, -3)$ and $(7, -1)$, and the line L_2 with slope -6 and passing through the point $(-1, \frac{3}{2})$.

   Solution. First, we find the slope m_1 and the y-intercept b_1 of the line L_1. We store m_1 in data register 56 and b_1 in 57:

| 5 | $x \leftrightarrow t$ | 3 | +/− | A | 7 | $x \leftrightarrow t$ | 1 | +/− | E | STO | 56 |
| $x \leftrightarrow t$ | STO | 57 |

Next we find b_2 and store it in register 58:

| 1 | +/− | $x \leftrightarrow t$ | 1.5 | A | 6 | +/− | B | STO | 58 |

Using $m_2 = -6$ and the stored data, we finally find the point of intersection:

| RCL | 56 | $x \leftrightarrow t$ | RCL | 57 | A | 6 | +/− | $x \leftrightarrow t$ |
| RCL | 58 | C′ |

The display shows $x = 0.5$. Press $x \leftrightarrow t$ for $y = -7.5$.

3. Find the point of intersection of the line $y = -6x + 1$ and the line L passing through the two points $(5, -27)$ and $(1.2, -4.2)$.

   Solution. First, we find the slope m and the y-intercept b of the line L.

| 5 | $x \leftrightarrow t$ | 27 | +/− | A | 1.2 | $x \leftrightarrow t$ | 4.2 | +/− | E |

Note that $m = -6$ so that L is parallel to the line $y = -6x + 1$: There is no point of intersection. Continuing as if we had not observed this fact, we proceed to calculate the point of intersection. Since we need m in the T-

17

register and b in the display, we begin by exchanging the contents of the display and T-register to perform Step 1, followed by Step 2:

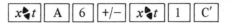

The display reads 9.9999999×10^{99} and no point of intersection exists.

EXERCISE 2.
DISTANCE FROM A POINT TO A LINE

The distance from a given point $P(x_1, y_1)$ to a specified nonvertical line L ($y = mx + b$) is defined to be the length d of the line segment PQ, such that Q lies on the line L and PQ is perpendicular to L (Figure 1.9). The program LINES calculates this distance.

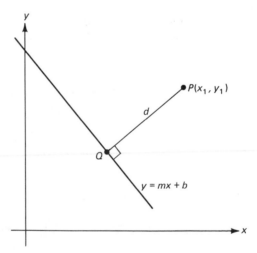

Figure 1.9 The distance d from a point P to a
given line L is the length PQ.

Calculating the Distance from a Point to a Nonvertical Line

Step 1: If the line is given in slope-intercept form, $y = mx + b$, enter m and press ⟨STO⟩ ⟨0⟩ ⟨5⟩ ; then enter b and press ⟨STO⟩ ⟨0⟩ ⟨6⟩ . Then perform Step 4.

Step 2: If the line is specified by giving two of its points, enter the x-coordinate of the first point into the T-register and the y-coordinate into the display; press ⟨A⟩ . Then enter the x-coordinate of the second point into the T-register and the y-coordinate into the display; press ⟨E⟩ . Then perform Step 4.

Step 3: If the line is specified by giving its slope and a point on the line, enter the x-coordinate of the point in the T-register and the y-coordinate into the display; press ⟨A⟩ . Then enter the slope m into the display and press ⟨B⟩ . Then perform Step 4.

Step 4: Enter the x-coordinate of the point $P(x_1, y_1)$ into the T-register and the y-coordinate into the display; press $\boxed{D'}$. The program halts with the distance d from the point P to the line L displayed.

Illustrations   **1.** Find the distance from the point $(3,-6)$ to the line $2x - 3y - 12 = 0$.

Solution. Write the equation in slope-intercept form: $y = \frac{2}{3}x - 4$. Next store the slope $m = \frac{2}{3}$ in data register 05 and the y-intercept $b = -4$ in data register 06:

(enter)	$\frac{2}{3}$	
(press)		$\boxed{STO}\ \boxed{05}$
(enter)	-4	
(press)		$\boxed{STO}\ \boxed{06}$

Then carry out Step 4:

(enter)	3	
(press)	$\boxed{x \blacktriangleleft t}$	Load the x-coordinate into the T-register.
(enter)	-6	Load the y-coordinate into the display.
(press)	$\boxed{D'}$	Calculate the distance.

The display shows $d = 3.328$ rounded to three decimals.

2. Find the distance from the point $(1,-7)$ to the line with slope $m = \frac{7}{5}$ that passes through the point $(4, \frac{14}{5})$.

Solution. First we enter the data for the line into LINES for conversion to slope-intercept form:

(enter)	4	
(press)	$\boxed{x \blacktriangleleft t}$	x-coordinate of point on line.
(enter)	$\frac{14}{5}$	y-coordinate of point on line.
(press)	$\boxed{A}$	
(enter)	$\frac{7}{5}$	Slope of line.
(press)	$\boxed{B}$	Convert to slope-intercept form.

The correct slope of the line is now stored in register 05, and the y-intercept is stored in register 06. Next we enter the coordinates of the data point and calculate the distance as stated in Step 4:

(enter)   1

(press) $\boxed{x \blacklozenge t}$ Load the x-coordinate into the T-register.

(enter)   −7   Load the y-coordinate into the display.

(press) $\boxed{D'}$ Calculate the distance.

The display shows $d = 3.2549$ rounded to four decimals.

3. Find the distance from the point $(-2,8)$ to the line through the points $(0,-5)$ and $(-10,0)$.

    Solution. We carry out the procedure outlined in Steps 2 and 4 as follows:

$$\boxed{0}\ \boxed{x \blacklozenge t}\ \boxed{-5}\ \boxed{A}\ \boxed{-10}\ \boxed{x \blacklozenge t}\ \boxed{0}\ \boxed{E}$$

The slope and y-intercept are now calculated correctly and stored by LINES. Next,

$$\boxed{-2}\ \boxed{x \blacklozenge t}\ \boxed{8}\ \boxed{D'}$$

The display shows $d = 10.733$ rounded to three decimals.

EXERCISE 3.
FITTING A STRAIGHT LINE TO DATA POINTS

In real life our predictions are never exactly fulfilled and our measurements usually contain some error. Thus our data measurements, even though they *should* lie perfectly along a straight line when plotted, they never quite do. We would, however, like to have an equation for the straight line that best approximates, in some sense, our measurements.

    To be more precise, suppose we have made n experimental observations yielding the data points,

$$(x_1,y_1), (x_2,y_2), \ldots, (x_n,y_n)$$

We want to find a single line

$$y = mx + b$$

to best "fit" these data points in the sense that the deviation between each observed value y_i and the predicted value $mx_i + b$, for all $i = 1, 2, \ldots, n$, will be minimized (Figure 1.10). Each deviation is the difference

$$y_i - (mx_i + b)$$

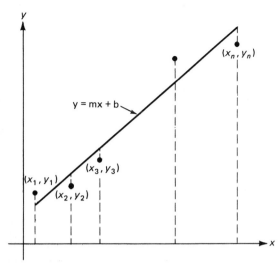

Figure 1.10 To fit a line to noncollinear data points, we choose a line that minimizes the deviations.

which measures the amount by which the predicted value of y (namely, $mx_i + b$) falls short of the actual observed value y_i. Because some of the differences will be positive and others will be negative, we minimize the sum of the squares of the deviations for our best-fitting line. The procedure for calculating the slope m and the y-intercept b for this best-fitting line is known as *the method of least squares*. The calculations are performed by LINES.

Calculating the Slope-Intercept Form of the Best-Fitting Line

Step 1: Press ⟦ A′ ⟧ to select and initialize the program.

Step 2: Enter the first data point (x_1, y_1): x_1 in the T-register and y_1 in the display. Then press ⟦ R/S ⟧ .

Step 3: Repeat Step 2 until all the data points have been entered. After each entry the display shows the total number of entries so far. If a data point is entered incorrectly, re-enter *the same incorrect point* and press ⟦ GTO ⟧ ⟦ ln x ⟧ ⟦ R/S ⟧ . Then enter the correct point using the procedure in Step 2, and continue.

Step 4: After entering all data points, press ⟦ B′ ⟧ . When the program halts, the slope m of the best-fitting line is in the display. Press ⟦ x⇄t ⟧ to obtain the y-intercept b from the T-register.

Step 5: To find a predicted y-value on the best-fitting line: Enter the x-coordinate into the display and press ⟦ E′ ⟧ . The program halts with the predicted y-value in the display.

Illustrations　1. In an experiment with a ball rolling down an inclined plane, the speed v (m/sec) at the end of t sec was observed as given in the following table:

t	1	2	3	4	5
v	1.98	3.84	5.91	7.74	9.78

21

To find the line that best fits the data, carry out the following keystrokes using LINES:

| A' | 1 | x⇕t | 1.98 | R/S | 2 | x⇕t | 3.84 | R/S | 3 | x⇕t | 5.91 |

| R/S | 4 | x⇕t | 7.74 | R/S | 5 | x⇕t | 9.78 | R/S | B' |

The display shows $m = 1.95$. Press $\boxed{x⇕t}$ for $b = 0$.
To find the predicted speed when $t = 4.67$ sec:

(enter)   4.67

(press) $\boxed{E'}$ The display shows $v = 9.1065$ m/sec.

2. The volume (V) of a gas at constant pressure was observed to vary with temperature (T) according to the following table:

T (°C)	$-20°$	$0°$	$30°$	$50°$
V (cm^3)	31.2	33.7	37.4	39.9

We will determine and graph the best-fitting line:

| A' | −20 | x⇕t | 31.2 | R/S | 0 | x⇕t | 33.7 | R/S | 30 | x⇕t | 37.4 |

| R/S | 50 | x⇕t | 3.9 | R/S | | | Oops! Error in last data entry. |

| 50 | x⇕t | 3.9 | GTO | ln x | R/S | Error corrected, enter correct data. |

| 50 | x⇕t | 39.9 | R/S | B' |

The display shows the slope $m = 0.124$, and the T-register contains the y-intercept $b = 33.688$ of the best-fitting line, correct to three decimals. A plot of the data points and of the best-fitting line is shown in Figure 1.11. When $T = 40°$ we can calculate the predicted volume as follows:

(enter)   40

(press) $\boxed{E'}$

The display shows the predicted volume to be $V = 38.65$ rounded to two decimal places. When $T = 30°$:

(enter)   30

(press) $\boxed{E'}$

The display shows $V = 37.412$ when $T = 30°$. This is very close to the actual observed value of $V = 37.4$.

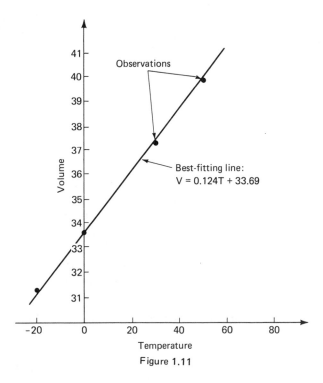

Figure 1.11

In the following problems give your answers correct to two decimal places. Use the program LINES.

1. Find the point of intersection of the given pairs of lines. Use the point-slope form of the lines in LINES.

   a. $y = -x - 1.11$
      $y = 2.7x - 5.92$

   b. $y = x + 42.16$
      $0.5y = 3x + 23.06$

   c. $x = y - 1$
      $x = 2y + 1$

   d. $4x - 7y = -5$
      $-3x + 2y = 8$

2. Find an equation of the line that passes through the intersection of the lines $y = x - 5$ and $y = -2x + 4$ and the point $(4, -3)$.

3. Find an equation of the line that passes through the intersection of the lines $11x + 7y - 12 = 0$ and $9x - 2y - 13 = 0$ and the point $(7, -5)$.

4. Find an equation of the line that passes through the intersection of the lines $5x - 4y + 8 = 0$ and $3x + 2y - 6 = 0$ and that is perpendicular to the line $7x - 4y + 13 = 0$.

5. Find the point at the foot of the perpendicular from the point $(4, 1.5)$ to the line $2x + 3y = 17$.

6. In each of the following find the distance from the given point to the given line:

a. $y = \dfrac{4}{3}x + \dfrac{8}{3}$, $(2,6)$

b. $8x - 6y - 21 = 0$, $(4,-2)$

c. $\sqrt{2}\,y - \pi x = 17$, $(1.7,-4.2)$

d. $1.63x + 3.84y - 19.6 = 0$, $(-\sqrt{5},-1.25)$

e. $4x + y = 3\sqrt{17}$, $(0,0)$

7. Find the distance between the parallel lines $x + y - 5 = 0$ and $4x + 4y + 9 = 0$. (Hint: Choose any point on one of the lines, and calculate the distance from that point to the second line.)

8. Find the distance between the parallel lines $2x - 3y + 9 = 0$ and $6x - 9y - 15 = 0$.

9. The vertices of a triangle are $A(0,0)$, $B(6,0)$, and $C(3,4)$. Find the distance from the vertex A to the side BC, and find the point Q at the foot of the perpendicular from A to BC.

10. Fit a straight line to the points $(1,16)$, $(3,26)$, $(4,32)$, and $(5,40)$.

11. Find an equation of the straight line that best fits the data

x	1.0	2.3	3.7	4.2	6.1	7.0
y	3.6	3.0	3.2	5.1	5.3	6.8

What is the predicted value of y when $x = 4.65$?

12. By means of the least squares technique, find the straight line that best represents the Index of Industrial Production from 1963 to 1968 based on the following data from the *Economic Report of the President,* 1971 (Washington, D.C.: U.S. Government Printing Office, 1971).

Year	1963	1964	1965	1966	1967	1968
Index	79	84	91	99	100	105

What is the predicted index for the year 1972?

13. Assume the following table represents the growth of a population of fruit flies over a given six-week period.

t (days)	7	14	21	28	35	42
P (number of observed flies)	8	41	133	250	280	297

Using the method of least squares, predict how many fruit flies there will be after 60 days.

14. The American College Test (ACT) scores of 19 students were compared to their grade point averages (GPAs) after one year in college, with the following tabled results.

ACT score	18	19	21	23	24	25	27	29
GPA	2.1	2.3	2.6	2.6	2.8	3.1	3.5	3.8

Predict the GPA of a student with an ACT score of 28.

15. In an experiment, the following data were obtained giving the temperature T of a coil of wire in degrees Centigrade based on the resistance r of the coil measured in ohms:

r (ohms)	10.421	10.939	11.321	11.799	12.242	12.668
T (°C)	10.50	29.49	42.70	60.01	75.51	91.05

Using the method of least squares, predict the temperature of a coil of wire with resistance 12.125 ohms.

16. In an experiment it was found that a given deflection D in mm. on a galvanometer corresponded to a measured current I in microampheres (μamps), as shown in the following table:

D (mm)	29.1	48.2	72.7	92.0	118	140	165	199
I (μamps)	0.0493	0.0821	0.123	0.154	0.197	0.234	0.274	0.328

Predict the current for a deflection of 127 mm.

17. The following table gives the elongation e in in/in for a given stress S on a square steel wire measured in pounds per square inch (lb/in^2).

S ($\times 10^{-3}$)	5	10	20	30	40	50	60	70	80	90	100
e ($\times 10^5$)	0	19	57	94	134	173	216	256	297	343	390

Predict the elongation for a stress of 65,500 lb/in^2.

Section 1.4 Functions and Quadratic Equations

One of the most fundamental concepts in mathematics is that of a *function*. The common meaning of the noun "function" as "role," "capacity," or "performance" has little connection with its mathematical meaning. Perhaps the synonym that comes closest to expressing the mathematical meaning of function is "rule" or "algorithm." Any specific process that can be applied to the numbers in a certain collection, and that yields numbers, can usually be described by means of a particular function. For example, the process that says "take any given number and square it" is a function. Or the rule that assigns the value 0 to every negative number and the value 1 to every nonnegative number is another function.

The calculator keyboard of your TI-59 is equipped with many "black box" functions. For instance, when you enter a number into the "input" display and press the function key $\boxed{x^2}$, the mechanism for squaring the display value is activated and the "output" result of the operation is then shown in the display. The keys $\boxed{\sqrt{x}}$, $\boxed{1/x}$, $\boxed{\sin x}$, $\boxed{\cos x}$, $\boxed{\ln x}$, $\boxed{\text{INV}}$

$\boxed{\log x}$ are all examples of function processes: For each input number, exactly one output result is produced. Note that, if the function key is to produce a nonflashing output result in the display, the value of the input number is sometimes restricted. For instance, the key $\boxed{\sqrt{x}}$ does not operate on negative values.

> **Definition.** A *function* consists of a domain and a rule. The domain is a collection of real numbers and the rule assigns to each number in the domain one and only one number.

It is customary to denote functions by the lower case letters f, g, or h. If x represents a number in the domain of the function f, then the value assigned by f to x is written $f(x)$ and is read "f of x." The function *must* make an assignment to each number in its domain. The collection of all values $f(x)$ for a given f, as x varies over the domain, is called the *range* of the function f. Notice that a function can assign *only one* number to any given number in its domain.

Returning to our calculator keyboard illustrations:

> Any number that can be entered into your TI-59 belongs to the domain of the function key $\boxed{x^2}$.
>
> For the key $\boxed{\sqrt{x}}$, the display entry must be nonnegative: The domain is the collection of nonnegative numbers.
>
> For the key $\boxed{1/x}$, the domain is the set of nonzero numbers.
>
> For $\boxed{\text{INV}}$ $\boxed{\sin x}$, the domain is $-1 \leqslant x \leqslant 1$.

If a number is entered into the calculator that lies outside the domain of a particular function key, then the result is a flashing display when the key is pressed or activated.

The idea of function is central to the study of calculus. It is important because any particular function expresses a relationship between the input numbers and the output results. The understanding of various *relationships* is essential to any scientific inquiry, whether it be an investigation in physics, astronomy, meteorology, economics, or psychology. Sometimes the functional relationship can be described by means of a formula or equation where the domain is understood to be the numbers for which the formula or equation is meaningful. Other times the relationship may be too complicated to describe algebraically, or perhaps it cannot be quantified. In the remainder of this book you will study many examples of functions that have proven useful to understanding physical reality, from the smallest particles of atomic physics to distant stars in the far reaches of space. Wherever we look we encounter functions.

EXERCISE 1.
GRAPHS OF FUNCTIONS

A useful way to visualize a specific function is by graphing the curve it represents in the *xy*-plane. More precisely, if f is a function, then *the graph of f* is the collection of ordered pairs (x,y) for which $y = f(x)$ and x varies over the domain of f. If we imagine a plot of the points (x,y) for every possible input value x, we obtain a single "curve" in the plane. Let's consider several examples.

Usually the domain values of a function constitute an infinite collection of numbers, such as an interval of values on the real number line. It would then be impossible to list *all* the numbers in the domain together with the corresponding function values. To assist us in obtaining a graph of the function f, we make up a table of values for selected values of x in the domain, together with the corresponding function values $f(x)$. We then plot the points $(x, f(x))$ in the xy-plane, where $y = f(x)$. Finally, we connect all these points by a single curve. In a later chapter, we will discuss and analyze significant features of this graph, but here we can give an intimation of some of these features in the several illustrations that follow.

Consider, for instance, the function f given according to the formula

$$f(x) = x^2 - x - 2$$

A table listing selected values of x and the corresponding values of $f(x)$ is given in Figure 1.12. A plot of the graph of the function f is shown in Figure 1.13. Notice how we have filled in the points between the tabled values in order to obtain a smooth curve, called a *parabola*. We are making some assumptions about the function when we do this, and these assumptions will be brought out in a later chapter.

x	-2.0	-1.5	-1.0	-0.5	0	0.5	1.0	1.5	2.0	2.5	3.0
$y = f(x)$	4.0	1.75	0	-1.25	-2.0	-2.25	-2.0	-1.25	0	1.75	4.0

Figure 1.12 A table of values for $f(x) = x^2 - x - 2$.

Several features concerning the graph are apparent from Figure 1.13. For instance, the graph is *rising upward* to the right when $x > 0.5$, and it is *falling downward* toward the right when $x < 0.5$. Where $x = 0.5$ the graph appears to give a *minimum value* of $y = -2.25$ for the function.

Another illustration is the function g given by

$$g(x) = x^3 - 4x$$

The table and graph of g are shown in Figure 1.14. The graph is rising upward to the right when $x < -1$ or $x > 1$; it is falling downward to the right when $-1 < x < 1$. When $x = -1$, the graph appears to give a high point value of $y = 3$; when $x = 1$, there is a low point value of $y = -3$. Notice that the graph crosses the x-axis, and hence has a y-value of zero, when $x = -2$, $x = 0$, and $x = 2$.

Systematic procedures for graphing general functions are covered further along in the book.

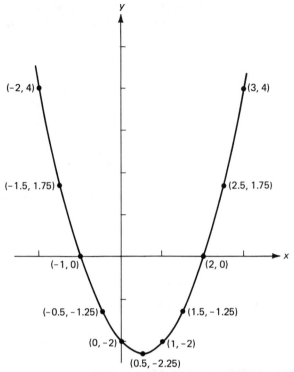

Figure 1.13 Graph of $f(x) = x^2 - x - 2$.

Figure 1.14 Graph of $g(x) = x^3 - 4x$.

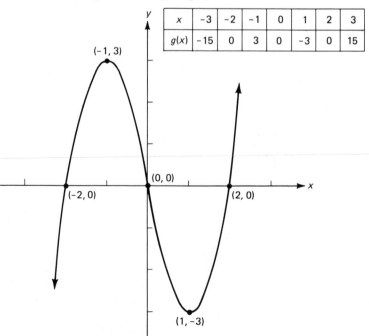

x	-3	-2	-1	0	1	2	3
$g(x)$	-15	0	3	0	-3	0	15

EXERCISE 2.
GRAPHING QUADRATIC FUNCTIONS

A function of the form

$$f(x) = ax^2 + bx + c \qquad\qquad (1.9)$$

where a, b, and c are constants and $a \neq 0$, is called a *quadratic function*. For example,

$$f(x) = x^2 \qquad g(x) = 3 - x^2 \qquad h(x) = 2x^2 - \sqrt{3}\,x + \pi$$

are all quadratic functions.

Quadratic functions can be readily analyzed using the program called QUADS. This program performs a variety of tasks, one of which assists the user in plotting the graph of any quadratic function in the form of Equation 1.9.

Calculating the Values of a Quadratic Function

Step 1: Read sides 1 and 2 of the magnetic card QUADS into your TI-59.

Step 2: Enter the coefficient a of the x^2 term, and press $\boxed{A}$.

Step 3: Enter the coefficient b of the x term, and press $\boxed{R/S}$.

Step 4: Enter the coefficient c, and press $\boxed{R/S}$.

Step 5: Enter the domain value x_0, and press $\boxed{B}$. The program halts with the value $f(x_0)$ in the display.

Illustrations 1. Consider the quadratic function $f(x) = -2x^2 + 3x - 5$. First, enter the co-efficients of f according to Steps 2-4:

$$\boxed{2}\;\boxed{+/-}\;\boxed{A}\;\boxed{3}\;\boxed{R/S}\;\boxed{5}\;\boxed{+/-}\;\boxed{R/S}$$

To evaluate $f(x_0)$ when $x_0 = 3$:

(enter)   3

(press) $\boxed{B}$ The display shows $f(3) = -14$.

To calculate additional values of f:

(enter)   7

(press) $\boxed{B}$ The display shows $f(7) = -82$.

(enter)   −2

(press) $\boxed{B}$ The display shows $f(-2) = -19$.

(enter)   −π

(press) $\boxed{B}$ The display shows $f(-\pi) = -34.164$ rounded to three decimal places.

2. We can use QUADS to calculate a table of function values for

$$g(x) = \pi x^2 + \sqrt{2}\, x - \sqrt{5}$$

to two decimal places. First, we enter the coefficients of g:

$$\boxed{\pi}\ \boxed{A}\ \boxed{2}\ \boxed{\sqrt{x}}\ \boxed{R/S}\ \boxed{5}\ \boxed{\sqrt{x}}\ \boxed{+/-}\ \boxed{R/S}$$

By entering each value of x and pressing $\boxed{B}$ in succession, we obtain the following table:

x	−1.25	−1.0	−0.75	−0.50	−0.25	0	0.25	0.50	0.75	1.0
$g(x)$	0.90	−0.51	−1.53	−2.16	−2.39	−2.24	−1.69	−0.74	0.59	2.32

A plot of the graph of g is shown in Figure 1.15. The curve is a parabola. Notice that the function has a minimum value somewhere near $x = -0.25$. Also, the graph crosses the x-axis between $x = -1.25$ and $x = -1.0$, and again between $x = 0.5$ and $x = 0.75$.

Figure 1.15 Graph of the quadratic $g(x) = \pi x^2 + \sqrt{2}\, x - \sqrt{5}$.

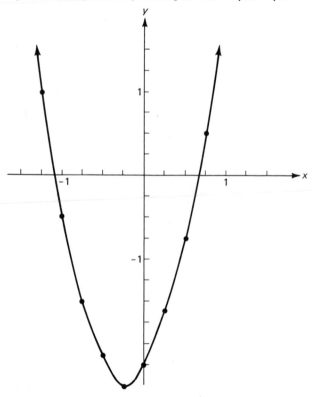

EXERCISE 3.
SOLVING QUADRATIC EQUATIONS

An equation of the form

$$ax^2 + bx + c = 0 \qquad\qquad (1.10)$$

where a, b, and c are constants and $a \neq 0$, is called a *quadratic equation.* A number r is called a *root* of the equation if a true arithmetic statement results when r is substituted for the variable x in the equation.

In elementary algebra the roots of quadratic equations are found using the quadratic formula,

$$r = \frac{-b \pm \sqrt{b^2 - 4ac}}{2a} \qquad\qquad (1.11)$$

You may recall that every quadratic equation has either two distinct real roots, one double root, or two complex roots, depending on whether the expression $b^2 - 4ac$ is positive, zero, or negative, respectively. The program QUADS calculates the real roots (if they exist) for any specified quadratic equation. The formula used is a modification of Equation 1.11 to reduce the roundoff error.

Calculating the Roots of a Quadratic Equation

With both sides of QUADS read into your TI-59 calculator, perform:

Step 1: Enter the coefficient a of the x^2 term, and press $\boxed{\text{A}}$.
Step 2: Enter the coefficient b of the x term, and press $\boxed{\text{R/S}}$.
Step 3: Enter the coefficient c, and press $\boxed{\text{R/S}}$.
Step 4: Press $\boxed{\text{D}}$. The program halts with the first root displayed. Press $\boxed{x \leftrightarrows t}$ to display the second root. If the roots are complex, the display shows 9.9999999×10^{99}.

Illustrations 1. To solve the quadratic equation $x^2 - 3x - 3 = 0$, perform the following keystroke sequence:

$\boxed{1}\ \boxed{\text{A}}\ \boxed{3}\ \boxed{+/-}\ \boxed{\text{R/S}}\ \boxed{\text{R/S}}\ \boxed{\text{D}}$ ($r_1 = 3.791$ rounded to three places)

$\boxed{x \leftrightarrows t}$ ($r_2 = -0.791$)

2. Solve the quadratic equation $x^2 + 2.46x + 1.5129$:

$\boxed{1}\ \boxed{\text{A}}\ \boxed{2.46}\ \boxed{\text{R/S}}\ \boxed{1.5129}\ \boxed{\text{R/S}}\ \boxed{\text{D}}$ ($r_1 = -1.23$)

$\boxed{x \leftrightarrows t}$ ($r_2 = -1.23$)

31 The equation has the double root -1.23.

3. Solve the quadratic equation $2x^2 + 3x + 6 = 0$:

| 2 | A | 3 | R/S | 6 | R/S | D |

The display shows 9.9999999×10^{99} so the roots are complex: There are no real roots.

The graphs of quadratic functions are always parabolas. The parabola may be *concave upward* or *concave downward* (Figure 1.16). The roots of a quadratic equation are precisely the values of x where the graph of the associated quadratic function crosses the x-axis. The three types of roots are related to the graph of the function (Figure 1.17). The graphs shown in Figure 1.17 are all concave upward. They could just as well be concave downward.

PROBLEMS 1.4

In each of Problems 1–10, graph the given quadratic function by first making a table of function values. Then find the roots of the quadratic equation $f(x) = 0$. Specify whether the graph is concave upward or concave downward.

1. $f(x) = x^2 - 5x + 4$
2. $f(x) = -x^2 - 2x + 3$
3. $f(x) = 6x^2 + 11x + 4$
4. $f(x) = 3x^2 - 10x - 8$
5. $f(x) = -2x^2 - 8x + 3$
6. $f(x) = \sqrt{2}\,x^2 - \sqrt{3}\,x + 1$
7. $f(x) = 1.2x^2 - 3.4x + 7.1$
8. $f(x) = \frac{1}{5}x^2 - \frac{2}{3}x + \frac{1}{17}$
9. $f(x) = \frac{2 - \sqrt{3}}{5}x^2 - 29$
10. $f(x) = x - \frac{13}{17}x^2$

Figure 1.16

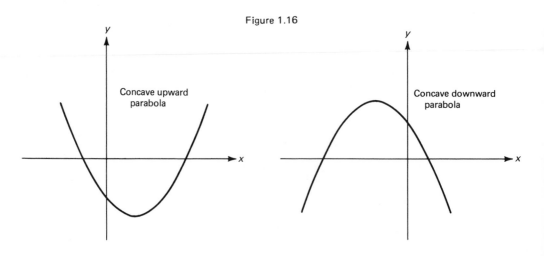

Concave upward parabola

Concave downward parabola

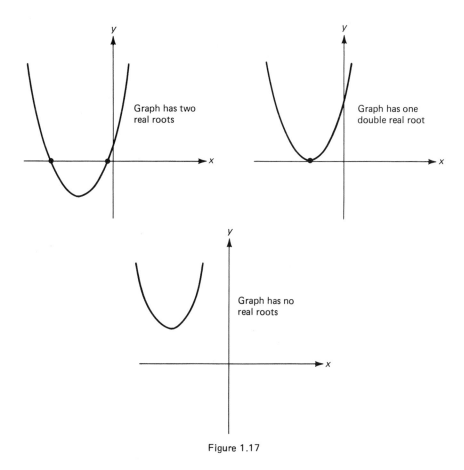

Figure 1.17

Section 1.5 Slope of a Curve and Quadratic Functions

One of the key concerns in calculus is that of finding the tangent line to a curve at a specified point. Historically there were several reasons for interest in this problem, apart from its purely geometric significance. In the seventeenth century, for instance, it was known that the direction of motion of a body moving along a curved path (such as a planet) at any point on the path is the same as the direction of the tangent to the path. The direction of the tangent is also important in optics when investigating the passage of light through a lens.

In elementary geometry, tangents to circles are studied. A line is *tangent* to a given circle if it meets the circle in exactly one point. However, that definition is inadequate for arbitrary curves, as can be seen from Figure 1.18: In Figure 1.18a the line is tangent to the curve yet meets the curve in more than one point. In Figure 1.18b the line meets the curve in exactly one point yet fails to be tangent. Clearly, a more precise notion of a tangent line is required. Since the tangent line at a point will be known if the slope of the line is found (using the point-slope equation of a line), we need only some method for determining the required slope. The idea behind one method is described as follows.

33

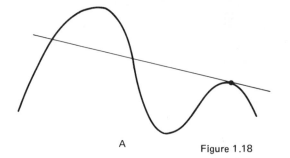

A

Figure 1.18

B

Suppose that a curve is given as the graph of a function f and that $P(x_1,y_1)$ is a point on the curve. Choose another point $Q(x_2,y_2)$ on the curve and draw the secant line through the points P and Q. This arrangement is illustrated in Figure 1.19. In the figure, Q is to the right of the point P, but it could just as well be to the left. The slope of this secant line is given by

$$m_{\text{sec}} = \frac{y_2 - y_1}{x_2 - x_1} = \frac{\Delta y}{\Delta x} \qquad (1.12)$$

Now imagine the point Q moving along the curve toward P. The secant line through P and Q will rotate. As Q gets closer and closer to the point P along the curve the secant line through P and Q approaches the limiting position of *the tangent* to the curve at P. For most curves that you ordinarily encounter in applications, such a limiting position does exist. As the secant line gets closer and closer to the limiting tangent line, the slope of the secant varies by smaller and smaller amounts and approaches a constant limiting value. This limiting value is called the *slope of the tangent to the curve at P*, or more

Figure 1.19

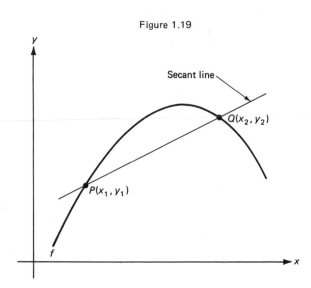

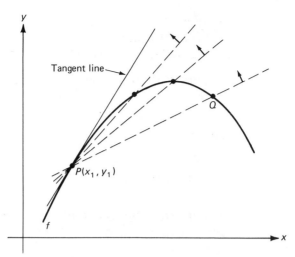

Figure 1.20 As Q moves along the curve toward P, the secant line approaches the limiting position of the tangent line.

briefly, the *slope of the curve at P*. In mathematical symbols we can write the slope $m_{\tan}$ of the tangent to the curve at P as

$$m_{\tan} = \begin{array}{c} \text{limiting value as } \Delta x \\ \text{approaches zero of} \end{array} \quad m_{\sec} = \lim_{\Delta x \to 0} \frac{\Delta y}{\Delta x} \tag{1.13}$$

From Equation 1.12, $x_2 = x_1 + \Delta x$, $y_2 = f(x_2) = f(x_1 + \Delta x)$, and $y_1 = f(x_1)$, the Equation 1.13 can be rewritten as:

$$m_{\tan} = \lim_{\Delta x \to 0} \frac{\Delta y}{\Delta x} = \lim_{\Delta x \to 0} \frac{f(x_1 + \Delta x) - f(x_1)}{\Delta x} \tag{1.14}$$

Since the limiting value in Equation 1.14 depends on the function f and the point x_1, it is written as $f'(x_1)$ (read "f-prime at x_1"). The number $f'(x_1)$, if it exists, is called the *derivative of the function f at x_1* and is defined by:

$$f'(x_1) = \lim_{\Delta x \to 0} \frac{f(x_1 + \Delta x) - f(x_1)}{\Delta x} \tag{1.15}$$

Geometrically, the derivative $f'(x_1)$ represents the slope of the tangent line to the curve $y = f(x)$ at the point $P(x_1, f(x_1))$.

There are techniques and rules associated with the process of finding derivatives for arbitrary functions, and we investigate some of these in Chapter 3. We also investigate the idea of the limiting concept more carefully. For purposes of this introductory chapter we have developed calculator programs that find derivative values for special kinds of functions.

35

EXERCISE 1.
FINDING THE SLOPE
OF A QUADRATIC FUNCTION

The program QUADS produces the correct slope $m_{tan} = f'(x_1)$ of a quadratic function

$$f(x) = ax^2 + bx + c$$

for specified $x = x_1$.

Calculating the Slope of a Quadratic Function
With both sides of QUADS read into your TI-59, perform:

Step 1: Enter the coefficient a of the x^2 term, and press $\boxed{A}$.
Step 2: Enter the coefficient b of the x term, and press $\boxed{R/S}$.
Step 3: Enter the coefficient c, and press $\boxed{R/S}$.
Step 4: Enter the domain value x_1 and press $\boxed{B}$. The program will halt with $f(x_1)$ displayed.
Step 5: Press $\boxed{C}$ and the program will halt with the slope $f'(x_1)$ displayed.
Step 6: If the slope is desired at another domain point, say $x_1 = z$, enter the number z and repeat Steps 4 and 5.

Illustration To find the slope of the quadratic $f(x) = -2x^2 + 3x - 5$ when $x = 0.5$, carry out the following keystrokes:

$$\boxed{2}\ \boxed{+/-}\ \boxed{A}\ \boxed{3}\ \boxed{R/S}\ \boxed{5}\ \boxed{+/-}\ \boxed{R/S}\ \boxed{0.5}\ \boxed{B}$$

The display shows $f(0.5) = -4$. To obtain the slope:

(press) $\boxed{C}$ The slope $f'(0.5) = 1.0$ is displayed.

To calculate additional values of f and f':

(enter)   −1.0

(press) $\boxed{B}$ The display shows $f(-1) = -10$.

(press) $\boxed{C}$ The display shows $f'(-1) = 7$.

(enter)   3.0

(press) $\boxed{B}$ The display shows $f(3) = -14$.

36 (press) $\boxed{C}$ The display shows $f'(3) = -9$.

EXERCISE 2.
FINDING THE TANGENT LINE
TO A QUADRATIC CURVE

The program QUADS produces the slope and y-intercept of the tangent line to a quadratic curve at a specified point. Moreover, it gives any desired value along the tangent line.

Calculating the Slope-Intercept Form of the Tangent Line

Step 1: Enter the coefficients of the quadratic function $f(x) = ax^2 + bx + c$ as in Exercise 1:

$$a \boxed{A} \quad b \boxed{R/S} \quad c \boxed{R/S}$$

Step 2: Enter the domain value x_1 where the tangent line is desired, and press $\boxed{E}$. The program halts with the slope $f'(x_1)$ of the tangent line at $(x_1, f(x_1))$ in the display.

Step 3: Press $\boxed{x \leftrightarrow t}$ and the y-intercept of the tangent line is displayed.

Step 4: To find the y-value *along the tangent line* for any value of x, enter the x-value into the display and press $\boxed{E'}$. The program halts with the corresponding y-value of the tangent line in the display.

Repeat Step 4 for additional tangent line values as desired.

Illustration   Find an equation of the tangent line to the quadratic curve

$$f(x) = \frac{1}{2}x^2 - 7x + 9$$

when $x = 8.5$. Find the value along the tangent line when $x = 6.25$.

   Solution. To obtain the tangent line, perform the following keystroke sequence:

$$\boxed{0.5} \boxed{A} \boxed{-7} \boxed{R/S} \boxed{9} \boxed{R/S} \boxed{8.5} \boxed{E}$$

The display shows the slope of the tangent as $m = 1.5$. To obtain the y-intercept,

(press) $\boxed{x \leftrightarrow t}$ The y-intercept is $b = -27.125$.

Thus the slope-intercept equation of the tangent line is $y = 1.5x - 27.125$. To find the value along the tangent line when $x = 6.25$:

(enter)   6.25

(press) $\boxed{E'}$ The display shows -17.75 as the y-value of tangent at $x = 6.25$.

To find the value of the tangent line when $x = 11.0$:

(enter)　　　11.0

(press)　　　$\boxed{\text{E}'}$　　The display shows $y = -10.625$.

To find the value *of the quadratic* function when $x = 11.0$:

(enter)　　　11.0

(press)　　　$\boxed{\text{B}}$　　The display shows $f(11.0) = -7.5$.

Thus the tangent line and function values differ by the amount 3.125 (neglecting the sign of the difference) when $x = 11.0$. This is sketched in Figure 1.21.

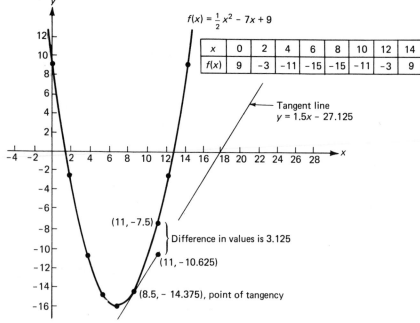

$f(x) = \frac{1}{2}x^2 - 7x + 9$

x	0	2	4	6	8	10	12	14
f(x)	9	-3	-11	-15	-15	-11	-3	9

Tangent line
$y = 1.5x - 27.125$

$(11, -7.5)$

Difference in values is 3.125

$(11, -10.625)$

$(8.5, -14.375)$, point of tangency

Figure 1.21 The difference between the tangent line value and the quadratic function value is shown for $x = 11$. The difference decreases as x gets closer and closer to the value 8.5.

PROBLEMS 1.5

In each of Problems 1–6, find the slope of the given quadratic function at the indicated domain value. Give your answers to three decimal places.

1. $f(x) = 6x^2 + 11x - 4$　　$x = -1$

2. $f(x) = -\frac{1}{3}x^2 + \frac{1}{5}x - \frac{1}{17}$　　$x = \frac{1}{8}$

3. $f(x) = \sqrt{2}\,x^2 - 2.71$　　$x = \sqrt{3}$

4. $f(x) = -\frac{1}{\pi}x^2 + x - \sqrt{2}$　　$x = -2.5$

5. $f(x) = x - \dfrac{13}{17}x^2$ $x = -3.2$

6. $f(x) = \dfrac{1 - \sqrt{5}}{2}x^2 + 1.9x$ $x = \dfrac{1}{\pi}$

In each of Problems 7–10, find the slope-intercept form for the equation of the tangent line to the given quadratic function at the specified domain value. Use two decimal place accuracy.

7. $f(x) = 3x^2 - \dfrac{1}{5}x + 7$ $x = 1.5$

8. $f(x) = -\dfrac{2}{3}x^2 + \dfrac{1}{7}x - \dfrac{1}{9}$ $x = \dfrac{1}{4}$

9. $f(x) = \dfrac{2 - \sqrt{3}}{5}x^2 + x$ $x = \pi$

10. $f(x) = 2 - \dfrac{4}{9}x - \dfrac{2}{15}x^2$ $x = -\dfrac{1}{\sqrt{3}}$

11. Establish that the curve $y = x^2 - 3.8x + 3.61$ is tangent to the x-axis.

12. Find the tangent line to the quadratic

$$f(x) = 7 - 2x - x^2 \quad \text{at } x = 3.1$$

a. What is the value of the tangent when $x = 2.97$?

b. What is the difference (neglecting sign) between the quadratic and the tangent line when $x = 3.02$? When $x = 3.08$? When $x = 3.09$? Sketch the graph of the quadratic and the tangent line, and show these differences on your graph.

Section 1.6 Fitting a Quadratic to Data Points

Section 1.3 presented the method of least squares for finding the best-fitting line to a given collection of data points. It may happen, however, that a straight line does not provide a very good representation of the data points that are determined through some experiment. Upon plotting the data points, you may find that they are more accurately represented by a quadratic curve, that is, by a parabola (Figure 1.22). In such a case we would seek a single quadratic function

$$y = ax^2 + bx + c$$

that best fits the observed data points (x_1, y_1), (x_2, y_2), ..., (x_n, y_n). Thus we want to obtain the coefficients a, b, and c so that the deviation between each observed value y_i and the predicted value

$$ax_i^2 + bx_i + c$$

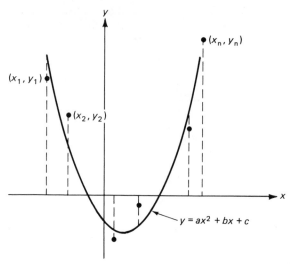

Figure 1.22 To fit a quadratic to the data points, we choose the quadratic that minimizes the deviations.

is minimized for each $i = 1, 2, \ldots, n$. That is, we minimize the sum of the squares of the deviation differences

$$y_i - (ax_i^2 + bx_i + c)$$

The required calculations are performed by QUADS.

EXERCISE 1.
MOTION OF A PROJECTILE

In a certain experiment a projectile is fired from the ground. At the end of each one-half second, an instrument relays its height above the ground to an observer and the information is recorded, as shown in the table in Figure 1.23. A plot of these data points reveals that they are not represented by a straight line, but more nearly by a parabola. We will use the program QUADS to find the parabola that best fits the data.

Calculating the Best-Fitting Quadratic Function
With both sides of QUADS read into your TI-59, perform

Step 1: Clear memory: press CMs .

Step 2: Enter the first data point (x_1,y_1): x_1 in the T-register and y_1 in the display. Then press A′ .

Step 3: Enter the second data point (x_2,y_2) with x_2 in the T-register and y_2 in the display. Then press R/S .

Step 4: Repeat Step 3 until all data points have been entered. After each entry, the display shows the total number of data points entered so far.

Step 5: After all data points have been entered, press $\boxed{\text{B}'}$. The program halts with the coefficient a of the x^2 term for the quadratic in the display.

Press $\boxed{\text{R/S}}$ for b, the coefficient of the x term.

Press $\boxed{\text{R/S}}$ for the coefficient c.

Step 6: To find a predicted y-value on the quadratic curve:

Enter the x into the display and press $\boxed{\text{B}}$. The program halts with the predicted y-value in the display. Press $\boxed{\text{C}}$ if you want the predicted slope.

Illustrations   1. Using the data for the projectile from Figure 1.23 carry out the following keystroke sequence:

The display shows $a = -8$. Press $\boxed{\text{R/S}}$ for $b = 32$, and press $\boxed{\text{R/S}}$ for $c = 5$. Thus the best-fitting quadratic is given by

$$y = -8x^2 + 32x + 5$$

Figure 1.23   Plot of projectile motion resembles a parabolic arc.

Time (sec)	0.5	1.0	1.5	2.0	2.5	3.0	3.5	4.0
Height (m)	19	29	35	37	35	29	19	5

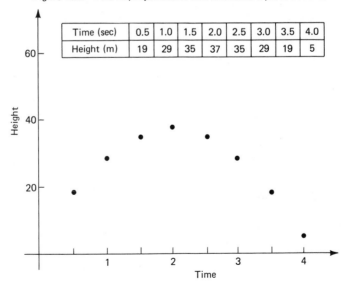

To find the predicted value when $x = 1.83$ sec:

(enter)   1.83

(press) $\boxed{\text{B}}$ The display shows the predicted
$y = 36.7688$ m.

(press) $\boxed{\text{C}}$ The display shows the predicted slope $m = 2.72$ at this time value.

To find an equation of the predicted tangent line when $x = 1.83$ sec:

(enter)   1.83

(press) $\boxed{\text{E}}$ The display shows 2.72 as the slope of the predicted tangent.

(press) $\boxed{x \updownarrow t}$ The display shows 31.7912 as the y-intercept of the predicted tangent.

This procedure for finding the tangent line is identical to that used in Exercise 2 of the preceding section.

2. You might ask, "How long after firing will the same projectile be expected to hit the ground?" Since ground level is reached when the height is zero, we seek the roots to our best-fitting quadratic $y = -8x^2 + 32x + 5$. Continuing with the same example:

(press) $\boxed{\text{D}}$ The display shows 4.15 sec, rounded to two decimals. This is the predicted time after firing when the projectile is expected to reach the ground.

(press) $\boxed{\text{B}}\boxed{\text{C}}$ The display shows −34.41 as the predicted slope when the projectile strikes the ground. In Chapter 3 you will see that this number actually gives the *speed* of the projectile when it hits the ground. The number −34.41 is negative because the projectile is *falling* when it hits.

PROBLEMS 1.6

In each of Problems 1-4, find the quadratic function that best fits the tabled data. Give the coefficients correct to two decimal places.

1.

x	−1	0	2	3	4
y	8	1	11	28	53

2.

x	−1.5	−1.0	−0.5	0	0.5	1.0	1.5
y	−17.895	−12.62	−8.695	−6.12	−4.895	−5.02	−6.495

3.

x	0.1	0.2	0.3	0.4	0.5
y	0.06	0.12	0.36	0.68	0.98

4.

x	1	3	4	5	7	9
y	3.80	9.01	13.64	19.56	35.46	56.68

5. The distance traveled by a ball rolling down an inclined plane was measured as follows:

t (sec)	0.5	1.0	1.5	2.0	2.5
s (m)	0.7	3.4	7.2	12.6	20.1

a. Fit a quadratic function to the data, and predict the distance the ball has rolled after 2.25 sec.

b. How fast is the ball predicted to travel when $t = 2.25$ sec? (This answer is given by the slope of the quadratic at $t = 2.25$.)

6. The times of sunrise and sunset at thirty-day intervals are recorded in the following table:

DATE	MAY 1	MAY 31	JUNE 30
Day	0	30	60
Sunrise (hr:min)	4:52	4:17	4:16
Sunset (hr:min)	19:02	19:39	19:48

a. Complete the following table giving the length of each recorded day in minutes:

Day	0	30	60
Length (min)			

b. Fit a quadratic function to the data tabled in part a.

c. Predict the length of the day for 49, 50, 51, and 52 days after May 1. Which day is the longest day? What is the corresponding date of the longest day?

7. If the brakes of a car are operating satisfactorily, the car should stop at a given distance s after the brakes are applied for a given speed v, as shown in the following table:

v (mph)	10	15	20	25	30	35	40	50
s (ft)	9.2	20.8	37	58	83.3	104	148	231

Fit a quadratic function to the data and predict the stopping distance required when the car is traveling 45 mph.

8. In an alloy of lead and zinc containing x percent of lead, the melting point T in degrees Centigrade (°C) was found as recorded in the following table:

x (percent)	40	50	60	70	80	90
T (°C)	186°	205°	226°	250°	276°	304°

Fit a quadratic function to the data and predict the melting point of an alloy with 65 percent lead.

9. A rock was dropped from a tall building, and the distance s it had fallen after t seconds was recorded as shown in the following table:

t (sec)	0	0.5	1.0	1.5	2.0
s (ft)	0	5	16	35	65

Predict how far the rock will fall after 3 sec and how fast it will be falling (that is, its speed).

10. The following table gives the resistance R in pounds per ton (lb/ton) for a train travelling at a speed of v mph:

v (mph)	20	40	60	80	100	120
R (lb/ton)	5.5	9.1	14.9	22.8	33.3	46.0

What is the predicted resistance for a train travelling at 107.5 mph?

11. The following table gives the experimental results for the coefficient of expansion γ of mercury between $0°C$ and $x°C$:

x	0	100	150	200	250	300	360
$\gamma \times 10^8$	18179	18216	18261	18323	18403	18500	18641

Fit a quadratic function to the data and predict the coefficient of expansion of mercury between $0°C$ and $276°C$.

12. The temperature (T) of a heated body cooling in air was taken (in degrees Fahrenheit) each minute and tabulated as follows:

time (min)	0	1	2	3	4	5	6
T ($°F$)		84.9	79.9	75.0	70.7	67.2	64.3	61.9

The temperature of the surrounding air was $20°$ F. Predict the temperature of the body after 10 min.

13. The speed of the water in the Mississippi River was taken at various depths and tabled as follows:

Depth (ft)	0	2	4	6	8
Speed (mph)	3.195	3.253	3.252	3.181	3.059

Predict the speed at a depth of 12 ft.

Section 1.7 Polynomial Functions

A *polynomial* is a function of the form

$$f(x) = a_n x^n + a_{n-1} x^{n-1} + \ldots + a_2 x^2 + a_1 x + a_0$$

where n is a nonnegative integer and $a_n, a_{n-1}, \ldots, a_2, a_1, a_0$ are constants. If $a_n \neq 0$, the number n is called the *degree* of the polynomial. The constants $a_n, a_{n-1}, \ldots, a_2, a_1, a_0$ are called the *coefficients* of the polynomial. The function $f(x) = 0$ is a polynomial (where each coefficient is zero), but no degree is assigned to it.

For example, the function $f(x) = 2x^5 - 2.7x^2 + 1$ can be written as

$$f(x) = 2x^5 + 0x^4 + 0x^3 - 2.7x^2 + 0x + 1$$

so it is a polynomial of degree 5. The quadratic functions are all polynomials of degree 2. The function $f(x) = 3.1$ is a *constant* polynomial and has degree 0. The function $f(x) = 0$ is also a constant polynomial, but its degree is not defined. The functions $f(x) = x^{1/2}$ and $f(x) = 2 + x + x^{-3}$ are not polynomials because they contain terms with powers of x that are not nonnegative integers. Since many important relationships in the sciences and applied mathematics can be expressed in this form, polynomials make up a very useful and significant class of functions to be investigated.

EXERCISE 1.
GRAPHS OF POLYNOMIALS

It can be established that the graph of any polynomial function of degree n is an unbroken curve that intersects the x-axis no more than n times. The prepared program POLYPROBE is designed to assist you in plotting the graphs of polynomial functions.

Plotting the Graph of a Polynomial Function

Step 1: Read both sides of the magnetic card POLYPROBE into your TI-59, with standard partitioning.

Step 2: Enter the degree n of the polynomial into the display and press $\boxed{C'}$. The number n cannot exceed 25.

Step 3: Enter the coefficients $a_n, a_{n-1}, \dots, a_2, a_1, a_0$ one at a time, beginning with the coefficient of the highest power of x and progressing to the lowest power. If a coefficient is zero, it must be entered as 0. After each entry, press $\boxed{\text{R/S}}$.

Step 4: Enter the starting value x_0, and press $\boxed{D'}$.

Step 5: Enter the increment Δx, and press $\boxed{E'}$.

Step 6: The following keys, when pressed, produce the indicated results:

Press $\boxed{A}$ to calculate $f(x + \Delta x)$

Press $\boxed{B}$ to calculate $f(x - \Delta x)$.

Press $\boxed{E}$ to display the current value of x.

Press $\boxed{A'}$ to reduce Δx by the factor 10.

Press $\boxed{B'}$ to increase Δx by the multiple 10.

These keys permit you to step forward or backward in exploring the values of the polynomial $f(x)$ to facilitate your graph plot and to reveal important characteristics of the polynomial function.

Illustrations   1. Let's graph the polynomial function

$$f(x) = x^4 - 9x^2 - 4x + 20$$

for values of x over the interval $-3 \leqslant x \leqslant 3$. First, read both sides of POLYPROBE into your calculator. Then:

(enter)	4		
(press)		$\boxed{C'}$	Load the degree $n = 4$.
(enter)	1		
(press)		$\boxed{R/S}$	Load the leading coefficient $a_4 = 1$.
(enter)	0		
(press)		$\boxed{R/S}$	Load $a_3 = 0$.
(enter)	-9		
(press)		$\boxed{R/S}$	Load $a_2 = -9$.
(enter)	-4		
(press)		$\boxed{R/S}$	Load $a_1 = -4$.
(enter)	20		
(press)		$\boxed{R/S}$	Load $a_0 = 20$.
(enter)	-3.5		
(press)		$\boxed{D'}$	Load initial $x_0 = -3.5$.
(enter)	0.5		
(press)		$\boxed{E'}$	Load $\Delta x = 0.5$.
(press)		$\boxed{Fix}\,\boxed{1}$	Set the calculator to display one digit past the decimal point.
(press)		$\boxed{A}$	The display shows $f(-3.5 + 0.5) = 32.0$
(press)		$\boxed{E}$	The display shows the current value of x: $x = -3.0$.

By repeatedly pressing $\boxed{A}$ and $\boxed{E}$, you obtain the table of values shown in Figure 1.24, along with the corresponding graph of the polynomial. Observe that the graph is a single unbroken curve and that it has no corners or angles. These features are characteristic of polynomials. The graph crosses the x-axis near $x = 1.5$ and again near $x = 2.75$. We will investigate the use of POLYPROBE in locating these roots precisely. Note also that the graph has a high point at the point labeled A, and low points at B and C. We will also investigate the use of POLYPROBE to locate high and low points of polynomials.

2. Consider the polynomial

$$f(x) = x^3 - 4x^2 - x + 6$$

x	-3	-2.5	-2	-1.5	-1	-.5	0	0.5	1	1.5
$f(x)$	32.0	12.8	8.0	10.8	16.0	19.8	20.0	15.8	8.0	-1.2

x	2	2.5	3
$f(x)$	-8.0	-7.2	8.0

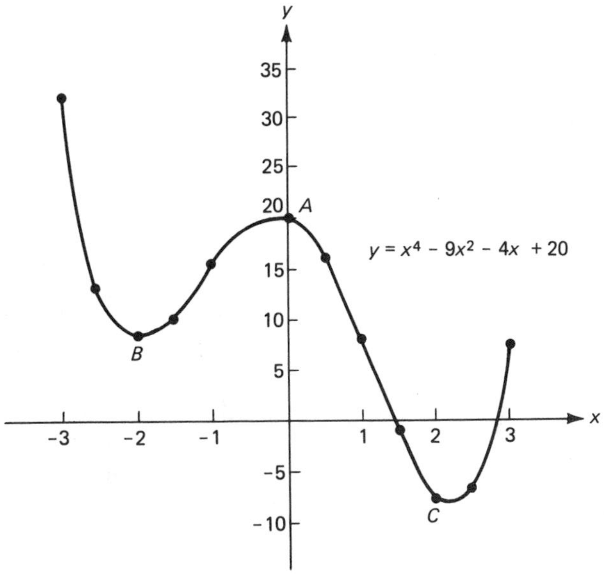

$$y = x^4 - 9x^2 - 4x + 20$$

Figure 1.24

Using a starting value of $x_0 = -2.5$ and an increment of $\Delta x = 0.5$, we determine the table of values shown in Figure 1.25, along with the graph of the polynomial. The graph appears to cross the x-axis near the values $x = -1, x = 1$, and $x = 4$. The curve is unbroken and has no corners or angles. It has a high point at A and a low point at B.

EXERCISE 2.
ROOTS OF POLYNOMIAL FUNCTIONS

A *root* of a function $y = f(x)$ is a number $x = r$ for which $f(r) = 0$. In other words, it corresponds to the location where the graph of the function crosses the x-axis. The program POLYPROBE can be used to locate the roots of a polynomial function to any desired degree of accuracy within the limitations of the calculator. This is accomplished by working interactively with the calculator.

As an illustration we will locate the root of the polynomial graphed in Figure 1.25, which lies between 1 and 2. First be sure the program POLYPROBE and the coefficients of the polynomial $f(x) = x^3 - 4x^2 - x + 6$ are still loaded into your calculator according to Steps 1-3 in Exercise 1. Next carry

x	-2	-1.5	-1	-.5	0	.5	1	1.5	2	2.5	3
$f(x)$	-16.0	-4.9	2.0	5.4	6.0	4.6	2.0	-1.1	-4.0	-5.9	-6.0

x	3.5	4	4.5
$f(x)$	-3.6	2.0	11.6

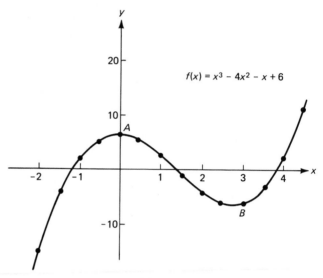

$$f(x) = x^3 - 4x^2 - x + 6$$

Figure 1.25

out the following procedures, noting the value of the display and the corresponding comment at each stage:

| Fix | 4 |

Set the calculator to display 4 digits past the decimal point.

| 1 | D′ |

Load $x_0 = 1$.

| 0.1 | E′ |

Load $\Delta x = 0.1$.

PRESS	DISPLAY	COMMENT
A	1.3910	We are left of the root; $f(x)$ is positive.
A	0.7680	Continue searching to the right.
A	0.1370	
A	-0.4960	Have crossed past the root. We are closer on the left side.
B	0.1370	Return to the left side of the root.
A′	0.0100	New decreased value of Δx.
A	0.0737	Continue searching to the right.
A	0.0104	

48

A	−0.0530	Have crossed past the root again.
B	0.0104	Back up because we were closer on the left side.
A'	0.0010	New decreased value of Δx.
A	0.0040	Continue searching to the right.
A	−0.0023	Have crossed past the root again and we are closer on the right side.
A'	0.0001	New decreased value of Δx.
B	−0.0017	Start searching to the left.
B	−0.0010	
B	−0.0004	
B	0.0002	Have crossed past the root.
A'	0.0000	Now $\Delta x = 0.00001$
A	0.0002	Search to the right.
A	0.0001	
A	0.0000	$f(x)$ is now zero to four decimal places.
E	1.3216	Display the current value of x.

Since $\Delta x = 0.00001$, the root $r = 1.3216$ is correct to all four decimal places shown. Of course, if desired, we could continue to narrow down the root to the limit of accuracy dictated by the calculator. This same process will locate the other two roots −1.1774 and 3.8558 within 0.00001.

EXERCISE 3.
SLOPES OF POLYNOMIALS

The slope of any curve was defined in Section 1.5 as the slope of the tangent line to the curve at the specified point. The value of the slope is given by the derivative of the function representing the curve. The program POLYPROBE calculates the derivative of any polynomial function.

Calculating the Slope of a Polynomial Function

With both sides of POLYPROBE read into your TI-59, perform the following:

Step 1: Enter the degree and coefficients of the polynomial into memory as in Steps 2 and 3 of Exercise 1 for plotting the graph.

Step 2: Enter the value x_0 at which the slope is desired; press $\boxed{D'}$.

Step 3: Press $\boxed{A}$ to calculate $f(x_0)$.

Step 4: Press $\boxed{C}$ to calculate the slope $f'(x_0)$.

Remark. If you are stepping forward or backward in exploration of the values of a polynomial, so that Steps 1–3 have already been effected, merely pressing $\boxed{C}$ gives the derivative $f'(x)$ at the current value of x in memory.

1. To find the slope of the polynomial

$$f(x) = -2x^5 + 3x^4 - \frac{1}{2}x + 1$$

when $x = 2.3$, carry out the following keystrokes with POLYPROBE:

| 5 | C′ | −2 | R/S | 3 | R/S | 0 | R/S | 0 | R/S | −0.5 | R/S | 1 | R/S |

| 2.3 | D′ | A | The display shows $f(2.3) = -44.92456$ |

| C | The display shows $f'(2.3) = -134.337$ |

2. Let us plot the values of the polynomial

$$f(x) = 1 + 2x^2 - x^4$$

together with the slopes, starting at $x_0 = -2.0$ in increments of $\Delta x = 0.5$. First we load the polynomial into memory together with the values of $x_0 - \Delta x = -2.5$ and Δx:

| 4 | C′ | −1 | R/S | 0 | R/S | 2 | R/S | 0 | R/S | 1 | R/S | −2.5 | D′ |
| 0.5 | E′ |

Next we obtain values of the polynomial and its slope values by carrying out the following procedures, with accuracy to one decimal place:

PRESS	DISPLAY	COMMENT
A	−7.0	Current polynomial value $f(x)$.
C	24.0	Current slope $f'(x)$.
E	−2.0	Current value of x.
A	0.4	Next polynomial value.
C	7.5	Next slope value.
E	−1.5	New current value of x.

Continuing in this manner we obtain the tabled values in Figure 1.26. When the points from the table are plotted, and a tangent is drawn at each point, we obtain Figure 1.26a. We can then draw a good picture of the curve as shown in Figure 1.26b. Observe from the graph in Figure 1.26b that at the high points A and C, and at the low point B, the derivative has value 0: that is, the tangent line is horizontal at those points. Note also that the curve is *symmetric about the y-axis*: For each point (x,y) on the graph, the point with coordinates $(-x,y)$ is also on the graph. Symmetry about the y-axis is characteristic of polynomials that contain only even powers of x, as in this particular example.

x	-2	-1.5	-1	-0.5	0	0.5	1	1.5	2
f(x)	-7	0.4	2	1.4	1	1.4	2	0.4	-7
f'(x)	24	7.5	0	-1.5	0	1.5	0	-7.5	-24

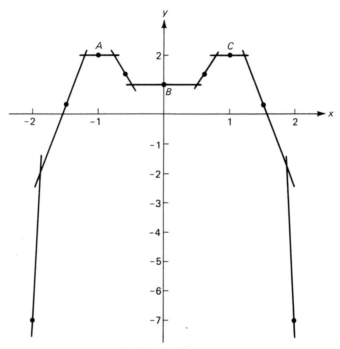

Figure 1.26a

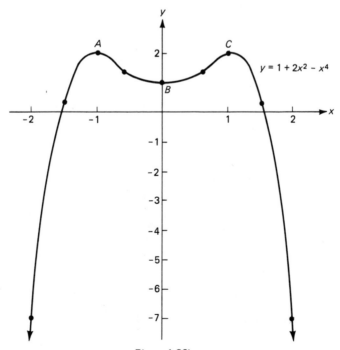

Figure 1.26b

EXERCISE 4.
MAXIMUM AND MINIMUM VALUES

When the graph of a function $y = f(x)$ is rising upward and to the right, the slope of the tangent line must be positive; that is, the value of the derivative is positive. On the other hand, where the curve is falling downward and to the right, the derivative must be negative. Thus the regions of rise and fall are usually separated by high or low points where the derivative is zero and the tangent line is horizontal. This is illustrated by the points marked A, B, and C in Figures 1.26a and 1.26b. If a high point occurs at $x = c$, the value $f(c)$ is called a *relative maximum* of the function $y = f(x)$; if a low point occurs at $x = c$, then $f(c)$ is called a *relative minimum* value. If the function has a tangent line at a relative maximum or relative minimum, then the tangent line must be horizontal so that the value of the derivative is zero there.

The program POLYPROBE can be used to find the relative maximum and minimum values of a polynomial function. For instance, consider again the polynomial investigated in Exercise 1:

$$f(x) = x^3 - 4x^2 - x + 6$$

Its graph is shown again in Figure 1.27. It has a high point at A occurring to the left of $x = 0$, and a low point at B occurring to the left of $x = 3$. We will use POLYPROBE to locate the points A and B. With both sides of POLYPROBE read into your calculator, carry out the following procedures:

(enter)	3		
(press)		C'	Load the degree $n = 3$.
(enter)	1		
(press)		R/S	Load the leading coefficient $a_3 = 1$.
(enter)	−4		
(press)		R/S	Load the remaining three coefficients.
(enter)	−1		
(press)		R/S	
(enter)	6		
(press)		R/S	
(enter)	−0.5		
(press)		D'	Load the starting value $x_0 = -0.5$.
(enter)	0.1		
(press)		E'	Load the increment $\Delta x = 0.1$.
(press)		Fix 4	Set the display to four decimal places.

52

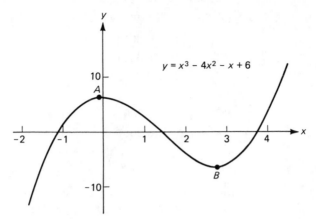

$$y = x^3 - 4x^2 - x + 6$$

Figure 1.27

PRESS	DISPLAY	COMMENT
A	5.6960	Begin search to the right.
A	5.9130	
A	6.0320	
A	6.0590	Must be nearing the maximum.
A	6.0000	
C	−1.0000	Slope is negative, we are right of the maximum.
B	6.0590	Back up.
C	−0.1700	Slope still negative.
A′	0.0100	New decreased value of Δx.
B	6.0603	Continue search to the left.
C	−0.0837	
B	6.0607	
C	0.0032	Slope is positive, we are left of the maximum.
A′	0.0010	New decreased value of Δx.
A	6.0607	Search to the right.
C	−0.0055	Slope negative.
A′	0.0001	Decrease Δx.
B	6.0607	Search to the left.
C	−0.0046	
B	6.0607	Continue search to the left.
C	−0.0038	
B	6.0607	
C	−0.0029	
B	6.0607	
C	−0.0020	
B	6.0607	

PRESS	DISPLAY	COMMENT
C	−0.0012	
B	6.0607	
C	−0.0003	
B	6.0607	
C	0.0006	Slope positive; passed the maximum.
A	6.0607	Step forward; slope closer to zero on the right side.
E	−0.1196	Display the current value of x.

Since $\Delta x = 0.0001$, we can state that the maximum value occurs at $x = -0.1196$ within $\Delta x = 0.0001$. The relative maximum value is 6.0607; so the point A has coordinates $(-0.1196, 6.0607)$.

    Similarly we can locate the relative minimum value of −6.2088 occurring at $x = 2.7863$ within $\Delta x = 0.0001$.

    A few comments are in order. You do not need to write down each result as it is generated on the calculator. With POLYPROBE, learn to use the calculator interactively by responding dynamically to what you see generated and displayed. The program is designed that way to assist you in locating roots and maximum/minimum values. The only time you should copy something down is when you have results worth copying. If you decide or are instructed to graph a polynomial, plot the information directly from the calculator. Here is a summary of the labels used in POLYPROBE for easy reference.

LABELS USED IN POLYPROBE

C'	Load the degree $n \leqslant 25$ and coefficients of the polynomial.
D'	Load the starting value of x.
E'	Load the increment Δx.
A	$f(x + \Delta x)$
B	$f(x - \Delta x)$
C	Slope at the current value of x.
E	Display the current value of x.
A'	$\Delta x \longleftarrow \Delta x/10$
B'	$\Delta x \longleftarrow 10\Delta x$

PROBLEMS 1.7

In each of Problems 1–5, graph the given polynomial function, locate its roots, and find the relative maximum and minimum values and where these occur. Give your answers correct to three decimal places.

    1. $f(x) = x^3 - 2x^2 - 8x + 6$

    2. $f(x) = -x^3 + 8x - 6$

3. $f(x) = 6x^4 + 7x^3 - 13x^2 - 4x + 4$

4. $f(x) = -x^4 + 10x^2 - 9$

5. $f(x) = x^5 - 3x^4 + 5x^3 - 6x^2 + 2x - 1$

6. Find the real cube root of 7 to six decimal places by solving the equation $x^3 - 7 = 0$.

7. Find the real roots of $x^4 - 3x^3 - 4x^2 + 10x + 6$ correct to five decimal places.

8. Find the real root of $x^3 - 3x - 12 = 0$ correct to four decimal places.

9. The depth x to which a solid sphere, floating in water, will sink is a positive root of the equation

$$x^3 - 3rx^2 + 4r^3s = 0$$

where r is the radius of the sphere and s is the specific gravity of the material. Find the depth to which a spherical cork of diameter 12 cm will sink if the specific gravity of cork is 0.24. Give your answer correct to five decimals.

10. A rectangular box with no top is to be constructed from a piece of cardboard 17 cm wide and 23 cm long by cutting out a square, whose side has a length x from each corner, and then bending up the sides. Find the size of the corner if the volume of the box must equal 250 cm^3. Give your answer correct to five decimals.

11. A covered box of height h is to be cut from a rectangular piece of cardboard 8 in by 18 in, according to the pattern shown in Figure 1.28. Find the volume of the box if $h = 1$ in. For what other value of h will the box have this same volume?

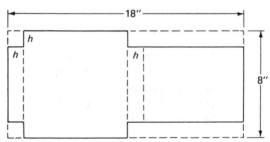

Figure 1.28

12. A rectangular tank has dimensions 6 m by 8 m by 10 m. Each side is to be increased by an equal amount x m.

   a. Determine x in order to double the capacity of the tank.

   b. Determine x if the capacity is to increase to 600 m^3.

13. A uniform beam of length L is freely supported at the origin and attached horizontally at the other end (Figure 1.29). The beam sags because of its weight. It can be shown that the greatest sag occurs at a properly selected root of the equation

$$8x^3 - 9Lx^2 + L^3 = 0$$

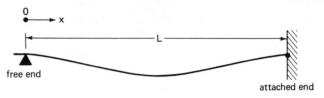

Figure 1.29

Find the point x where the greatest sag occurs, assuming that the beam is 10 m long.

14. Evaluate the polynomial function,

$$f(x) = x^{18} - 2x^{17} + 3x^{16} - 4x^{15} + 5x^{14} - 6x^{13} + 7x^{12} - 8x^{11}$$
$$+ 9x^{10} - 10x^9 + 9x^8 - 8x^7 + 7x^6 - 6x^5 + 5x^4 - 4x^3$$
$$+ 3x^2 - 2x + 1$$

and its derivative, for $x = -2, -\sqrt{2}, -1, 0, \sqrt{3}, \pi$ correct to one decimal place.

Section 1.8 Other Forms of Polynomial Expressions

There are occasions when it is desirable to divide a polynomial of the nth degree by a binomial of the form $x - x_0$, where x_0 is a fixed constant. Also it is sometimes necessary to express a polynomial in powers of the binomial $x - x_0$ rather than in powers of x.

EXERCISE 1.
THE REMAINDER THEOREM

If a polynomial of degree n is divided by a binomial of the form $x - x_0$, the quotient will be another polynomial of degree $n - 1$, and the remainder will be a constant (which will be zero if the division is exact). For instance, if $p(x) = 2x^4 + 7x^3 + 11x - 12$ is divided by $x + 4$, then the quotient is $q(x) = 2x^3 - x^2 + 4x - 5$ and the remainder is 8 because

$$2x^4 + 7x^3 + 11x - 12 = (2x^3 - x^2 + 4x - 5)(x + 4) + 8$$

More generally,

$$p(x) = q(x)(x - x_0) + R \qquad (1.16)$$

where $p(x)$ denotes the original polynomial, $q(x)$ the quotient polynomial, and R the constant remainder. Equation 1.16 is true for all values of x, and in particular when $x = x_0$. In that case we can see that

56 $p(x_0) = R$ $\qquad (1.17)$

because $q(x)(x - x_0)$ is zero when $x = x_0$. This fact is stated precisely in the following result:

> **The Remainder Theorem.** If the polynomial $p(x)$ is divided by $x - x_0$, the remainder is the value $p(x_0)$.

From Equation 1.16 it is clear that if the remainder $p(x_0)$ is equal to zero, then $x - x_0$ is a factor of the polynomial $p(x)$. Thus as a corollary to the Remainder Theorem we have . . .

> **The Factor Theorem.** The binomial $x - x_0$ is a factor of the polynomial $p(x)$ if and only if $p(x_0) = 0$.

Thus we see that $x - x_0$ is a factor of a given polynomial precisely when x_0 is a root of the polynomial.

The program POLYPROBE calculates the quotient $q(x)$ and the remainder R in Equation 1.16 when dividing a given polynomial $p(x)$ by the binomial $x - x_0$.

Calculating the Quotient and the Remainder

With both sides of POLYPROBE read into your TI-59, perform the following:

Step 1: Enter the degree and coefficients of the polynomial into memory, as in Steps 2 and 3 of Exercise 1 in Section 1.7.

Step 2: Enter the value x_0 for division by the term $x - x_0$.

Step 3: Press $\boxed{\text{GTO}}$ $\boxed{\div}$ and then $\boxed{\text{R/S}}$. When the program halts, the coefficient of highest degree in $q(x)$, for the power x^{n-1}, will be in the display.

Step 4: By pressing $\boxed{\text{R/S}}$ repeatedly, you can display the remaining co-efficients for $q(x)$ sequentially, from the highest to the lowest powers of x.

Step 5: After all the coefficients of $q(x)$ have been revealed, the display reads 9.9999999×10^{99} to signal the termination of the division. Press $\boxed{\text{R/S}}$ to find the value of the remainder.

Illustrations   1. To divide the polynomial $p(x) = 3x^5 - 5x^3 + 1$ by $x - 2$, carry out the following procedures:

(enter)	5		
(press)		$\boxed{\text{C}'}$	Load the degree $n = 5$.
(enter)	3		
(press)		$\boxed{\text{R/S}}$	Load the leading coefficient $a_5 = 3$.
(enter)	0		
(press)		$\boxed{\text{R/S}}$	Load the remaining coefficients.

(enter)	-5	
(press)	R/S	
(enter)	0	
(press)	R/S	
(enter)	0	
(press)	R/S	
(enter)	1	
(press)	R/S	
(enter)	2	Load $x_0 = 2$ for division by $x - 2$.
(press)	GTO ÷	
(press)	R/S	Display shows 3., the coefficient of x^4 in the quotient $q(x)$.
(press)	R/S	Display shows 6., coefficient of x^3.
(press)	R/S	Display shows 7.
(press)	R/S	Display shows 14.
(press)	R/S	Display shows 28.
(press)	R/S	Display shows 9.9999999×10^{99} signaling termination of the division.
(press)	R/S	Display shows the remainder $R = 57$.

Therefore

$$3x^5 - 5x^3 + 1 = (3x^4 + 6x^3 + 7x^2 + 14x + 28)(x - 2) + 57$$

with

$$q(x) = 3x^4 + 6x^3 + 7x^2 + 14x + 28 \quad \text{and} \quad R = p(2) = 57$$

2. In dividing $2x^3 - 5x^2 + 5x + 11$ by $x + 1$ (so that $x_0 = -1$), we obtain

$$q(x) = 2x^2 - 7x + 12 \quad \text{and} \quad R = -1$$

EXERCISE 2.
COEFFICIENTS IN POWERS OF $x - x_0$

At times it is desirable to express a given polynomial

$$p(x) = a_n x^n + a_{n-1} x^{n-1} + \ldots + a_1 x + a_0$$

in powers of the binomial $x - x_0$:

$$p(x) = b_n (x - x_0)^n + b_{n-1}(x - x_0)^{n-1} + \ldots + b_1(x - x_0) + b_0$$

The coefficients $b_n, b_{n-1}, \ldots, b_1, b_0$ are easily calculated using POLYPROBE.

Calculating the Coefficients in Powers of $x - x_0$

With both sides of POLYPROBE read into your TI-59, perform the following:

Step 1: Enter the degree and coefficients of the original polynomial as before when using POLYPROBE.

Step 2: Enter the value x_0 for the binomial $x - x_0$ and press $\boxed{\text{D}'}$.

Step 3: Press $\boxed{\text{D}}$. When the program halts, the coefficient b_0 is displayed; that is the constant coefficient.

Step 4: Press $\boxed{\text{D}}$. The coefficient b_1 of the term $(x - x_0)$ is displayed.

Step 5: Press $\boxed{\text{D}}$ repeatedly. The coefficients $b_2, b_3, \ldots, b_n$ are displayed, progressing from the lowest powers of $(x - x_0)$ to the highest powers.

After the last coefficient b_n has been revealed, further pressing of the key $\boxed{\text{D}}$ continues to display b_n.

Illustrations 1. To express the polynomial

$$p(x) = 6x^4 - 53x^3 + 184x^2 - 295x + 186$$

in powers of $x - 3$, carry out the following procedures:

(enter)	4		
(press)		$\boxed{\text{C}'}$	Load the degree $n = 4$.
(enter)	6		
(press)		$\boxed{\text{R/S}}$	Load the leading coefficient $a_4 = 6$.
(enter)	−53		
(press)		$\boxed{\text{R/S}}$	Load the remaining coefficients.
(enter)	184		
(press)		$\boxed{\text{R/S}}$	
(enter)	−295		
(press)		$\boxed{\text{R/S}}$	
(enter)	186		
(press)		$\boxed{\text{R/S}}$	
(enter)	3		
(press)		$\boxed{\text{D}'}$	Load $x_0 = 3$ for powers of $x - 3$.
(press)		$\boxed{\text{D}}$	Display shows $b_0 = 12$.
(press)		$\boxed{\text{D}}$	Display shows $b_1 = 26$.

(press) | $\boxed{D}$ | Display shows $b_2 = 31$.

(press) | $\boxed{D}$ | Display shows $b_3 = 19$.

(press) | $\boxed{D}$ | Display shows $b_4 = 6$.

Thus:

$$p(x) = 12 + 26(x-3) + 31(x-3)^2 + 19(x-3)^3 + 6(x-3)^4$$

If the key $\boxed{D}$ is pressed again, the display continues to show $b_4 = 6$.

2. Expressing the same polynomial in powers of $x + \frac{1}{2}$ (so that $x_0 = -\frac{1}{2}$), we obtain

$$p(x) = 386.5 - 521.75(x+\tfrac{1}{2}) + 272.5(x+\tfrac{1}{2})^2 - 65(x+\tfrac{1}{2})^3 + 6(x+\tfrac{1}{2})^4$$

PROBLEMS 1.8

In each of Problems 1–10, divide each polynomial by the binomial indicated and obtain the quotient and remainder.

1. $6x^4 + 7x^3 - 13x^2 - 4x + 4$ by $x - \frac{1}{2}$

,2. $x^3 - 3x^2 + 4x - 6$ by $x - 2.3$

3. $x^4 - 3x^3 - 4x^2 + 10x + 6$ by $x + 3.8$

4. $2x^5 - 3x^4 + 5x^3 - 6x^2 + 2x - 1$ by $x - 1.05$

5. $x^4 - 9x^2 - 4x + 20$ by $x + 4.1$

6. $x^{10} - 1$ by $x - 1$

7. $7x^5 - 6x^3 + 2$ by $x + 3$

8. $1.2x^4 - 5.31x^2 + 1.7$ by $x - 1.3$

9. $x^6 - x^5 + x^4 - x^3 + x^2 - x + 1$ by $x + 1$

10. $\frac{1}{5}x^5 - \frac{1}{4}x^4 + \frac{1}{3}x^3 - \frac{1}{2}x^2 + x - 1$ by $x - \frac{1}{6}$

In Problems 11–15, express each polynomial in powers of the binomial indicated.

11. $x^4 - 4x^3 + 3x^2 - 2x + 5$ in powers of $x - \frac{1}{2}$

12. x^5 in powers of $x + 1$

13. $\frac{1}{4}x^5 + \frac{1}{2}x^3 - x + \frac{1}{5}$ in powers of $x - 1$

14. $x^7 - 1$ in powers of $x - 1$

15. $x^{12} + 2x^{11} + 3x^{10} + 4x^9 + 5x^8 + 6x^7 + 7x^6 + 6x^5 + 5x^4 + 4x^3$
    $+ 3x^2 + 2x + 1$ in powers of $x + 2$

The calculus was created primarily for the investigation of several major problems of concern in the seventeenth century. One of these was finding the tangent to a curve, which we briefly investigated in Section 1.5. A second problem was finding the area bounded by a plane curve, and we will now treat this problem for polynomials.

To compute the area of a plane figure, we begin with a square whose sides are of one unit length. If the unit of length is one centimeter, the corresponding unit of area associated with the square will be one square centimeter. From this basic definition, you can easily calculate the area of any rectangle using the familiar product of the length times the width. Since the area of any triangle is equal to one-half the area of a rectangle with the same base and altitude, the areas of triangular and polygonal figures also present no computational difficulty. The problem arises when you ask for the area of a plane figure bounded by a *curve*. How does one compute, for example, the area of a circle or the area of a segment of a parabola? These questions were raised by the ancient Greeks.

In the third century BC the Greek mathematician Archimedes devised a process known as the "method of exhaustion," which he used to calculate the area of a parabolic segment and the area of a circle. Basically, his idea was to inscribe in the parabolic segment or circle a polygon whose area could be computed easily. By choosing another inscribed polygon whose interior includes that of the former one, a better approximation to the area of the plane figure could be obtained. In continuing to choose inscribed polygons in succession, each having an interior that includes the former ones, gradually the whole area of the original region will be "exhausted." Archimedes used an ingenious technique especially suited to the circle and parabolic segment for his calculations. However, his method was the germ of the idea that eventually led to the seventeenth century invention of the integral calculus.

To understand how Archimedes' approach can be modified, consider the problem of finding the area of the region R bounded by the parabola $f(x) = x^2$, the x-axis, and the vertical line $x = 2$, as shown in Figure 1.30.

Let us inscribe rectangles in the region R, as shown in Figure 1.31. Then the sum of the areas of all the rectangles is less than the total area of the region R. If we inscribe more and narrower rectangles, as shown in Figure 1.32, the sum of the areas of the rectangles is still less than the area of R, but the approximation is a much better one. As we continue to inscribe more and more rectangles, their bases become smaller and smaller, tending to zero, and the sum of the areas of all the rectangles gets closer and closer to the actual area of the region R.

Instead of using inscribed rectangles, we can circumscribe rectangles about R (Figure 1.33). In this case the sum of the areas of all the circumscribed rectangles will exceed the area of the region R. Nevertheless, as the bases of the circumscribed rectangles become smaller and smaller, the sum of their areas gets closer and closer to the area of R (Figure 1.34). All this suggests that the area of R can be defined as *the limit* of these inscribed or

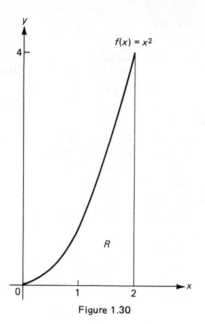

Figure 1.30

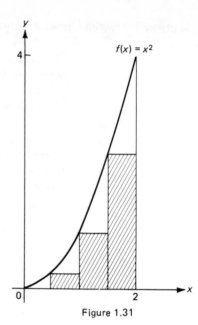

Figure 1.31

circumscribed rectangles. We will make this limiting idea more precise in a later chapter.

You can follow the same procedure when dealing with an area like the one shown in Figure 1.35. Here the region whose area we seek is bounded above by the curve $y = f(x)$, below by the x-axis, to the left by the vertical line $x = a$, and to the right by the vertical line $x = b$. We show the area being approximated by inscribed rectangles. As the bases of these rectangles get

Figure 1.32

Figure 1.33

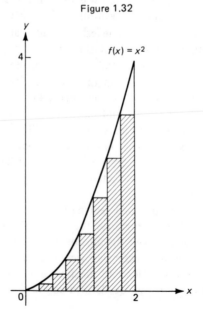

62

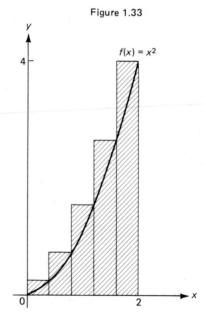

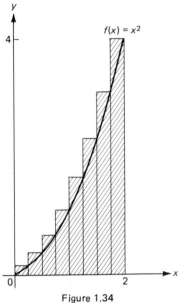

Figure 1.34

closer and closer to zero, the sum of the areas of the rectangles gets closer and closer to the area of the region shown in the figure.

The numerical calculations required in the limiting process for the area in Figure 1.35 can become very tedious and involved. However, a thorough investigation of the procedure, which we will carry out in the chapter on integration, reveals that simple methods do exist for calculating the limiting number that gives the area. Discussing these methods in greater detail is beyond our present level so far in this text, but in the case of polynomial curves the correct calculations are given in POLYPROBE.

Figure 1.35

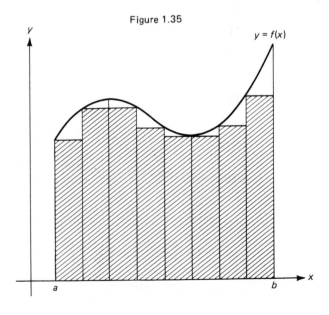

EXERCISE 1.
AREA BENEATH A POSITIVE
POLYNOMIAL CURVE

Suppose that $y = f(x)$ is a polynomial whose values are nonnegative for the interval $a \leqslant x \leqslant b$ (Figure 1.35).

Calculating the Area Beneath a Polynomial

With both sides of POLYPROBE read into your TI-59, perform the following:

Step 1: Enter the degree and coefficients of the polynomial into memory as in Steps 2 and 3 of Exercise 1 in Section 1.7.

Step 2: Enter the left end-point a of the interval $a \leqslant x \leqslant b$, and press $\boxed{x \leftrightarrow t}$.

Step 3: Enter the right end-point b of the interval $a \leqslant x \leqslant b$. Press $\boxed{\text{GTO}}$ $\boxed{\text{Int}}$ $\boxed{\text{R/S}}$. The program will halt with the area beneath the curve from $x = a$ to $x = b$ shown in the display.

Illustrations   1. To find the area beneath the curve $y = x^2$ from $x = 0$ to $x = 2$, carry out the following procedures with POLYPROBE in your calculator:

(enter)	2		
(press)		$\boxed{C'}$	Load the degree $n = 2$.
(enter)	1		
(press)		$\boxed{\text{R/S}}$	Load the leading coefficient $a_2 = 1$.
(enter)	0		
(press)		$\boxed{\text{R/S}}$	Load the remaining coefficients.
(enter)	0		
(press)		$\boxed{\text{R/S}}$	
(enter)	0		
(press)		$\boxed{x \leftrightarrow t}$	Load the left end-point $a = 0$.
(enter)	2		Now the right end-point $b = 2$.
(press)		$\boxed{\text{GTO}}$ $\boxed{\text{Int}}$	Position the pointer at area routine.
(press)		$\boxed{\text{R/S}}$	Calculate the area.

The program halts with the area $A = 2.667$, rounded to three decimals, in the display.

2. To find the area beneath the polynomial

$$f(x) = x^4 - 9x^2 - 4x + 20$$

64

from $x = -3$ to $x = 1$ (Figure 1.24), carry out the following keystrokes:

The display shows the area $A = 60.8$ square units.

3. To find the area beneath the polynomial $f(x) = 6 - x - x^2$ over the interval $-3 \leqslant x \leqslant 2$ (Figure 1.36), carry out the following keystrokes:

The display shows the area $A = 20.833$ square units, to three decimal places.

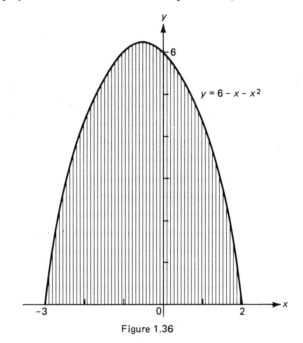

Figure 1.36

EXERCISE 2.
AREA TRAPPED BETWEEN THE x-AXIS
AND A POLYNOMIAL WITH NEGATIVE VALUES

Consider the polynomial

$$y = x^2 + 2x$$

whose graph is shown in Figure 1.37. Let's determine the area trapped between the curve and the x-axis over the interval $-3 \leqslant x \leqslant 1$. From the graph we see

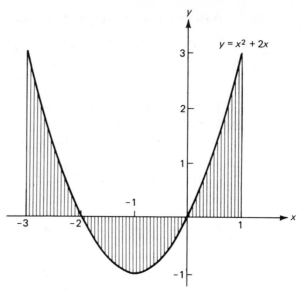

Figure 1.37

that the curve has positive values for $-3 < x < -2$ and $0 < x < 1$, but negative values for $-2 < x < 0$. Thus the heights of the rectangles of $-2 < x < 0$ will be considered negative and give an associated *negative* signed area. Let us first calculate that signed area using POLYPROBE:

The display shows -1.333 rounded to three decimals. Thus the area is the absolute value of this number, or 1.333 square units.

Next we find the two areas associated with the positive values of the polynomial:

$$\boxed{2}\ \boxed{C'}\ \boxed{1}\ \boxed{R/S}\ \boxed{2}\ \boxed{R/S}\ \boxed{0}\ \boxed{R/S}\ \boxed{-3}\ \boxed{x \text{▲} t}\ \boxed{-2}$$
$$\boxed{GTO}\ \boxed{Int}\ \boxed{R/S}$$

The display shows 1.333 rounded to three decimals for the area beneath the curve from $x = -3$ to $x = -2$ (Figure 1.37).

The display shows 1.333 for the area from $x = 0$ to $x = 1$. From the symmetry of the graph it should not be surprising that these last two areas have the same numerical value. So the total area trapped between the curve and the x-axis over $-3 \leqslant x \leqslant 1$ is the sum of these three areas, rounded to two decimals:

$A = 1.333 + 1.333 + 1.333 = 4.00$ square units

If we had simply tried to find the area using $a = -3$ and $b = 1$, the region for $-2 < x < 0$ would have been assigned its *negative* value -1.333 yielding the *algebraic sum*

$1.333 + (-1.333) + 1.333 = 1.333$

rather than the area trapped between the curve and the x-axis. We verify this with the following keystrokes:

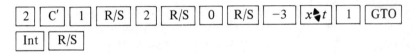

The display does show the algebraic sum 1.333 rounded to three decimals.

In summary, in finding the area trapped between the x-axis and a polynomial curve, we must:

1. determine where the polynomial has negative values
2. calculate the negative-signed area associated with those values,
3. then change the sign to plus, and
4. add the area beneath the x-axis to the positive-signed areas associated with the positive values of the curve.

As a second illustration, consider the polynomial shown in Figure 1.38:

$f(x) = x^3 - 4x^2 - x + 6$

Figure 1.38

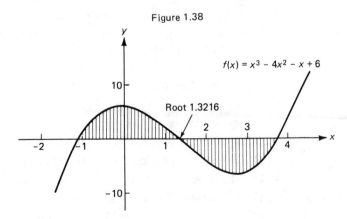

In Exercise 2 of Section 1.7 we found the root $r = 1.3216$ correct to four decimals. The signed area for $-1 < x < 1.3216$ will be positive and negative for the interval $1.3216 < x < 3.5$. We calculate each signed area separately:

| 3 | C' | 1 | R/S | −4 | R/S | −1 | R/S | 6 | R/S | −1 |

| $x \updownarrow t$ | 1.3216 | GTO | Int | R/S |

The display shows the positive signed area 9.657840589.

| 3 | C' | 1 | R/S | −4 | R/S | −1 | R/S | 6 | R/S | 1.3216 |

| $x \updownarrow t$ | 3.5 | GTO | Int | R/S |

The display shows the negative signed area -9.517215589.

The total area trapped between the x-axis and the polynomial from $x = -1$ to $x = 3.5$ is then given by

$$A = 9.657840589 + 9.517215589 = 19.175 \text{ square units,}$$

rounded to three decimals.

PROBLEMS 1.9

In each of Problems 1–5, find the area beneath the given nonnegative polynomial over the indicated interval, correct to three decimal places.

1. $y = x^4 + 3x^2 + 6$ from $x = 0$ to $x = 3$

2. $y = \sqrt{2}x^2 + \frac{1}{3}x - 1$ from $x = 1.5$ to $x = 4.75$

3. $y = 6x^5 + 5x^4 + 4x^3 + 3x^2 + 2x + 1$ from $x = \frac{1}{3}$ to $x = \frac{18}{19}$

4. $y = 7x^3 + \sqrt{3}x^2 - 2x + 6$ from $x = -1$ to $x = 4$

5. $y = x^{12} + 2x^{11} + 3x^{10} + 4x^9 + 5x^8 + 6x^7 + 7x^6 + 6x^5 + 5x^4 + 4x^3 + 3x^2 + 2x + 1$ from $x = 1.09$ to $x = \pi$

In Problems 6–15, find the area trapped between the x-axis and the given polynomial curve over the indicated interval, correct to three decimal places.

6. $y = x^2 - 7x + 6$ from $x = 1$ to $x = 6$

7. $y = x^2 - 7x + 6$ from $x = 2$ to $x = 8$

8. $y = 3 + 2x - x^2$ from $x = -2$ to $x = 2$

9. $y = 3 + 2x - x^2$ from $x = -2$ to $x = 5$

10. The curve in Problem 1 of Problem Section 1.7 from $x = -2$ to $x = 4$.

11. The curve in Problem 2 of Problem Section 1.7 from $x = -3$ to $x = 2$.

12. The curve in Problem 3 of Problem Section 1.7 from $x = -2$ to $x = 1$.

13. The curve in Problem 5 of Problem Section 1.7 from $x = -1$ to $x = 2$.

14. $y = x^4 - 9x^2 - 4x + 20$ from $x = -3$ to $x = 2$

15. $y = 2x^3 - 6x^2 + 3x + 2$ from $x = -1$ to $x = 2$

2

Functions, Limits, and Continuity

The polynomial functions investigated in the last chapter are especially easy to study. Polynomials are formed by merely summing powers of a variable multiplied by a constant, and so the only arithmetic processes involved are addition, subtraction, and multiplication. Much more could be said about polynomial behavior, and deeper results than we have mentioned are examined in modern algebra. But we must go on to other functions that are also important in science and in applied mathematics. Among these are the algebraic, trigonometric, and exponential functions.

You are going to study these functions in this chapter. In particular, we introduce the "limit" concept, which is fundamental to the calculus, which provides the basis for studying functional behavior. In later chapters you will see how it is used to find quantities like velocity and acceleration of a moving body at every instant of time, the rate of increase of profit per unit increase of production, the lengths of curves, and many other quantities.

Before you begin your study of this chapter, record the two programs PROBE and LIMIT, listed in Appendix A, on separate magnetic cards. Each program uses standard 479.59 partitioning and is to be recorded on a single side of a card. After recording each program, be sure it reads correctly back into your TI-59 calculator. We assume you are now thoroughly familiar with this procedure. After recording the cards, you are ready to begin your study of this chapter.

Section 2.1 Combining Functions and Rational Functions

In many applications a function arises as a combination of other functions. For example, suppose a car is headed due north and at any time t is located $f(t)$ miles north of a city P. A second car is headed due south and at any time t is located $g(t)$ miles south of P. Then the distance $s(t)$ between the two cars at any time is the sum of their individual distances from P (Figure 2.1). In other words,

$$s(t) = f(t) + g(t)$$

The function s is called the *sum* of the functions f and g, and it is written $s = f + g$.

Each of the four arithmetic operations can be used to combine functions. If f and g are functions, define the *sum* $f + g$, the *difference* $f - g$, the *product* fg, and the *quotient* f/g by the rules

$$(f + g)(x) = f(x) + g(x)$$
$$(f - g)(x) = f(x) - g(x)$$
$$(fg)(x) = f(x)g(x)$$
$$(f/g)(x) = f(x)/g(x) \quad g(x) \neq 0$$

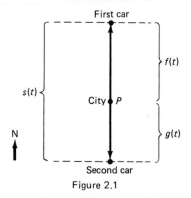

Figure 2.1

In each case the domain consists of the values of x for which both $f(x)$ and $g(x)$ are defined and the arithmetic operation makes sense. In the case of division we exclude the values of x when the denominator $g(x)$ equals zero, since division by zero is not permitted. We consider several examples of these functions in this section.

The prepared program PROBE* is designed to assist you in studying these new functions by plotting their graphs. PROBE can produce values for any function that can be keyed into your TI–59. The use of the program requires that you key in a subroutine for the function you wish to investigate. Let's review the overall characteristics of the program.

*PROBE first appeared in the Naval Postgraduate School publication *Calculator Calculus* by Herbert D. Peckham and the author.

PROBE uses program steps 000 through 133, and memory locations 01 through 04. The balance of the program steps (134 through 479) and memory locations (00, and 05 through 59) are available for your use while evaluating $f(x)$. When PROBE jumps to the subroutine to evaluate $f(x)$, x is in the display. Consequently one of your first steps in the subroutine should be to store the value of x away where it is always available while computing $f(x)$. The first two steps in the subroutine for $f(x)$ *must* be

because PROBE assumes that the subroutine to calculate $f(x)$ is located at label C'. As is the case with all subroutines, the last two steps *must* be

| INV | SBR |

Each of the subparts of the program is accessed by one of the special labels on your calculator. These labels are as follows:

D' This loads the starting value of x into the program.

E' The increment Δx is loaded with this label.

A Two things are accomplished when this key is pressed. First, the value of x is replaced by $x + \Delta x$, then $f(x)$ is computed using the new value of x. Repeated use of this key permits you to step forward in x, displaying the value of $f(x)$ at each step.

B This is the same as the previous label except that x is replaced by $x - \Delta x$, and you step backward.

C This label causes the central difference approximation for $f'(x)$ to be computed using

$$\frac{f(x + \Delta x/2) - f(x - \Delta x/2)}{\Delta x}$$

We will explain this calculation in Section 3.2.

D This label causes the forward difference approximation for $f'(x)$ to be computed using

$$\frac{f(x + \Delta x) - f(x)}{\Delta x}$$

This calculation will be explained in Section 3.1.

A' In your investigation of $f(x)$ you may discover that Δx is too large. This key causes Δx to be replaced by $\Delta x/10$.

B' If a larger value of Δx is required, this key causes Δx to be replaced by $10 \Delta x$.

Any time you wish to see the current value of x displayed, press this label.

Before illustrating the use of PROBE, it will be helpful to point out the best method for evaluating a polynomial on your calcuator. If

$$p(x) = a_n x^n + a_{n-1} x^{n-1} + \ldots + a_1 x + a_0$$

is a given polynomial, then it is best evaluated in its *nested form*

$$p(x) = \{\ldots [(a_n x + a_{n-1})x + a_{n-2}]x + \ldots + a_1\} x + a_0$$

For instance,

$$p(x) = 2x^5 - 8x^4 + 9x^3 - 13x^2 + 4x + 6$$

can be evaluated as

$$p(x) = \{[((2x - 8)x + 9)x - 13]x + 4\} x + 6 \tag{2.1}$$

In this nested form there is no need for the power $\boxed{y^x}$ key: All that is needed is to multiply and add, and even the parentheses key can be avoided. To evaluate Equation 2.1 when $x = 3.0125$, for instance, carry out the following keystrokes:

3.0125	STO	00	$\times$	2	$-$	8	$=$	$\times$	RCL	00	$+$
9	$=$	$\times$	RCL	00	$-$	13	$=$	$\times$	RCL	00	$+$	4
$=$	$\times$	RCL	00	$+$	6	$=$

The display shows -16.535 rounded to three decimals. We are now ready to illustrate the use of PROBE in evaluating and graphing functions.

EXERCISE 1.
SUMMING TWO FUNCTIONS

Consider the functions $f(x) = x^2 - x - 2$ and $g(x) = x^3 - 4x$ (Figures 2.2a and 2.2b). We form a new function from f and g by summing them:

$$(f + g)(x) = f(x) + g(x) = (x^2 - x - 2) + (x^3 - 4x)$$
$$= x^3 + x^2 - 5x - 2$$

The value of the sum $f + g$ at a point x is obtained by adding together the numbers $f(x)$ and $g(x)$. For instance,

$$(f + g)(1) = f(1) + g(1) = (-2) + (-3) = -5$$

Let's use PROBE to calculate a table of values for the sum $f + g$.

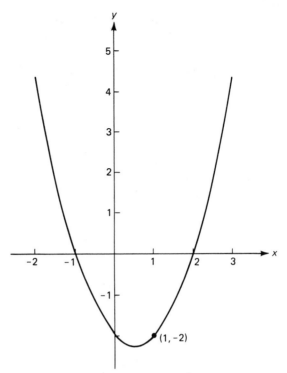

Figure 2.2a Graph of $f(x) = x^2 - x - 2$.

Figure 2.2b Graph of $g(x) = x^3 - 4x$.

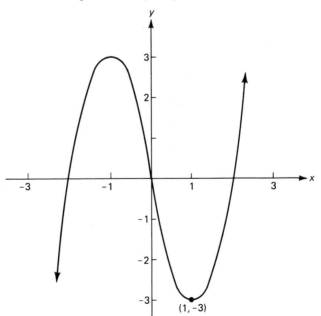

Finding a Table of Function Values

Step 1: Read side 1 of the magnetic card PROBE into your TI-59 with standard partitioning.

Step 2: Key in the particular function to be investigated as follows:

| GTO | 134 | LRN | Position the program pointer to location 134, the entry of the subroutine for the function evaluation, and switch the calculator to the learn mode.

| Lb1 | C' | Required statements to label the subroutine.

| STO | 00 | First statement stores the current value of x.

Next key in the keystrokes for the particular function $h(x)$ to be investigated. In our example,

$$h(x) = x^3 + x^2 - 5x - 2$$

and is keyed in as follows:

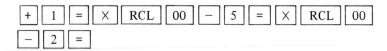

After the function is keyed in, press

| INV | SBR | Required statements to return from the subroutine.

| LRN | Switch the calculator back to the calculate mode.

Step 3: Verify that the subroutine was keyed in correctly.

Step 4: Calculate the table using the special label keys for PROBE. For our particular function $h = f + g$, perform the following keystrokes:

(enter)	−4		
(press)		D'	Load initial $x_0 = -4.0$.
(enter)	0.5		
(press)		E'	Load increment $\Delta x = 0.5$.
(press)		Fix 2	Set the calculator display for two digits past the decimal point.
(press)		A	The display shows $h(x) = -15.13$.
(press)		E	The display shows the current x value, $x = -3.50$. Thus $h(-3.5) = -15.13$

By repeatedly pressing $\boxed{A}$ and $\boxed{E}$, you obtain the following table of values:

x	$h(x) = x^3 + x^2 - 5x - 2$
−3.5	−15.13
−3.0	−5.00
−2.5	1.13
−2.0	4.00
−1.5	4.38
−1.0	3.00
−0.5	0.63
0	−2.00
0.5	−4.13
1.0	−5.00
1.5	−3.88
2.0	0.00
2.5	7.38
3.0	19.00

The graph of $h = f + g$ is shown in Figure 2.3. If f and g are both polynomial functions, as in our example, the sum $f + g$ is also a polynomial function.

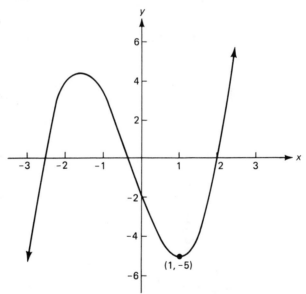

Figure 2.3 Graph of $f(x) + g(x) = x^3 + x^2 - 5x - 2$.

EXERCISE 2.
MULTIPLYING TWO FUNCTIONS

For the functions f and g given in Exercise 1, the product is given by

$$(fg)(x) = f(x)g(x) = (x^2 - x - 2)(x^3 - 4x)$$
$$= x^5 - x^4 - 6x^3 + 4x^2 + 8x$$

Using PROBE we calculate a table of values for the product over the interval $-3 \leqslant x \leqslant 3$. Key in the following keystrokes:

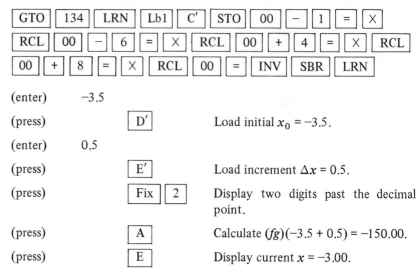

(enter)		−3.5		
(press)			D′	Load initial $x_0 = -3.5$.
(enter)		0.5		
(press)			E′	Load increment $\Delta x = 0.5$.
(press)			Fix 2	Display two digits past the decimal point.
(press)			A	Calculate $(fg)(-3.5 + 0.5) = -150.00$.
(press)			E	Display current $x = -3.00$.

Repeatedly press $\boxed{A}$ and $\boxed{E}$ to obtain the following table:

x	$(fg)(x) = x^5 - x^4 - 6x^3 + 4x^2 + 8x$
−3.0	−150.00
−2.5	−37.97
−2.0	0.00
−1.5	4.59
−1.0	0.00
−0.5	−2.34
0	0.00
0.5	4.22
1.0	6.00
1.5	3.28
2.0	0.00
2.5	9.84
3.0	60.00

A graph of the product fg is shown in Figure 2.4. As is the case with the sum (or difference), the product of polynomial functions is again a polynomial function. Yet the quotient of two polynomials does not, in general, yield another polynomial but rather a different kind of function. Quotients of polynomials are called *rational functions*.

If f and g are both polynomials, then the domain of the rational function

$$h(x) = \frac{f(x)}{g(x)}$$

consists of all points x for which $f(x)$ and $g(x)$ are both defined and $g(x) \neq 0$ (since division by zero is undefined).

Let's examine the graphs of several rational functions to investigate the various types of behavior that can occur.

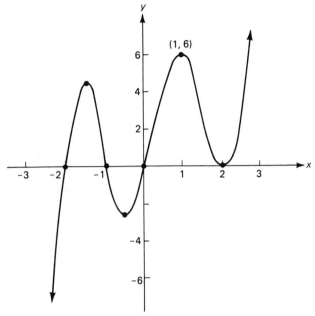

Figure 2.4 Graph of $f(x)g(x) = x^5 - x^4 - 6x^3 + 4x^2 + 8x$.

EXERCISE 3.
HORIZONTAL AND VERTICAL ASYMPTOTES

Consider the rational function

$$f(x) = \frac{x + 2}{x - 3}$$

Observe that x cannot equal 3 because the denominator cannot be 0. Let's see what happens to the graph of f near $x = 3$. Using PROBE, key in the following keystrokes for the subroutine to evaluate $f(x)$:

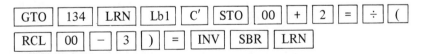

Let's calculate a table of values as x gets closer to 3 "from the left":

(enter)	1.9		
(press)		D′	Load initial $x_0 = 1.9$.
(enter)	0.1		
(press)		E′	Load increment $\Delta x = 0.1$.

78 Successively press ⬚A and ⬚E to obtain the following table, with entries rounded to one decimal place:

x	2.0	2.1	2.2	2.3	2.4	2.5	2.6	2.7	2.8	2.9
f(x)	−4.0	−4.6	−5.3	−6.1	−7.3	−9.0	−11.5	−15.7	−24.0	−49.0

Decrease Δx, and allow x to advance more slowly toward 3: press ⬚A′ and then press ⬚A and ⬚E successively to obtain:

x	2.91	2.92	2.93	2.94	2.95	2.96	2.97	2.98	2.99
f(x)	−54.6	−61.5	−70.4	−82.3	−99.0	−124.0	−165.7	−249.0	−499.0

We observe that the values of $f(x)$ become larger in absolute value as x gets closer to 3 "from the left." Next, let's examine the behavior as x gets closer to 3 "from the right":

(enter)   4.1

(press)   ⬚D′   Load initial $x_0 = 4.1$.

(press)   ⬚B′   Multiply $\Delta x = 0.01$ by 10 to increase the increment to $\Delta x = 0.1$.

Successively press ⬚B and ⬚E to "back up" on $x = 3$, obtaining the table:

x	4.0	3.9	3.8	3.7	3.6	3.5	3.4	3.3	3.2	3.1
f(x)	6.0	6.6	7.3	8.1	9.3	11.0	13.5	17.7	26.0	51.0

Now decrease Δx by pressing ⬚A′ , and continue to back up:

x	3.09	3.08	3.07	3.06	3.05	3.04	3.03	3.02	3.01
f(x)	56.6	63.5	72.4	84.3	101.0	126.0	167.7	251.0	501.0

Observe again that the values of $f(x)$ become larger in absolute value as x gets closer to 3. Mathematically, this situation is described by saying that the graph of the function f is getting closer to the line $x = 3$ "asymptotically," and that the line $x = 3$ is called a *vertical asymptote*. The situation is depicted in Figure 2.5.

Next let's see what happens to the graph of f as the values of x become large in absolute value. First we consider the case when x is positive and grows large.

(enter)   −5.0

(press)   ⬚D′   Load initial $x_0 = -5.0$.

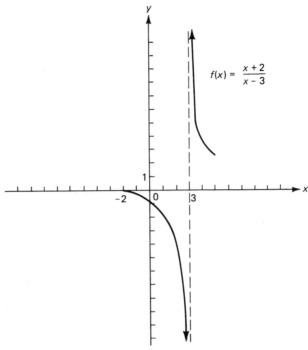

Figure 2.5 The graph of *f* has the vertical asymptote *x* = 3.

$$f(x) = \frac{x+2}{x-3}$$

(enter) 10.0

(press) E' Load Δx = 10.0.

Successively press A and E to obtain the following table, with entries rounded to one decimal place:

x	5	15	25	35	45	55	65	75	85	95	105	115
f(x)	3.5	1.4	1.2	1.2	1.1	1.1	1.1	1.1	1.1	1.1	1.0	1.0

As the values of *x* become larger in absolute value the values of *f(x)* get closer and closer to 1. For negative values of *x* we obtain,

x	−5	−15	−25	−35	−45	−55	−65	−75	−85	−95	−105	−115
f(x)	0.4	0.7	0.8	0.9	0.9	0.9	0.9	0.9	0.9	0.9	1.0	1.0

Again the values of *f(x)* get closer and closer to 1 as *x* grows large in absolute value. [The fact that the calculator actually *shows* 1.0 eventually is due to roundoff error. Mathematically, the values of *f(x)* never quite reach 1.] Thus we say that *f(x)* approaches 1 "asymptotically," and that the line *y* = 1 is called a *horizontal asymptote*. Notice that if *x* > 3, then *f(x)* > 1, and if *x* < 3, then *f(x)* < 1. The completed graph of *f* showing its overall behavior is given in Figure 2.6.

79

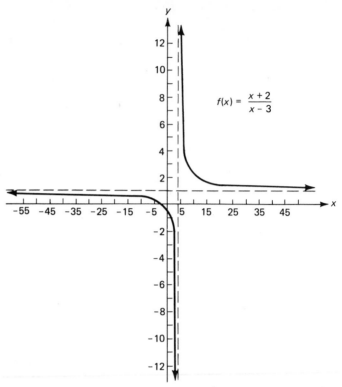

Figure 2.6 The graph of f has the horizontal asymptote $y = 1$ as well as the vertical asymptote $X = 3$.

EXERCISE 4.
SYMMETRY ABOUT THE y-AXIS

Let's determine a table of values, and plot the graph, for the rational function

$$g(x) = \frac{x^2}{1 + x^2}$$

over the interval $-4 \leqslant x \leqslant 4$. Observe that there are no restrictions on x in order that the formula for $g(x)$ be arithmetically valid. Using PROBE, key in the following keystrokes for the subroutine to evaluate $g(x)$:

GTO	134	LRN	Lb1	C′	x²	÷	(	CE	+	1	)

=	INV	SBR	LRN

First we consider positive values of x. We want more detail for smaller values of x, so for $0 \leqslant x \leqslant 1$ we use the increment $\Delta x = 0.25$, and for $1 \leqslant x \leqslant 4$, the increment $\Delta x = 0.5$.

(enter)   −0.25

80   (press)   D′   Load initial $x_0 = -0.25$.

(enter)   0.25

(press) $\boxed{E'}$ Load increment $\Delta x = 0.25$.

Successively press $\boxed{A}$ and $\boxed{E}$ for the following table, changing the increment to 0.5 when the current value of x reaches 1:

x	0	0.25	0.50	0.75	1.0	1.5	2.0	2.5	3.0	3.5	4.0
$g(x)$	0	0.06	0.20	0.36	0.50	0.69	0.80	0.86	0.90	0.92	0.94

For negative values of x we obtain,

x	−0.25	−0.50	−0.75	−1.0	−1.5	−2.0	−2.5	−3.0	−3.5	−4.0
$g(x)$	0.06	0.20	0.36	0.50	0.69	0.80	0.86	0.90	0.92	0.94

Notice that the values $g(x)$ and $g(-x)$ are the same. This situation is described
mathematically by saying that $g(x)$ is *symmetric about the y-axis.* In fact, in
this example,

$$g(-x) = \frac{(-x)^2}{1 + (-x)^2} = \frac{x^2}{1 + x^2} = g(x)$$

The graph of $g(x)$ is given in Figure 2.7. Observe from the graph that $y = 1$ is
a horizontal asymptote of g (you should verify this with your calculator).

In general, if a function f is represented by an expression that remains
unchanged when $-x$ is substituted for x in the expression, then $f(x) = f(-x)$
and the graph is said to be *symmetric about the y-axis.* In this situation, the
point $(-x,y)$ is on the graph whenever the point (x,y) is on the graph. The
function f is also said to be an *even function.*

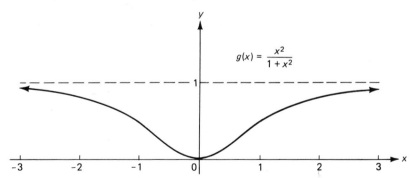

Figure 2.7 The graph of g is symmetric about the y-axis, and the line $y = 1$ is a horizontal
asymptote.

EXERCISE 5.
SYMMETRY ABOUT THE ORIGIN

Let's obtain the graph for the rational function

$$h(x) = \frac{4x}{x^2 + 1}$$

for $-5 \leqslant x \leqslant 5$. Key in the following keystrokes for the PROBE subroutine to evaluate $h(x)$:

GTO	134	LRN	Lb1	C′	STO	00	×	4	=	÷	(

RCL	00	x^2	+	1	)	=	INV	SBR	LRN

For positive values of x with an increment $\Delta x = 0.5$, we obtain the following table using PROBE:

x	0	0.5	1.0	1.5	2.0	2.5	3.0	3.5	4.0	4.5	5.0
$f(x)$	0	1.6	2.0	1.8	1.6	1.4	1.2	1.1	0.9	0.8	0.8

For negative values of x we obtain,

x	−0.5	−1.0	−1.5	−2.0	−2.5	−3.0	−3.5	−4.0	−4.5	−5.0
$f(x)$	−1.6	−2.0	−1.8	−1.6	−1.4	−1.2	−1.1	−0.9	−0.8	−0.8

Notice that the values $h(-x)$ equal the values $-h(x)$; we say that $h(x)$ is *symmetric about the origin.* To verify this,

$$h(-x) = \frac{4(-x)}{(-x)^2 + 1} = -\frac{4x}{x^2 + 1} = -h(x)$$

The graph of h is given in Figure 2.8. It is not difficult to verify that $y = 0$ is a horizontal asymptote. In general, if a function f is represented by an expression that changes sign when $-x$ is substituted for x in the expression, then $f(-x) = -f(x)$ and the graph of f is *symmetric about the origin.* In this situation, the point $(-x, -y)$ is on the graph whenever the point (x, y) is on the graph. The function f is also said to be an *odd function.*

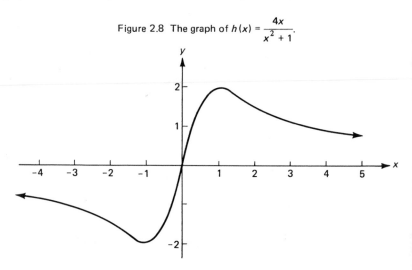

Figure 2.8 The graph of $h(x) = \dfrac{4x}{x^2 + 1}$.

EXERCISE 6.
ANOTHER EXAMPLE
OF A RATIONAL FUNCTION

Consider the rational function

$$r(x) = \frac{3x^2 - 1}{x^3}$$

First observe that $r(-x) = -r(x)$ so that the graph is symmetric about the origin. Moreover, we must restrict x so that $x \neq 0$. Key in the following keystrokes for PROBE:

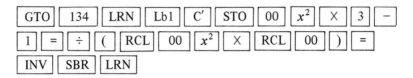

Due to the symmetry we obtain a table of $r(x)$ for positive values of x only:

x	0.25	0.5	0.75	1.0	1.25	1.5	1.75	2.0	2.5	3.0	4.0	5.0
$r(x)$	−52.0	−2.0	1.6	2.0	1.9	1.7	1.5	1.4	1.1	0.96	0.73	0.59

Backing up on $x = 0$ "from the right" we obtain the following table:

x	0.10	0.09	0.08	0.07	0.06	0.05	0.04	0.03	0.02	0.01
$r(x)$	−970	−1338	−1916	−2873	−4580	−7940	−15550	−36937	−124850	−999700

Thus we observe from the table that the vertical line $x = 0$ is a vertical asymptote. Finally, for large positive values of x, we find that $y = 0$ is a horizontal asymptote:

x	10	50	100	250	500	1000
$r(x)$	0.3	0.06	0.03	0.01	0.01	0.00

In obtaining this last table of values, we loaded $\Delta x = 0.0$, then each value of x individually using the key D′ and then pressing A . The graph of $r(x)$ showing its behavior is given in Figure 2.9.

EXERCISE 7.
ROOTS OF FUNCTIONS

The program PROBE can be used to locate the roots of any function that can be keyed in as a subroutine, with the root found to any desired degree of accuracy within the limitations of the calculator.

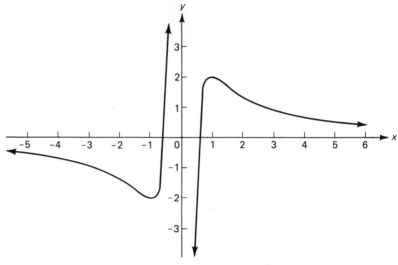

Figure 2.9 The graph of $r(x) = \dfrac{3x^2 - 1}{x^3}$.

As an illustration we will locate the root of the rational function

$$r(x) = \frac{3x^2 - 1}{x^3}$$

that lies between 0 and 1 (Figure 2.9). First be sure the program PROBE and the subroutine for $r(x)$ are still loaded into your calculator from Exercise 6. Next carry out the following procedures, noting the value of the display and the corresponding comment at each stage:

| Fix | 4 | | Set the calculator to display 4 digits past the decimal point. |

| 0.5 | D' | | Load $x_0 = 0.5$. |

| 0.1 | E' | | Load $\Delta x = 0.1$. |

PRESS	DISPLAY	COMMENT
A	0.3704	We are right of the root, $f(x)$ is positive.
B	−2.0000	Have crossed past the root. We are closer on the right side.
A	0.3704	Return to the right side of the root.
A'	0.0100	New decreased value of Δx.
B	0.2157	Continue searching to the left.
B	0.0472	
B	−0.1366	Have crossed past the root again.
A	0.0472	Return to the right side because we are closer to the root.

A'	0.0010	New decreased value of Δx.
B	0.0295	Continue searching to the left.
B	0.0117	
B	−0.0063	Have crossed past the root, and we are closer on the left side.
A'	0.0001	New decreased value of Δx.
A	−0.0045	Continue searching to the right.
A	−0.0027	
A	−0.0009	
A	0.0009	Have crossed past the root.
A'	0.0000	Now $\Delta x = 0.00001$
B	0.0007	Search to the left.
B	0.0005	
B	0.0004	
B	0.0002	
B	0.0000	$r(x)$ is zero to four decimal places.
E	0.5774	Display the current value of x.

Since $\Delta x = 0.00001$, the root 0.5774 is correct to all four decimal places shown.

PROBLEMS 2.1

In each of Problems 1-12, graph the given rational function, locate its roots, horizontal and vertical asymptotes (if any), and identify any symmetries.

1. $f(x) = \dfrac{x^2 + 1}{x^2 - 1}$

2. $f(x) = \dfrac{x^4 + 3}{x}$

3. $f(x) = \dfrac{x - 2}{x^2 - 9x + 20}$

4. $f(x) = \dfrac{4}{x^2 - 9}$

5. $f(x) = \dfrac{x(x - 1)}{x^2 - 4}$

6. $f(x) = \dfrac{5}{3x - 7}$

7. $f(x) = \dfrac{x - \frac{1}{3}}{x^2 - 2}$

8. $f(x) = \dfrac{7}{x^2 + 5}$

9. $f(x) = \dfrac{2x^2 + 1}{2x^2 - 3x}$

10. $f(x) = \dfrac{x^3}{x^3 + 1}$

11. $f(x) = \dfrac{x^4 + 1}{(x - 1)(x + 2)}$

12. $f(x) = \dfrac{x(x - 2)}{(x^2 - 1)(x - 3)}$

13. In physics, Boyle's law states that the pressure p and the volume v of a certain container of gas satisfies the equation $p = 3{,}000/v$. The pressure is measured in pounds per square inch (lb/in^2) and the volume in cubic inches (in^3). Obtain a table of values and sketch the graph of $p = 3{,}000/v$ for positive values of v.

14. Suppose the cost C in thousands of dollars to remove x percent of a pollutant from the environment is given by

$$C(x) = \frac{6.65x}{100 - x}$$

Graph the function $C(x)$. Is it possible to remove *all* the pollutant from the environment?

15. A manufacturer estimates that if x machines are used, the cost C of a production run will be

$$C(x) = 19.5x + \frac{2{,}351}{x}$$

dollars. Graph this cost function. From the graph, estimate how many machines the manufacturer should use to minimize the cost.

16. Newton's law of gravitation says that the force of attraction between two particles of matter varies inversely as the square of the distance between them. If F denotes the force and x the distance, then

$$F(x) = \frac{C}{x^2}$$

for some constant C. If the force of attraction upon a meteorite 1,000 mi above the earth's surface is 10 lb, what would the meteorite weigh at the surface? Assume the radius of the earth is 4,000 mi.

In Problems 17–23, find the roots of the given functions correct to four decimal places.

17. $f(x) = \dfrac{1}{x^2} + 2x$

18. $f(x) = \dfrac{x(x - 0.4) - 1.4}{x + 1}$

19. $f(x) = x^2 - \dfrac{5}{x}$

20. $f(x) = x - 4 + \dfrac{5}{x + 2}$

21. $f(x) = \dfrac{x^2 - 3x + 1}{x + 1}$

22. $f(x) = \dfrac{x^3 - 4x^2 - x + 6}{x^2 + 5x + 6}$

23. $f(x) = \dfrac{x^5 - 3x^4 + 5x^3 - 6x^2 + 2x - 1}{x^2 - 4}$

Section 2.2 Algebraic Functions

Another process that can be applied to real numbers is root extraction, although we sometimes have to restrict the numbers to be nonnegative. If we combine the process of root extraction with the operations of addition, subtraction, multiplication, and division, and if we then apply these processes to polynomials, we obtain new functions. A function defined in terms of polynomials and roots of polynomials is called an *algebraic function;* it is obtained by arithmetic processes. Thus

$$f(x) = \sqrt{1 - x^2} \qquad g(x) = \frac{x^{1/3}}{(x^2 + 1)^{3/2}} \qquad h(x) = \left(x - \frac{1}{\sqrt{x}}\right)^2$$

are examples of algebraic functions. Let's investigate the graphs of several of these functions.

EXERCISE 1.
THE SQUARE ROOT FUNCTION

If x is a positive real number, the (positive) *square root* of x, written $\sqrt{x}$, is the *positive* real number that, when squared, is x. Symbolically

$$\sqrt{x} \cdot \sqrt{x} = x$$

Notice from the definition that $\sqrt{x}$ is always positive. This is a source of confusion for many students of arithmetic. The equation

$$y^2 = x \qquad x > 0 \tag{2.2}$$

has *two* possible solutions: One solution is $\sqrt{x}$ (which is positive), and the other is $-\sqrt{x}$ (which is negative). Therefore, $\sqrt{x}$ itself does not mean "plus or minus the square root of x," but is simply the positive solution $y = \sqrt{x}$ to the quadratic equation 2.2.

Using the square root key $\boxed{\sqrt{x}}$ on your TI-59, it is easy to obtain the following table of values of the square root function for nonnegative x:

x	0	1	2	3	4	5	6
$y = \sqrt{x}$	0.0	1.00	1.41	1.73	2.00	2.24	2.45

The graph is given in Figure 2.10.

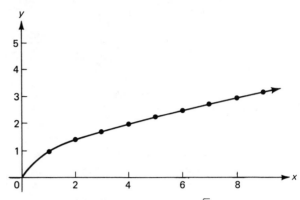

Figure 2.10 The graph of $y = \sqrt{x}, x \geqslant 0$.

EXERCISE 2.
THE FUNCTION $y = 1 - x^{2/3}$

Using the program PROBE, key in the following keystrokes to evaluate this function:

| GTO | 134 | LRN | Lb1 | C' | x^2 | y^x | 3 | $1/x$ | = | +/- |

| + | 1 | = | INV | SBR | LRN |

The following table is then easily obtained:

x	−5	−4	−3	−2	−1	0	1	2	3	4	5
y	−1.92	−1.52	−1.08	−0.59	0.0	1.0	0.0	−0.59	−1.08	−1.52	−1.92

The graph is shown in Figure 2.11. Observe that it is symmetric about the y-axis.

Composition of Functions

Suppose that f and g are given functions. Let x be in the domain of g. If $g(x)$ belongs to the domain of f, then a unique number results by applying f to $g(x)$. As x varies, we obtain in this way a new function $f \circ g$, called the *composition of f and g*, whose rule is

$$(f \circ g)(x) = f[g(x)]$$

and whose domain consists of all numbers x in the domain of g for which the number $g(x)$ belongs to the domain of f. The notation "$f \circ g$" is read "f of g" or "f composed with g."

For instance, if $f(x) = x^2 + 1$ and $g(x) = 3x - 1$, then

$$(f \circ g)(x) = f[g(x)] = f(3x - 1) = (3x - 1)^2 + 1 = 9x^2 - 6x + 2$$

For the same functions, if we take the composition in the reverse order, we get

$$(g \circ f)(x) = g[f(x)] = g(x^2 + 1) = 3(x^2 + 1) - 1 = 3x^2 + 2$$

In general, therefore, the composition $g \circ f$ is a different function from $f \circ g$. Composition is a powerful way to obtain new functions from old ones.

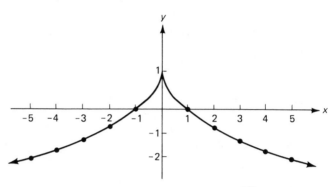

Figure 2.11 The graph of $y = 1 - x^{2/3}$.

EXERCISE 3.
THE ABSOLUTE VALUE FUNCTION

The *absolute value* of a number x equals x if x is nonnegative, and equals $-x$ if x is negative. The absolute value of x is written $|x|$. Thus

$$|3| = 3 \quad \text{and} \quad |-3| = -(-3) = 3$$

The absolute value of a number corresponds to its distance from 0 on the real number line. The graph of the absolute value function

$$y = |x|$$

is shown in Figure 2.12.

The following equations summarize the main properties of absolute value. The symbols a and b denote arbitrary real numbers that may be positive, negative, or zero. Of course, if a is negative then $-a$ is positive.

$$|-a| = |a| \geqslant 0 \tag{2.3}$$

$$\left| \frac{1}{a} \right| = \frac{1}{|a|} \qquad a \neq 0 \tag{2.4}$$

$$|ab| = |a||b| \tag{2.5}$$

$$|a + b| \leqslant |a| + |b| \tag{2.6}$$

$$|a-b| \geqslant |a|-|b| \tag{2.7}$$

$$||a|-|b|| \leqslant |a+b| \tag{2.8}$$

Equation 2.6 is called the *triangle inequality* for absolute value. In words, it says that the absolute value of a sum is less than or equal to the sum of the absolute values.

The absolute value and square root functions are related by the equation

$$\sqrt{x^2} = |x| \tag{2.9}$$

Equation 2.9 holds for every real number x because $|x|$ is nonnegative and

$$|x| \cdot |x| = |x^2| = x^2$$

Thus the absolute value of x satisfies the requirements demanded of the number that is the square root of x^2 and establishes 2.9. From Equation 2.9 we also see that the absolute value function is the composition $f \circ g$, where $f(x) = \sqrt{x}$ and $g(x) = x^2$.

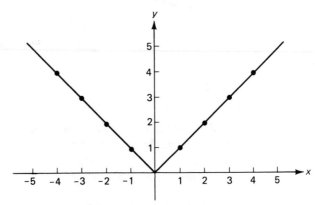

Figure 2.12 The graph of the absolute value function $y = |x|$.

Next let's investigate how absolute value can be used to express the distance between two real numbers. Suppose that c is a fixed number on the number line and that x is any other number whose distance from c is less than some positive constant δ. Then it must be true that

$$c - \delta < x < c + \delta$$

or equivalently

$$-\delta < x - c < \delta \tag{2.10}$$

(See Figure 2.13.) Now the inequalities in the expression 2.10 hold if and only if

$$|x - c| < \delta \tag{2.11}$$

That is, the inequalities in 2.10 and 2.11 are equivalent. Thus *the distance be-tween two numbers x and c being smaller than some positive constant δ is equivalent to the inequality* $|x - c| < \delta$. Moreover, the measure of the distance between two numbers is obtained by taking the absolute value of their difference. This property of absolute value will be useful in studying the behavior of functions.

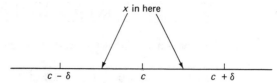

Figure 2.13 The distance between x and c is smaller than δ whenever x lies between $c - \delta$ and $c + \delta$.

EXERCISE 4.
THE UPPER UNIT SEMICIRCLE

A *circle* is the path of a point (x,y) whose distance from a fixed point (h,k), called the *center*, is a constant *r*, called the *radius*. Using the distance formula (1.1) from Chapter 1, this translates into

$$(x - h)^2 + (y - k)^2 = r^2 \tag{2.12}$$

Thus Equation 2.12 represents an equation of the circle with center (h, k) and radius *r*. In particular, if $(h,k) = (0,0)$ is the origin and $r = 1$, we obtain the *unit circle*

$$x^2 + y^2 = 1 \tag{2.13}$$

For nonnegative values of *y*, we get the upper unit semicircle function

$$y = \sqrt{1 - x^2}$$

whose graph is shown in Figure 2.14. Notice that the domain of this function is $-1 \leqslant x \leqslant 1$, since taking the square root of a negative number is not permitted.

Figure 2.14 The graph of the upper unit semicircle
$y = \sqrt{1 - x^2}$.

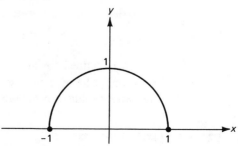

EXERCISE 5.

THE FUNCTION $y = x/\sqrt{1 + x^2}$

Using the program PROBE, key in the following keystrokes to evaluate this function:

| GTO | 134 | LRN | Lb1 | C′ | STO | 00 | x^2 | + | 1 | = |

| $\sqrt{x}$ | 1/x | × | RCL | 00 | = | INV | SBR | LRN |

Next obtain the following table of values:

x	0	0.5	1.0	1.5	2.0	2.5	3.0	3.5	4.0	5.0	9.0
y	0	0.45	0.71	0.83	0.89	0.93	0.95	0.96	0.97	0.98	0.99

Since $(-x, -y)$ is on the graph whenever (x, y) is there, the graph is symmetric about the origin. Observe also that the lines $y = -1$ and $y = 1$ are horizontal asymptotes. The graph is shown in Figure 2.15.

EXERCISE 6.

THE FUNCTION $y = \sqrt{x}\,(x - 4.5)^2/3.5$

Using the program PROBE, key in the following keystrokes to evaluate this function:

| GTO | 134 | LRN | Lb1 | C′ | STO | 00 | $\sqrt{x}$ | × | (| RCL |

| 00 | − | 4.5 |) | x^2 | ÷ | 3.5 | = | INV | SBR | LRN |

Notice that the function is defined only for nonnegative values of x. Thus we obtain the following table:

x	0	0.25	0.50	0.75	1.00	1.25	1.50	1.75	2.00	2.50	3.00
y	0	2.58	3.23	3.48	3.50	3.37	3.15	2.86	2.53	1.81	1.11

x	3.50	4.00	4.50	5.00	5.50	6.00	6.50	7.00
y	0.53	0.14	0	0.16	0.67	1.57	2.91	4.72

The graph is shown in Figure 2.16.

EXERCISE 7.

THE FUNCTION $y = x^{1/3} + x^{2/3}$

This function is defined for all values of x. Since the power key y^x on your TI-59 cannot be used to raise negative values to a power, you will have to test the current value of x and use the calculation

92 $y = - (|x|^{1/3}) + (x^2)^{1/3}$

whenever $x \leqslant 0$. Figure 2.17 is a flow chart describing the logic of the routine to calculate y.

Now key in the following keystrokes for this function evaluation, as a subroutine to PROBE:

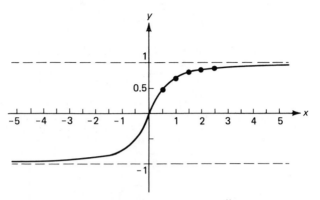

Figure 2.15 The graph of $y = \dfrac{x}{\sqrt{1 + x^2}}$.

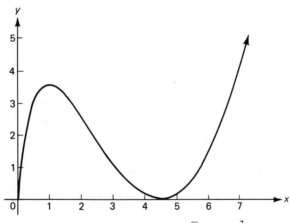

Figure 2.16 The graph of $y = \dfrac{\sqrt{x}\,(x - 4.5)^2}{3.5}$.

Figure 2.17 Flow chart to calculate $y = x^{1/3} + x^{2/3}$.

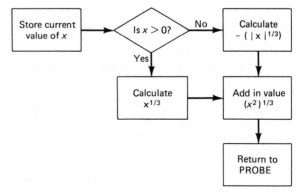

| GTO | 134 | LRN | Lb1 | C′ | STO | 00 | CP | INV | $x \geqslant t$ |

| $|x|$ | y^x | 3 | $1/x$ | Lb1 | SUM | + | RCL | 00 | x^2 | y^x | 3 |

| $1/x$ | = | INV | SBR | Lb1 | $|x|$ | $|x|$ | y^x | 3 | $1/x$ | = |

| +/− | GTO | SUM | LRN |

Next obtain the following table of values:

x	−5.0	−4.5	−4.0	−3.5	−3.0	−2.5	−2.0	−1.5	−1.0
y	1.21	1.07	0.93	0.79	0.64	0.48	0.33	0.17	0

x	−0.5	−0.25	0	0.25	0.50	0.75	1.0	1.5	2.0	2.5
y	−0.16	−0.23	0	1.03	1.42	1.73	2.00	2.46	2.85	3.20

x	3.0	3.5	4.0	5.0	6.0
y	3.52	3.82	4.11	4.63	5.12

The graph is shown in Figure 2.18.

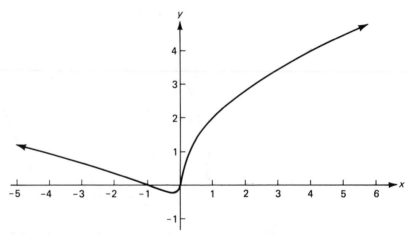

Figure 2.18 The graph of $y = x^{1/3} + x^{2/3}$.

EXERCISE 8.
THE FUNCTION $y = x^{1/3}(x-1)^{2/3}$

This function is defined for all values of x, but you must make the same adjustments in calculating y for negative values of x as in Exercise 7. Thus key in the following keystrokes for PROBE:

| GTO | 134 | LRN | Lb1 | C′ | STO | 00 | CP | INV | $x \geqslant t$ |

| $|x|$ | y^x | 3 | $1/x$ | Lb1 | Prd | × | (| RCL | 00 | − | 1 |) |

| x^2 | y^x | 3 | $1/x$ | = | INV | SBR | Lb1 | $|x|$ | $|x|$ | y^x | 3 |

| $1/x$ | = | +/− | GTO | Prd | LRN |

Next obtain the following table of values:

x	-5.0	-4.0	-3.0	-2.0	-1.0	-0.75	-0.50	-0.25	0
y	-5.65	-4.64	-3.63	-2.62	-1.59	-1.32	-1.04	-0.73	0

x	0.25	0.50	0.75	1.00	1.25	1.50	2.0	2.5	3.0	4.0	5.0
y	0.52	0.50	0.36	0	0.43	0.72	1.26	1.78	2.29	3.30	4.31

The graph is shown in Figure 2.19.

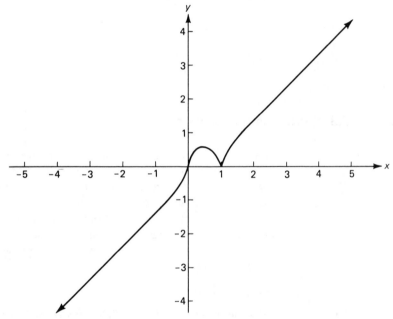

Figure 2.19 The graph of $y = x^{1/3} (x - 1)^{2/3}$.

PROBLEMS 2.2

In each of Problems 1-10, graph the given algebraic function. Identify any symmetries and horizontal or vertical asymptotes.

1. $y = x^{1/3}$

2. $y = \sqrt{x - x^2}$

3. $y = \sqrt{9 + x^2}$

4. $y = 2x + 3x^{2/3}$

5. $y = \dfrac{x^2 + x + 7}{\sqrt{2x + 1}}$

6. $y = \sqrt{\dfrac{x}{x + 1}}$

7. $y = x - x^{1/3}$

8. $y = \sqrt{x} - \dfrac{x}{2}$

9. $y = (x^{1/3} - 1)^2$

10. $y = (|x| - 2.5)^2$

In Problems 11-14 find the roots of the given functions correct to four decimal places.

11. $y = 4x - 3x^{4/3}$

12. $y = 3x^{5/3} - \dfrac{22}{\sqrt{5}} x^{2/3}$

13. $y = 2x + 3x^{2/3}$

14. $y = 2\sqrt{x} - 5x^{1/4} + \dfrac{23}{8}$

Section 2.3 Trigonometric Functions

Much of the phenomena we observe in the real world is periodic or cyclic: for instance, the annual motion of the earth around the sun, the movement of the ocean tides, the cycles of sunspots, sound waves and radio waves, yearly business cycles, and alternating electrical current. All these phenomena can be investigated through a class of functions, called the *trigonometric functions,* which play an indispensable role in modern science and applied mathematics. In this section we investigate the elementary properties of the trigonometric functions and their graphs.

Measuring Angles

An angle of measure θ is said to be of *standard position* in a cartesian coordinate system when the vertex of the angle is at the origin and the initial side lies along the positive x-axis. Positive angles are measured counterclockwise and negative angles are measured clockwise from the positive x-axis (Figure 2.20).

In geometry you learned to measure angles in degrees ($^\circ$), minutes ($'$), and seconds ($''$): There are 180° in a straight angle, 90° in the angle formed by two perpendicular lines, and so on. Furthermore, each degree is divided into 60 equal parts called *minutes,* and each minute is divided into 60 *seconds.*

Another way of measuring an angle is by *radian* measure. This is the way angles are measured in calculus. If the vertex of an angle is placed at the center of a circle of radius r, and if the angle cuts out an arc of the circle r units long, then the angle is of measure one *radian* (Figure 2.21). More generally, the number of radians in an angle θ that cuts out an arc of the circle s units long is given by

$$\theta = \frac{s}{r}$$

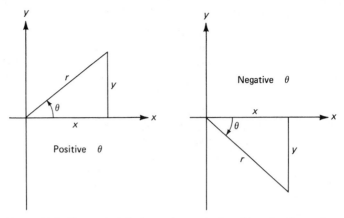

Figure 2.20 The angle θ is shown in standard position. Positive angles are measured counterclockwise, and negative angles clockwise, from the positive x-axis.

This is depicted in Figure 2.22. We say that the angle θ is being measured in *radians.* Notice that a radian measure is the quotient of two lengths s and r, so it is a *real number.* That is the reason we use radian measure in calculus: We can, for instance, add and multiply real numbers, but we cannot multiply degrees.

The length of the arc of a semicircle of radius r is πr units. Therefore, a straight angle measures π radians. An angle of $1°$ then measures $\pi/180 \approx 0.01745$ radians. On the other hand, one radian measures $180/\pi \approx 57.29577$ degrees. Thus:

1. To convert degrees to radians, multiply by $\pi/180$.
2. To convert radians to degrees, multiply by $180/\pi$.

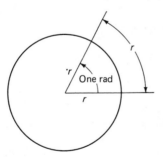

Figure 2.21 An angle of measure one radian.

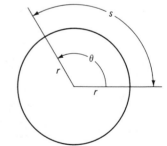

Figure 2.22 An angle θ of measure s/r radians.

Using these rules you can easily establish the following conversion table.

Degrees	0	15	30	45	60	75	90	120	135	150	180
θ (radians)	0	$\dfrac{\pi}{12}$	$\dfrac{\pi}{6}$	$\dfrac{\pi}{4}$	$\dfrac{\pi}{3}$	$\dfrac{5\pi}{12}$	$\dfrac{\pi}{2}$	$\dfrac{2\pi}{3}$	$\dfrac{3\pi}{4}$	$\dfrac{5\pi}{6}$	π

Now consider the unit circle $x^2 + y^2 = 1$. For each *nonnegative* real number t there can be associated a unique point P_t on the unit circle in the following way: Measure off the distance t along the circumference of the unit circle from the point $Q(1,0)$ in the *counterclockwise* direction (Figure 2.23). Thus, if $t = 2\pi$ we go counterclockwise around the circle and get back to the starting point $Q(1,0)$; if $t = 7\pi/2$ we go counterclockwise around the circle and reach the point $(0,-1)$; if $t = 4\pi$ we go twice around the circle and get back to $Q(1,0)$; and so forth.

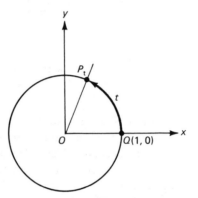

Figure 2.23   The point P_t for $t \geqslant 0$ is located a distance t counterclockwise from $Q(1,0)$ along the circumference of the unit circle $x^2 + y^2 = 1$.

Similarly, if t is a *negative* real number we locate the point P_t on the circle by measuring off the distance $|t|$ along the circumference from $Q(1,0)$ in the *clockwise* direction. Thus if $t = -\pi$ we go clockwise around the circle and reach the point $(-1,0)$; if $t = -4\pi$ we go twice around the circle in the clockwise direction and get back to $Q(1,0)$; and so forth. Thus

$$P_{2\pi} = P_{4\pi} = P_{-2\pi} = P_0 = Q(1,0)$$

Notice that for each point P on the unit circle $x^2 + y^2 = 1$, there is exactly one value of t in the interval $0 \leqslant t < 2\pi$ such that the point P_t is the point P: t is the length of the arc from $Q(1,0)$ around the circle to P in the counterclockwise direction. However, for every integer n the point $P_{t+2n\pi}$ also coincides with the point P. When $|n|$ is larger than 1, we may "wrap around" the circle several times before reaching the terminal point P; and if n is negative, we go in a clockwise direction. We can think of t, or $t + 2n\pi$, as the radian angle swept out by the line segment $\overline{OQ}$ as we wrap around the unit circle to reach the terminal point. In this way every real number can be considered as a radian angle.

Now let t be any real number whatsoever. We define the numbers $\cos t$ (cosine t) and $\sin t$ (sine t) as the x and y coordinates, respectively, of the point P_t (Figure 2.24). That is,

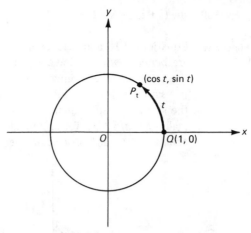

Figure 2.24 cos t and sin t are the x and y coordinates of the point P_t on the unit circle.

cos t = x-coordinate of P_t

sin t = y-coordinate of P_t

(2.14)

Thus cos t and sin t are functions defined for all radian angles t. From the definitions, we immediately obtain the values for these functions given in the following table:

t	cos t	sin t
0	1	0
$\pi/2$	0	1
π	−1	0
$3\pi/2$	0	−1
2π	1	0

Moreover, since (cos t, sin t) is a point on the unit circle $x^2 + y^2 = 1$, it is true that

$$\cos^2 t + \sin^2 t = 1 \qquad (2.15)$$

and $-1 \leqslant \cos t \leqslant 1$ and $-1 \leqslant \sin t \leqslant 1$ for all values of t. Equation 2.15 expresses the fundamental relationship between the sine and cosine functions.

It is also immediate from the definitions in 2.14 and the ways in which P_t and P_{-t} are obtained, that

$$\cos(-t) = \cos t \qquad (2.16)$$

$$\sin(-t) = -\sin t \qquad (2.17)$$

Furthermore, since $P_t = P_{t+2\pi}$, it is also true that

$\cos(t + 2\pi) = \cos t$ (2.18)

Equations 2.18 and 2.19 express the fact that the sine and cosine functions are *periodic* with period 2π. The periodic nature of these functions makes them fundamentally important in applications. The graphs of $x = \cos t$ and $y = \sin t$ are shown in Figure 2.25. From the graph in Figure 2.25 we see that the sine and cosine functions have the same values at $t = \pi/4$ and, more generally, $t = \pi/4 + n\pi$ for any integer n; for odd integers n, this common value equals $-\sqrt{2}/2$, and for even integers n it is $\sqrt{2}/2$.

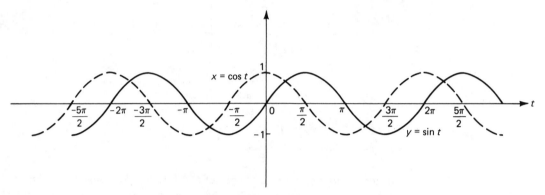

Figure 2.25 The graphs of the sine (solid curve) and cosine (dashed curve) functions are periodic with period 2π.

Whenever the real number t satisfies $0 < t < \pi/2$, we can associate with the point P_t on the unit circle a right triangle OAP_t as shown in Figure 2.26. In this figure, the angle θ between OA and OP_t has radian measure t. From the figure we obtain the *right-triangle definitions* of the sine and cosine for θ:

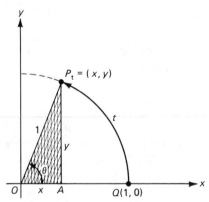

Figure 2.26 Right triangle OAP_t associated with P_t when $0 < t < \pi/2$.

$$\cos t = x = \frac{x}{1} = \frac{\text{Adjacent side}}{\text{Hypotenuse}}$$

$$\sin t = y = \frac{y}{1} = \frac{\text{Opposite side}}{\text{Hypotenuse}}$$

Other Trigonometric Functions

The two functions $\sin t$ and $\cos t$ are the basic trigonometric functions, but there are four others, the tangent, cotangent, secant and cosecant functions. These four functions are defined as follows:

$$\tan t = \frac{\sin t}{\cos t} \qquad\qquad \cot t = \frac{\cos t}{\sin t}$$

$$\sec t = \frac{1}{\cos t} \qquad\qquad \csc t = \frac{1}{\sin t}$$

Of course in using these definitions you must be sure not to divide by zero. Thus the functions $\tan t$ and $\sec t$ are not defined when $t = \pi/2 + n\pi$ for all integers n; and the functions $\cot t$ and $\csc t$ are not defined when $t = n\pi$.

If we divide Equation 2.15 by $\cos^2 t$, we obtain

$$1 + \tan^2 t = \sec^2 t \tag{2.20}$$

which expresses the fundamental relationship between the tangent and secant functions. A similar formula pertains to the cotangent and cosecant functions when Equation 2.15 is divided by $\sin^2 t$.

The values of the six trigonometric functions are provided by your TI-59 calculator. Be sure to press the second key $\boxed{\text{Rad}}$ before you begin to evaluate these functions, to switch your calculator into radian mode. For further instructions, see the author's book *Calculator Clout,* Chapter 5. The graphs of the tangent, secant, cotangent, and cosecant functions are shown in Figure 2.27. Observe the periodicity of these functions. For instance, the tangent and cotangent functions are periodic of period π. Notice also the vertical asymptotes.

Sum and Difference Identities

Many identities hold true for the trigonometric functions. You have already encountered several of these in Equations 2.15 through 2.20, but there are others of fundamental importance. The following sum and difference identities are especially useful in changing the form of a trigonometric expression: For all real numbers s and t,

$$\cos (s + t) = \cos s \cos t - \sin s \sin t \tag{2.21}$$

$$\cos (s - t) = \cos s \cos t + \sin s \sin t \tag{2.22}$$

$$\sin (s + t) = \sin s \cos t + \cos s \sin t \tag{2.23}$$

$$\sin (s - t) = \sin s \cos t - \cos s \sin t \tag{2.24}$$

The identity 2.22 follows from the fact that the length of the chord joining the two points $P(\cos t, \sin t)$ and $Q(\cos s, \sin s)$ on the unit circle is equal to the positive square root of $2 - 2 \cos (s - t)$ (Figure 2.28). Thus

101 $\qquad \sqrt{(\cos s - \cos t)^2 + (\sin s - \sin t)^2} = \sqrt{2 - 2 \cos (s - t)}$

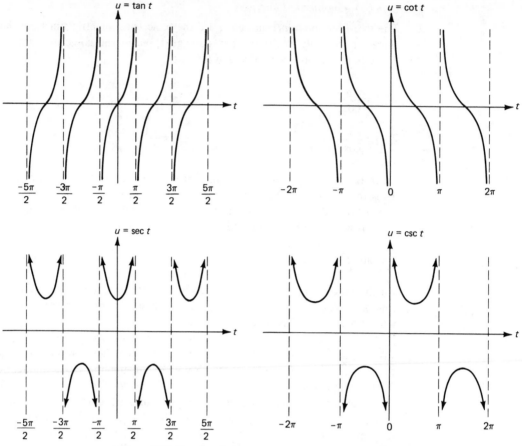

Figure 2.27 Graphs of the tangent, cotangent, secant, and cosecant functions showing the vertical asymptotes associated with them.

which simplifies algebraically to identity 2.22. The fact that the chord length PQ in Figure 2.28 is given by $\sqrt{2 - 2\cos(s - t)}$ follows from computing the distance between the points $(1,0)$ and $[\cos(s - t), \sin(s - t)]$. You may wish to make that calculation as an exercise.

The remaining sum and difference identities can be deduced from 2.22 using the identities 2.16, 2.17, and

$$\sin t = \cos\left(\frac{\pi}{2} - t\right) \tag{2.25}$$

$$\cos t = \sin\left(\frac{\pi}{2} - t\right) \tag{2.26}$$

These last two identities are readily apparent from the graphs of the sine and cosine functions shown in Figure 2.25.

Law of Cosines

Consider any triangle ABC labeled as shown in Figure 2.29. The *law of cosines* generalizes the Theorem of Pythagoras and gives the relationship

102

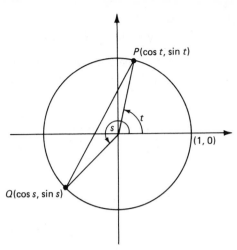

Figure 2.28 The arc of the unit circle joining
P and Q is subtended by the central angle $s - t$.

$$c^2 = a^2 + b^2 - 2ab \cos \gamma \qquad (2.27)$$

In words the law of cosines is as follows:

> The square of the length of any side of a triangle equals the sum of the squares of the lengths of the other two sides minus twice their product times the cosine of the angle between the other two sides.

If $\gamma = 90°$, then $\cos \gamma = 0$ and Equation 2.27 is simply the Pythagorean Theorem.

Equation 2.27 is deduced by setting up a cartesian coordinate system with C at the origin and the angle γ in standard position with A along the positive x-axis. The coordinates of A, B, and C are then $C(0,0)$, $A(b,0)$, and $B(a \cos \gamma, a \sin \gamma)$. Calculation of the distance between A and B using the distance formula, and equating the result to c, then gives Equation 2.27. We leave the details to an exercise.

Trigonometric identities abound, but we have presented only the key results. Additional identities are given in the exercises at the end of this section. Let's now use the program PROBE to plot the graphs of several functions involving the fundamental trigonometric functions.

Figure 2.29 In triangle ABC the side c is
opposite to the angle γ.

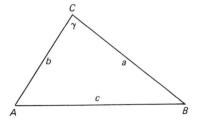

EXERCISE 1.

THE FUNCTION $f(x) = 5 \sin x \cos^2 x$

Since the sine and cosine functions are periodic of period 2π we graph this function for the interval $0 \leqslant x \leqslant 2\pi$. Using PROBE, key in the following keystrokes for the subroutine to evaluate $f(x)$:

We will use the increment $\Delta x = \pi/8$ and calculate a table of values for $f(x)$ over the interval $0 \leqslant x \leqslant 2\pi$.

(press)	Rad	Set your calculator to radian mode.
(enter)	$-\pi/8$	
(press)	D'	Load $x_0 = -\pi/8$.
(press)	+/−	
(press)	E'	Load $\Delta x = \pi/8 \approx 0.3927$.
(press)	Fix 2	Display 2 digits past the decimal point.
(press)	A	Calculate $f(0) = 0.00$.
(press)	E	Display current $x = 0.00$.

Repeatedly press A and E to obtain the following table:

x	0.00	0.39	0.79	1.18	1.57	1.96	2.36	2.75	3.14	3.53
$f(x)$	0.00	1.63	1.77	0.68	0.00	0.68	1.77	1.63	0.00	−1.63

x	3.93	4.32	4.71	5.11	5.50	5.89	6.28
$f(x)$	−1.77	−0.68	0.00	−0.68	−1.77	−1.63	0.00

The graph of f is given in Figure 2.30. Using PROBE you can locate the maximum values of 1.92 for f when $x = 0.59$ and $x = 2.51$ (the minimum values are −1.92 at $x = 3.77$ and $x = 5.65$).

EXERCISE 2.

A GENERAL SINE CURVE

Consider the curve given by

$$f(x) = 2 \sin (3x - \pi) + 1$$

Using PROBE, key in this function as a subroutine using the following keystrokes:

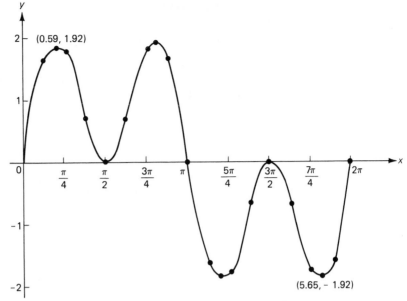

Figure 2.30 Graph of $y = 5 \sin x \cos^2 x$.

With your calculator in radian mode, set $x_0 = -\pi/12$ and $\Delta x = \pi/12 \approx 0.26$ to obtain the following table of values from PROBE:

x	0.0	0.3	0.5	0.8	1.0	1.3	1.6	1.8	2.1	2.4	2.6	2.9
$f(x)$	1.0	−0.4	−1.0	−0.4	1.0	2.4	3.0	2.4	1.0	−0.4	−1.0	−0.4

x	3.1	3.4	3.7	3.9	4.2	4.5	4.7	5.0	5.2	5.5	5.8	6.0	6.3
$f(x)$	1.0	2.4	3.0	2.4	1.0	−0.4	−1.0	−0.4	1.0	2.4	3.0	2.4	1.0

The graph of f is given in Figure 2.31. Notice how one complete cycle of the sine curve occurs over the interval $\pi/3 \leqslant x \leqslant \pi$. The curve begins at $x = \pi/3$ (*the phase shift*) and covers an interval of length of $2\pi/3$ (*the period* of f). The *amplitude* of the function is 2, which equals half the difference between the largest value 3 and the smallest value −1. Finally, notice that the sine curve is shifted upwards by 1 (*the vertical shift*).

A function of the form

$$f(x) = A \sin \left[\frac{2\pi}{B} (x - C) \right] + D \tag{2.28}$$

is known as a *general sine function*. Here $|A|$ is the *amplitude*, B is the *period*, C is the *phase shift*, and D is the *vertical shift*. If we rewrite the expression for the function in the prior example in this new form (2.28), we obtain,

105

$$f(x) = 2 \sin (3x - \pi) + 1$$

$$= 2 \sin \left[\frac{2\pi}{2\pi/3} \left(x - \frac{\pi}{3} \right) \right] + 1$$

and we see that $A = 2$, $B = 2\pi/3$, $C = \pi/3$, and $D = 1$ in agreement with the graph given in Figure 2.31.

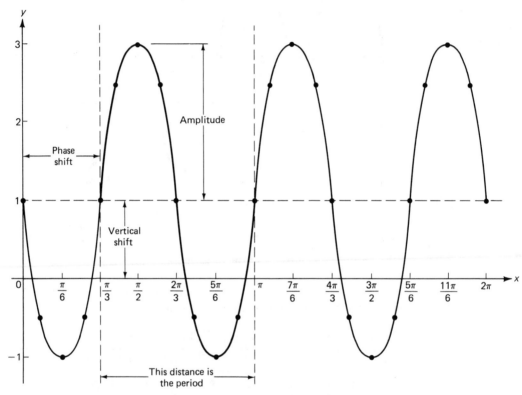

Figure 2.31 Graph of $f(x) = 2 \sin (3x - \pi) + 1$.

EXERCISE 3.
ROOTS OF A TRIGONOMETRIC FUNCTION

Let's use PROBE to locate a root between 2 and 3, correct to 6 decimal places, of the function

$$f(x) = 2x - 3 \sin x - 5$$

The keystrokes for the subroutine to calculate $f(x)$ are as follows:

| GTO | 134 | LRN | Lbl | C' | STO | 00 | × | 2 | − | 3 | × |

| RCL | 00 | sin | − | 5 | = | INV | SBR | LRN |

Now make sure your calculator is in radian mode: Press $\boxed{\text{RAD}}$. Then load $\Delta x = 0.1$ and $x_0 = 1.9$ to begin your search for the root, as in Exercise 1 of Section 2.1. The root, correct to 6 decimals, is $r = 2.883237$.

PROBLEMS 2.3

In each of Problems 1-6, convert the angle given in degrees to radian measure correct to five decimal places.

1. $27.5°$

2. $217.75°$

3. $322° \ 14' \ 57''$

4. $-12.1°$

5. $579.2°$

6. $176° \ 27' \ 46''$

In Problems 7-12, convert the angle given in radian measure to decimal degrees correct to two decimal places.

7. 2.01327

8. 0.86439

9. -1.68721

10. 4.92116

11. $17\pi/5$

12. $-19\pi/6$

Determine the values given in Problems 13-18.

13. $\sin 4$

14. $\cos (4° \ 17' \ 37'')$

15. $\tan (121° \ 14' \ 38'')$

16. $\cot (-26.39)$

17. $\sec (-19.214)$

18. $\csc (246° \ 8'')$

In each of Problems 19-29, graph the given function over the indicated interval.

19. $y = \sin x - \cos x \qquad 0 \leqslant x \leqslant 8$

20. $y = \sin \left(\frac{\pi}{2}x^{2/3}\right) \qquad 0 \leqslant x \leqslant 4$

21. $y = x^2 - \cos x \qquad -4 \leqslant x \leqslant 4$

22. $y = 2 \cos \frac{2\pi x}{3} \qquad 0 \leqslant x \leqslant 2\pi$

23. $y = -4 \sin \left(\frac{x}{3} + \frac{\pi}{2}\right) \qquad 0 \leqslant x \leqslant 2\pi$

24. $y = 2 \sin (5 - 3x) \qquad 0 \leqslant x \leqslant 4$

25. $y = x \cos x \qquad 0 \leqslant x \leqslant 2\pi$

26. $y = \tan \left(x - \frac{\pi}{6}\right) \qquad -\frac{\pi}{3} < x < \frac{2\pi}{3}$

27. $y = 2 \csc (\pi x - \frac{1}{2})$ $0 \leqslant x \leqslant 3$

28. $y = \cos 2x + 2 \cos x$ $0 \leqslant x \leqslant 4\pi$

29. $y = \dfrac{\sin x}{x}$ $-\pi \leqslant x \leqslant 3\pi$ $x \neq 0$

What value would you assign to y at $x = 0$ for the graph to be "connected" or in one piece?

30. Show that the length of the chord PQ in Figure 2.28 equals $\sqrt{2 - 2 \cos (s - t)}$ using the hint given in the text.

31. Establish identity 2.23 using identities 2.22, 2.25, and 2.26.

32. Establish identity 2.21 using identities 2.22, 2.16, and 2.17.

33. Establish the *law of cosines* (2.27) using the hint given in the text.

In Problems 34–37, use the law of cosines to find the specified unknown parts of the given triangle, labeled as shown in Figure 2.32. Give your answer correct to two decimal places.

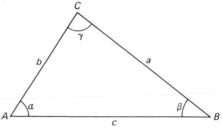

Figure 2.32

34. c if $a = 21.5$, $b = 13.7$, and $\gamma = \pi/3$

35. a if $b = 17.2$, $c = 41.5$, and $\alpha = 15°$

36. γ if $a = 3.1$, $b = 4.3$, and $c = 4.9$

37. β if $a = 4.25$, $b = c = 9.75$

38. Find the diameter of the moon if it subtends an angle of $31' 6''$ at the eye and its distance from the earth is 240,000 mi.

39. The end of a 5-ft pendulum swings through an arc 4 in in length. Determine the angle through which it swings, giving your answer in degrees-minutes-seconds.

40. Establish the *double-angle formulas:*

$$\sin 2x = 2 \sin x \cos x$$

$$\cos 2x = \cos^2 x - \sin^2 x = 1 - 2 \sin^2 x$$

41. Establish the *half-angle formulas:*

$$\cos^2 \left(\frac{x}{2} \right) = \frac{1 + \cos x}{2}$$

$$\sin^2 \left(\frac{x}{2} \right) = \frac{1 - \cos x}{2}$$

42. Two ships leave harbor at the same time. The first sails N 14° W at 22 knots (a knot is one nautical mile per hour). The second sails N 38° E at 19 knots. After 2 hrs and 25 min, how far apart are the ships?

Section 2.4 Exponential Functions

Certain mathematical functions are important because they describe relationships that occur in a wide variety of situations in science, business, economics, and other areas. The exponential function, for instance, describes population growth, growth of money when interest is earned at a rate "compounded continuously," growth in energy use, radioactive decay in "carbon 14 dating," increase in sales activity, and so forth.

In high school algebra you learned the meaning of the symbol b^x when b is a positive real number and the exponent x is a *rational number,* that is x is of the form p/q. In symbols,

$$b^{p/q} = \sqrt[q]{b^p}$$

so that $b^{p/q}$ is the qth *root of b multiplied by itself p times.* For instance,

$$3^{1/2} = \sqrt{3} \qquad 5^{2/3} = \sqrt[3]{5 \cdot 5} \qquad (0.1)^{3/5} = \sqrt[5]{0.001}$$

If the exponent x is an *irrational number,* then the calculation of b^x is quite a different story: It is accomplished by successive approximations. For instance, to calculate 2^π, we use the decimal representation $\pi = 3.14159\ldots$ and determine the successive values

$$2^{3.1} \quad = 2^{31/10} \qquad = 8.5741877$$

$$2^{3.14} \quad = 2^{314/100} \qquad = 8.815240927$$

$$2^{3.141} \quad = 2^{3141/1000} \quad = 8.821353305$$

$$2^{3.1415} \ = 2^{31415/10000} = 8.824411082$$

and so on, until eventually we find $2^\pi \approx 8.824977827$ correct to 9 decimal places. Of course, you can calculate all these powers $2^{3.1}$, $2^{3.14}$, $2^{3.141}$, $2^{3.1415}$, ..., even 2^π, on your TI–59 using the $\boxed{y^x}$ key. Do these calculations now. We are interested here, however, in the *meaning* assigned to the number 2^π in order to establish its connection to what has previously been taught about exponents.

Now that b^x makes sense for all real numbers x, we can define an exponential function. Whenever b is a positive real number, then

$$y = b^x$$

is an *exponential function.* The number b is called *the base* of the exponential

109 function.

Let's consider the graphs of several exponential functions and determine some of their characteristics.

EXERCISE 1.
THE GRAPH OF $y = 2^x$

Using PROBE, key in the following subroutine to evaluate this function:

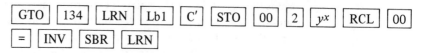

Now obtain the following table of function values:

x	−10.0	−8.0	−6.0	−4.0	−2.0	−1.5	−1.0	−0.5	0.0	0.5	1.0
y	0.00	0.00	0.02	0.06	0.25	0.35	0.50	0.71	1.00	1.41	2.00

x	1.5	2.0	2.5	3.0	3.5	4.0	5.0	6.0	8.0	10.0
y	2.83	4.00	5.66	8.00	11.31	16.0	32.0	64.0	256.0	1024.0

The graph of $y = 2^x$ is portrayed in Figure 2.33. Notice that the graph is
concave upward and rises upward toward the right. Also, it is asymptotic
to the x-axis: as $x \to -\infty$, $y \to 0$. (Although the table shows the value $y = 0$
when $x = -10$, the value of y is actually the very small positive number
0.0009765625.) Exponential functions *never* reach the value zero, but only
approach it in the asymptotic sense.

Figure 2.33 Graph of the exponential function $y = 2^x$.

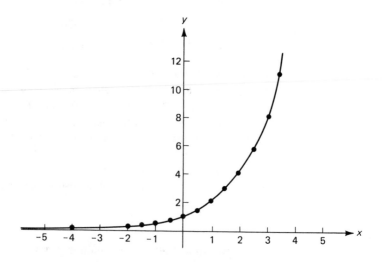

EXERCISE 2.

THE GRAPH OF $y = \left(\dfrac{1}{2}\right)^x$

Using PROBE you can obtain the following table of values for this function:

x	−10.0	−8.0	−6.0	−4.0	−2.0	−1.5	−1.0	−0.5	0.0	0.5	1.0
y	1024.0	256.0	64.0	16.0	4.00	2.83	2.00	1.41	1.00	0.71	0.50

x	1.5	2.0	2.5	3.0	3.5	4.0	6.0	8.0	10.0
y	0.35	0.25	0.18	0.13	0.09	0.06	0.02	0.00	0.00

The graph of $y = \left(\dfrac{1}{2}\right)^x$ is shown in Figure 2.34. Notice that the graph of this exponential function is also concave upward, but that it is *decreasing* downward toward the right. Again the x-axis is a horizontal asymptote, but in this case $y \to 0$ as x gets larger in the *positive* direction. This graph is typical of exponential functions $y = b^x$ when $0 < b < 1$.

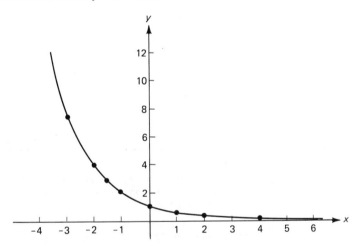

Figure 2.34 Graph of the exponential function $y = (1/2)^x$.

EXERCISE 3.

THE NUMBER *e*

AND COMPOUND INTEREST

The exponential function that occurs most often in real world applications is $y = e^x$. The number *e* is an irrational number that is approximately equal to 2.718281828459. This number corresponds to the point on the x-axis for which the area trapped beneath the curve of $y = 1/x$ and above the x-axis, and between the vertical lines $x = 1$ and $x = e$, equals exactly *one* square unit. This is depicted in Figure 2.35. For large values of the positive integer *n*, a good approximation to *e* is given by

$$e \approx \left(1 + \frac{1}{n}\right)^n$$

For example, when $n = 1,000,000$ the approximation yields

$$\left(1 + \frac{1}{1,000,000}\right)^{1,000,000} \approx 2.718280469$$

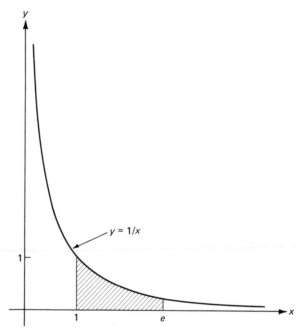

Figure 2.35 The number e on the x-axis is such that the shaded region trapped beneath the graph of $y = 1/x$ is exactly one square unit.

The calculation for $y = e^x$ is given by the keystrokes $\boxed{\text{INV}}$ $\boxed{\ln x}$ on your TI-59, where the value of x is in the display when the keys are pressed. The graph of $y = e^x$ is shown in Figure 2.36. The notation $y = \exp x$ is sometimes used instead of $y = e^x$.

Interest is said to be *compounded continuously* if the amount A of a principal P after n years at an annual rate r (expressed as a decimal) is given by the exponential

$$A = Pe^{rn}$$

The following keystrokes calculate the amount that $100 will become after 25 years with interest compounded continuously at an annual rate of 7.05 percent.

$\boxed{0.0705}$ $\boxed{\times}$ $\boxed{25}$ $\boxed{=}$ $\boxed{\text{INV}}$ $\boxed{\ln x}$ $\boxed{\times}$ $\boxed{100}$ $\boxed{=}$

(Answer: $582.70)

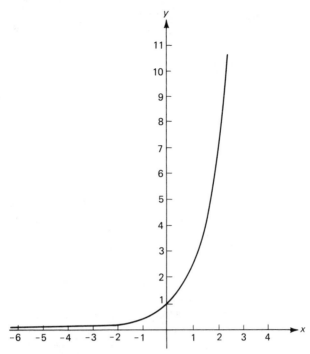

Figure 2.36 Graph of the exponential function $y = e^x$.

EXERCISE 4.
EXPONENTIAL GROWTH AND DECAY

A quantity Q that increases according to the rule $Q = Ce^{kx}$, where C and k are positive constants, is said to experience *exponential growth*. If C is positive and k is negative, Q is said to experience *exponential decay*. Money that earns interest compounded continuously is an example of exponential growth. Also, in the absence of environmental limitations, populations increase exponentially. Radioactive substances illustrate exponential decay, which provides the basis for carbon 14 dating. Quantities that grow or decay exponentially are characterized by the fact that their *rate* of increase or decrease is proportional to the amount currently present. You will see why this is so in the next chapter.

The consumption of energy during the twentieth century is an example of a quantity that has grown exponentially, at an annual rate of about 7 percent.* Let's examine some of the implications of this growth.

Suppose that in the year 1900 the world was using 1 "unit" of energy, whatever that might have been (possibly measured in so many trillion kilowatt hours of electricity, or in so many million barrels of oil, or whatever). At a 7 percent growth rate, after x years the amount of energy consumed will be $Q = e^{0.07x}$. Making a table of values for this function we obtain the following:

*See the article, Albert A. Bartlett, "Forgotten Fundamentals of the Energy Crisis," *American Journal of Physics*, 46(9) (September 1978).

x	Year	Consumption Q
0	1900	1.00
10	1910	2.01
20	1920	4.06
30	1930	8.17
40	1940	16.44
50	1950	33.12
60	1960	66.69
70	1970	134.29
80	1980	270.43
90	1990	544.57
100	2000	1,096.63

From the table you can see that the amount of energy used doubles about
every 10 years: in 1920 twice as much energy was used as in 1910, in 1930
twice as much as in 1920, and so forth. By the year 1980, we were consuming
270 times as much energy as in the year 1900. Unless the growth rate is de-
creased, by the end of this century we will be consuming over a thousand
times as much energy as we were using at the beginning!

Now there's a curious law about the exponential growth curve, which
has to do with the area beneath the curve. In Figure 2.37 the shaded area beneath the curve from 1900 to 1970 represents the *total amount* of energy
consumed during that seventy-year timespan. Likewise, the area beneath the
graph from 1970 to 1980 represents the amount of energy used in the decade
of the seventies. In another chapter it will be established that *these two areas
are very nearly equal.* The amount of energy used in the seventies about
equals the total amount used previously from 1900 to 1970. Moreover, unless
the growth rate is slowed, the amount of energy we will use during the eighties
will likewise nearly equal all the energy consumed from 1900 up to 1980.

Figure 2.37 The graph shows that energy consumption doubles every 10
years. The shaded region represents total energy use from 1900 to 1970,
which equals the area beneath the curve from 1970 to 1980.

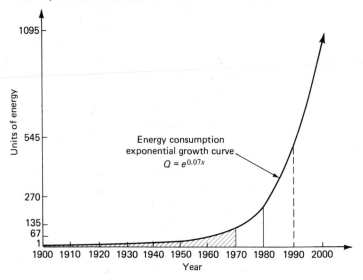

Energy consumption
exponential growth curve
$Q = e^{0.07x}$

Units of energy

Year

Since most of our energy comes from oil, a nonrenewable resource, you now see what is behind the energy crisis.

Even if tomorrow we discovered a vast and new oil field that contains as much oil as we've already used so far, it would provide only a mere 10–12 more years of supply: *A doubling of the resource results in only a small increase in its life expectancy.* Moreover, according to the *Global 2000 Report,* "During the 1990s world oil production will approach geological estimates of maximum production capacity, even with rapidly increasing petroleum prices."*

EXERCISE 5.
AN EXPONENTIAL MODEL:
LEARNING CURVES

The graph of a function of the form $y = A - Be^{-kx}$, where A, B, and k are positive constants, is sometimes called a *learning curve.* Such curves have been found to describe the relationship between the efficiency with which an individual does a certain job and the amount of training or experience the individual has had.

For example, the daily output y of a worker who has been on the job for x weeks might be determined by experiment to satisfy

$$y = 65 - 50e^{-0.4x}$$

When a new worker comes on the job, he or she would have $x = 0$ weeks of experience and could produce only

$$y(0) = 65 - 50 = 15$$

units of daily output. After 3 weeks experience on the job, an average new employee would be expected to produce

$$y(3) = 65 - 50e^{-1.2} \approx 50$$

units of daily output. As the number of weeks increases, the daily output grows closer and closer to 65 units because the exponential term $e^{-0.4x}$ approaches zero. In fact, after 12 weeks on the job the daily output is

$$y(12) = 65 - 50e^{-4.8} \approx 64.5885$$

PROBLEMS 2.4

In each of Problems 1–8, graph the given function over the specified interval. Identify any symmetries and horizontal and vertical asymptotes.

***The Global 2000 Report to the President,* prepared by the Council on Environmental Quality and the Department of State of the United States, (Washington, D.C.: U.S. Government Printing Office, September 1980).

1. $y = e^x + e^{-x}$ $\quad -4 \leqslant x \leqslant 4$

2. $y = 3^{-x}$ $\quad -3 \leqslant x \leqslant 5$

3. $y = \dfrac{e^x}{1 + e^x}$ $\quad -\infty < x < \infty$

4. $y = \dfrac{1}{1 + e^{1-x}}$ $\quad -\infty < x < \infty$

5. $y = xe^x$ $\quad -3 \leqslant x \leqslant 2$

6. $y = \dfrac{1}{1 - e^x}$ $\quad -\infty < x < \infty$

7. $y = e^{-x^2}$ $\quad -\infty < x < \infty$

8. $y = e^x \cos x$ $\quad -2\pi \leqslant x \leqslant 3\pi$

9. Suppose that, due to inflation, money is losing value at the rate of 12 percent a year. What is the value of $1 after 5 years? Estimate the cost of a $6,329 car at today's dollars in 5 more years, due to the inflation factor alone.

10. It is estimated that the population of a certain country x years from now will be $P(x) = 65e^{0.021x}$ million.

    a. What is the population of the country today?

    b. What will the population be in 10 years? 20 years?

11. The rate of decay of a radioactive substance is described by giving its *half-life*, the time it takes for half of a sample to decompose. If the radioactive substance decays at the rate of r percent annually (given as a decimal number), then the amount $y(t)$ after t years satisfies the equation

    $$y(t) = Ce^{rt}$$

    The half-life of radium-226 is 1,620 years. What percentage of a sample of radium-226 remains after 325 years?

12. Find a solution to the equation $e^x = x^3$ between $x = 1$ and $x = 2$, using PROBE.

13. In the inversion of raw sugar, the amount $A(t)$ of raw sugar present at time t hours is given by an exponential of the form

    $$A(t) = Se^{kt}$$

    where S is the original amount of raw sugar, and k is a constant. If 1,000 lb of raw sugar has been reduced to 800 lb after 10 hrs, how much sugar is present after 36 hrs?

14. A cool glass of water is removed from a refrigerator on a hot summer day and placed in a room whose temperature is $30°$ Celsius. According to *Newton's law of heating*, the temperature of the water t minutes later is given by a function of the form

    $$H(t) = 30 - Be^{-kt}$$

If the temperature of the water was $11°$ Celsius when it left the refrigerator and $17°$ Celsius after 20 min, what is the temperature of the water after 45 min?

15. According to a law of physics, the barometric pressure $p(x)$ in inches of mercury at x miles above sea level is given approximately by

$$p(x) = 29.92e^{-0.2x} \qquad x \geqslant 0$$

Find the barometric pressure at 9,000 ft above sea level.

16. Experimental results indicate that the air pressure $p(x)$ measured in "atmospheres" (where the pressure at sea level is 1 atmosphere) at x meters above sea level approximately satisfies

$$p(x) = e^{-0.000125x} \qquad x \geqslant 0$$

Find the atmospheric pressure outside a jet plane flying across the ocean at 37,250 ft (1 m equals 3.280840 ft).

17. After an experiment a sociologist found that the fraction of a population who have heard a rumor after d days is approximately

$$P(d) = \frac{Ae^{kd}}{1 - A(1 - e^{kd})}$$

where A is the fraction of people who initially heard the rumor and k is a constant. If $k = 0.15$, find the percentage of people who heard the rumor after 7 days if 4 percent initially heard it.

18. If a mortgage loan of amount L is taken out at an annual interest rate r and paid back at a monthly payment M, then the balance $B(t)$ owing on the loan after t months (assuming B declines "continuously") is given by the formula

$$B(t) = \frac{12M}{r} + (L - \frac{12M}{r}) e^{rt/12}$$

Find the balance remaining after 5 years on a $70,000 mortgage borrowed at 9.75 percent annually if the monthly payments are $611.

Section 2.5 Continuity of Functions

Previously, to obtain a table of values in order to plot certain points on the graph, which were then connected by an unbroken curve that "looked reasonable," we used PROBE as standard procedure. When we did so, we were making assumptions because we really had no information about the graph in between the points given by the table. For example, if the tabled points were plotted as in Figure 2.38, a graph through the points could look like either Figure 2.39a or Figure 2.39b. Moreover, if two adjacent points on the graph happen to lie on opposite sides of a vertical asymptote, as shown in Figure 2.39c, it would not even be correct to connect them because the function val-

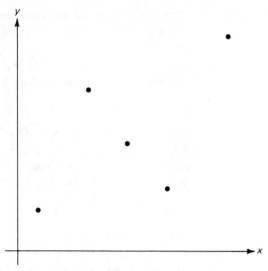

Figure 2.38

ues are growing arbitrarily large in absolute value in the vicinity of a vertical asymptote.

How, then, do we know which graph—if any—is correct? One way to find out is by taking smaller and smaller step sizes, with the increment Δx, in order to determine many more points on the graph. However, such a procedure becomes very tedious and time-consuming. If we could at least identify in advance those points near which we should make such a detailed study, it would cut out an enormous amount of work. In graphing rational functions, for instance, we looked for values of x making the denominator zero as possible locations for a vertical asymptote. Using small values of Δx near such a location then revealed the precise nature of the functional behavior. Other "clues" can be discovered to single out points of particular significance near which the local behavior of a function needs to be studied. The concept of a "limit" will help us in our search for these clues.

We are not going to give precise mathematical definitions here, and we're not going to prove anything. Rather, we are going to convey a qualitative feeling for the "limiting processes" involved, based on your intuition and supported by quantitative calculations you make on your calculator.

EXERCISE 1.
CONTINUITY OF A FUNCTION
AT A POINT

Consider the function $f(x) = x^3$. At the point $x = 2$, the value of this function is $f(2) = 8$. Let's examine the values of f near 2 using your calculator. You will find the following table of values:

118

x	$f(x)$	x	$f(x)$
1.90	6.859	2.10	9.261
1.95	7.415	2.09	9.129
1.97	7.645	2.05	8.615
1.99	7.881	2.01	8.121
1.991	7.892	2.005	8.060
1.995	7.940	2.003	8.036
1.999	7.988	2.001	8.012

What the table reveals is that a small change in x produces only a small change in $f(x) = x^3$ near the point $x = 2$. Moreover, we can keep the change in $f(x)$ as

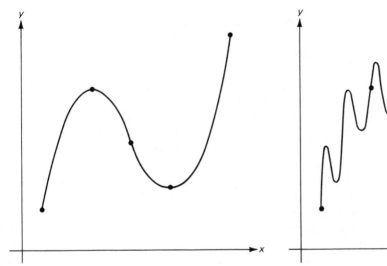

Figure 2.39a

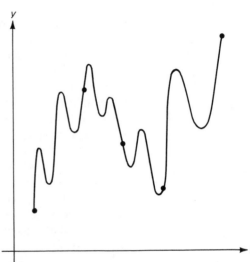

Figure 2.39b

Figure 2.39c

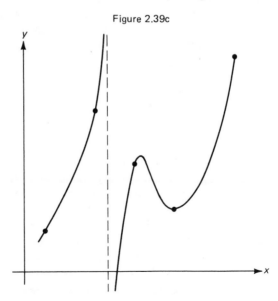

small as we want by keeping the change in x sufficiently small. As x gets closer and closer to 2, either from the left of 2 or the right of 2, $f(x)$ gets closer and closer to $f(2) = 8$. This is the idea behind "continuous" variation.

More generally, the following provides an intuitive statement of continuity:

> The function f is *continuous at the point $x = a$* if a small change in x away from a produces only a small change in $f(x)$ away from $f(a)$, and if we can make the change in $f(x)$ as small as we please by keeping x sufficiently close to a. Thus, *as x approaches a, the function values $f(x)$ approach $f(a)$.*

Whenever a function fails to be continuous at a point, we say that it is *discontinuous* there, or that it has a *discontinuity* at that point. If a function has no points of discontinuity, then it is continuous everywhere over its domain, or simply *continuous*. Since arithmetic operations, such as addition and multiplication, react to small input changes with only small output changes, all the polynomial functions are continuous everywhere. Likewise, the rational functions are continuous at all points excluding the roots of the denominator when division by zero is attempted. Notice that we suspected vertical asymptotes of the rational function might be located at these zeros, and we investigated the local behavior of the function near them using PROBE. When a function is everywhere continuous, like a polynomial function, its graph is connected in one piece. When there are points of discontinuity, such as at a vertical asymptote, the graph is broken into pieces with the breaks occurring at the places of discontinuity. Figure 2.9 provides an example of a function with a discontinuity at $x = 0$ where a vertical asymptote is located. The graph of the function is broken into two pieces, one on each side of the asymptote. The graphs of the trigonometric functions $\tan t$, $\cot t$, $\sec t$, and $\csc t$ in Figure 2.27 exhibit similar behavior and reveal that these functions are broken into many pieces. You will see in the examples to follow that discontinuities can occur for reasons other than the presence of vertical asymptotes.

EXERCISE 2.
JUMP DISCONTINUITIES:
THE GREATEST INTEGER FUNCTION

The greatest integer function $y = [x]$ is defined for every real number x, where $[x]$ is specified as the largest integer less than or equal to x. Thus, $[1.25] = 1$, $[4] = 4$, $[\pi] = 3$, and so forth. For negative values of x, the definition is the same: $[-1.25] = -2$ because among all the negative integers smaller than -1.25, the integer -2 is the greatest one. Likewise, $[-4] = -4$ and $[-\pi] = -4$. The graph of the greatest integer function is shown in Figure 2.40. Notice how the graph "jumps" to a new level at each integer value, remains at that constant level between two consecutive integers, and then jumps to a new level again as x progresses through an integer value. We say that the function has a *jump discontinuity* occurring at each integer point of its domain. At each jump discontinuity, the function suddenly jumps from one value to another without taking on any of the intervening values.

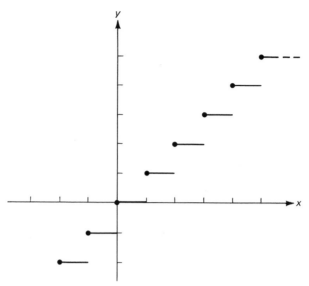

Figure 2.40 The graph of the greatest integer function $y = [x]$.

EXERCISE 3.
DISCONTINUITY WHERE FUNCTION VALUES
GROW ARBITRARILY LARGE

The function $y = 1/x$ is defined for all values of x except $x = 0$. The following table shows that the function values become larger and larger as x approaches zero through positive values:

x	$y = 1/x$
0.1	10.
0.01	100.
0.001	1,000.
0.0001	10,000.
0.00001	100,000.
0.000001	1,000,000.
0.0000001	10,000,000.

Thus the y-axis is a vertical asymptote (Figure 2.41). You can also see from the table that the values of $y = 1/x$ do not get close to any particular finite value as x gets closer and closer to zero: A small change in the value of x away from zero produces large changes in the function values $1/x$. This is an example of a function that has a discontinuity at a point because the function values are growing arbitrarily large in absolute value near that point. We say that the function is **unbounded** near the point. Although this function is discontinuous at $x = 0$, it *is* continuous at all the other nonzero points.

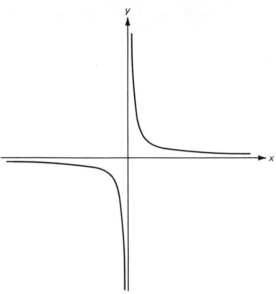

Figure 2.41 The graph of $y = 1/x$ has a discontinuity at $x = 0$.

DISCONTINUITY WHERE FUNCTION VALUES
OSCILLATE INFINITELY OFTEN

Consider the function $g(x) = \sin 1/x$, which is defined for all values of x except $x = 0$. Let's examine the behavior of g near $x = 0$. Using PROBE, obtain the following table of values:

x	$\sin 1/x$	x	$\sin 1/x$	x	$\sin 1/x$
2.000	0.479	0.200	−0.959	0.019	0.700
1.800	0.527	0.180	−0.665	0.018	−0.838
1.600	0.585	0.160	−0.033	0.017	0.762
1.400	0.655	0.140	0.758	0.016	−0.326
1.200	0.740	0.120	0.887	0.015	−0.639
1.000	0.841	0.100	−0.544	0.014	0.737
0.900	0.896	0.080	−0.066	0.013	0.999
0.800	0.949	0.070	0.989	0.012	0.997
0.700	0.990	0.060	−0.818	0.011	0.196
0.600	0.995	0.050	0.913	0.010	−0.506
0.500	0.909	0.040	−0.132	0.009	−0.915
0.400	0.598	0.030	0.941	0.008	−0.616
0.300	−0.191	0.020	−0.262	0.007	−0.996

A graph showing the plot of this table of values is provided in Figure
122 2.42. Notice that the graph switches from positive to negative values at $x = 0.3$

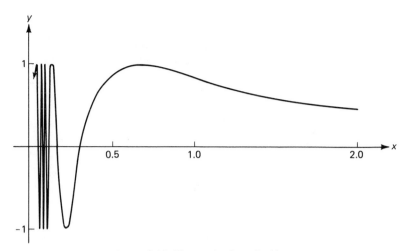

Figure 2.42 The graph of $y = \sin 1/x$.

and then begins to oscillate back and forth across the x-axis as x decreases toward zero. Moreover, as x gets nearer and nearer to zero, this oscillation becomes ever more rapid: The function values shift from positive to negative, and back again to positive values, for smaller and smaller changes in the value of x. You can see this behavior in the table. The graph actually oscillates infinitely many times between $y = -1$ and $y = +1$ as x decreases toward zero: Whenever x has the value $2/n\pi$, the value of $g(x)$ is ± 1. And as $n = 1, 2, 3, \ldots$, etc. increases, the number $2/n\pi$ gets closer and closer to zero. So a small change in x away from 0 can produce a change in $g(x)$ by as much as 2 units. In other words, it is impossible to keep the change in $g(x)$ small by keeping x close to 0. In the vicinity of zero, the function g assumes each value between $y = -1$ and $y = +1$ infinitely often. Accordingly, g fails to be continuous at $x = 0$. However, g is continuous at all nonzero values of x.

Whenever two functions are continuous, the same holds true of their sum, difference, product, quotient, and composition at all points for which no attempt is made at division by zero. The polynomial, sine, cosine, and exponential functions are all everywhere continuous (although we are not proving this). Thus any new functions formed from them by the basic function operations just mentioned are also continuous. For instance,

$$\sin (x^2 + 5x - 1) \qquad \tan 2x \qquad e^{x^3} \qquad \cos (2^x) \qquad \frac{3x^4 - x + 1}{x^2 - 5}$$

are all examples of functions that are continuous at every point for which there is no division by zero. All the functions you will encounter in this book will be continuous except, possibly, at some isolated points.

123

1. a. Compute how close $f(x) = 5x - 3x^2$ is to $f(1) = 2$ when x is near 1. Do this by setting $h = x - 1$ and completing the following table:

h	x	$f(x)$	$f(x) - f(1)$
0.2	1.2	1.68	−0.32
0.1	____	____	____
0.05	____	____	____
0.01	____	____	____
0.001	____	____	____
0.0001	____	____	____
−0.2	0.8	2.08	0.08
−0.1	____	____	____
−0.05	____	____	____
−0.01	____	____	____
−0.001	____	____	____
−0.0001	____	____	____

b. Compute how close $f(x)$ is to $f(2) = -2$ when x is near 2 following the same procedure as in part a. How does the table you obtain now differ from that found in part a?

In each of Problems 2-9, find the values of x, if any, where the function is discontinuous. In some instances you may wish to use the program PROBE for root finding.

2. $f(x) = 3x^2 - 4x + 1$

3. $f(x) = \sqrt{x - 1}$

4. $f(x) = \dfrac{x}{x^2 + 4}$

5. $f(x) = \dfrac{x}{x^2 - 4}$

6. $f(x) = \dfrac{|x|}{x}$

7. $f(x) = \cos\left(\dfrac{x + 1}{2 - x}\right)$

8. $f(x) = \dfrac{x^2 - 1}{x^3 - 2x^2 - 8x + 6}$

9. $f(x) = \dfrac{x^3 - 1}{1 - \sin^2 x}$

Section 2.6 Limits of Functions

In providing an intuitive statement of continuity of a function $f(x)$ at a point $x = a$, we used such phrases as "whenever x is near to a" or "for x approaching a" to then describe a similar condition to be satisfied by the function values $f(x)$. The phrases are meant to convey a dynamic process in the functional relationship between the values of x and the values of $f(x)$. In this section we explore this "limiting" process a little more generally.

Consider again the function $f(x) = x^3$ near $x = 2$ investigated in Exercise 1 of the preceding section. As x gets closer and closer to the number 2, the function values $f(x)$ get closer and closer to $f(2) = 8$. In other words, as x approaches 2, $f(x)$ approaches $f(2)$. If we use the arrow symbol ($\rightarrow$) for the word "approaches," the last statement could be expressed symbolically as

$$f(x) \rightarrow f(2) \quad \text{as} \quad x \rightarrow 2$$

With this symbology, our more general statement of continuity of $f(x)$ at the point $x = a$ would be written

$$f(x) \rightarrow f(a) \quad \text{as} \quad x \rightarrow a \tag{2.29}$$

The number $f(a)$ is also called the *limit* of $f(x)$ as x approaches a. This terminology leads to the notation

$$\lim_{x \rightarrow a} f(x) = f(a) \tag{2.30}$$

Each of expressions 2.29 and 2.30 mean the same thing, and we will use the notations interchangeably. The main idea is that the function values are tending to some "target" number as the domain values get closer and closer to a fixed number a.

Now it may happen that for some function f the values $f(x)$ do approach some "target" value L as x approaches a, but this target value is *not* $f(a)$. For instance, if you consider the function

$$f(x) = \frac{\sin x}{x}$$

it would be impossible for $f(x)$ to "target" in on $f(0)$ as x approaches 0 because there is no number $f(0)$. Nevertheless, it does turn out that $f(x)$ approaches a fixed number L as x approaches 0, and we say that L is the *limit* of $f(x)$ as x approaches 0. In Exercise 1 you will see that $L = 1$. More generally,

The number L is said to be the *limit* of $f(x)$ as x approaches a if $f(x) \rightarrow L$ as $x \rightarrow a$. We also write $\lim_{x \rightarrow a} f(x) = L$.

The program LIMIT* is designed to investigate the value of $f(x)$ as x approaches some value a. The program uses program steps 000 through 087, and memory locations 01 through 03. You must write a subroutine for LIMIT that specifies the keystrokes for evaluating $f(x)$. Program steps 088 through 479, as well as memory steps 00 and 04 through 59, are available for your use in writing that subroutine. The first two program steps in the subroutine for $f(x)$ *must* be

| Lb1 | | C′ |

because that label identifies the location of the subroutine for $f(x)$. As with every subroutine, the last two steps *must* be

| INV | | SBR |

You are free to use the $\boxed{=}$ key in your subroutine for $f(x)$. The current value of x may be recalled from memory location 01 in the evaluation of $f(x)$; this value of x is also in the display upon entry into the subroutine.

In investigating the limit of $f(x)$ as x approaches a, the values of x may be smaller than a or they may be larger. If x approaches a through values to the left of a, we write $x \to a^-$; if x approaches a through values to the right of a, we write $x \to a^+$. The program LIMIT investigates the approach from each side separately.

Like our previous programs, LIMIT is controlled by predefined labels. The purpose and use of each of these labels is now discussed.

D′   This loads the starting value of x into the program.

A′   This loads the quantity a, which x is approaching, into the program: thus $x \to a^-$ or $x \to a^+$.

E′   This loads the "step size factor" g into the program. For example, if $g = 2$, then x moves toward a by stepping $\frac{1}{2}$ of its current distance from a. The stepping is accomplished by the keys explained below.

A   This key investigates the limit of $f(x)$ as $x \to a^-$. It is assumed that x is less than a. Each time the key is pressed, the current value of x is replaced by the new value

$$x + \frac{1}{g}(a - x)$$

The value of f is then computed at this new x, and displayed.

---

*LIMIT first appeared in Herbert D. Peckham and the author, *Calculator Calculus* (Naval Postgraduate School publication).

This key investigates the limit of $f(x)$ as $x \to a^+$. It is assumed that x is greater than a. Each time the key is pressed, the current value of x is replaced by the new value

$$x - \frac{1}{g}(x - a)$$

The value of f is then computed at this new x, and displayed.

C   This key is used to investigate the limit of $f(x)$ as x approaches 0. If the value of x initially loaded is positive, then $x \to 0^+$; if it is negative then $x \to 0^-$. Each time the key is pressed, the current value of x is replaced by the new value x/g. The value of f is then computed at this new x, and displayed.

D   This key is used to investigate the limit of $f(x)$ as x tends to infinity. If the value of x initially loaded is positive, then $x \to +\infty$; if it is negative, then $x \to -\infty$. Each time the key is pressed, the current value of x is replaced by the new value gx. The value of f is then computed at this new x, and displayed.

E   Any time you wish to see the current value of x displayed, press this label.

The following exercises not only illustrate the use of LIMIT, but they also demonstrate how the programmable calculator provides a nice way to get at the idea of a limit in an intuitive manner.

EXERCISE 1.
AN IMPORTANT LIMIT: $\lim\limits_{x \to 0} (\sin x)/x = 1$

We use the program LIMIT to calculate this limit. The number x is assumed to be in radians so be sure your calculator is in that mode: Press ⎡Rad⎤ . With LIMIT read into your calculator, key in the following keystrokes for the subroutine to evaluate $\sin x/x$:

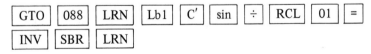

First we examine the limit from the left side, $x \to 0^-$:

(enter)   −1

(press)   ⎡D'⎤   Load initial $x_0 = -1.0$.

(enter)   2

(press)   ⎡E'⎤   Load step factor $g = 2$.

(press) Fix 4 Display four digits past the decimal point.

By repeatedly pressing the key C , you can watch the sequence of numbers below as they develop. If you wish to see the current value of x displayed at each stage, press E alternately with C .

Cycle Number	$\dfrac{\sin x}{x}$	Current x
1	0.9589	−0.5000
2	0.9896	−0.2500
3	0.9974	−0.1250
4	0.9993	−0.0625
5	0.9998	−0.0313
6	1.0000	−0.0156
7	1.0000	−0.0078
8	1.0000	−0.0039
9	1.0000	−0.0020
10	1.0000	−0.0010
11	1.0000	−0.0005
12	1.0000	−0.0002
13	1.0000	−0.0001
14	1.0000	−0.0001
15	1.0000	0.0000

Next we investigate the limit from the right side, $x \to 0^+$:

(enter)   1

(press) D′ Load initial $x_0 = 1.0$.

Now repeatedly press C .

Cycle Number	$\dfrac{\sin x}{x}$	Current x
1	0.9589	0.5000
2	0.9896	0.2500
3	0.9974	0.1250
4	0.9993	0.0625
5	0.9998	0.0313
6	1.0000	0.0156
7	1.0000	0.0078
8	1.0000	0.0039
9	1.0000	0.0020
10	1.0000	0.0010
11	1.0000	0.0005
12	1.0000	0.0002
13	1.0000	0.0001
14	1.0000	0.0001
15	1.0000	0.0000

We conclude that the value of the limit of $f(x) = \sin x/x$ as x approaches 0 is equal to the number 1. It seems clear that by Step 6 the process has reached this limiting value (at least to five significant digits). Notice that it is not necessary to display the current value of x. We did so for you to observe how near x is to zero when the function values get close to 1.

In calculating this limit, if x is measured in *degrees* rather than in radians, the limit you would obtain is

$$\lim_{x \to 0} \frac{(\sin x^\circ)}{x} = \frac{\pi}{180} \approx 0.0175$$

In calculus we want to avoid this factor $\pi/180$ in all calculations, and so we use radian measure in all operations with trigonometric functions.

EXERCISE 2.
ANOTHER IMPORTANT LIMIT: $\lim_{x \to 0} (1 + x)^{1/x} = e$

With LIMIT read into your calculator, key in the following keystrokes to evaluate $(1 + x)^{1/x}$:

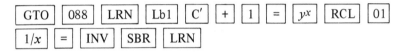

To calculate the right-hand limit, $x \to 0^+$:

(enter)	10		
(press)		$\boxed{D'}$	Load initial $x_0 = 10.0$.
(enter)	2		
(press)		$\boxed{E'}$	Load step factor $g = 2$.
(press)		$\boxed{\text{Fix}}$ $\boxed{4}$	Display 4 digits past the decimal point.

By repeatedly pressing the key $\boxed{C}$, you can watch the sequence of numbers below as they target in on the limiting value.

Cycle Number	Result		Cycle Number	Result
1	1.4310		11	2.7117
2	1.6505		12	2.7150
3	1.9131		13	2.7166
4	2.1745		14	2.7175
5	2.3874		15	2.7179
6	2.5324		16	2.7181
7	2.6192		17	2.7182
8	2.6670		18	2.7182
9	2.6922		19	2.7183
10	2.7051		20	2.7183

Clearly, by Step 19, the process has converged (at least to five significant digits) to the value 2.7183. You may recognize this number as e, studied in

Section 2.4. A similar table results when you load $x_0 = -10$ and calculate the left-hand limit, $x \to 0^-$. We conclude that

$$\lim_{x \to 0} (1 + x)^{1/x} = e \approx 2.7183$$

So far so good. But if you go on pressing $\boxed{C}$ to continue the table calculated for $x \to 0^+$, strange things begin to happen.

Cycle Number	Result	Cycle Number	Result
21	2.7183	34	2.7179
22	2.7183	35	2.7179
23	2.7183	36	2.7086
24	2.7183	37	2.6901
25	2.7183	38	2.6901
26	2.7183	39	2.6901
27	2.7183	40	2.6901
28	2.7182	41	2.4100
29	2.7182	42	2.4100
30	2.7182	43	2.4100
31	2.7179	44	1.0000
32	2.7179	45	1.0000
33	2.7179	46	1.0000

At Step 28 the process moves away from the value of 2.7183 and finally settles out at 1.0000 at Step 44. The reason for this behavior is that the calculator handles only thirteen digits in calculations (but displays only the ten most significant digits). A little thought reveals why this causes a problem. Remember that we started with $x = 10$. In Step 1, this becomes $10/2 = 5$. In Step 2, x was $5/2 = 2.5$ or $10/2^2$. Thus, at Step 28, the value of x was $10/2^{28}$ or 0.00000003725290321. At this point the calculator must try to compute

$$(1 + 0.00000003725290321)^{1/0.00000003725290321}$$

And here's the rub. Since the calculator can handle only thirteen significant digits, the addition in the parenthesis produces 1.000000037252 instead of 1.00000003725290321. Actually the problem began developing before Step 28, but we simply didn't see the change in the results since we were looking at only four places past the decimal. By Step 44, x is so small that $(1 + x)$ looks like 1.0 to the calculator, and 1.0 raised to any power is still 1.0, hence the observed results. It would be instructive for you to repeat this exercise but with all the digitis displayed so you can watch the limit develop and then "blow up."

The only reason that the limit of 2.7183 developed in the first place was that a delicate mathematical balance is established between the rate at which $(1 + x)$ decreases and the rate at which the exponent $(1/x)$ increases. As soon as the crucial parts of the computation become lost, because the calculational machine handles only N digits (whatever N is), rapid error build-up takes place and the limit "blows up." The fundamental problem is that any calculating device handles only a finite number of significant digits while mathematical theory assumes an infinite number of digits will be processed. Ultimately any calculator or computer is susceptible to this problem. Practically, though, the problem can be controlled and lived with easily. Our purpose here is merely to alert you to a potential problem and one that you should watch out for when using your calculator. If you see strange things happening in your calculations, truncation error may not be the cause, but it certainly should be considered a possible candidate.

EXERCISE 3.
AN EXAMPLE WHEN
THE LEFT- AND RIGHT-HAND
LIMIT VALUES DIFFER

Consider the function

$$f(x) = \frac{1}{3 + 2^{1/(x-1)}}$$

which is not defined when $x = 1$. Let's investigate the limiting behavior of f as x approaches 1. With LIMIT read into your calculator, key in the following subroutine to calculate $f(x)$:

| GTO | 088 | LRN | Lb1 | C' | 3 | + | 2 | y^x | (| RCL | 01 |
| $-$ | 1 |) | $1/x$ | = | $1/x$ | INV | SBR | LRN |

To calculate the left-hand limit $x \to 1^-$,

(enter)	1		
(press)		A'	Load $a = 1$.
(enter)	-1		
(press)		D'	Load initial $x_0 = -1.0$.
(enter)	2		
(press)		E'	Load step factor $g = 2$.

By repeatedly pressing A , you obtain the following results:

Cycle Number	Result
1	0.2857
2	0.3077
3	0.3265
4	0.3329
5	0.3333
6	0.3333

Next calculate the right-hand limit $x \to 1^+$:

(enter) 2

(press) $\boxed{D'}$ Load initial $x_0 = 2.0$.

Repeatedly press $\boxed{B}$ to obtain:

Cycle Number	Result
1	0.1429
2	0.0526
3	0.0039
4	0.0000
5	0.0000
6	0.0000

Since the value of the left-hand limit, $\frac{1}{3}$, differs from the right-hand limit, 0, we conclude that *the limit of $f(x)$ as $x \to 1$ does not exist.* In other words, the function values $f(x)$ are not close to a *single* specific value whenever x is sufficiently near 1: When x is slightly to the left of 1, $f(x)$ is near $\frac{1}{3}$; but when x is just to the right of 1, $f(x)$ is near 0.

EXERCISE 4.
HORIZONTAL ASYMPTOTES

In looking for a possible horizontal asymptote for a function f we examined the behavior of f as x got larger and larger in absolute value; that is, as $x \to \infty$ or $x \to -\infty$. We can easily investigate such behavior using LIMIT. For example, key in the function $y = x/\sqrt{1 + x^2}$ as a subroutine to be called by LIMIT (the graph of this function is shown in Figure 2.15):

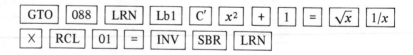

$\boxed{\text{GTO}}\ \boxed{088}\ \boxed{\text{LRN}}\ \boxed{\text{Lb1}}\ \boxed{C'}\ \boxed{x^2}\ \boxed{+}\ \boxed{1}\ \boxed{=}\ \boxed{\sqrt{x}}\ \boxed{1/x}$
$\boxed{\times}\ \boxed{\text{RCL}}\ \boxed{01}\ \boxed{=}\ \boxed{\text{INV}}\ \boxed{\text{SBR}}\ \boxed{\text{LRN}}$

To determine the limit as $x \to \infty$,

(enter) 1

(press) $\boxed{D'}$ Load initial $x_0 = 1.0$ (a positive value).

(enter) 2

(press) $\boxed{E'}$ Load step factor $g = 2$.

Repeatedly press the key $\boxed{D}$ to obtain

Cycle Number	Result
1	0.8944
2	0.9701
3	0.9923
4	0.9981
5	0.9995
6	0.9999
7	1.0000
8	1.0000
9	1.0000

Thus $x/\sqrt{1 + x^2} \to 1$ as $x \to \infty$. To determine the limit as $x \to -\infty$,

(enter) -1

(press) $\boxed{D'}$ Load initial $x_0 = -1.0$ (a negative value).

Repeatedly press the key $\boxed{D}$ to obtain:

Cycle Number	Result
1	−0.8944
2	−0.9701
3	−0.9923
4	−0.9981
5	−0.9995
6	−0.9999
7	−1.0000
8	−1.0000
9	−1.0000

Thus $x/\sqrt{1 + x^2} \to -1$ as $x \to -\infty$. The lines $y = 1$ and $y = -1$ are therefore horizontal asymptotes, in agreement with the results found in Exercise 5 of Section 2.2.

In the opening discussion for this section you saw that a function f is continuous at the point $x = a$, provided that $f(x) \to f(a)$ as $x \to a$. In other words, the number a must belong to the domain of f (otherwise $f(a)$ doesn't exist as a number), and both the left- and right-hand limits must exist and equal that same value:

$$\lim_{x \to a^-} f(x) = f(a) \quad \text{and} \quad \lim_{x \to a^+} f(x) = f(a) \tag{2.31}$$

The conditions in Equations 2.31 are both necessary and sufficient for the continuity of f at a. Thus we see that the function

$$f(x) = \frac{1}{3 + 2^{1/(x-1)}}$$

in Exercise 3 fails to be continuous at $x = 1$ because the left- and right-hand limits differ. Moreover, since f targets in on different values from the left and right sides of $x = 1$, there is no way we can "patch up" this function to make it continuous at $x = 1$. However, sometimes a function can be patched, as you will see in the next example.

EXERCISE 5.
A REMOVABLE DISCONTINUITY

The function

$$f(x) = \frac{x^2 - 9}{x^2 + x - 12}$$

is not defined when $x = 3$ because 3 is a root of the denominator. Thus f is discontinuous at 3. Let's examine the limit of f as x approaches 3. With LIMIT loaded into your calculator, key in the following subroutine to evaluate $f(x)$:

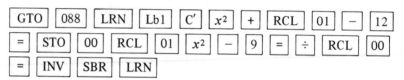

The calculations for the left- and right-hand limits as x approaches 3 are as follows ($g = 2$):

Cycle Number	$x \to 3^-$		Cycle Number	$x \to 3^+$
1	0.8462		1	0.8667
2	0.8519		2	0.8621
3	0.8545		3	0.8596
4	0.8559		4	0.8584
5	0.8565		5	0.8578
6	0.8568		6	0.8575
7	0.8570		7	0.8573
8	0.8571		8	0.8572
9	0.8571		9	0.8572
10	0.8571		10	0.8572
			11	0.8572
			12	0.8571
			13	0.8571
			14	0.8571

So $f(x) \to 0.8571$ as $x \to 3$, correct to four decimal places. If we *define* $f(3)$ to be this limiting value 0.8571, then we have effectively "removed" the discontinuity and patched up the function. In this instance we say that $x = 3$ is a *removable* discontinuity.

Now notice that f is also discontinuous at $x = -4$ because the denominator is zero at -4. Moreover, using LIMIT, you find that

$$\lim_{x \to -4^-} f(x) = +\infty \qquad \text{and} \qquad \lim_{x \to -4^+} f(x) = -\infty$$

Thus the line $x = -4$ is a vertical asymptote of the function f. Since the limit of f as x approaches -4 fails to exist, there is no value we could assign to f at $x = -4$ so as to make the resultant function continuous. We cannot "patch up" f, and we say the function has an *essential* discontinuity at $x = -4$. A graph of f illustrating these conclusions is shown in Figure 2.43. Notice that the line $y = 1$ is a horizontal asymptote.

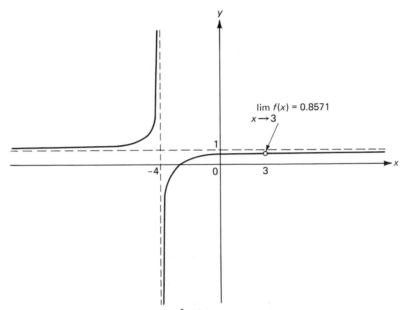

Figure 2.43 The graph of $f(x) = \dfrac{x^2 - 9}{x^2 + x - 12}$ has a limit as x approaches 3, but not as x approaches -4.

The Fundamental Limit Laws

Several laws are related to limits, in connection with the basic operations for functions, which we list here without any formal proofs. Understood is that all the functions in question are defined throughout some interval containing the limit point a, except possibly at a itself. Similar statements can be made about one-sided limits when the functions in question are defined on the *same* side of a.

Rule 1: If $f(x) \to L$ and $g(x) \to M$ as $x \to a$, then

      a. $f(x) + g(x) \to L + M$

      b. $f(x) g(x) \to LM$

      c. $\dfrac{1}{f(x)} \to \dfrac{1}{L}$, provided that $L \neq 0$ as $x \to a$.

Rule 2: If $f(x) \to L$ as $x \to a$, and if $g(z)$ is continuous at $z = L$, then $g[f(x)]$ $\to g(L)$ as $x \to a$.

Rule 3: If $f(x) \to L$ and $g(x) \to L$ as $x \to a$, and if $f(x) \leq h(x) \leq g(x)$ for all x near a, then $h(x) \to L$ as $x \to a$.

Much more can be said concerning limits and concerning the properties of continuous functions. We will discuss some of those results further on in the text. Our approach here has been a qualitative one, based on your intuition as you observed functional behavior using your calculator. In advanced mathematics courses, proofs are given to the limit laws, and the deeper implications of the limiting process are rigorously studied.

PROBLEMS 2.6

In each of Problems 1–24, use LIMIT to calculate the given limit. Give your answers correct to four decimal places.

1. $\lim\limits_{x \to 2} (4 - x + 3x^2)$

2. $\lim\limits_{x \to -1} \dfrac{x - 4}{x + 3}$

3. $\lim\limits_{x \to 1} \dfrac{x^3 - 1}{x^2 - 1}$

4. $\lim\limits_{x \to \frac{1}{3}} |1 - 3x|$

5. $\lim\limits_{x \to -3} \sqrt[3]{\dfrac{x - 4}{6x^2 + 2}}$

6. $\lim\limits_{y \to 1} \sqrt{\dfrac{3y^2 - 2y + 1}{y^8 + 4y^2 + 7}}$

7. $\lim\limits_{x \to 0} \dfrac{\sqrt{x + 3} - \sqrt{3}}{x}$

8. $\lim\limits_{h \to 1} \dfrac{(1/\sqrt{h}) - 1}{1 - h}$

9. $\lim\limits_{x \to \infty} \left(1 + \dfrac{1}{x}\right)^x$

10. $\lim\limits_{x \to \infty} \left(1 + \dfrac{2}{x}\right)^x$

11. $\lim\limits_{x \to 0} \dfrac{e^{2x} - 1}{x}$

12. $\lim\limits_{x \to \infty} \dfrac{\sin (3/x)}{2/x}$

13. $\lim\limits_{x \to 0} \dfrac{\sin x - \tan x}{x^3}$

14. $\lim\limits_{x \to 1} x^{1/(1-x)}$

15. $\lim\limits_{x \to 3} \left(\dfrac{6}{x^2 - 9} - \dfrac{1}{x - 3} \right)$

16. $\lim\limits_{y \to 2} \dfrac{1 - (2/y)}{y^2 - 4}$

17. $\lim\limits_{x \to 0^+} (x + 1)^{\cot x}$

18. $\lim\limits_{x \to 0} \dfrac{4^x - 2^x}{x}$

19. $\lim\limits_{x \to \infty} xe^{-x}$

20. $\lim\limits_{x \to 0} \dfrac{e^{2x} - 1}{x}$

21. $\lim\limits_{x \to 0} \dfrac{\sin x - x \cos x}{x^3}$

22. $\lim\limits_{x \to \infty} \dfrac{x^2 - 5}{2x^2 + 3x}$

23. $\lim\limits_{x \to \pi/2^-} \left(x \tan x - \dfrac{\pi}{2} \sec x \right)$

24. $\lim\limits_{x \to 0} \dfrac{\tan x - x}{x - \sin x}$

In Problems 25–29 determine whether you can define $f(a)$ so as to make f continuous at a.

25. $f(x) = \dfrac{1 - \cos x}{x}$ $a = 0$

26. $f(x) = \begin{cases} 4 - x^2 & \text{if } x \leqslant -1 \\ 1 + x^2 & \text{if } x > -1 \end{cases}$ $a = -1$

27. $f(x) = \dfrac{|x - 4|}{x - 4}$ $a = 4$

28. $f(x) = \dfrac{3x^2 - 1}{x^3}$ $a = 0$

29. $f(x) = \dfrac{x^3 + x^2 - x - 1}{x^2 + 2x - 3}$ $a = 1$

In Problems 30–33, find all horizontal and vertical asymptotes of the graph of f.

30. $f(x) = \dfrac{2x - 1}{x + 6}$

31. $f(x) = \dfrac{x^2 + 1}{x^2 - 1}$

32. $f(x) = \dfrac{x(x - 1)}{x^2 - 4}$

33. $f(x) = \sqrt{\dfrac{x}{x+1}}$

34. If the graph of a function $y = f(x)$ and that of a straight line $y = mx + b$ approach each other as x becomes infinite, the line is called an *asymptote* of the curve. Show that the line $y = 2x - 1$ is an asymptote of the curve

$$y = \frac{2x^3 - x^2 + 7}{x^2 + 4}$$

35. In an experiment it was found that by applying a force to a particular muscle, the muscle extended beyond its usual length by an amount A, satisfying

$$A = \frac{(2.1 - t)}{(2.1 + t^2)}$$

where A is measured in centimeters and t is the time in seconds after the force is initially applied. Find $\lim\limits_{t \to 0.9} A$ and $\lim\limits_{t \to 2} A$.

36. If a body of mass m is dropped from a great height, and if it is assumed that the force of the air resistance is proportional to the velocity, then its velocity as a function of time is given by

$$v = \frac{mg}{k}(1 - e^{-kt/m})$$

where g is the acceleration due to gravity and k is a constant. Find v as t tends to infinity. This limiting velocity is called the *terminal velocity* of the falling body.

37. If a body of mass m is dropped from a great height, and if it is assumed that the force of the air resistance is proportional to the square of the velocity, then its velocity as a function of time is given by

$$v = \sqrt{mg/k}\left[\frac{e^{2\sqrt{kg/m}\,t} - 1}{e^{2\sqrt{kg/m}\,t} + 1}\right]$$

where g is the acceleration due to gravity and k is a constant. Find the terminal velocity.

3

Differentiation

In the first chapter we introduced the idea of a line *tangent* to a curve at P as the limiting position of the secant line joining P to a second point Q advancing along the curve toward P. This limiting process is called *differentiation*. In calculus, "differentiating" a function means "finding the derivative" of the function.

In the present chapter you will see that the derivative of a function is also interpreted as an exact rate of change. This idea is important because many physical laws involve relationships among varying quantities, and these relationships are often stated in the form of equations involving derivatives of the various quantities. For example, the speed of a falling object is related to the distance it has fallen; the velocity of a rocket is related to its changing mass as it burns up fuel; the rate of inflation depends on the rate of energy consumption; the charge in an electrical circuit is related to the current and its change; and so forth. By investigating and solving such equations we come to understand, and to make predictions about, the physical world.

Our approach is to use the TI-59 calculator to find derivatives and to analyze functional behavior. Some technical questions are involved when calculating derivatives numerically on a computing device. For instance, how do you know that the limit specifying the derivative actually exists? Such questions are considered in books on numerical analysis, and we will not address them here. You will not have any difficulties with the well-behaved functions studied in this book or with those that you are most likely to encounter in many applications.

This chapter examines the derivative as an exact rate of change, considers two numerical methods for finding derivative values, and relates the derivative concept to continuity. The second derivative is investigated and related to the shape of a curve and to the acceleration of a particle along a straight line. Numerous applications of the derivative are studied, and the formal rules for analytically calculating the derived function are presented.

Before you begin your study of this chapter, record the programs DERIVE, TANGENT, and CHAIN on separate magnetic cards. Each program is listed in Appendix A and uses standard 479.59 partitioning.

Section 3.1 Rate of Change of a Function

In Section 1.5 the derivative of a function was defined and found to correspond to the slope of the tangent line. Symbolically, the derivative of the function f at the point $x = a$ is given by the limit

$$f'(a) = \lim_{\Delta x \to 0} \frac{f(a + \Delta x) - f(a)}{\Delta x} \tag{3.1}$$

It represents the slope of the tangent line to $y = f(x)$ at the point $(a, f(a))$. We now consider the derivative idea from a different point of view. We begin with an illustration of the idea.

Average and Instantaneous Velocity

Suppose you are driving a car from one city to another. You know that the cities are 110 mi apart and that it takes you exactly 2 hrs to complete the trip. You would then say that your average velocity is 55 mph because

$$\frac{\text{Distance traveled}}{\text{Elapsed time}} = \frac{110}{2} = 55$$

More generally, suppose a particle is moving along a straight line. We can coordinatize the line by assigning 0 to the starting position and the positive direction to the direction of the particle's motion. At each instant of time t, the particle has a unique position s representing the distance it has traveled from the starting position. Thus position s is a function of time t,

$$s = f(t)$$

The situation is depicted in Figure 3.1. Notice that the variable time does not appear directly in the figure; only the positions of the particle along the coordinate line are shown. Time enters indirectly because it determines what these positions are on the line.

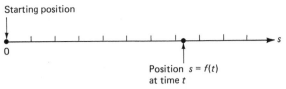

Starting position

0

Position $s = f(t)$
at time t

Figure 3.1 Position of a particle moving along a straight line as a function of time.

Now at a particular instant of time the particle will be at position $f(t)$ along the coordinate line, and, after a change in time Δt, the particle will be at a new position $f(t + \Delta t)$. Thus the change in the position, representing the distance traveled over the time span Δt, is

Distance traveled = $\Delta s = f(t + \Delta t) - f(t)$

In accordance with your intuitive notion of average velocity, it follows that

$$\text{Average velocity} = \frac{\text{Distance traveled}}{\text{Elapsed time}} = \frac{\Delta s}{\Delta t} = \frac{f(t + \Delta t) - f(t)}{\Delta t}$$

For instance, if a particle moves 140 ft in 7 sec, then $\Delta s = 140$ and $\Delta t = 7$. So the average velocity is $\Delta s / \Delta t = 20$ ft/sec.

When a particle is in motion, it has an exact or *instantaneous velocity* at each instant of time. For a moving car this would correspond to the exact reading of its (perfect) speedometer at each instant of time. Suppose you want to determine this instantaneous velocity at the particular moment $t = t_0$. By allowing time to change by a very small increment Δt to a new time $t_0 + \Delta t$, and measuring the distance traveled Δs over that interval of time, you could approximate the instantaneous velocity v_0 at time t_0 by the average velocity during the time interval:

$$v_0 \approx \frac{\Delta s}{\Delta t} = \frac{f(t_0 + \Delta t) - f(t_0)}{\Delta t}$$

As the interval of time Δt becomes smaller and smaller, the difference between the average velocity and the instantaneous velocity likewise becomes smaller and smaller. That is, as Δt approaches 0, the average velocity approaches the instantaneous velocity. Symbolically,

$$\text{Instantaneous velocity at time } t_0 = v_0 = \lim_{\Delta t \to 0} \frac{f(t_0 + \Delta t) - f(t_0)}{\Delta t}$$

In other words, the exact velocity at a particular instant t_0 is the derivative value $f'(t_0)$ of the position function $s = f(t)$ with respect to time. Because t_0 is an arbitrary instant of time, it is customary to drop the subscripts and write more simply

141

Instantaneous velocity $= v = \lim\limits_{\Delta t \to 0} \dfrac{\Delta s}{\Delta t} = f'(t)$ $\qquad\qquad$ (3.2)

where $s = f(t)$ denotes position, measured as distance from the start along the coordinate line, as a function of time.

Average and Instantaneous Rate of Change

The preceding discussion of velocity illustrates a more general idea. Let $y = f(x)$ be any function of x. If x is changed by an amount Δx, then the function value changes from $f(x)$ to $f(x + \Delta x)$. Accordingly, the change in y over the interval from x to $x + \Delta x$ is

$$\Delta y = f(x + \Delta x) - f(x)$$

The *average rate of change* in y over the Δx interval is then the ratio $\Delta y/\Delta x$. Thus

Average rate of change of $f(x)$ $= \dfrac{\Delta y}{\Delta x} = \dfrac{f(x + \Delta x) - f(x)}{\Delta x}$ $\qquad\qquad$ (3.3)

As Δx becomes smaller and smaller, the average rate of change approaches the *instantaneous rate of change*. So we obtain the definition

Instantaneous rate of change of $f(x)$ $= \lim\limits_{\Delta x \to 0} \dfrac{\Delta y}{\Delta x} = \dfrac{dy}{dx} = f'(x)$ $\qquad\qquad$ (3.4)

Equation 3.4 gives a second interpretation of the derivative concept.

For example, the formula $A = x^2$ specifies the area of a square with side length x. If the side length is changed by an amount Δx, then the average rate of change of the area is the quotient $\Delta A/\Delta x$. If originally $x = 5$ and $\Delta x = 0.1$, then

$$\frac{\Delta A}{\Delta x} = \frac{(5.1)^2 - 5^2}{0.1} = 10.1$$

So the area increases by an average rate of 10.1 square units per unit change in side length. On the other hand, to calculate the instantaneous rate of change when $x = 5$, first determine

$$\Delta A = (5 + \Delta x)^2 - 5^2 = 10\Delta x + \Delta x^2$$

From this you find the derivative dA/dx when $x = 5$:

$$A'(5) = \lim\limits_{\Delta x \to 0} \frac{\Delta A}{\Delta x} = \lim\limits_{\Delta x \to 0} (10 + \Delta x) = 10$$

which means that the area increases at the exact rate of change of 10 square units per unit change in side length.

The program PROBE calculates the average rate of change of a function according to Equation 3.3.

Calculating the Average Rate of Change of a Function

Step 1: With PROBE read into your TI-59 calculator, key in the particular function to be investigated in the usual way. (See the instructions in Step 2 of Exercise 1 in Section 2.1 if you need to refresh your memory on how to do so.)

Step 2: Load the original value x_0 at which the average rate of change is desired, using the second key $\boxed{D'}$.

Step 3: Load the increment value Δx, using the second key $\boxed{E'}$.

Step 4: Calculate the average rate of change $\Delta y/\Delta x$ by pressing the key $\boxed{D}$.

Calculating the Instantaneous Rate of Change of a Function

Step 5: After performing Steps 1-4 above, decrease Δx by pressing the second key $\boxed{A'}$. Then press $\boxed{D}$ again to display the new average rate of change with this diminished value of Δx.

Step 6: Continue to decrease Δx by $\boxed{A'}$ and to display $\Delta y/\Delta x$ by $\boxed{D}$, repeatedly, watching the sequence of numbers target in on the limiting value giving the derivative at the point x_0.

We will illustrate the use of PROBE to find derivatives in several applied examples.

EXERCISE 1.
RATE OF CHANGE
IN THE AREA OF A SQUARE

Key in the function $A(x) = x^2$ as a subroutine to PROBE:

$\boxed{\text{GTO}}$ $\boxed{134}$ $\boxed{\text{LRN}}$ $\boxed{\text{Lb1}}$ $\boxed{C'}$ $\boxed{x^2}$ $\boxed{\text{INV}}$ $\boxed{\text{SBR}}$ $\boxed{\text{LRN}}$

To calculate the rate of change at $x = 5$,

(enter)	5		
(press)		$\boxed{D'}$	Load $x_0 = 5.0$.
(enter)	0.1		
(press)		$\boxed{E'}$	Load $\Delta x = 0.1$.
(press)		$\boxed{D}$	Display $\Delta A/\Delta x = 10.1$.

Thus the average rate of change is 10.1 in agreement with our previous arithmetic. To find $A'(5)$, repeatedly press $\boxed{A'}$ followed by $\boxed{D}$ to obtain the following table:

Cycle Number	Δx	$\Delta A / \Delta x$
1	0.01	10.01
2	0.001	10.001
3	0.0001	10.0001
4	0.00001	10.00001
5	0.000001	10.

Thus you see that by Step 5 the process has converged to the derivative value $A'(5) = 10$, as we determined previously.

EXERCISE 2.
VELOCITY OF A BULLET

A bullet is fired straight upward. Its height h in ft after t sec satisfies the equation $h = 960t - 16t^2$. Let's find the velocity dh/dt after 7.1 sec. With PROBE loaded into your calculator, key in the expression for h:

$\boxed{GTO}$ $\boxed{134}$ $\boxed{LRN}$ $\boxed{Lb1}$ $\boxed{C'}$ $\boxed{STO}$ $\boxed{00}$ $\boxed{\times}$ $\boxed{960}$ $\boxed{-}$ $\boxed{16}$

$\boxed{\times}$ $\boxed{RCL}$ $\boxed{00}$ $\boxed{x^2}$ $\boxed{=}$ $\boxed{INV}$ $\boxed{SBR}$ $\boxed{LRN}$

To calculate the velocity at $t = 7.1$,

(enter)	7.1		
(press)		$\boxed{D'}$	Load $t = 7.1$.
(enter)	0.1		
(press)		$\boxed{E'}$	Load $\Delta t = 0.1$.

Repeatedly press $\boxed{A'}$ followed by $\boxed{D}$ to obtain

Cycle Number	Δt	$\Delta h / \Delta t$
1	0.01	732.64
2	0.001	732.784
3	0.0001	732.7984
4	0.00001	732.7999
5	0.000001	732.8

Thus the desired velocity is $h'(7.1) = 732.8$ ft/sec. Since the velocity is positive, the bullet is *rising* when $t = 7.1$ sec.

To find additional velocities we can use $\Delta t = 10^{-6}$ as in Step 5 and simply change the times. For instance,

(enter)	4		
(press)		$\boxed{D'}$	Load $t = 4.0$.
(press)		$\boxed{D}$	Calculate $h'(4) = 832$.
(enter)	26		
(press)		$\boxed{D'}$	Load $t = 26.0$.
(press)		$\boxed{D}$	Calculate $h'(26) = 128$.
(enter)	39		
(press)		$\boxed{D'}$	Load $t = 39.0$.
(press)		$\boxed{D}$	Calculate $h'(39) = -288$.

The negative velocity when $t = 39$ sec indicates that the bullet has already reached its maximum height and is now *falling* back to earth at the rate of 288 ft/sec.

The program PROBE can also be used to determine the maximum height reached by the bullet and the time when that height is reached. When the bullet reaches its highest point, its velocity will be zero because at that instant the bullet has ceased to rise and is poised to fall. Since $h'(26) = 128$ and $h'(39) = -288$, the highest point is reached sometime between $t = 26$ and $t = 39$ sec. Load $t = 26$ and $\Delta t = 0.5$ with the keys $\boxed{D'}$ and $\boxed{E'}$, and step along with the function:

PRESS	DISPLAY	COMMENT
A	14,204.	Height in ft.
E	26.5	$t = 26.5$ sec.
A	14,256.	
A	14,300.	
A	14,336.	
A	14,364.	
A	14,384.	
A	14,396.	
A	14,400.	
A	14,396.	We have gone past the maximum.
B	14,400.	Back up to previous height.
A'	0.05	Decrease Δt.
D	−0.8	Calculate the derivative.
A'	0.005	Decrease Δt.
D	−0.08	
A'	0.0005	
D	−0.008	
A'	0.00005	

D	−0.0006	
A′	0.000005	
D	0.	Velocity is zero.
E	30.	Time t = 30.0 sec.

Thus the maximum height attained by the bullet is 14,400 ft after 30 sec have elapsed.

When the bullet strikes the ground, its height above the surface of the earth is zero. Using PROBE to find the roots of the function $h(t)$, you obtain 0.0 and 60.0 as the roots. Thus the bullet strikes the ground 60 sec after being fired. To find the velocity when it strikes the ground, load $\Delta t = 10^{-6}$ and $t = 60$ to compute $\Delta h/\Delta t$:

(enter)	60		
(press)		$\boxed{\text{D}'}$	
(enter)	0.000001		
(press)		$\boxed{\text{E}'}$	
(press)		$\boxed{\text{D}}$	Calculate $h'(60) = -960.0$.

Thus the velocity is −960 ft/sec when t = 60 sec. The negative sign means that the motion is directed downward.

EXERCISE 3.
MARGINAL COST

In business, the instantaneous rate of change of the total production cost with respect to the number of units produced is called the *marginal cost*. In other words, marginal cost is the derivative of the total cost. It is measured in dollars per unit ($/unit) and approximates the cost of producing one additional unit of the output commodity at a given level of production.

For example, suppose the total cost in dollars of producing x television sets is $C(x) = 2{,}735 + 109x - 0.15x^2$. Let's find the marginal cost when 100 television sets have been produced. With PROBE read into your calculator, key in the cost function:

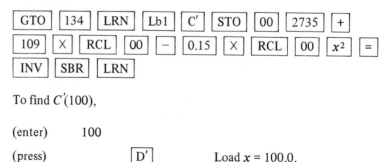

To find $C'(100)$,

(enter)	100		
(press)		$\boxed{\text{D}'}$	Load x = 100.0.

(enter)	0.1		
(press)	$\boxed{\text{E}'}$		Load $\Delta x = 0.1$.
(press)	$\boxed{\text{Fix}}$	$\boxed{2}$	Display two decimal digits.
(press)	$\boxed{\text{D}}$		Calculate $\Delta C/\Delta x = 78.99$.

Repeatedly press $\boxed{\text{A}'}$ followed by $\boxed{\text{D}}$ to obtain the following table:

Cycle Number	$\Delta C/\Delta x$
1	79.00
2	79.00
3	79.00

Thus $C'(100) = 79$ dollars per television set, the approximate cost of producing the 101st set. The *actual* cost of producing the 101st television set is the difference between the cost of producing 101 sets and the cost of producing 100 sets:

$$\text{Actual cost of 101st set} = C(101) - C(100)$$
$$= \$12,213.85 - \$12,135.00$$
$$= \$78.85$$

Note that the marginal cost is close to, but not exactly equal to the actual cost of producing the one additional set. So marginal cost is a close approximation to the actual cost of producing one additional unit.

The idea of the preceding example can be generalized. Economists often call the derivative of a function the *marginal value* of the function. It estimates the change in the function, at a given level, resulting from a one unit increase in the value of the independent variable. For example, the derivative of a profit function estimates the change in profit, at a given level of production, that results from increasing the production by one unit. Economists also write of marginal products, marginal revenue, marginal utility, and so on.

PROBLEMS 3.1

1. Find the average rate of change of the function $y = x^3 - 6x + 8$ from $x = 0.5$ to $x = 0.6$; from $x = 1.27$ to $x = 1.39$.

2. If a body falls from rest under the action of gravity the distance in ft it will fall is given by the formula $s = 0.5 \, gt^2$, where t is the time in sec and $g \approx 32.16$ is the acceleration of gravity. What is the velocity of the falling body when

   a. $t = 11.5$ sec?

   b. the body has fallen 127 ft?

3. The area of a circle is given by $A = \pi r^2$. At what rate is the area increasing when $r = 6.21$?

4. A particle moves along a straight line so that after t sec, its distance from a specified reference point is

$$D(t) = 12.5t + \frac{7.1}{t + 0.9}$$

meters. What is the velocity at the end of 3.5 sec?

5. Suppose the total cost in dollars of manufacturing x units is $C(x) = 0.2x^3 - 0.5x^2 + 475x + 225$.

   a. Estimate the cost of manufacturing the 14th unit.

   b. Compute the actual cost of manufacturing the 14th unit.

6. A marble rolls up a smooth inclined plane. After t seconds its distance s ft from the starting position is given by $s = 144t - 9t^2$.

   a. Find the velocity when $t = 5.1$ sec.

   b. Find the time when the marble stops and begins to roll back down the inclined plane.

   c. How far does the marble roll up the inclined plane?

7. The pressure P of a given amount of gas in a spherical balloon is given by the formula $P = k/r^3$, where k is a constant and r is the radius of the balloon.

   a. Find k if the pressure is 15 lb/in^2 when $r = 20$ ft.

   b. Find the pressure when r increases to 23.5 ft.

   c. Find the rate of change of the pressure with respect to the radius when $r = 21$ ft.

8. Often sales of a new product grow rapidly and then level off with time. For example, suppose the sales S of a certain commodity after x years is given by

$$S(x) = 200 - 170e^{-0.3x}$$

Find the rate of change of sales after five years.

9. Suppose that the population of a certain city for the next several years is approximated by the formula

$$P = \frac{250,000}{1 + 160e^{-0.4x}}$$

where x is the time in years. Find the rate of change of the population when $x = 3$ yrs.

In each of Problems 10–14, find the rate of change of the given function at the specified point, correct to two decimal places.

10. $f(x) = 4 + (x - 1)^{2/3}$ $x = 2.5$

11. $f(x) = \dfrac{x^2}{x - 3}$ $x = 4.7$

12. $f(x) = (2x + 1) \sqrt{6x + 7}$ $x = \sqrt{2}$

13. $f(x) = x^3 - \dfrac{1}{x^2} + 2\sqrt{x} - \dfrac{3}{x}$ $x = 13.1$

14. $f(x) = \sin \sqrt{x^2 - 4}$ $x = \pi$

15. Find the rate of change of the area of an equilateral triangle with respect to its side length x when $x = 5$.

16. If two bodies are a distance r apart, then the gravitational force $F(r)$ exerted by one body on the other body is given by

$$F(r) = \frac{k}{r^2} \qquad \text{for } r > 0$$

where k is a positive constant. Suppose the force of attraction upon a meteorite 1,300 mi above the earth's surface is 23 lb. Assume the radius of the earth is 3,959 mi.

a. Determine the constant k.

b. What would the meteorite weigh at the surface of the earth?

c. What is the rate of change of the force when the meteorite is 125 mi above the earth's surface?

Section 3.2 Differentiation by Central Differences

We have used the average rate of change

$$\frac{f(a + \Delta x) - f(a)}{\Delta x}$$

for small Δx to approximate the derivative value $f'(a)$. Geometrically, this means that the slope of the secant line passing through the two points $(a, f(a))$ and $(a + \Delta x, f(a + \Delta x))$ on the graph of f approximates the slope of the tangent line at the point $(a, f(a))$. This is depicted in Figure 3.2. It is not clear

Figure 3.2 The slope of the secant line approximates the slope of the tangent line for small Δx.

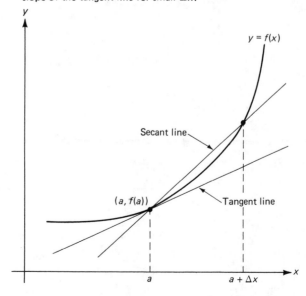

how "small" Δx should be for a fairly good approximation to $f'(a)$. Our procedure is to begin with some initial value of Δx, calculate the average rate of change, decrease Δx by a factor of 10, and then calculate a new average rate of change with this diminished value. Then we decrease Δx again, and so on, until we discern very little or no difference between the successive values for the rate of change as it appears in the display of the calculator. This method for calculating derivatives is known as the *forward difference* or *full-increment* method.

A second method for calculating the derivative of a function is known as the *central difference* or *half-increment* method. In this method you pick the slope of the secant line joining the two points $(a - \frac{\Delta x}{2}, f(a - \frac{\Delta x}{2}))$ and $(a + \frac{\Delta x}{2}, f(a + \frac{\Delta x}{2}))$ on the graph of f to approximate the slope of the tangent line when $x = a$. As Δx becomes smaller and smaller, the slope of the secant line gets closer and closer to the slope of the tangent line (Figure 3.3). In the case of central differences, the slope of the secant line is

$$\frac{f(a + \frac{\Delta x}{2}) - f(a - \frac{\Delta x}{2})}{\Delta x} \tag{3.5}$$

where Δx is "small." The central difference method for approximating the derivative $f'(a)$ is also built into PROBE. Let's compare the two methods with an example.

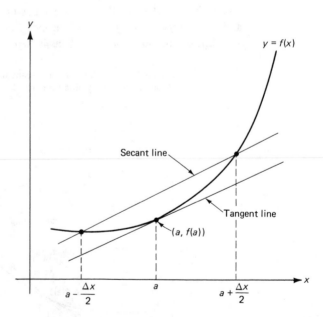

Figure 3.3 The central difference approximation of the slope of the tangent line at $x = a$ by the slope of the secant line.

EXERCISE 1.
TWO METHODS FOR FINDING SLOPES

We want to find the slope of the tangent line to the function

$$f(x) = \frac{2}{1 + 3e^{-2x}}$$

when $x = 1.75$. With PROBE loaded into your TI-59, enter the subroutine for the function f:

| GTO | 134 | LRN | Lb1 | C' | × | 2 | +/− | = | INV | ln x |

| × | 3 | + | 1 | = | 1/x | × | 2 | = | INV | SBR | LRN |

First we will calculate $f'(1.75)$ by forward differences accurate to five decimals: set Fix 5 . Then

(enter)	1.75	
(press)	D'	Load $x = 1.75$.
(enter)	0.1	
(press)	E'	Load $\Delta x = 0.1$.

PRESS	DISPLAY	COMMENT
D	0.28036	First approximation to $f'(1.75)$.
A'	0.01000	Decrease Δx.
D	0.30214	Second approximation to $f'(1.75)$.
A'	0.00100	Decrease Δx.
D	0.30441	Third approximation to $f'(1.75)$.
A'	0.00010	Decrease Δx.
D	0.30464	Fourth approximation to $f'(1.75)$.
A'	0.00001	Decrease Δx.
D	0.30466	Fifth approximation to $f'(1.75)$.
A'	0.00000	Decrease Δx.
D	0.30467	Sixth approximation to $f'(1.75)$.

The key C in PROBE calculates the derivative by central differences. Thus

| (enter) | 0.1 | |
| (press) | E' | Reload $\Delta x = 0.1$. |

PRESS	DISPLAY	COMMENT
C	0.30494	First approximation to $f'(1.75)$.
A'	0.01000	Decrease Δx.

C	0.30467	Second approximation to $f'(1.75)$.
A'	0.00100	Decrease Δx.
C	0.30467	Third approximation to $f'(1.75)$.

For the particular function $f(x) = 2/(1 + 3e^{-2x})$, it is clear that the central difference method for calculating the derivative converges much more rapidly than the forward difference method. This is often the case with elementary functions. Questions concerning the convergence of numerical methods are investigated in numerical analysis and are beyond the scope of this book.

For most of the functions you will encounter, use the central difference method to calculate the derivative. Note, however, that this method requires the function to be defined (that is, to have values) on both sides of the point $x = a$. If the formula for $f(x)$ is valid only to the left of $x = a$, then you can calculate only the *left-hand derivative* by the forward difference method with *negative* Δx. Likewise, if the formula for $f(x)$ is valid only to the right of $x = a$, then calculate the *right-hand derivative* by the forward difference method with *positive* Δx. *The derivative of a <u>continuous</u> function exists at $x = a$ if and only if these left- and right-hand derivatives exist and have the same value.*

EXERCISE 2.
LEFT- AND RIGHT-HAND DERIVATIVES

Consider the function given by

$$f(x) = \begin{cases} x^3 + 2 & x \leqslant 1 \\ 3x & x > 1 \end{cases}$$

Notice that $\lim_{x \to 1^-} (x^3 + 2) = \lim_{x \to 1^+} 3x = 3$ so that f is continuous at $x = 1$ (which you can verify with the LIMIT program). We will find the left- and right-hand derivatives at $x = 1$. With PROBE loaded in your calculator, enter the formula $x^3 + 2$ to calculate the derivative from the left:

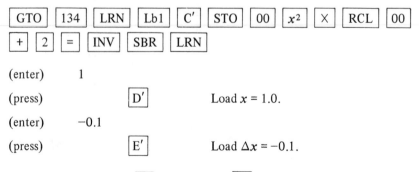

| GTO | 134 | LRN | Lb1 | C' | STO | 00 | x² | X | RCL | 00 |

| + | 2 | = | INV | SBR | LRN |

(enter)   1

(press)   D'   Load $x = 1.0$.

(enter)   −0.1

(press)   E'   Load $\Delta x = -0.1$.

By repeatedly pressing D followed by A' , you obtain the left-hand derivative value 3.0000 in five steps. Now enter the formula $3x$ to calculate the derivative from the right:

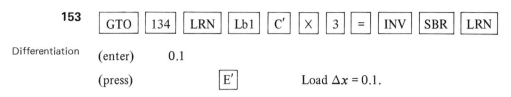

(enter) 0.1

(press) $\boxed{\text{E}'}$ Load $\Delta x = 0.1$.

Again, repeatedly press $\boxed{\text{D}}$ followed by $\boxed{\text{A}'}$, and you obtain the right-hand derivative value 3.0000. Since these values both exist and are equal, the continuous function f is differentiable at $x = 1$ and $f'(1) = 3$.

To calculate the derivative of f at a value other than 1, use central differences. For instance, to find $f'(-5.2)$, enter the formula $x^3 + 2$ for $f(x)$, then

(enter) −5.2

(press) $\boxed{\text{D}'}$

(enter) 0.1

(press) $\boxed{\text{E}'}$

Now repeatedly press $\boxed{\text{C}}$ followed by $\boxed{\text{A}'}$ to obtain $f'(-5.2) = 81.12$.

Next consider the function

$$g(x) = \begin{cases} x^2 + 2 & x \leqslant 1 \\ 3x & x > 1 \end{cases}$$

Since $\lim\limits_{x \to 1^-} (x^2 + 2) = \lim\limits_{x \to 1^+} 3x = 3$, g is also continuous at $x = 1$. Now calculate the left-hand derivative of g at $x = 1$:

$$\boxed{\text{GTO}} \; \boxed{134} \; \boxed{\text{LRN}} \; \boxed{\text{Lbl}} \; \boxed{\text{C}'} \; \boxed{x^2} \; \boxed{+} \; \boxed{2} \; \boxed{=} \; \boxed{\text{INV}}$$
$$\boxed{\text{SBR}} \; \boxed{\text{LRN}}$$

Load $x = 1$ and $\Delta x = -0.1$ to obtain the left-hand derivative value 2.0000 by the forward-difference method (using the keys $\boxed{\text{D}}$ and $\boxed{\text{A}'}$).

On the other hand, the right-hand derivative of g at $x = 1$ has the value 3.0000 (just as was the case for f previously). Since these two derivative values are unequal, the continuous function g is *not* differentiable at $x = 1$; that is, there is no number we can call $g'(1)$. Geometrically, the graph of g has a "corner" when $x = 1$, but the graph of f does not. At a "corner," the graph of a function cannot have a tangent line. We say that the graph fails to be "smooth" at a point if there is no tangent line there. Thus differentiability is a "smoothness" condition.

The function g is differentiable at all values of x other than 1. To calculate any such derivative value, you would employ the central difference method via the keys $\boxed{\text{C}}$ and $\boxed{\text{A}'}$. For instance, $g'(-5.2) = -10.4$.

Differentiability and Continuity

An important property of differentiable functions is that they are always continuous. More precisely,

> If a function is differentiable at a point $x = a$, then it is continuous there.

This last result is sometimes used to determine where a function is continuous. But be careful about what the result says! It does *not* say that a continuous function has a derivative. On the contrary, the preceding example illustrated a function g that is continuous and yet that fails to have a derivative at some point. What it *does* say is that it is impossible to have differentiability without continuity.

EXERCISE 3.
MARGINAL REVENUE

An equation that relates the price p per unit with the quantity demanded is called a *demand equation.* For example, the equation

$$p(x) = \frac{107}{x+2} - \frac{4}{x}$$

where p denotes the dollar price per unit for x units, is a demand equation. If the price per unit is multiplied by the number of units sold, then the revenue the manufacturer receives for selling x units is

$$r(x) = xp(x)$$

or

$$r(x) = \frac{107x}{x+2} - 4$$

in the case of our example. The exact rate of change of the revenue function r is called the *marginal revenue.* Thus

$$\text{Marginal revenue} = \frac{dr}{dx}$$

Let's calculate the marginal revenue when 12 units are sold. With PROBE loaded into your calculator, key in the above revenue function $r(x)$:

| GTO | 134 | LRN | Lb1 | C′ | STO | 00 | + | 2 | = | 1/x |

154 | X | 107 | X | RCL | 00 | − | 4 | = | INV | SBR | LRN |

Load $x = 12$ and $\Delta x = 0.1$ and repeatedly press $\boxed{C}$ followed by $\boxed{A'}$ to obtain $r'(12) = 1.0918$. Thus after 12 units have been sold, the sale of one more unit increases revenue by about $1.09.

PROBLEMS 3.2

In each of Problems 1-22, compute the derivative of the given function at the specified point, correct to two decimal places. Use the central difference method in PROBE.

1. $y = (x^3 - 2)^4$ $x = -1.5$

2. $y = (1 - x^2 + x^4)^{1/3}$ $x = 1.0$

3. $y = (1 - x^2)^{-1/2}$ $x = 0.25$

4. $y = (3 - 2x)^5 (x^2 - 2)^4$ $x = 1.9$

5. $y = \sqrt{\dfrac{x}{1-x}}$ $x = 0.69$

6. $y = \dfrac{x^4 - 12x^2}{(x^2 - 4)^2}$ $x = 0.23$

7. $y = x(x - 1)^{2/3}(x + 2)^{1/3}$ $x = 2.0$

8. $y = xe^{-x/2}$ $x = -1.75$

9. $y = x^2 e^{\sqrt{x}}$ $x = 1.67$

10. $y = \sin^2 5x$ $x = 1.0$ (radian mode)

11. $y = \dfrac{\sin 3\sqrt{x}}{\sqrt{x}}$ $x = 2.1$

12. $y = \sin x \sin 2x$ $x = \pi/4$

13. $y = \sin x^2$ $x = \pi/8$

14. $y = x^2 \sin x - 2 \sin x + 2x \cos x$ $x = \pi/4$

15. $y = \tan\left(\cos \dfrac{2}{x}\right)$ $x = 4/\pi$

16. $y = x \sin 1/x$ $x = 2/\pi$

17. $y = e^{\sin x}$ $x = 1.0$

18. $y = x 3^x$ $x = 1.2$

19. $y = e^{-x} \cos 2x$ $x = \pi/8$

20. $y = \dfrac{1}{1 + e^{-x}}$ $x = 2.09$

21. $y = x^x$ $x = 2.0$

22. $y = x^{\sin x}$ $x = 1.0$

In Problems 23-27, find the left- and right-hand derivatives of the given functions at the specified points. State whether each function is or is not differentiable at the point. Be sure to check continuity.

23. $f(x) = \begin{cases} x^4 + 1 & x > 1 \\ 2x^2 & x \leqslant 1 \end{cases}$ at $x = 1$

24. $f(x) = \begin{cases} \sin x & x \geqslant 0 \\ |x| & x < 0 \end{cases}$ at $x = 0$

25. $f(x) = \begin{cases} e^{x^2} & x > 1 \\ 2e^x & x \leqslant 1 \end{cases}$ at $x = 1$

26. $f(x) = \sin |x|$ at $x = 0$

27. $f(x) = \cos |x|$ at $x = 0$

28. Suppose a revenue function r is given by

$$r(x) = \begin{cases} 3x + 2 & 0 \leqslant x \leqslant 1 \\ 5x - x^2 + 1 & 1 < x \leqslant 4 \end{cases}$$

Show that there is a marginal revenue at $x = 1$, and calculate it.

29. A particle moves along a straight line so that its distance s in ft from the starting position after t sec is given by

$$s = \frac{\sqrt{t}}{1 + t + 3t^2}$$

Find the velocity of the particle after 0.25 sec and after 0.50 sec. Interpret your results.

30. The initial population in a bacteria colony is 15,000. After t hours the colony grows to a number $P(t)$ given by

$$P(t) = 15{,}000(1 + 0.94t + t^2)$$

Find the number of bacteria present after 5 hrs, and find the rate of change of P when $t = 5$.

Section 3.3 The Second Derivative

Consider a differentiable function $y = f(x)$. Then f is continuous, and at every value of x over some interval there is a derivative value $f'(x)$ giving the slope of the tangent line or the instantaneous rate of change of f at x. This defines a new function f' called the *derivative* or *derived function* associated with f. If this new function f' also has a derivative at x, we denote the value by $f''(x)$ or $f^{(2)}(x)$ and call it the *second derivative* of f at x. Thus the second derivative is the derivative of the first derivative. It is also customary to denote the first and second derivative functions by dy/dx and d^2y/dx^2, respectively. Let's examine the geometric meaning of the second derivative.

Suppose $y = f(x)$ has a second derivative at every number x over some interval. Since every differentiable function is continuous, the existence of f'' means that both of the functions f and f' are continuous. Whenever f' is continuous, we say that f is a *continuously differentiable* function. For such a function, a small change in x produces only a small change in the slope $f'(x)$ of the tangent. This means that the graph of f is a continuous curve whose tangent line turns continuously as x varies. Let's take a closer look at this idea.

Imagine a point P traversing the curve depicted in Figure 3.4. At the point marked A on the curve, the slope of the tangent is positive and the function is increasing. At B it is still increasing, but the tangent is not as steep as before, so the slope is less positive and the rate of increase has diminished. By the time this imagined point has moved along to the position C, the slope has diminished even more to become a negative value. That is, the slope function f' is decreasing in the movement of P along the curve from A to C. Since the sign of the derivative of a function signifies whether it is increasing or decreasing, this means that the derivative of f', namely the second derivative f'', is negative as P moves along the curve from A to C. Geometrically, the tangent line is turning continuously in the clockwise direction, and the curve itself lies below the tangent line everywhere from A to C. Mathematically we say that the curve is *concave downward*.

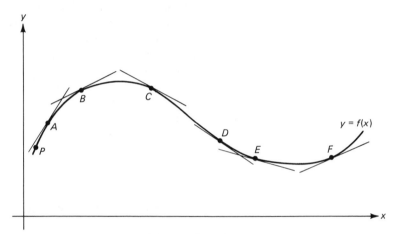

Figure 3.4 At the points *A, B,* and *C* the curve lies below the tangent line and is concave downward. At *D, E,* and *F* the curve lies above the tangent line and is concave upward. As the point *P* moves from *A* to *C,* the tangent line turns clockwise; from *D* to *F* it turns counterclockwise.

Similarly, at the point marked D the slope of the tangent line is negative, and at E it is also negative. However, at E the slope is less negative than it is at D so the slope has increased in value. By the time the moving point P reaches the position F, the slope has increased to a positive value. Thus, f' is increasing along the curve from D to F, and consequently the second derivative f'' is positive there. In Figure 3.4 you see that the tangent line turns continuously in the counterclockwise direction in the movement of P from D to F, and the curve lies everywhere above the tangent line. In this situation we say that the curve is *concave upward*. In summary, the curve is:

1. *concave upward* if the second derivative is *positive,* and
2. *concave downward* if the second derivative is *negative.*

A curve that is shaped concave upward is cupped to "hold water"; when it is shaped concave downward it would "spill water."

Associated with the specific point $x = a$ and function f are three numbers: $f(a)$, $f'(a)$, and $f''(a)$. The number $f(a)$, the value of the function when $x = a$, allows you to locate the point $(a, f(a))$ on the graph of f. The second number $f'(a)$ measures the slope of the graph at that point and tells you how steeply the graph is rising (a positive value) or falling (a negative value) there. The third number $f''(a)$ measures the tendency of the graph to "bend" at the point in question. Larger absolute values for $f''(a)$ mean that the graph will tend to bend away from the tangent line more. For a straight line, the second derivative $f''(a)$ is zero, but at the sharpest turning point around a hairpin curve, the absolute value of $f''(a)$ is large. Thus f'' gives a measure of the amount of *curvature* that is present in a curve.

Intuitively we get an understanding of curvature from circles. Small circles, those with small radii, have large curvatures; large circles have much less curvature. The expression "turning on a dime" is meant to convey a high degree of maneuverability because a dime is the smallest of our coins and its curvature is greater than that of a penny, nickle, or quarter.

The second derivative alone does not provide the exact measure of curvature: The slope of the curve itself must also be taken into account. It is customary to denote curvature by the Greek letter κ (kappa). Although we are not going to give the derivation, the formula for the curvature of the curve $y = f(x)$ when $x = a$ is

$$\kappa = \frac{|f''(a)|}{[1 + [f'(a)]^2]^{3/2}} \tag{3.6}$$

Thus κ is a measure of the local bending in the curve away from the tangent line when $x = a$.

In Figure 3.4 you can see that the curve is concave downward at the point marked C, but concave upward at D. Thus at some point along the curve from C to D, the curve changes its direction of concavity. A point on the curve where the direction of concavity changes is called a *point of inflection*. At an inflection point the sign of the second derivative changes. This change may take place because the second derivative is zero at that point or because it fails to exist there (for instance, the second derivative might become infinite).

The program DERIVE calculates the derivative, second derivative, and curvature of any second differentiable function that can be keyed into your calculator. Like the other prepared programs you have been using, DERIVE requires you to key in a subroutine for the function f that you wish to investigate. The program uses program steps 000 through 159, and storage locations 01 through 05. Program steps 160 through 479 and memory locations 00, and 06 through 59 are available for your use while evaluating $f(x)$. DERIVE uses the following *central difference* expressions to calculate the first and second derivative values:

$$f'(x) = \frac{f(x + \Delta x) - f(x - \Delta x)}{2\Delta x} \tag{3.7}$$

and

$$f''(x) = \frac{f(x + \Delta x) - 2f(x) + f(x - \Delta x)}{\Delta x^2} \qquad (3.8)$$

where the increment Δx is sufficiently small: the smaller the value of Δx, the better the approximation to the derivatives. Practically, you will experiment with the values of Δx until you achieve the desired accuracy.

The rationale for Equation 3.7 was discussed previously, although we have made a notational change of Δx to $2\Delta x$ to simplify the form of the equations. Since the quotients

$$\frac{f(x + \Delta x) - f(x)}{\Delta x} \quad \text{and} \quad \frac{f(x) - f(x - \Delta x)}{\Delta x}$$

provide good approximations to the derivative f' at the two "halfway" points

$$x + \frac{\Delta x}{2} \quad \text{and} \quad x - \frac{\Delta x}{2}$$

we apply Equation 3.7 to them and obtain the second derivative approximation

$$f''(x) = \frac{\dfrac{f(x + \Delta x) - f(x)}{\Delta x} - \dfrac{f(x) - f(x - \Delta x)}{\Delta x}}{\Delta x}$$

which simplifies algebraically to Equation 3.8. It is not so important that you understand this last derivation. You will be able to use DERIVE even if you do not. We just want you to see that there is nothing especially complicated or mysterious about Equation 3.8.

Using the Program DERIVE

When DERIVE jumps to the subroutine to determine a function value $f(x)$, the number x is assumed to be in the display. Thus one of your first steps in the subroutine should be to store the value of x away where it will always be available while computing $f(x)$. The first two steps in the subroutine for $f(x)$ *must* be

$$\boxed{\text{Lb1}} \quad \boxed{\text{C}'}$$

because DERIVE assumes that the subroutine for $f(x)$ is located at label C'. The last two steps must be

$$\boxed{\text{INV}} \quad \boxed{\text{SBR}}$$

Each of the subparts of the program is accessed by one of the special calculator labels as follows:

D'	This loads the value of x into the program.
E'	The increment Δx is loaded with this label.
A	The value $f(x)$ is computed and displayed (*not $f(x + \Delta x)$* as in PROBE).
B	The derivative value $f'(x)$ is computed and displayed, according to the central difference formula.
C	The second derivative $f''(x)$ is computed and displayed, according to the central difference formula.
D	The curvature κ is computed and displayed.
A'	This key causes Δx to be replaced by $\Delta x/10$.
B'	This key causes Δx to be replaced by $10\Delta x$.
E	To see the value of x, press this label.

Let's look at several examples.

EXERCISE 1.
CALCULATING DERIVATIVES

Consider the function

$$f(x) = x^2 e^x$$

We have to write a subroutine to evaluate this function. First, read DERIVE into your TI–59. Then key in the following keystrokes for $f(x)$:

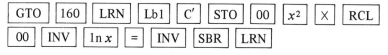

| GTO | 160 | LRN | Lb1 | C' | STO | 00 | x² | X | RCL |

| 00 | INV | 1n x | = | INV | SBR | LRN |

Note that for large positive values of x, the values of $f(x)$ will be large. It is not clear what happens for negative values of x, so we will explore that issue as we go along. Load $\Delta x = 0.001$ and set the display to three digits past the decimal point:

(enter)   0.001

(press) | E' |

(press) | Fix | | 3 |

Remember that the key | D' | loads the value of x each time. Now verify the table below using the label keys | A |, | B |, | C |, and | D | to control the calculations as described for the program DERIVE:

x	$f(x)$	$f'(x)$	$f''(x)$	κ
−5.0	0.168	0.101	0.047	0.046
−4.0	0.293	0.147	0.037	0.035
−3.5	0.370	0.159	0.008	0.007
−3.0	0.448	0.149	−0.050	0.048
−2.5	0.513	0.103	−0.144	0.141
−2.0	0.541	0.000	−0.271	0.271
−1.5	0.502	−0.167	−0.390	0.375
−1.0	0.368	−0.368	−0.368	0.304
−0.5	0.152	−0.455	0.152	0.114
0.0	0.000	0.000	2.000	2.000
0.5	0.412	2.061	7.007	0.583
1.0	2.718	8.155	19.028	0.034
1.5	10.084	23.529	45.937	0.004
2.0	29.556	59.112	103.447	0.001
3.0	180.770	301.283	461.967	0.000
4.0	873.570	1310.356	1856.337	0.000

A graph of the function is sketched in Figure 3.5. Notice from the table of values that the function values are increasing for $x = -5$ to $x = -2$ and that $f'(x)$ is positive over this interval. Now $f''(x)$ is positive for $x \leqslant -3.5$ and negative for $-3 \leqslant x \leqslant -1$. So the graph of f is concave upward for $x \leqslant -3.5$ and concave downward for $-3 \leqslant x \leqslant -1$. You can see that there is a point of inflection somewhere between $x = -3.5$ and $x = -3.0$ where the graph changes its direction of concavity. Since $f''(x)$ is close to zero at $x = -3.5$, the inflection point is somewhere in that vicinity. We now explore this region more closely:

x	$f''(x)$	x	$f''(x)$	x	$f''(x)$
−3.49	0.007	−3.45	0.003	−3.41	0.000
−3.48	0.006	−3.44	0.002	−3.40	−0.001
−3.47	0.005	−3.43	0.001	−3.39	−0.002
−3.46	0.004	−3.42	0.001	−3.38	−0.003

Figure 3.5 Graph of $y = x^2 e^x$. Inflection points occur when $x = -3.41$ and $x = -0.586$.

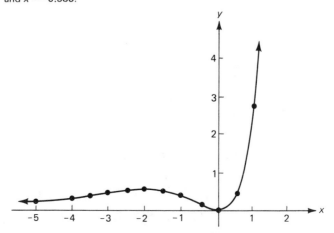

From this last table you can see that an inflection point occurs when $x = -3.41$. Since $f(-3.41) = 0.384$, the point $(-3.41, 0.384)$ is the desired inflection point.

Going back to the original table, observe that the derivative f' is zero at $x = -2$. Thus the tangent line to the graph at $(-2, 0.541)$ is horizontal and the function has a relative maximum. As x increases away from -2.0 the values of $f(x)$ decrease and $f'(x)$ is negative. The second derivative $f''(x)$ is also negative, so the graph is concave downward, until x reaches -0.5 when $f''(x)$ is positive again. Thus another inflection point occurs between $x = -1.0$ and $x = -0.5$. Since f'' is closer to zero at $x = -0.5$, the inflection point occurs more nearly in the vicinity of that value. In taking a closer look there, you can verify the following table:

x	$f''(x)$	x	$f''(x)$
−0.52	0.113	−0.59	−0.007
−0.54	0.077	−0.585	0.001
−0.56	0.042	−0.586	0.000
−0.58	0.009		

So the inflection point occurs at $x = -0.586$. For values of x larger than -0.586, the second derivative $f''(x)$ remains positive, and the curve is everywhere concave upward. At $x = 0$, the derivative f' is zero again, and the function has a relative minimum.

Finally, note the values of the curvature κ. The greatest curvature occurs at $x = 0$ when $\kappa = 2$. As x increases away from zero, the curvature decreases rapidly, eventually reaching zero when $x = 3$. This means that for $x \geqslant 3$, there is virtually no bending of the curve away from the tangent line: The curve is locally a straight line. In the negative direction, as x goes to $-\infty$, $f(x)$, $f'(x)$, $f''(x)$, and κ all approach zero. The x-axis is a horizontal asymptote of the curve.

EXERCISE 2.
ACCELERATION ALONG A STRAIGHT LINE

In Section 3.1 we discussed the motion of a particle moving along a straight line. The position s of the particle is a function of time t,

$$s = f(t)$$

and the instantaneous velocity v of the particle is the derivative of position with respect to time:

$$\text{Velocity} = v = \frac{ds}{dt} = f'(t)$$

The instantaneous rate of change of velocity with respect to time, called the *acceleration a*, is given by the formula

$$\text{Acceleration} = a = \frac{dv}{dt} = \frac{d^2s}{dt^2} = f''(t)$$

Thus acceleration is the second derivative of position with respect to time. It indicates the rate at which the speed of the motion of the particle is changing.

The *sign of the velocity* is related to the direction of motion of the particle.

1. If v is positive, the particle is moving away from the starting position toward the right.
2. If v is negative, the particle is moving toward the left.
3. If v is zero, the particle is instantaneously at rest.

The *sign of the acceleration* is related to the velocity.

1. If a is the same sign as the velocity, the particle is speeding up.
2. If a is opposite in sign to the velocity, it is slowing down.
3. If a is zero, the particle is moving at a constant speed.

Let's consider an illustration.

Suppose a particle is moving along a straight line according to the law

$$s = \frac{1}{3}t^3 - 7t^2 + 33t$$

With DERIVE read into your calculator, key in the following subroutine for $s = f(t)$:

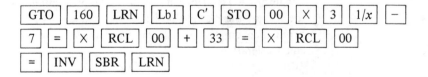

Now load $\Delta t = 0.01$ and set the display to two digits past the decimal point:

(enter)   0.01

(press) $\boxed{E'}$

(press) $\boxed{\text{Fix}}$ $\boxed{2}$

Using the key $\boxed{D'}$ to load each value of t, you obtain the following table using the keys $\boxed{A}$, $\boxed{B}$, and $\boxed{C}$:

t	s	v	a
0.0	0.00	33.00	−14.00
1.0	26.33	20.00	−12.00
2.0	40.67	9.00	−10.00
3.0	45.00	0.00	−8.00
4.0	41.33	−7.00	−6.00
5.0	31.67	−12.00	−4.00
6.0	18.00	−15.00	−2.00
7.0	2.33	−16.00	0.00
8.0	−13.33	−15.00	2.00
9.0	−27.00	−12.00	4.00
10.0	−36.67	−7.00	6.00
11.0	−40.33	0.00	8.00
12.0	−36.00	9.00	10.00
13.0	−21.67	20.00	12.00
14.0	4.67	33.00	14.00
15.0	45.00	48.00	16.00
16.0	101.33	65.00	18.00
18.0	270.00	105.00	22.00
20.0	526.67	153.00	26.00

From the table you see that the particle starts out (at time $t = 0$) at the starting position ($s = 0$) with an initial positive velocity ($v = 33$). When $t < 3$, the particle is moving to the right with acceleration opposite in sign to the velocity: It is slowing down. At $t = 3$, the particle is instantaneously at rest and has moved a maximum distance $s = 45$ to the right of the starting position. For $3 < t < 11$, the particle has reversed its direction and is moving to the left. During the first part of this motion $3 < t < 7$, the acceleration has the same sign as the velocity, and the particle is gaining speed (the negative velocity indicating motion to the left). When $7 < t < 11$, the acceleration of the particle is positive and opposite in sign to the velocity: The particle is slowing down again. It speeds past the starting position and continues moving left until $t = 11$, at which time it reaches its minimum position $s = −40.33$ to the left of the starting position, and reverses its direction of motion again. From then on, the particle moves to the right with ever increasing velocity and acceleration.

PROBLEMS 3.3

In each of Problems 1–10, calculate the values $f(a), f'(a), f''(a)$, and κ at the indicated point $x = a$. State whether the graph is concave upward or concave downward at the given point.

1. $f(x) = x^3 + 3x^2 + 4$ $x = -1.75$
2. $f(x) = x^5 - 4x^4 + 4x^3$ $x = 0.81$
3. $f(x) = 4x + 6x^{2/3}$ $x = -2.15$
4. $f(x) = (0.2)^{x+1} + 3$ $x = 1.09$
5. $f(x) = 2 \sin (3x + 1)$ $x = \pi/3$

6. $f(x) = \dfrac{x}{\sqrt{x^2 + 1}}$ $x = 1.97$

7. $f(x) = e^x - e^{-x}$ $x = 1.27$

8. $f(x) = xe^x$ $x = -2.13$

9. $f(x) = \sqrt{x}(x - 5)^2$ $x = 3.09$

10. $f(x) = \dfrac{\sqrt{1 - x^2}}{(x + 1)^{2/3}}$ $x = -0.67$

In Problems 11-16, find the points of inflection of the given function, accurate to three decimal places.

11. $f(x) = 3x^2 - x^{-2}$

12. $f(x) = (1 + x)^{2/3}(3 - x)^{1/3}$

13. $f(x) = \dfrac{1}{1 + x^2}$

14. $f(x) = xe^{-x}$

15. $f(x) = x^2 (1 + x)^2$

16. $f(x) = 2\sqrt{x} - x$

17. Suppose a particle moves along a straight line according to the formula

$$s = -t\sqrt{t + 1} \qquad t \geq 0$$

Find the velocity and acceleration when $t = 1.75$.

18. An object moves along a straight line according to the formula

$$s = 32.5t^2 - \frac{13}{6}t^3$$

for $0 \leq t \leq 10$. Assume t is measured in seconds and s in meters.

a. At what time is the acceleration zero?

b. What is the maximum velocity?

c. How far has the object gone when it reaches its maximum velocity?

19. A bullet is shot straight into the air with an initial velocity of 500 m/sec. Its height in meters after t seconds have elapsed is $h(t) = 500\,t - 4.905t^2$.

a. After how many seconds will the bullet begin to fall?

b. How high will the bullet go?

c. What is the acceleration at any time?

20. When a ball is dropped from a height of 123 m, its height s above the ground after t sec is given by

$$s = 123 - 4.905t^2$$

a. How fast is the ball dropping after 4.5 sec?

b. How far has the ball fallen after 4.5 sec?

c. After how many seconds will the ball hit the ground?

In many real world problems in science, engineering, and economics, you have to find optimal solutions. That is, you seek the fastest, the highest, the largest, the smallest, the cheapest, the most profitable, and so forth. In other words, you look for the extreme values of some function. The eighteenth-century mathematician Leonhard Euler even said that "nothing at all takes place in the universe in which some rule of maximum or minimum does not appear." The differential calculus is an important tool for investigating these problems.

We introduced the idea of relative extreme values of a function in Section 1.7. If a relative maximum or minimum of $y = f(x)$ occurs at $x = c$, and if the derivative $f'(c)$ exists, then $f'(c) = 0$ so the tangent line to the graph at $(c, f(c))$ is horizontal. It may happen, however, that a function has a relative extremum at $x = c$, but the derivative $f'(c)$ fails to exist. For instance, the graph may have a "corner" at the point where the maximum or minimum occurs, in which case no tangent line occurs there. This is depicted in Figure 3.6. In summary, *if f has a relative maximum or minimum at $x = c$, then either $f'(c) = 0$ or $f'(c)$ does not exist.*

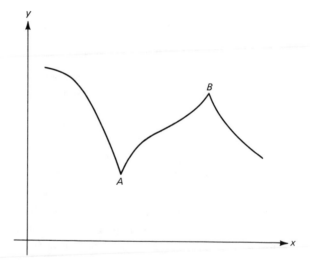

Figure 3.6 The graph has a relative minimum at A and a relative maximum at B, but the derivative does not exist at those locations (there is no tangent line).

In seeking the relative extrema of some function $y = f(x)$, we thus determine the values of x at which f' is zero or f' fails to exist. These values of x are called **critical points** of the function f. Once a critical point $x = c$ is located, concavity is helpful in identifying whether it gives a relative maximum or minimum. If the curve is concave upward at $x = c$, then locally the curve lies above the horizontal tangent line (if the tangent exists), and therefore a relative minimum occurs there. If the curve is concave downward at $x = c$, then locally the curve lies below the tangent line, giving a relative maximum there (Figure 3.7). Since the sign of the second derivative signifies the direction of concavity, when $f'(c) = 0$ these observations translate to:

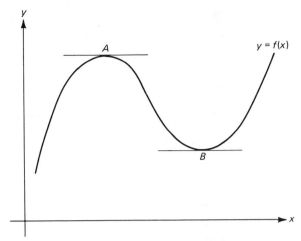

Figure 3.7 At the relative maximum *A*, the graph is concave downward; at the relative minimum *B*, it is concave upward.

1. *if $f''(c) > 0$, there is a relative minimum at $x = c$*; and
2. *if $f''(c) < 0$, there is a relative maximum at $x = c$*.

No conclusion can be drawn if $f''(c) = 0$.

The word "relative" signals that a maximum or minimum value is occurring *locally*. For instance, when the function f has a relative maximum at $x = c$, then

$$f(c) \geqslant f(c + \Delta x)$$

for all positive and negative values of Δx sufficiently near zero. On the other hand, if at some point $x = a$,

$$f(a) \geqslant f(x)$$

for *every* value of x in the domain of f, then it is said that f has an *absolute maximum* at $x = a$. Similarly, an *absolute minimum* is defined by reversing the inequality. At an absolute maximum or minimum, the derivative need not be zero.

An important result in mathematical analysis asserts that whenever a function f is continuous over a closed interval $I:a \leqslant x \leqslant b$, it has an absolute minimum value m and an absolute maximum value M. So there are numbers c_1 and c_2 in the interval I for which $f(c_1) = m, f(c_2) = M$, and

$$m \leqslant f(x) \leqslant M \quad \text{for all } x \text{ in } I$$

The numbers c_1 and c_2 may occur at an endpoint of the interval I, or they may occur interior to the interval. Whenever c_1 or c_2 occurs interior to I, it must be a critical point. Thus in seeking the absolute extrema of a continuous function $y = f(x)$ over a closed interval, look among all the critical points and also check the endpoints of the interval.

In solving a maxima or minima problem, you must first write an expression $f(x)$ for the quantity y that is to be a maximum or minimum: $y = f(x)$. This is usually the hardest part for the beginning calculus student. Once the function $y = f(x)$ is determined, you can use the program PROBE to search the domain $a \leqslant x \leqslant b$ of f for the critical points and investigate each of these points for a possible maximum or minimum. Finally, evaluate f at the endpoints of the interval over which it is defined for possible extreme values of y. The following exercises illustrate the procedure.

EXERCISE 1.
FINDING ABSOLUTE EXTREMA

Let's determine the absolute maximum and minimum values of the function

$$y = x^{3/2} (x-8)^{-1/2} \quad \text{over} \quad 10 \leqslant x \leqslant 16$$

With PROBE read into your calculator, key in the subroutine for y:

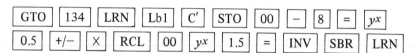

Load $x_0 = 9.5$ and $\Delta x = 0.5$, and set the display to two digits past the decimal point:

(enter)   9.5

(press) $\boxed{D'}$

(enter)   0.5

(press) $\boxed{E'}$

(press) $\boxed{\text{Fix}}$ $\boxed{2}$

Now, following the same procedures you have used before with PROBE, you can verify the following table:

x	y	y'	x	y	y'
10.0	22.36	−2.24	12.2	20.79	0.08
10.5	21.52	−1.23	12.5	20.83	0.19
11.0	21.06	−0.64	13.0	20.96	0.32
11.5	20.85	−0.26	13.5	21.15	0.43
11.6	20.82	−0.20	14.0	21.39	0.51
11.7	20.81	−0.14	14.5	21.66	0.57
11.8	20.79	−0.09	15.0	21.96	0.63
11.9	20.79	−0.04	15.5	22.28	0.67
12.0	20.78	0.00	16.0	22.63	0.71
12.1	20.79	0.04			

Thus the absolute minimum value is $y = 20.78$ when $x = 12.0$. Since the point $x = 12.0$ is interior to the interval $10 \leqslant x \leqslant 16$, the derivative y' is 0 there. The point $x = 12.0$ is the only critical point for y over the entire interval $10 \leqslant x \leqslant 16$. Thus the absolute maximum must occur at one of the endpoints of the interval. You can see from the table that it occurs at the endpoint $x = 16.0$ giving the absolute maximum value of $y = 22.63$. Notice that the derivative y' is not zero there.

EXERCISE 2.
INTENSITY OF ILLUMINATION

The intensity of illumination at any point varies inversely as the square of the distance between the point and the light source. Two lights, one having an intensity eight times that of the other, are 5 ft apart. How far from the stronger light is the total illumination least?

Solution. Let A and B denote the two light sources, and let x denote the distance from the stronger light source A (Figure 3.8). The intensity of illumination at P associated with the source A is $8/x^2$, and with B it is $1/(5-x)^2$, because the intensity at A is eight times that at B. Then setting I as the total illumination at point P, we have

$$I(x) = \frac{8}{x^2} + \frac{1}{(5-x)^2} \qquad 0 < x < 5$$

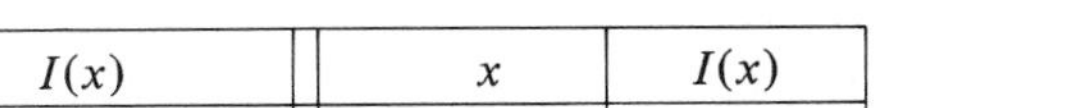

Figure 3.8

With PROBE loaded into your calculator, key in $I(x)$, load $x = 0.0$ and $\Delta x = 0.5$ to obtain the following table:

x	$I(x)$	x	$I(x)$
0.5	32.05	3.0	1.14
1.0	8.06	3.5	1.10
1.5	3.64	4.0	1.50
2.0	2.11	4.5	4.40
2.5	1.44		

From the table it is clear that we should explore the region around $x = 3.5$ for the minimum. Using PROBE you discover that the minimum illumination is 1.0800065 occurring at $x = 3.33$. There is no absolute maximum illumination because, as x gets close to either 0 or 5, the illumination becomes arbitrarily large. This does not contradict our discussion concerning absolute extrema because the interval $0 < x < 5$ of definition of the function $I(x)$ fails to be *closed* as required.

EXERCISE 3.
VOLUME OF A BOX

A rectangular box is to be made from a sheet of cardboard 15.5 in by 15.5 in by cutting a square from each corner and turning up the sides. Find the edge of this square that makes the volume of the box a maximum.

Solution. Let x represent the edge length of the square cut out of each corner of the cardboard sheet. Then the volume of the box is given by the formula

$$V(x) = x(15.5 - 2x)^2 \qquad 0 \leqslant x \leqslant 7.75$$

The problem is to determine x so that V is a maximum. Using PROBE you can verify the following table:

Δx	x	V	$\approx V'$	Δx	x	V	$\approx V'$
0.5	0.50	105.125	181.500	0.1	2.60	275.834	-1.020
0.5	1.00	182.250	128.500	0.01	2.59	275.841	-0.413
0.5	1.50	234.375	81.500	0.01	2.58	275.842	0.207
0.5	2.00	264.500	40.500	0.001	2.581	275.842	0.145
0.5	2.50	275.625	5.500	0.001	2.582	275.843	0.083
0.5	3.00	270.750	-23.500	0.001	2.583	275.843	0.021
				0.001	2.584	275.843	-0.041

From the table you see that the maximum volume $V = 275.843$ in^3 occurs when the edge length $x = 2.583$ in. Since $V'(2.583)$ is not quite zero, the solution is not exact. A more accurate result is $x = 2.583333333$, and this does give $V' = 0$.

EXERCISE 4.
DISTANCE BETWEEN SHIPS

At 7:30 AM, ship B is 75 mi due east of another ship A. Ship B is sailing due west at 12 mph, and ship A sails due north at 17 mph. If the two ships continue to follow these courses, at what time will they be nearest each other? And how near?

Solution. Let A_O and B_O be the positions of the ships at 7:30 AM, and let A and B denote their positions t hours later. Since the distance traveled equals the rate times the time of travel, after t hours A has gone $17t$ mi due north and B has gone $12t$ mi due west. The situation after t hours is depicted in Figure 3.9. From the figure, you see that the distance D between the two ships after t hours have elapsed is

170 $D = \sqrt{(17t)^2 + (75 - 12t)^2} \qquad t \geqslant 0$

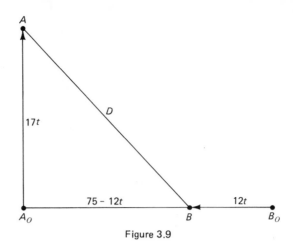

Figure 3.9

We want to find t when D is minimal. Using PROBE, verify the following table:

Δt	t	D	$\approx D'$	Δt	t	D	$\approx D'$
0.5	0.50	69.522	−9.810	0.01	2.09	61.273	0.081
0.5	1.00	65.253	−7.137	0.01	2.08	61.273	0.010
0.5	1.50	62.444	−3.998	0.001	2.079	61.273	0.003
0.5	2.00	61.294	−0.553	0.001	2.078	61.273	−0.004
0.1	2.10	61.274	0.152				

From the table, the ships are at the closest distance $D = 61.273$ mi when $t = 2.079$ hrs approximately (because D' is not quite zero). Now 2.079 hrs translates to 2 hrs, 4 min, 44 sec. So the ships are nearest each other at 9:34:44 AM when they are 61.273 mi apart.

EXERCISE 5.
AUXILIARY VARIABLES

Sometimes the quantity that is to be maximized or minimized is naturally expressed in terms of several variables. These variables are then related by formulas or equations that allow for the elimination of all the variables but one. Then the quantity to be maximized or minimized is expressed in terms of this one variable, and the solution obtained by the method used before. The next example illustrates this procedure.

Suppose a spring is situated at distances of 29 ft and 73 ft from two straight roads intersecting at right angles. Of all the straight paths passing by the spring and connecting the two roads, find the one of shortest length.

Solution. Consider the situation in Figure 3.10. Let D denote the length
171 of the path passing by the spring. Let x and y denote the distances as shown

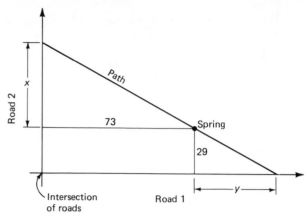

Figure 3.10

schematically in the figure. The problem is to minimize the length D of the path.

From the diagram and the Pythagorean Theorem,

$$D = (x^2 + 73^2)^{1/2} + (29^2 + y^2)^{1/2}$$

Using similar triangles in the figure, we can eliminate the auxiliary variable y:

$$\frac{x}{73} = \frac{29}{y} \quad \text{or} \quad y = \frac{29 \cdot 73}{x}$$

Substitution into the expression for D gives

$$D = (x^2 + 73^2)^{1/2} + \left[29^2 + \frac{(29 \cdot 73)^2}{x^2} \right]^{1/2} \quad x > 0$$

We want to determine x so that D is minimal.

x	D	Δx	x	D	$\approx D'$
10.0	287.359	0.10	53.9	139.565	0.008
20.0	185.441	0.10	53.8	139.564	0.004
30.0	155.217	0.10	53.7	139.564	0.001
40.0	143.590	0.01	53.69	139.564	0.001
50.0	139.801	0.01	53.68	139.564	0.001
60.0	140.165	0.01	53.67	139.564	0.000
51.0	139.687	0.01	53.66	139.564	0.000
52.0	139.611				
53.0	139.572				
54.0	139.566				
55.0	139.593				

The table reveals that the minimum path length is $D = 139.564$ ft occurring when $x = 53.66$ ft. So the path crosses road 2 at a point $29 + 53.66 = 82.66$

ft from the intersection, and it crosses road 1 at a point $73 + y = 73 + 39.452$ = 112.452 ft from the intersection.

EXERCISE 6.
MAXIMIZING PROFITS

A manufacturing company can sell x thousand items per week at a price $P = 9.5 - x$ thousand dollars, and it costs $C = 1.5 + 3\sqrt{x}$ thousand dollars to make the items. How many items should be produced in order to maximize the profit?

Solution. The amount of revenue earned each week from the sale of x thousand items is

$$xP = 9.5x - x^2$$

The weekly profit Q in thousands of dollars is the revenue minus cost:

$$Q = xP - C = 9.5x - x^2 - 1.5 - 3\sqrt{x}$$

For values of x beyond 10, Q is negative, so Q has its maximum value somewhere over the interval $0 \leqslant x \leqslant 10$. Using PROBE, you can verify the following table:

x	Q	Δx	x	Q	$\approx Q'$
0.5	0.879	0.1	4.90	14.399	−0.978
1.0	4.000	0.1	4.80	14.487	−0.785
1.5	6.826	0.1	4.70	14.556	−0.592
2.0	9.257	0.1	4.60	14.606	−0.399
2.5	11.257	0.1	4.50	14.636	−0.207
3.0	12.804	0.1	4.40	14.647	−0.015
3.5	13.888	0.01	4.39	14.647	0.004
4.0	14.500	0.001	4.391	14.64721	0.002
4.5	14.636	0.001	4.392	14.64721	0.000
5.0	14.292	0.001	4.393	14.64721	−0.002

It is clear from the table that the maximum weekly profit is $Q = \$14,647.21$, when $1,000x = 4,392$ items are produced.

EXERCISE 7.
INSCRIBING A CYLINDER IN A CONE

Find the circular cylinder of maximum volume that can be inscribed in the cone with an altitude of 17 in and a base radius of 3 in.

Solution. Let h denote the height of the cylinder and r its radius. From the geometry of the configuration shown in Figure 3.11, the portion of the cone lying above the cylinder is similar to the entire cone itself. Thus

$$\frac{17-h}{r} = \frac{17}{3}$$

or

$$h = 17\left(1 - \frac{r}{3}\right)$$

Now we want to maximize the volume V of the cylinder where

$$V = \pi r^2 h = 17\pi r^2 \left(1 - \frac{r}{3}\right) \qquad 0 \leqslant r \leqslant 3$$

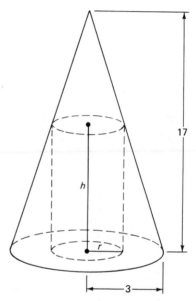

Figure 3.11

Using PROBE, verify the following table:

Δr	r	V	$\approx V'$	Δr	r	V	$\approx V'$
0.5	0.50	11.126	38.943	0.01	1.99	71.204	1.062
0.5	1.00	35.605	52.294	0.01	2.00	71.209	0.000
0.5	1.50	60.083	38.943	0.01	2.01	71.204	−1.074
0.5	2.00	71.209	−1.113	0.01	2.02	71.188	−2.158

From the table you see that $V = 71.209$ in^3 is the maximum volume occurring when $r = 2.00$ in. Notice that $\Delta r = 0.5$ does not give a good estimate to V' at $r = 2$; $\Delta r = 0.01$ gives $V'(2) = 0$, verifying that $r = 2$ is a critical point. When $r = 2$, $h = 17/3$. So the cylinder of maximum volume that can be inscribed in the cone has a height of 17/3 in and a radius of 2 in.

EXERCISE 8.
COST OF TRANSPORTATION

A truck driver is paid $7.85 per hour to drive 475 mi. For speeds between 40 and 65 mph, the truck gets $537/x$ mpg when driven at a constant speed of x mph. If gasoline costs $1.40 per gallon, what is the most economical speed between 40 and 65 mph at which to drive the truck?

Solution. From the formula

Distance = Rate $\times$ Time

the total driving time is $475/x$ hrs. The cost of the driver is the time spent driving multiplied by the wage, or

$$\text{Labor cost} = (\frac{475}{x})(7.85) \text{ dollars}$$

The cost of the gasoline is the number of gallons used times the cost per gallon. Since the truck gets $537/x$ mpg, the amount of gas used for the trip is 475 times $x/537$. Thus

$$\text{Cost of gas} = (\frac{475x}{537})(1.40) \text{ dollars}$$

We want to minimize the total cost

$$C(x) = \frac{(475)(7.85)}{x} + \frac{(475)(1.40)}{537} x \qquad 40 \leqslant x \leqslant 65$$

Using PROBE, verify the following table:

x	C		Δx	x	C	$\approx C'$
40	142.75		0.1	55.0	135.91	0.01
45	138.59		0.1	54.9	135.90	0.00
50	136.49		0.1	54.8	135.91	0.00
55	135.91					
60	136.45					

The table reveals that the minimum cost of the trip is $C = \$135.90$ when the truck is driven at $x = 54.9$ mph.

Summary The most difficult part of solving a maxima or minima problem is setting up the expression for the quantity y to be maximized or minimized in terms of *one* independent variable x. Here are some guidelines to help you with that process.

Step 1: Read the problem carefully so you clearly understand exactly *what* quantity is to be maximized or minimized. If the problem involves

geometric magnitudes, draw a figure that clearly shows their relationships, as specified in the problem. Be sure to label your figure
with appropriate constants and variables.

Step 2: From known relationships–such as the geometric relationships expressed in your figure or a physical relationship like Distance = Rate ×
Time–derive equations connecting all the variables in the problem.
If there are auxiliary variables, they have to be connected to the one
independent variable x by equations.

Step 3: Express the quantity y to be maximized or minimized as a function
of the single independent variable x. If the equation for y involves
auxiliary variables, you have to make substitutions for them in terms
of x. Do so by solving the equations connecting the auxiliary variables to x: Each auxiliary variable must be expressed in terms of x
alone prior to the substitution in the equation for y. You need as
many auxiliary equations as you have auxiliary variables to accomp-
lish that task.

Step 4: With the function $y = f(x)$ determined, use PROBE to locate the extreme values of y, just as illustrated in the examples given. If the
independent variable is limited, $a \leqslant x \leqslant b$, examine the endpoints
$x = a$ and $x = b$ for possible extreme values of y.

PROBLEMS 3.4

In each of Problems 1–10, find the absolute maximum and minimum values
of the given function over the specified interval. One or both of these values
may not exist. Give your answer accurate to three decimal places.

1. $f(x) = x^3 - 7x^2 - 5x + 19$ $\quad -1 \leqslant x \leqslant 3$

2. $f(x) = \pi x^2 e^{-1.5x}$ $\quad 0 \leqslant x \leqslant 4.7$

3. $f(x) = x\sqrt{2x - x^2}$ $\quad 0 \leqslant x \leqslant 2$

4. $f(x) = x^{3/2} (x - 17)^{-1/2}$ $\quad 17 < x < 94$

5. $f(x) = (3x - x^2)^{1/3}$ $\quad 0 < x < 3$

6. $f(x) = \sin x + 2 \cos x$ $\quad 0 \leqslant x < \pi$

7. $f(x) = 2 \sec x + \tan x$ $\quad -\pi/2 < x < \pi/2$

8. $f(x) = \dfrac{x}{2} + \sin x$ $\quad 0 < x \leqslant 3\pi$

9. $f(x) = x - \sqrt{1 - x^2}$ $\quad -1 \leqslant x \leqslant 1$

10. $f(x) = \cos 4x + 2 \sin 2x$ $\quad 0 \leqslant x \leqslant \pi$

Solve the following applied maximum and minimum problems. Report your
answers to three decimal places.

11. Find a positive number that, when summed with its reciprocal, gives a
minimum value.

12. A wire 5 m in length is cut in two. One part is bent into the shape of a
circle, and the other part into an equilateral triangle. Find the length of
each part if the sum of their areas is a minimum.

13. Divide 19 into two parts (not necessarily integers) in such a way that the product of one part with the cube of the other is a maximum.

14. A man is in a row boat 1.75 mi offshore from the nearest point P on a straight beach. His destination is a town located 3.2 mi down the beach from P. If the man can row 3 mph and walk 4.5 mph, find the point C on the beach to which the man should row to reach the town in the least possible time.

15. Find the dimensions of the rectangle of largest area that can be inscribed in a semicircle of radius 6.31 m.

16. A landscape architect plans a rose garden in the shape of a rectangle plus a semicircular area at each end. The perimeter of the garden is to be fenced with 225 ft of fencing. Find the dimensions of the garden if the rectangular part has as large an area as possible.

17. A truck burns diesel fuel at the rate of

$$G(x) = \frac{1}{29.6}\left(\frac{77}{x} + \frac{x}{41.5}\right)$$

gallons per mile when traveling at the speed x mph. If fuel costs $1.37 per gallon, find the speed to minimize the cost of running the truck for a 785-mi trip.

18. A manufacturer estimates that if x is the number of thousands of units of some commodity produced, then the cost and revenue functions are given by

$$C(x) = \frac{x^3}{2.9} - 4.1x^2 + 9x \quad \text{and} \quad R(x) = 11x - 1.5x^2$$

How many units should be produced to maximize the profit?

19. Find the point on the curve $y = \sqrt{x}$ nearest the point $(1.37, 2.49)$.

20. A woman starts bicycling across a 70-ft-long river bridge at the rate of 11.2 ft/sec, exactly when a motorboat passes directly beneath the center of the bridge. The boat is traveling at the rate of 9.3 ft/sec. Find the shortest horizontal distance between the woman and the boat.

21. An isosceles triangle ABC has legs 5 cm long and a base AB of 8 cm. If P is a point interior to the triangle and equidistant from A and B, such that the sum of the distances PA, PB, PC is the least possible, how far is P from C?

22. A cylindrical tank, open at the top, is to hold 10,000 ft³ of water. The cost of building the bottom of the tank is $27.50 per square foot, and that of the vertical surface is $15.50 per square foot. Find the radius of the tank so that the cost is a minimum.

23. A hallway with a width of 4.5 ft meets another hallway 6.2 ft wide at right angles. A steel girder of length L is to be moved on rollers around the corner of the intersecting passageways. Neglecting the width of the girder, what is the maximum length of the girder so it will just go around the corner? The situation is depicted in Figure 3.12.

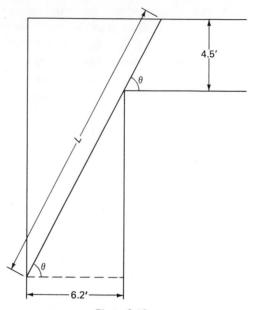

Figure 3.12

Section 3.5 The Tangent Line Approximation: Differentials

Suppose that $y = f(x)$ is a differentiable function at $x = x_0$. Then the derivative $f'(x_0)$ gives the slope of the tangent line to the graph of the function at the point $(x_0, f(x_0))$. Thus an equation of the tangent line L is

$$L(x) = f'(x_0)(x - x_0) + f(x_0) \tag{3.9}$$

When the increment $\Delta x = x - x_0$ is sufficiently small, the y value $L(x)$ on the tangent line is very close to the actual function value $f(x)$. Let's examine the amount of error involved in this approximation.

For the independent variable x, define *the differential of x*, written dx, to be the increment Δx. That is,

$$dx = \Delta x \tag{3.10}$$

Next define *the differential of the dependent variable y* by

$$dy = f'(x_0)\, dx \tag{3.11}$$

where $y = f(x)$. The value of dy depends on two quantities: the number x_0 and the value of $dx = \Delta x$.

If we rewrite Equation 3.9 using the definition in 3.11, we obtain

178 $L(x) = dy + f(x_0)$

$$L(x) - f(x_0) = dy$$

Moreover, since $L(x_0) = f(x_0)$, this last equation can be written as

$$L(x) - L(x_0) = dy \tag{3.12}$$

So Equation 3.12 reveals that the differential dy of the function $y = f(x)$ measures the change in values along the tangent line. On the other hand, the increment Δy measures the change in the values of the function itself:

$$f(x) - f(x_0) = \Delta y \tag{3.13}$$

The situation is depicted in Figure 3.13. Since

$$\lim_{\Delta x \to 0} \frac{\Delta y}{\Delta x} = f'(x_0)$$

is equivalent to

$$\lim_{\Delta x \to 0} \frac{\Delta y - f'(x_0)\Delta x}{\Delta x} = 0 \tag{3.14}$$

you can see that the numbers Δy and $dy = f'(x_0)\Delta x$ are close together when Δx is small. The limit in Equation 3.14 expresses the fact that the difference $\Delta y - dy$ goes to zero faster than does the increment Δx. Thus the tangent line L provides a good local approximation to f near x_0. Upon examining Figure 3.13, you see that the difference $\Delta y - dy$ measures the error involved in using the tangent line value $L(x)$ to approximate the function value $f(x)$. We will sometimes write df for dy and Δf for Δy.

The program TANGENT calculates the differential for a specified function f at a given point x_0 and associated with a particular increment Δx. The program calls f as a subroutine keyed in by the user. TANGENT uses program steps 000 through 131, and storage locations 01 through 07. Program steps 132 through 479 and memory locations 00, and 08 through 59 are available for use while evaluating $f(x)$. TANGENT uses the central difference approximation

$$f'(x_0) = \frac{f(x_0 + h) - f(x_0 - h)}{2h}$$

where $h = 0.0001$, for the first derivative calculation. This is an accurate enough approximation for the functions you will encounter in this book.

Using the Program TANGENT

TANGENT assumes the subroutine for $f(x)$ is located at label C'. Thus the first two steps of your subroutine must be

$\boxed{\text{Lb1}}$ $\boxed{C'}$

and the last two steps must be

$\boxed{\text{INV}}$ $\boxed{\text{SBR}}$

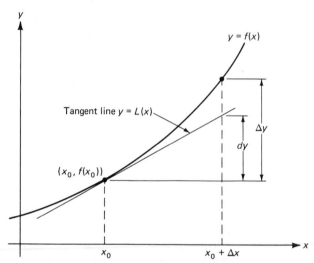

Figure 3.13 The differential dy measures the change along the tangent line L, whereas Δy gives the change in the function f itself. When Δx is close to zero, dy and Δy are approximately equal.

Each calculation in TANGENT is controlled by one of the special calculator labels as follows:

D′	This loads the value x_0 into the program.
E′	This loads the differential $dx = \Delta x$ into the program, unless label B′ is used instead.
B′	This loads a value of x into the program and calculates the differential $dx = \Delta x = x - x_0$. Both numbers are stored.
A	The value $f(x_0)$ is computed and displayed.
B	The increment $\Delta y = f(x_0 + \Delta x) - f(x_0)$ is computed and displayed.
C	The slope m and y-intercept b of the tangent line at $(x_0, f(x_0))$ are computed. The slope $m = f'(x_0)$ is in the display, and the y-intercept $b = f(x_0) - f'(x_0)x_0$ is in the T-register.
D	The differential $dy = f'(x_0)\, dx$ is computed and displayed.
E	When this key is pressed, x_0 is displayed.

A' This key causes x_0 to be replaced by the new value $x_0 + \Delta x$ in order to step forward in f (positive Δx) or backward (negative

Δx). The new value $x_0 + \Delta x$ is displayed, and becomes the current x_0.

EXERCISE 1.
COMPUTING THE DIFFERENTIAL
AND TANGENT LINE

Consider the function $f(x) = \sqrt{1 + x^3}$. Let's compute the differential and an equation of the tangent line when $x = 2.5$ and $\Delta x = 0.01$. First, with TAN-GENT loaded in your calculator, key in the subroutine for the function f:

| GTO | 132 | LRN | Lb1 | C' | STO | 00 | x^2 | $\times$ | RCL | 00 |

| + | 1 | = | $\sqrt{x}$ | INV | SBR | LRN |

(enter)   2.5

(press)   D'   Load $x_0 = 2.5$.

(enter)   0.01

(press)   E'   Load $\Delta x = 0.01$.

(press)   Fix 4   Display four decimal digits.

(press)   D $df = 0.0230$ is in the display.

Thus the differential of f for $x_0 = 2.5$ and $\Delta x = 0.01$ is the value 0.0230. To compute the tangent line:

(press)   C $f'(2.5) = 2.2993$ is in the display.

(press) $x \blacktriangleleft t$ $b = -1.6708$ is in the display.

Thus an equation of the tangent line at $x_0 = 2.5$ is

$L(x) = 2.2993x - 1.6708$

To obtain the value of the function at 2.5

(press)   A $f(2.5) = 4.0774$ is in the display.

EXERCISE 2.
COMPARING THE INCREMENT
AND THE DIFFERENTIAL

Consider the function

$f(x) = x^{1/3} + x^{2/3}$

whose graph is shown in Figure 2.18. We investigated this function in Exercise 7 of Section 2.2. Key in this function as a subroutine to TANGENT using exactly the same keystrokes you used in that previous exercise. Then, using the key $\boxed{D'}$ to enter x_0, the key $\boxed{E'}$ to enter Δx, the key $\boxed{B}$ to calculate Δf, and the key $\boxed{D}$ to calculate df, verify the following table (to four decimal places):

x_0	Δx	Δf	df	$\Delta f - df$
−0.25	0.50	1.2599	−0.1092	1.3691
	0.25	0.2331	−0.0546	0.2877
	0.10	−0.0159	−0.0218	0.0059
	0.01	−0.0021	−0.0022	0.0000
	0.001	−0.0002	−0.0002	0.0000
0.25	0.50	0.7072	0.9491	−0.2419
	0.25	0.3969	0.4746	−0.0777
	0.10	0.1746	0.1898	−0.0153
	0.01	0.0188	0.0190	−0.0002
	0.001	0.0019	0.0019	0.0000

You should make several observations from the table. First, notice how the value of the differential df depends on *both* the number x_0 and the differential Δx of the independent variable. The same value of Δx can produce different values of df at different points x_0. Second, the difference $\Delta f - df$ gets smaller and smaller as Δx tends to zero: The values of Δf and df are nearly equal for sufficiently small Δx. Finally, the difference $\Delta f - df$ can be positive or negative, and it can be quite large in comparison to Δx until Δx gets sufficiently close to zero.

EXERCISE 3.
ERROR OCCURRING IN MEASUREMENTS

Suppose a quantity x is measured and the measurement is used to calculate a second quantity y, where $y = f(x)$ is a known relationship. Then an error $\Delta x = dx$ in the measurement of x leads to an error Δy in the quantity y. The differential dy approximates the error Δy. The ratio $\Delta x/x$ is called the *relative error in x*, and $(100\Delta x)/x$ percent is called the *percentage error.* Similar definitions apply to the variable y.

For example, suppose you have a box of steel ball bearings from which you want to select all ball bearings of diameter 3/4 cm. You permit a deviation in the diameters of the ball bearings of 2.5 percent, and you are going to select the ball bearings by weighing them. If you use the weight of a 3/4-cm steel ball bearing that you have for a standard, what deviation from that weight will you permit when making your selections?

The weight of a ball bearing is its density times the volume. Since the density of steel is 7.6 gm/cm^3, the weight of a steel ball bearing of diameter $2r$ cm is

$$W = (7.6)\frac{4}{3}\pi r^3$$

At $2r = 0.75$ cm, we want to know ΔW when

$$\left|\frac{dr}{r}\right| \leqslant 0.025$$

Using TANGENT, key in the function W as a subroutine. Then

(enter)	0.375		
(press)		$\boxed{D'}$	Load $r_0 = 0.75/2$.
(enter)	0.009375		
(press)		$\boxed{E'}$	Load $\Delta r = (0.025)(0.75/2)$.
(press)		$\boxed{B}$	$\Delta W = 0.1291$ is in the display, rounded to four decimal places.

So the permissible deviation in weight from the standard ball bearing is approximately 0.13 gm. By pressing the key $\boxed{D}$, you obtain $dW = 0.1259$, which is a close estimate to ΔW.

The permissible percentage deviation in the weight is $(100\Delta W)/W$. To calculate W when $r = 0.375$,

(press)		$\boxed{A}$	1.6788, rounded to four decimals, is in the display.

Then $\Delta W/W = 0.0769$. The permissible deviation in W is therefore about 7.7 percent. This is estimated by $(100\,dW)/W = 7.5$ percent.

PROBLEMS 3.5

In each of Problems 1-10, calculate the differential df and the increment Δf for the given function at the specified point x_0 and differential dx. Give your answer to four decimal places.

1. $f(x) = x + \dfrac{1}{x}$ $x_0 = 1.25, dx = 0.01$

2. $f(x) = e^{x^2}$ $x_0 = 2.1, dx = 0.005$

3. $f(x) = x^4 - 3x^2 + 1.7x - 4$ $x_0 = -2.75, dx = -0.015$

4. $f(x) = \sin(e^x)$ $x_0 = \pi/2, dx = -0.17$

5. $f(x) = \dfrac{1}{1 + 3e^{-2x}}$ $x_0 = 1.1, dx = 0.012$

6. $f(x) = (1 - x^2 + x^4)^{1/3}$ $x_0 = 1.0, dx = 0.025$

7. $f(x) = x^2 e^{\sqrt{x}}$ $x_0 = 2.49, dx = -0.04$

8. $f(x) = x\, 3^x$ $x_0 = 3.7, dx = 0.25$

9. $f(x) = \cos^2(5x)$ $x_0 = \pi/4, dx = 0.01$

10. $f(x) = e^{-x} \sin x^2$ $x_0 = \pi/6, dx = 0.015$

In problems 11–15, calculate an equation of the tangent line to the given function for the specified point. Write your coefficients to two-place accuracy.

11. $f(x) = 3x^2 - x^{-1/3} + 4$ $x_0 = 1.65$

12. $f(x) = \sqrt{1 - x^2}$ $x_0 = 0.5$

13. $f(x) = \dfrac{1 - x}{1 + x}$ $x_0 = 2.71$

14. $f(x) = \tan x$ $x_0 = \pi/12$

15. $f(x) = \dfrac{\sin x}{x}$ $x_0 = 1.75$

16. Each of the six sides of a cubical box is 0.225 cm thick, and the inside volume of the box is 77 cm³. Find the volume of metal used to make the box.

17. The radius of a sphere is measured to be 1 ft with a deviation of no more than 0.025 in. What is the maximum error in the volume of the sphere? Give the differential estimate to this error.

18. The altitude of a certain right circular cone is $h = 2.6$ m. If the radius r of the base is increased from 75 cm to 83.25 cm, what is the increase in the volume of the cone? The volume of a cone is given by the formula
$$V = \frac{1}{3}\pi r^2 h.$$

19. The radius r of a sphere is measured to be 7.75 cm with a possible percentage error of 3 percent. Find the error and percentage error in the value of the surface area of the sphere that might occur because of the error in the radius. The surface area of a sphere is given by the formula $S = 4\pi r^2$.

20. The diameter of a circle is to be approximately 1.6 ft in length. How precisely must the diameter be measured for the area to be correct within 1 percent?

Section 3.6 Formal Rules of Differentiation

We have been using various calculator programs that find the value of the derivative of a function by the numerical technique of central differences. Each program called the specific function $y = f(x)$ as a subroutine and gave the value $f'(a)$ at a given point $x = a$. Thus we could obtain selected values of the derivative function $f'(x)$, although we did not have an analytic expression for the derivative. From formal rules of differentiation the derivative function $f'(x)$ can be obtained as an analytic expression from the original function $f(x)$. Since these rules are developed in any standard calculus text, we will not derive them here. Yet we are going to summarize these rules in this section and give examples illustrating their use.

Each differentiation formula is obtained by applying the limit process specified in the definition of the derivative. It is instructive to consider a specific example so you can see how the process works.

Consider the function $f(x) = x^3$. Let's calculate an expression for the derivative $f'(x)$ directly from the definition. We do so in several stages.

Step 1: First, write out $f(x + \Delta x)$ and $f(x)$:

$$f(x + \Delta x) = (x + \Delta x)^3$$
$$= x^3 + 3x^2 \, \Delta x + 3x(\Delta x)^2 + (\Delta x)^3$$
$$f(x) = x^3$$

Step 2: Subtract $f(x)$ from $f(x + \Delta x)$:

$$f(x + \Delta x) - f(x) = 3x^2 \, \Delta x + 3x(\Delta x)^2 + (\Delta x)^3$$

Step 3: Divide by Δx:

$$\frac{f(x + \Delta x) - f(x)}{\Delta x} = 3x^2 + 3x \, \Delta x + (\Delta x)^2$$

Step 4: Calculate the limit as Δx tends to zero:

$$f'(x) = \lim_{\Delta x \to 0} \frac{f(x + \Delta x) - f(x)}{\Delta x}$$
$$= \lim_{\Delta x \to 0} [3x^2 + 3x \, \Delta x + (\Delta x)^2]$$
$$= 3x^2$$

This four-step process is known as the *delta process* for calculating derivatives. The derivation thus obtained is an example of a more general rule of differentiation known as the *power rule:*

$$\frac{d}{dx}\left(x^n\right) = nx^{n-1}$$

We derived the rule for the case $n = 3$. The same method would work for any positive integer n. Additional work is required in the derivation for arbitrary real numbers, but it is true that the power rule is valid for any real number n.

You have seen how new functions can be obtained from other functions through the algebraic processes of addition, subtraction, multiplication, division, powers, and roots. Differentiation formulas give the derivatives of all these new functions, and we summarize those rules here.

Differentiation Formulas

In these formulas, u and v are assumed to be differentiable functions of x, and c is any constant.

1. $\frac{d}{dx}(c) = 0$

2. $\frac{d}{dx}(x^n) = nx^{n-1}$

3. $\frac{d}{dx}(cu) = c\frac{du}{dx}$

4. $\frac{d}{dx}(u+v) = \frac{du}{dx} + \frac{dv}{dx}$

5. $\frac{d}{dx}(uv) = u\frac{dv}{dx} + v\frac{du}{dx}$

6. $\frac{d}{dx}\left(\frac{u}{v}\right) = \frac{v\frac{du}{dx} - u\frac{dv}{dx}}{v^2} \qquad v \neq 0$

7. $\frac{d}{dx}\left(u^n\right) = nu^{n-1}\frac{du}{dx}$

Let's apply these rules in several examples.

EXERCISE 1.

Find dy/dx if $y = x^4 - 5x^3 + 6x^2 - x + 1$.

Solution. We find the derivatives of the separate terms and add the results:

$$\frac{dy}{dx} = \frac{d(x^4)}{dx} + \frac{d(-5x^3)}{dx} + \frac{d(6x^2)}{dx} + \frac{d(-x)}{dx} + \frac{d(1)}{dx}$$

$$= 4x^3 - 5\frac{d(x^3)}{dx} + 6\frac{d(x^2)}{dx} - \frac{d(x)}{dx} + 0$$

$$= 4x^3 - 5(3x^2) + 6(2x) - x^0$$

$$= 4x^3 - 15x^2 + 12x - 1$$

In general, if

$$y = a_n x^n + a_{n-1}x^{n-1} + \ldots + a_2 x^2 + a_1 x + a_0$$

is a polynomial, then

$$\frac{dy}{dx} = na_n x^{n-1} + (n-1)a_{n-1}x^{n-2} + \ldots + 2a_2 x + a_1$$

gives the derivative function.

EXERCISE 2.

Find dy/dx if $y = (x^2 - 1)(x^3 + 2x - 7)$.

Solution. We apply the product rule 5:

$$\frac{dy}{dx} = (x^2 - 1)\frac{d(x^3 + 2x - 7)}{dx} + (x^3 + 2x - 7)\frac{d(x^2 - 1)}{dx}$$

$$= (x^2 - 1)(3x^2 + 2) + (x^3 + 2x - 7)(2x)$$

$$= 5x^4 + 3x^2 - 14x - 2$$

EXERCISE 3.

Find dy/dx if $y = \dfrac{(3x + 5)}{(x^2 - 4x + 7)}$

Solution. We apply the quotient rule 6:

$$\frac{dy}{dx} = \frac{(x^2 - 4x + 7)\dfrac{d(3x + 5)}{dx} - (3x + 5)\dfrac{d(x^2 - 4x + 7)}{dx}}{(x^2 - 4x + 7)^2}$$

$$= \frac{(x^2 - 4x + 7)(3) - (3x + 5)(2x - 4)}{(x^2 - 4x + 7)^2}$$

$$= \frac{-3x^2 - 10x + 41}{(x^2 - 4x + 7)^2}$$

EXERCISE 4.

Find dy/dx if $y = (x^3 - 7x^2 + 4)^{-2}$.

Solution. The function y is of the form $y = u^{-2}$, where $u = x^3 - 7x^2 + 4$. Thus the power rule 7 applies:

$$\frac{dy}{dx} = -2(x^3 - 7x^2 + 4)^{-3}\frac{d(x^3 - 7x^2 + 4)}{dx}$$

$$= -2(x^3 - 7x^2 + 4)^{-3}(3x^2 - 14x)$$

EXERCISE 5.

Find dy/dx if $y = \dfrac{\sqrt[3]{x^2 - 5}}{(x + 1)}$.

Solution. The quotient rule 6 and power rule 7 both apply:

$$\frac{dy}{dx} = \frac{(x + 1)\dfrac{d(\sqrt[3]{x^2 - 5})}{dx} - (\sqrt[3]{x^2 - 5})\dfrac{d(x + 1)}{dx}}{(x + 1)^2}$$

$$= \frac{(x+1)\frac{1}{3}(x^2-5)^{-2/3}\frac{d(x^2-5)}{dx} - (x^2-5)^{1/3}(1)}{(x+1)^2}$$

$$= \frac{\frac{1}{3}(x+1)(x^2-5)^{-2/3}(2x) - (x^2-5)^{1/3}}{(x+1)^2}$$

$$= \frac{\frac{1}{3}(x^2-5)^{-2/3}[2x(x+1) - 3(x^2-5)]}{(x+1)^2}$$

$$= \frac{-x^2 + 2x + 15}{3(x^2-5)^{2/3}(x+1)^2}$$

In the first step we use the quotient rule, and in the second step we use the power rule. The remaining steps consist of algebraic simplification.

Using the differentiation rules given above, you can differentiate polynomial, rational, and algebraic functions. Next let's consider the trigonometric and exponential functions. The derivative formulas are summarized as follows:

8. $\dfrac{d}{dx}(\sin x) = \cos x$

9. $\dfrac{d}{dx}(\cos x) = -\sin x$

10. $\dfrac{d}{dx}(\tan x) = \sec^2 x$

11. $\dfrac{d}{dx}(\cot x) = -\csc^2 x$

12. $\dfrac{d}{dx}(\sec x) = \sec x \tan x$

13. $\dfrac{d}{dx}(\csc x) = -\csc x \cot x$

14. $\dfrac{d}{dx}(e^x) = e^x$

EXERCISE 6.

Find dy/dx if $y = e^x \sin^2 x$.

Solution. We indicate each differentiation rule as it is being applied in calculating the derivative.

$$\frac{dy}{dx} = e^x \frac{d(\sin^2 x)}{dx} + \sin^2 x \frac{d(e^x)}{dx} \qquad \text{rule 5}$$

$$= e^x (2 \sin x)\frac{d}{dx}(\sin x) + \sin^2 x \frac{d(e^x)}{dx} \qquad \text{rule 7}$$

$$= e^x (2 \sin x)(\cos x) + \sin^2 x \frac{d(e^x)}{dx} \qquad \text{rule 8}$$

$$= e^x (2 \sin x)(\cos x) + \sin^2 x \, (e^x) \qquad \text{rule 14}$$

$$= e^x \sin x \, (2 \cos x + \sin x) \qquad \text{simplification}$$

PROBLEMS 3.6

Find dy/dx in each of the following problems.

1. $y = 17x^3 - 9x^2 + 4x - 3$

2. $y = 2x^{-5} + 13x^{-2} + 4x + 7x^2$

3. $y = 15 + 4x^{1/7} - 2x^3 - 3x^{-5/3}$

4. $y = (14x - 3x^2 + 2x^{1/2})^4$

5. $y = (13 - x^4)(2 + x^2)^3$

6. $y = x\sqrt{x^4 - 2x + 3}$

7. $y = \dfrac{x^3 - x^2}{x + 1}$

8. $y = \dfrac{x^2 - 4x + 3}{3x^2 - 2x + 5}$

9. $y = \dfrac{1}{x} + \sqrt{x}$

10. $y = \dfrac{x^2 + 1}{(x - 2)(x^3 + 2)}$

11. $y = \left(\dfrac{x - 1}{x + 1}\right)^3$

12. $y = (3\sqrt{x} + 2x - 5)^{3/2}$

13. $y = \left[(4 - 3x^2)^{1/3} (2 - 5x)^3 \right]^2$

14. $y = e^{2x}$

15. $y = \tan^2 x + \sec x$

16. $y = e^x \tan x$

17. $y = e^{-x} \cos x$

18. $y = (e^x + e^{-x})^2$

19. $y = (\sin^2 x + \cos x)^{1/2}$

20. $y = x^3 e^x$

21. $y = x \sin x + \cos x$

22. $y = \tan x - x$

23. $y = \dfrac{1}{1 + e^{-x}}$

24. $y = x e^{-x}$

25. $y = \csc^2 x + \cot^3 x$

26. Using the delta process, derive the rule

$$\frac{d}{dx}\left(\frac{1}{x}\right) = -\frac{1}{x^2}$$

directly from the definition of the derivative.

27. Using the delta process, derive the rule

$$\frac{d}{dx}(\sin x) = \cos x$$

directly from the definition of the derivative. You may use the program LIMIT to calculate any limits about which you are unsure.

Section 3.7 The Chain Rule and Related Rates

We have summarized the rules of differentiation applied to sums, products, and quotients of functions. Another operation combining functions is composition, which was studied in Section 2.2. In this section you will investigate the rule for finding the derivative of the composition of two functions: This rule is known as the *chain rule*. You will also see some applied examples illustrating the use of the chain rule.

Consider the composite of f with g, $y = (f \circ g)(x)$ or $y = f[g(x)]$. If the function g has a derivative at $x = x_0$ and the function f has a derivative at $g(x_0)$, then the composite $f \circ g$ has a derivative at x_0 given by the following *chain rule:*

$$(f \circ g)'(x_0) = f'[g(x_0)]\, g'(x_0) \tag{3.15}$$

As x_0 varies we obtain the derivative function for the composition $y = f[g(x)]$:

$$\frac{dy}{dx} = f'[g(x)]g'(x) \tag{3.16}$$

Another way to view the chain rule is through the introduction of another variable. Suppose y is a differentiable function of u, and u is a differentiable of x. Then y is a differentiable function of x and the chain rule is

$$\frac{dy}{dx} = \frac{dy}{du} \cdot \frac{du}{dx} \tag{3.17}$$

To relate Equation 3.17 back to 3.16, let $u = g(x)$ and $y = f(u)$. Then y becomes a function of x, $y = (f \circ g)(x)$, when $g(x)$ is substituted for u in the expression $y = f(u)$. Equation 3.17 says that the derivative of the composite $y = f[g(x)]$ with respect to x equals the derivative of the function $y = f(u)$

with respect to u times the derivative of $u = g(x)$ with respect to x. That's exactly what Equation 3.16 expresses.

Let's consider a specific example, $y = \sin(x^2 + 1)$. Then $y = f[g(x)]$, where $f(u) = \sin u$ and $g(x) = x^2 + 1$. The derivative of f is the derivative of the sine, $f'(u) = \cos u$; and the derivative of g is $g'(x) = 2x$. Therefore, according to the chain rule,

$$\frac{dy}{dx} = \frac{d}{dx}\,[\sin(x^2 + 1)]$$

$$= f'[g(x)]\,g'(x)$$

$$= \cos[g(x)] \cdot 2x$$

$$= 2x \cos(x^2 + 1)$$

The prepared program CHAIN calculates the derivative of a composite function at a specified point. CHAIN uses program steps 000 through 103, and memory locations 01 through 08. You must key in subroutines to evaluate the two functions f and g. Program steps 104 through 479, as well as memory steps 00 and 09 through 59, are available for your use in writing those subroutines. The subroutine for f *must* be located beginning at step 104 with the label, Lb1 C'. The subroutine for g *must* be located at step 300 with the label, Lb1 B'. The last two steps in each subroutine *must* be INV SBR.

Using the Program CHAIN

When CHAIN jumps to the subroutine to determine a function value of either f or g, it assumes the number to be operated on is in the display. Thus you need to store that value away where it is available in the computation of f or g. Since f and g are computed independently, you can use the same storage address in each subroutine if you wish.

The calculation for the derivative $(f \circ g)'(x_0)$ is accomplished through the following procedures.

Step 1: Key in the subroutine for f at program step 104 with label C'. End the subroutine with [INV] [SBR] .

Step 2: Key in the subroutine for g at program step 300 with label B'. End the subroutine with [INV] [SBR] .

Step 3: Enter the number x_0 into the display and press [D'] . This loads the value of x_0 into the program and initializes $\Delta x = 0.0001$.

Step 4: Press [A] . This calculates $g(x_0)$.

Step 5: Press [B] . This calculates $g'(x_0)$.

Step 6: Press [C] . This calculates $f'[g(x_0)]\,g'(x_0)$.

To obtain correct results, you must execute the sequence of calculations in the order specified by these steps.

EXERCISE 1.
CALCULATING THE DERIVATIVE
OF A COMPOSITE

Let's find dy/dx for $y = 2u^3 + 5u^{1/2}$ and $u = (3x^2 - x + 4.5)^{2/3}$ when $x = 2.61$.
First key the subroutine for $y = f(u)$ into CHAIN:

| GTO | 104 | LRN | Lb1 | C' | STO | 00 | x^2 | × | RCL | 00 |

| × | 2 | + | 5 | × | RCL | 00 | $\sqrt{x}$ | = | INV | SBR | LRN |

Next key in the subroutine for $u = g(x)$:

| GTO | 300 | LRN | Lb1 | B' | STO | 00 | x^2 | × | 3 | − |

| RCL | 00 | + | 4.5 | = | y^x | (| 2 | ÷ | 3 |) | = |

| INV | SBR | LRN |

(enter)   2.61

(press)   D'   Load $x_0 = 2.61$. The value $\Delta x = 0.0001$ appears in the display.

(press)   A $g(2.61) = 7.928867689$ is in the display.

(press)   B $g'(2.61) = 3.47086026$ is in the display.

(press)   C $(f \circ g)'(2.61) = 1312.295786$ is in the display.

As a second illustration, let's find dy/dx when $y = \sin^3(7x^2 + 1)$ and $x = 0.5$ radians. First key in the subroutine for $f(u) = \sin^3 u$:

| GTO | 104 | LRN | Lb1 | C' | sin | STO | 00 | x^2 | × | RCL |

| 00 | = | INV | SBR | LRN |

Then key in the subroutine for $g(x) = 7x^2 + 1$:

| GTO | 300 | LRN | Lb1 | B' | x^2 | × | 7 | + | 1 | = |

| INV | SBR | LRN |

Be sure your calculator is in the radians mode: Press [Rad] . Enter $x_0 = 0.5$ with the key [D'] and press [A] , then [B] and [C] to find $dy/dx = -2.827$, rounded to three decimals.

Related Rates

You have seen several applications of the differential calculus in which it was required to find the rate of change of some quantity. Sometimes the quantity
192   is given as a function of one variable, say $y = f(x)$, but you want to know its

rate of change with respect to another variable t; that is, you seek dy/dt instead of dy/dx. Such problems, known as *related rates problems,* can be solved by means of the chain rule because

$$\frac{dy}{dt} = \frac{dy}{dx} \cdot \frac{dx}{dt} \qquad (3.18)$$

From the equation $y = f(x)$, the derivative $dy/dx = f'(x)$ can be determined. If you know $x = g(t)$, then $dx/dt = g'(t)$ can also be found. Or perhaps the rate of change dx/dt is given in the statement of the problem. In either case, you can find dy/dt by means of Equation 3.18.

The program CHAIN is designed to assist you in solving related rates problems. If $y = f(x)$ and $x = g(t)$ are both known functions, then you simply use CHAIN as before. But if the function g is not known, you then need the values $g(t_0)$ and $g'(t_0)$ directly given in the problem. These values are loaded into CHAIN with the special calculator keys as follows:

A'   This key loads the value of $g(t_0)$, if g is not given as a subroutine at label B'.

E'   This key loads the value of $g'(t_0)$ if g is not given as a subroutine at label B'.

D'   This key loads the value t_0 and initializes $\Delta t = 0.0001$.

Once these values are loaded, press the key $\boxed{\text{C}}$ to calculate

$$\frac{dy}{dt} = f'[g(t_0)]\, g'(t_0)$$

The value of t_0 is not actually used in the calculation.
Let's consider several examples.

EXERCISE 2.
RATE OF INCREASE
OF A CIRCULAR AREA

When a pebble is dropped into a still pool of water, it causes concentric ripples on the water's surface. If the outer ripple increases in diameter at the rate of 3 m/sec, how fast is the area of the disturbed surface increasing at the end of 8 sec?

Solution. Let $x(t)$ denote the diameter of the outer circular ripple at any time t. We are given that $dx/dt = 3$ m/sec. We seek dA/dt when $t = 8$ for the area of the disturbed surface

$$A = \pi \left(\frac{x}{2}\right)^2$$

Since distance equals rate × time, we also know that $x = 3 \cdot 8 = 24$ m at the end of 8 sec. With CHAIN loaded in your calculator, enter the function $A = f(x)$ and the given information as follows:

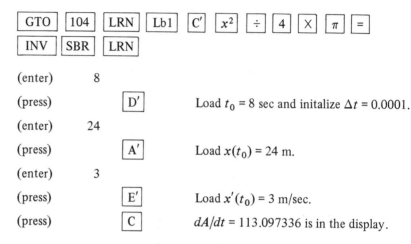

| GTO | 104 | LRN | Lb1 | C' | x^2 | ÷ | 4 | × | π | = |
| INV | SBR | LRN |

(enter)	8		
(press)		D'	Load $t_0 = 8$ sec and initalize $\Delta t = 0.0001$.
(enter)	24		
(press)		A'	Load $x(t_0) = 24$ m.
(enter)	3		
(press)		E'	Load $x'(t_0) = 3$ m/sec.
(press)		C	$dA/dt = 113.097336$ is in the display.

Thus the area of the disturbed surface is increasing approximately at the rate of 113.1 m^2/sec 8 sec after the pebble hits the pool.

EXERCISE 3.
A SLIDING LADDER

A ladder 8 m long leans against a vertical wall. If the lower end is being moved away from the wall at the rate of 1.7 m/sec, how fast is the top sliding down the wall when the lower end is 3.5 m from the wall.

Solution. Let $y(t)$ denote the height of the top of the ladder above the ground, and $x(t)$ the distance of the lower end from the wall, at any time t. The situation is depicted in Figure 3.14. We are given that $dx/dt = 1.7$ m/sec and seek dy/dt when $x = 3.5$ m. Applying the Pythagorean Theorem to the right triangle in the figure,

$$y = \sqrt{64 - x^2}$$

With CHAIN loaded in your calculator, enter $y = f(x)$ as a subroutine:

| GTO | 104 | LRN | Lb1 | C' | x^2 | +/− | + | 64 | = | $\sqrt{x}$ |
| INV | SBR | LRN |

(press)		D'	Initialize $\Delta t = 0.0001$.
(enter)	3.5		
(press)		A'	Load $x(t_0) = 3.5$ m.

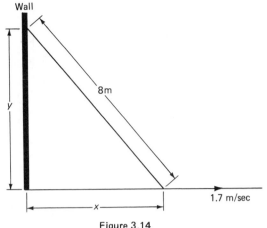

Wall

8m

1.7 m/sec

x

Figure 3.14

(enter)   1.7

(press) $\boxed{\text{E}'}$ Load $x'(t_0) = 1.7$ m/sec.

(press) $\boxed{\text{C}}$ $dy/dt = -0.827107171$.

Thus the top of the ladder is descending (minus sign) at approximately 0.83 m/sec.

EXERCISE 4.
A MOVING SHADOW

A light is at the top of a tower 110 ft high. A ball is dropped from the same height from a point 17 ft from the light. If the ball falls according to the law $s = 16t^2$, how fast is the shadow of the ball moving along the ground 1.5 sec after its release?

Solution. Let $x(t)$ denote the distance of the shadow along the ground from the base of the light tower at any time t. The situation is depicted in Figure 3.15. We want to find dx/dt when $t = 1.5$ sec.

From similar triangles in the figure,

$$\frac{x}{110} = \frac{17}{s} \quad \text{or} \quad x = \frac{1{,}870}{s} \quad \text{where } s = 16t^2$$

With CHAIN in your calculator, load $x = f(s)$ and $s = g(t)$ as subroutines:

$\boxed{\text{GTO}}$ $\boxed{104}$ $\boxed{\text{LRN}}$ $\boxed{\text{Lb1}}$ $\boxed{\text{C}'}$ $\boxed{1/x}$ $\boxed{\times}$ $\boxed{1870}$ $\boxed{=}$ $\boxed{\text{INV}}$

$\boxed{\text{SBR}}$ $\boxed{\text{LRN}}$ $\boxed{\text{GTO}}$ $\boxed{300}$ $\boxed{\text{LRN}}$ $\boxed{\text{Lb1}}$ $\boxed{\text{B}'}$ $\boxed{x^2}$ $\boxed{\times}$ $\boxed{16}$ $\boxed{=}$

$\boxed{\text{INV}}$ $\boxed{\text{SBR}}$ $\boxed{\text{LRN}}$

195

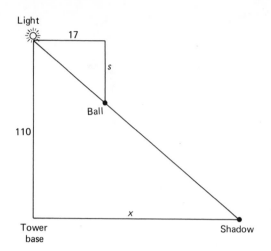

Light

17

s

Ball

110

Tower
base

x

Shadow

Figure 3.15

(enter)   1.5

(press)   D'   Load t_0 = 1.5 sec and initialize Δt = 0.0001.

(press)   A   s = 36 ft.

(press)   B ds/dt = 48 ft/sec.

(press)   C dx/dt = −69.2592624 ft/sec.

Thus the shadow is moving *toward* the base of the tower (indicated by the minus sign) at approximately 69.3 ft/sec.

EXERCISE 5.
A REVOLVING BEACON

A revolving beacon located 3 mi from a straight shoreline makes one revolution every 17 sec. Find the speed of the spot of light along the shore when it is $\sqrt{3}$ mi away from the point on the shore nearest the light.

Solution. Let $y(t)$ denote the distance of the light spot along the shore from the point on the shore nearest the beacon, at any time t. Let $\theta(t)$ denote the angle the light ray makes with the perpendicular to the shore line. We will assume the beacon rotates counterclockwise. The situation is depicted in Figure 3.16. We want to find dy/dt when $y = \sqrt{3}$ mi.

Since the beacon makes one revolution every 17 sec, we find that

$$\frac{d\theta}{dt} = \frac{60}{17}(2\pi)$$

radians per minute. From trigonometric considerations in the figure,

$$y = 3 \tan \theta$$

196   Also, when $y = \sqrt{3}$, $\tan \theta = \sqrt{3}/3$ so that $\theta = 30°$ or $\pi/6$ rad.

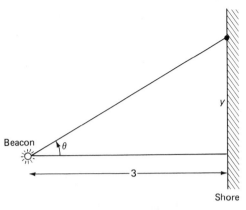

Figure 3.16

Now, with CHAIN in your calculator, key in the subroutine $y = f(\theta) = 3 \tan \theta$ at location 104. Make sure your calculator is in the radians mode. Then,

(press)		$\boxed{D'}$	Initialize $\Delta t = 0.0001$.
(enter)	$\pi/6$		
(press)		$\boxed{A'}$	Load θ.
(enter)	$\dfrac{60}{17}(2\pi)$		
(press)		$\boxed{E'}$	Load $d\theta/dt$.
(press)		$\boxed{C}$	$dy/dt = 88.70379257$.

So the spot of light is moving approximately 88.7 mi/min away from the point on the shore nearest the light.

Summary The following strategy will help you in solving related rates problems:

Step 1: Read the problem carefully and select the quantity whose rate of change is desired. If the problem involves geometric magnitudes, draw a figure that clearly shows their relationships, and label your figure with appropriate constants and variables. Your figure should be valid for all time values being considered.

Step 2: Find an equation relating the quantity y having the unknown rate of change to a single variable x for which (a) the function $x = g(t)$ is known, or (b) the rate of change dx/dt is known.

Step 3: Determine the value of x and its derivative dx/dt at the instant $t = t_0$ specified in the problem. These values may be given explicitly in the problem, or they need to be found (possibly with the aid of the program CHAIN).

Step 4: Using CHAIN, calculate the rate of change dy/dt at the specified instant t_0.

197

In each of Problems 1–5, find the derivative dy/dx at the specified point. Use the program CHAIN, and give your answer to three decimal places.

1. $y = u^5 - 2u^3 + 4u^2 - u + 2$ $u = \sqrt{x} + x^{-2}, x = 2.17$

2. $y = \dfrac{u^2}{u^3 + 2u}$ $u = x^{3/2} + x^{1/2} + 1, x = 8.76$

3. $y = u^{2/3} + \sin u$ $u = \tan x, x = \pi/6$

4. $y = \cos(\sqrt{u} + 1)$ $u = x^3 + 2x^2 - x + 1, x = 4.49$

5. $y = e^{\sec u}$ $u = x^2 - x^{-1}, x = 1.09$

6. If a point traces the circle $x^2 + y^2 = 4$ and if $dx/dt = \frac{3}{7}$ when the point reaches $(1, -\sqrt{3})$, find dy/dt there.

In Problems 7–14, find analytic expressions for dy/dx using the chain rule.

7. $y = (5x^4 - 3x^3 + 4x - 3)^{2/3}$

8. $y = \sqrt{x + \dfrac{1}{x}}$

9. $y = x \cos(5x - 2)$

10. $y = \dfrac{\sec 3\sqrt{x}}{\sqrt{x}}$

11. $y = (3 - e^{-5x})^4$

12. $y = \sin(e^{-x^2})$

13. $y = e^{\tan x^3}$

14. $y = e^{-2x} \sin x$

15. The sides of a square are increasing at the rate of 0.015 cm/sec. At what rate is the area of the square increasing when the side length is 5 cm?

16. A man 5 ft 11 in tall is walking at the rate of 2.93 ft/sec toward a street light 17.25 ft high. At what rate is the length of his shadow changing?

17. A triangular trough is 12 ft long, 3 ft wide at the top, and 3 ft deep. Water is poured into the trough at the rate of 5 ft^3/min.

    a. How fast is the surface rising when the depth is 1.5 ft?

    b. When the depth is 2 ft?

18. A 37-ft-long rope is attached to a weight and passed over a pulley 18 ft above the ground. The other end of the rope is pulled away along the ground at the rate of 4 ft/sec. At what rate is the weight rising at the instant when the other end of the rope is 14 ft from its initial point?

19. The volume of a spherical balloon is increasing at the rate of 5.5 in^3/sec. At what rate is the radius of the balloon increasing when the radius is 2.25 in?

20. A truck, traveling due west at 55 mph, and a car, traveling south at 30 mph, leave an intersection at the same time.

    a. At what rate is the distance between them changing when the truck has traveled 75 mi?

    b. When the car has traveled 75 mi?

21. It is estimated that t years from now, the population of a certain suburban community will be

$$p(t) = \frac{105}{1 + 6e^{-0.07t}}$$

thousand people. An environmental study indicates that the average daily level of carbon monoxide in the air will be $c(p) = 0.45\sqrt{p^2 + 1.05p + 54}$ parts per million (ppm) when the population is p thousand. What is the rate of change in the level of carbon monoxide three years from now?

22. A swimming pool is 110 ft long, 40 ft wide, 12 ft deep at the deep end, and 4 ft deep at the shallow end, the bottom being rectangular. If the pool is filled by pumping water into it at the rate of 60 ft^3/min, how fast is the water level rising when it is 9 ft deep at the deep end?

23. A baseball diamond is a square 90 ft on each side. A player is running from home to first base at the rate of 26 ft/sec. When he has run three-quarters of the way, at what rate is his distance from second base changing?

24. Suppose the cost C of producing x units of a product is given by $C = 3,600 + 15x + 0.12x^2$. If the price per unit p is given by the equation $x = 1,150 - 2.25p$, find the rate of change of cost with respect to the price per unit when $p = 95$.

25. A walk is perpendicular to a long wall, and a woman strolls along it away from the wall at the rate of 3 ft/sec. There is a light 9 ft from the walk and 26 ft from the wall.

    a. How fast is her shadow moving along the wall when she is 18 ft from the wall?

    b. When she is 23 ft from the wall?

26. A rectangle is inscribed in a circle of radius 7 cm. If the length of the rectangle is decreasing at 2 cm/sec, how fast is the area changing at the instant when the length is 9 cm?

27. At an altitude of 1,800 m, a parachutist jumps from an airplane and falls $4.9t^2$ m after t sec. The air pressure p decreases with altitude at the constant rate of 0.096 units/m. At what time does dp/dt reach 1.95 units/sec?

4

Integration

In this chapter we cover the second major limiting operation in the calculus, namely, the definite integral. First we present the integral as the limit of a sum of rectangular regions. You are already acquainted with this approach from the calculation of area under a polynomial curve treated in the first chapter. Now the idea will be generalized to the area associated with arbitrary continuous functions. Next we improve on the numerical calculation of the integral using trapezoidal and parabolic approximations instead of rectangles. Then the Fundamental Theorem of Calculus is discussed, and the integration process is viewed as an "undoing" or reversal of the differentiation process. From that point of view the natural logarithm function can be presented as an integral.

There are numerous applications of the definite integral. It is used to calculate the area between two curves, the length of a curve in the plane, and the area of a surface of revolution. It is also used to determine the distance traveled by a moving particle when its speed or acceleration is known. Moreover, volumes of solids obtained by revolving curves about the coordinate axes are given by integrals, and the integral is used to define the average value of a continuous function over an interval. Finally the inverse trigonometric functions are investigated because their derivatives lead to useful integration formulas.

Before you commence your study of this chapter, record the programs RECTANGLES, INTEGRATE, and MEASURES on separate magnetic cards. Each program is listed in Appendix A, uses standard 479.59 partitioning, and can be recorded on a single side of a card.

Section 4.1 Area as a Limit

In Chapter 1 we considered finding the area beneath a polynomial curve. The idea of the area beneath a positive continuous curve $y = f(x)$ and above the x-axis—bounded on the left by the vertical line $x = a$ and on the right by the vertical line $x = b$—was presented as the limiting number associated with the sums of inscribed and circumscribed rectangles, which gradually exhaust the area of the region R. Figure 4.1 illustrates a typical case of inscribed rectangles. As the bases of the inscribed rectangles get closer and closer to zero, the sum of their areas gets closer and closer to the area of the region R shown in the figure.

Let's examine this limiting process a little more carefully. We will consider the case of inscribed rectangles, with the case for circumscribed rectangles being entirely analogous. First, we obtain the bases of the inscribed rectangles by choosing an arbitrary positive integer n and dividing the interval $a \leqslant x \leqslant b$ into n subintervals of length $\Delta x = (b - a)/n$. The endpoints of the subintervals are labeled $a, x_1, x_2, \ldots, x_{n-1}, b$ (as shown in Figure 4.1). Next

Figure 4.1 The area of the region R is approximated by inscribed rectangles of width $(b - a)/n$. The height of each rectangle occurs at the point m_i in the ith subinterval where f assumes its minimum value. The area of R is defined as the limit of the areas of the approximation regions as n tends to $+\infty$.

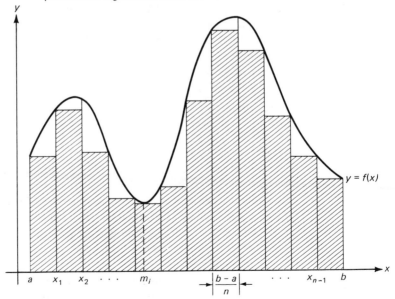

draw vertical lines through the points $a, x_1, x_2, \ldots, x_{n-1}, b$ to divide the region R into n strips of equal width Δx. In each of the closed subintervals

$$[a, x_1], [x_1, x_2], \ldots, [x_{n-1}, b]$$

choose a point at which f assumes its minimum value. (These points do occur because f is continuous over each of the closed subintervals. That result is established in advanced calculus.) If these minimum values occur at the points $m_1, m_2, \ldots, m_n$, then the heights of the inscribed rectangles are $f(m_1)$, $f(m_2), \ldots, f(m_n)$. The sum $\underline{S}_n$ of the areas of the inscribed rectangles is then

$$\underline{S}_n = f(m_1) \, \Delta x + f(m_2) \, \Delta x + \ldots + f(m_n) \, \Delta x$$

$$= \sum_{k=1}^{n} f(m_k) \, \Delta x$$

(The sigma notation Σ means "the sum of all terms of the form . . ." and is discussed in Section 11.2 of *Calculator Clout*.) The number $\underline{S}_n$ is called the *lower Riemann sum* associated with the continuous function f and the subdivision points $a, x_1, x_2, \ldots, x_{n-1}, b$.

If maximum values over each of the closed subintervals occur at the points $M_1, M_2, \ldots, M_n$ then in like manner we obtain the *upper Riemann sum*

$$\overline{S}_n = \sum_{k=1}^{n} f(M_k) \, \Delta x$$

which represents the sum of the areas of the circumscribed rectangles. Each number $\underline{S}_n$ and $\overline{S}_n$, the first too small and the second too large, approximates the area we seek.

The *exact* area of the region R is defined to be the limit of the upper and lower Riemann sums as the widths of the rectangles tend to zero. Since $\Delta x = (b - a)/n$ tends to 0 as n tends to $+\infty$, we have

$$\text{Area of } R = \lim_{n \to \infty} \sum_{k=1}^{n} f(m_k) \, \Delta x = \lim_{n \to \infty} \sum_{k=1}^{n} f(M_k) \, \Delta x$$

Computationally there are difficulties in calculating the lower and upper Riemann sums because we generally do not know the locations of the points $m_1, m_2, \ldots, m_n$ and $M_1, M_2, \ldots, M_n$ where the minimum and maximum values of f occur in each of the subintervals. However, if the function is *increasing* over the entire interval $a \leqslant x \leqslant b$ then each minimum value occurs at the left endpoint of the subinterval, and each maximum value at the right endpoint. If the function is *decreasing* over $a \leqslant x \leqslant b$, then the roles of the endpoints are reversed.

The prepared program RECTANGLES calculates the upper and lower Riemann sums for any positive continuous function f that is increasing or decreasing over the entire interval $a \leqslant x \leqslant b$. The function f is keyed in by the user to be called as a subroutine by the main program. RECTANGLES uses program steps 000 through 087, and storage locations 01 through 04, 58, and 59. Program steps 088 through 479, as well as memory locations 00 and 05 through 57, are available for use while evaluating $f(x)$.

Using the Program RECTANGLES

Step 1: With RECTANGLES read into your calculator, go to program step 088 and key in the subroutine for $f(x)$. The first two steps of your subroutine must be

$$\boxed{\text{Lb1}} \quad \boxed{\text{C}'}$$

and the last two steps must be

$$\boxed{\text{INV}} \quad \boxed{\text{SBR}}$$

Step 2: Back in the calculate mode, enter the number of rectangles n and press $\boxed{\text{E}}$. The program halts with the number n displayed.

Step 3: Enter the left endpoint a, and press $\boxed{\text{A}}$. The program halts with a displayed.

Step 4: Enter the right endpoint b, and press $\boxed{\text{B}}$. The program halts with $(b - a)/n$ displayed.

If f is an *increasing* function over $a \leqslant x \leqslant b$:

Step 5: Press $\boxed{\text{C}}$. The program halts with the *lower* sum in the display. Press $\boxed{x \blacktriangle t}$ for the upper sum.

If f is a *decreasing* function over $a \leqslant x \leqslant b$:

Step 5: Press $\boxed{\text{C}}$. The program halts with the *upper* sum in the display. Press $\boxed{x \blacktriangle t}$ for the lower sum.

EXERCISE 1.
RIEMANN SUMS
FOR AN INCREASING FUNCTION

Let's calculate a table of upper and lower Riemann sums for the function

$$f(x) = \sqrt{1 + x^2} \quad \text{over} \quad 0 \leqslant x \leqslant 10$$

Since the derivative $f'(x) = x(1 + x^2)^{-1/2}$ is positive whenever $x > 0$, the function f is increasing everywhere over the given interval. We will create a table of values of the Riemann sums for $n = 10, 100, 200, 500,$ and $1,000$ rectangles.

With RECTANGLES read into your calculator, key in the subroutine for $f(x)$:

| GTO | 088 | LRN | Lb1 | C′ | x^2 | + | 1 | = | $\sqrt{x}$ | INV |

| SBR | LRN |

(enter)	10		
(press)		E	Load $n = 10$.
(enter)	0		
(press)		A	Load $a = 0$.
(enter)	10		
(press)		B	Load $b = 10$.
(press)		C	The program halts with the lower sum $\underline{S}_{10} = 47.30615757$ displayed.
(press)		x⯈t	The upper sum $\overline{S}_{10} = 56.35603319$ is displayed.

To obtain the Riemann sums when $n = 100$:

(enter)	100		
(press)		E	Load $n = 100$.
(enter)	0		
(press)		A	Load $a = 0$.
(enter)	10		
(press)		B	Load $b = 10$.
(press)		C	The program halts with the lower sum $\underline{S}_{100} = 51.296825$ displayed.
(press)		x⯈t	The upper sum $\overline{S}_{100} = 52.20181256$ is displayed.

Continue to change the number of rectangles, and you obtain the following table of Riemann sums (the program runs for about 20 minutes when $n = 1,000$):

n	$\underline{S}_n$	$\overline{S}_n$
10	47.30615757	56.35603319
100	51.296825	52.20181256
200	51.52244999	51.97494377
500	51.65802399	51.8390215
1,000	51.70324849	51.79374725

The true area under the curve turns out to be $A = 51.74848958$. So, even with 1,000 rectangles, the upper and lower Riemann sums are accurate only to the first decimal place. Later you will see how to improve on the accuracy without having to increase the number of rectangles but merely by altering their heights.

EXERCISE 2.
RIEMANN SUMS
FOR A DECREASING FUNCTION

The function $f(x) = 2x - x^2$ is decreasing over the interval $1 \leqslant x \leqslant 2$ because $f'(x) = 2 - 2x$ is negative there. To calculate the Riemann sums for $n = 200$, for instance, key in the subroutine for $f(x)$:

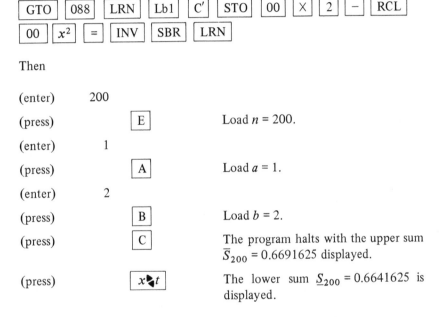

| GTO | 088 | LRN | Lb1 | C' | STO | 00 | X | 2 | − | RCL |

| 00 | x^2 | = | INV | SBR | LRN |

Then

(enter)	200		
(press)		E	Load $n = 200$.
(enter)	1		
(press)		A	Load $a = 1$.
(enter)	2		
(press)		B	Load $b = 2$.
(press)		C	The program halts with the upper sum $\overline{S}_{200} = 0.6691625$ displayed.
(press)		x⮀t	The lower sum $\underline{S}_{200} = 0.6641625$ is displayed.

In calculating the upper and lower sums to approximate the area, we have taken the heights of the rectangles to be the largest or smallest value of f, respectively, over each of the subintervals. We could take instead the heights of the rectangles to be the values of f at the *midpoint* of each of the subintervals. This is illustrated for the case $n = 6$ rectangles in Figure 4.2. From the figure you can see that some of the rectangles include portions outside the region R whose area we seek, but that other portions of R are excluded from these rectangular regions. These tend to cancel each other out, often giving a better approximation to the area of R than the corresponding upper or lower sums. The use of this approximation to the area is called the *midpoint rule*. We will denote the midpoint sum by S_n when using n rectangles. It is always true that

$$\underline{S}_n \leqslant S_n \leqslant \overline{S}_n$$

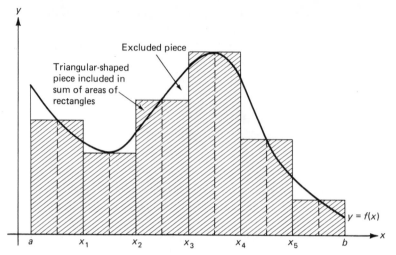

Figure 4.2 The area under the curve is approximated by rectangles whose heights are the values of the function f at the midpoint of each subinterval.

from which it follows that S_n gets closer and closer to the exact area of the region R as n tends to infinity.

Another advantage to the midpoint rule is that it presents no computational difficulties. The rule is easy to apply to any continuous function f so that f need not be everywhere increasing or decreasing.

The program RECTANGLES also calculates an approximation to the area beneath a curve using the midpoint rule. The procedures are exactly the same as for computing the upper and lower Riemann sums except that Step 5 is replaced by the following:

Step 5': Press ⃞D⃞ . The program halts with the midpoint approximation S_n in the display.

The next example illustrates the procedure.

EXERCISE 3.
CALCULATING AREA
BY THE MIDPOINT RULE

Consider again the function

$$f(x) = \sqrt{1 + x^2} \qquad \text{over } 0 \leqslant x \leqslant 10$$

To calculate the area trapped between the curve and the x-axis over the given interval by the midpoint rule, first key in $f(x)$ as a subroutine to RECTANGLES, just as in Exercise 1. Then

206

(enter)	10		
(press)		$\boxed{\text{E}}$	Load $n = 10$.
(enter)	0		
(press)		$\boxed{\text{A}}$	Load $a = 0$.
(enter)	10		
(press)		$\boxed{\text{B}}$	Load $b = 10$.
(press)		$\boxed{\text{D}}$	The program halts with the midpoint sum $S_{10} = 51.70734331$ in the display.

By changing the value of n and repeating the above entry procedures with the keys $\boxed{\text{E}}$, $\boxed{\text{A}}$, $\boxed{\text{B}}$, and $\boxed{\text{D}}$, you obtain the following table:

n	S_n
10	51.70734331
100	51.74807498
200	51.74838593
500	51.74847299
1,000	51.74848543

Notice the tremendous improvement in the midpoint approximations over the upper and lower sums found in Exercise 1.

EXERCISE 4.
CALCULATING AREA FOR AN ARBITRARY
POSITIVE CONTINUOUS FUNCTION

As a final example, let's calculate the area of the function

$$f(x) = \cos x \quad \text{over } -\pi/2 \leqslant x \leqslant \pi/2$$

Notice that the function is neither increasing nor decreasing over the entire interval. Now use the midpoint rule to calculate the approximations to the exact area (be sure your calculator is in the radians mode before you begin your calculations), and obtain the following table:

n	S_n
10	2.008248408
100	2.000082249
200	2.000020562
500	2.000003290
1,000	2.000000822

Finding areas by the method of rectangles, even with the midpoint rule, is slow because large numbers of rectangles are usually required for a satisfactory level of accuracy. Other numerical methods for obtaining area are faster, because fewer computations are required, and they give the same level of accuracy. You will study two of these methods in the following sections.

PROBLEMS 4.1

In each of Problems 1–10, find an approximation to the area beneath the specified function over the given interval for $n = 200$ rectangles by:

a. upper Riemann sums,

b. lower Riemann sums, and

c. the midpoint rule.

1. $y = x^3$ $1 \leqslant x \leqslant 2$
2. $y = \sqrt{x}$ $2 \leqslant x \leqslant 5$
3. $y = 1/x$ $1 \leqslant x \leqslant 2$
4. $y = \cos x$ $-\pi/2 \leqslant x \leqslant 0$
5. $y = 10 - 3x - x^2$ $-1.25 \leqslant x \leqslant 1.69$
6. $y = e^x$ $-1 \leqslant x \leqslant 3$
7. $y = x^3 + 2x + 1$ $0 \leqslant x \leqslant 2$
8. $y = \dfrac{1}{\sqrt{3x + 1}}$ $0.75 \leqslant x \leqslant 5.1$
9. $y = x^{1/3}(x - 1)^{2/3}$ $1 \leqslant x \leqslant 3$
10. $y = e^x \cos x$ $3\pi/2 \leqslant x \leqslant 2\pi$
11. Find the upper and lower Riemann sums, along with the midpoint sum, for the function $y = x^3$ over the interval $0 \leqslant x \leqslant 1$ using $n = 100, 200, 500,$ and $1{,}000$.
12. Find the upper and lower Riemann sums, as well as the midpoint sum, for the function $y = e^x \cos x$ over the interval $0 \leqslant x \leqslant \pi/2$ using $n = 100, 200, 500,$ and $1{,}000$.

In Problems 13–20, use the midpoint rule with $n = 200$ rectangles to approximate the area associated with the specified function over the given interval.

13. $y = 12 - x - x^2$ $-3 \leqslant x \leqslant 3$
14. $y = 4 + 3x - x^3$ $-2 \leqslant x \leqslant 2$
15. $y = \dfrac{\sqrt{x}(x - 4.5)^2}{3.5}$ $0 \leqslant x \leqslant 4.5$
16. $y = xe^{5x}$ $0 \leqslant x \leqslant 10$
17. $y = \sec x$ $-\pi/4 \leqslant x \leqslant \pi/3$
18. $y = x \sin(x^2)$ $0 \leqslant x \leqslant \sqrt{\pi}$
19. $y = \dfrac{4}{1 + x^2}$ $0 \leqslant x \leqslant 1$
20. $y = \sin x \cos x$ $0 \leqslant x \leqslant \pi/2$

Section 4.2 Numerical Integration

In the preceding section we gave three equivalent ways of obtaining the area under a nonnegative continuous curve $y = f(x)$ over a closed interval $a \leqslant x \leqslant b$. The area is the limit of the upper Riemann sums, the lower Riemann sums, and the midpoint sums. All three methods are but special cases of a more general limiting process that applies to arbitrary (not necessarily nonnegative) continuous functions.

We now assume only that f is continuous on the closed interval $a \leqslant x \leqslant b$. We define the lower and upper sums of f over $[a,b]$ for n subintervals of equal length $\Delta x = (b - a)/n$ in the same way as before:

$$\underline{S}_n = \sum_{k=1}^{n} f(m_k) \Delta x$$

and

$$\overline{S}_n = \sum_{k=1}^{n} f(M_k) \Delta x$$

where for any integer k between 1 and n, m_k and M_k are the points in the kth subinterval at which the minimum and maximum values of f occur. As the number of subintervals n tends to infinity, so that $\Delta x \to 0$, the lower and upper sums converge to a *unique* number called *the definite integral of f from a to b.* This integral is denoted by

$$\int_a^b f(x)\, dx$$

Thus

$$\int_a^b f(x)\, dx = \lim_{n \to \infty} \sum_{k=1}^{n} f(m_k) \Delta x = \lim_{n \to \infty} \sum_{k=1}^{n} f(M_k) \Delta x$$

The numbers a and b are called, respectively, the *lower* and *upper limits of integration,* and the function f is called the *integrand.*

In obtaining the definite integral by this limiting process, you need not evaluate f at the points of minimum and maximum values in each subinterval, nor do the subintervals need to be of equal lengths. But the lengths of *all* the subintervals must decrease to zero as the number of subintervals increases to infinity in the limiting process. The midpoint rule is just a special case of this more general process.

So if f is continuous over $[a,b]$, and if we divide the interval $[a,b]$ into n subintervals (not necessarily of equal length) using the subdivision points $a < x_1 < x_2 < \ldots < x_{n-1} < b$, then

$$\int_a^b f(x)\, dx = \lim_{n \to \infty} \sum_{k=1}^{n} f(x_k^*) \Delta x_k$$

where x_k^* is an *arbitrary* point in the kth subinterval, Δx_k is the *length* of the kth subinterval, and all the Δx_k decrease to zero in the limiting process.

In the particular case when f is a nonnegative function over the interval $[a,b]$, the definite integral can be interpreted as area.

> **Definition.** If f is a nonnegative continuous function over the interval $a \leqslant x \leqslant b$, then
>
> $$\int_a^b f(x)\, dx$$
>
> is defined to be the *area* of the region R lying beneath the graph of f, above the x-axis, and between the vertical lines $x = a$ to the left and $x = b$ to the right.

In studying applications of the definite integral in later sections you will see that numerous other interpretations can be assigned to the definite integral. For purposes of the present section we will now consider two numerical approaches popularly used to calculate definite integrals.

It is clear from your previous work that a large number of rectangular strips is required to obtain a satisfactory numerical approximation to the definite integral with rectangles, even using the midpoint rule. Yet the method of rectangles is easy to improve upon. For ease of discussion, we will illustrate this point with a nonnegative curve.

Consider a piece of a positive curve $y = f(x)$ that forms the top of a double strip as shown in Figure 4.3. Each strip is of width Δx. Instead of forming rectangles out of the two vertical strips, as done previously, we connect the tops of the vertical lines, having heights $f(a)$, $f(x_1)$, and $f(b)$, with straight lines. In this way we form two trapezoids as shown in the figure. We then approximate the area beneath the curve from a to b by the sum of the areas of these two trapezoids. The areas of the first and second trapezoids are

$$\left[\frac{f(a) + f(x_1)}{2}\right]\Delta x \quad \text{and} \quad \left[\frac{f(x_1) + f(b)}{2}\right]\Delta x$$

Figure 4.3 The area under the curve from a to b is approximated by two trapezoids.

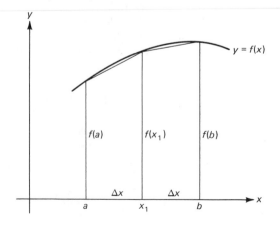

respectively. The total area is the sum of these two terms:

$$\text{Area} \approx [f(a) + 2f(x_1) + f(b)] \frac{\Delta x}{2}$$

Let's generalize the situation to $y = f(x)$ over $a \leqslant x \leqslant b$ using n subintervals, each of width $\Delta x = (b - a)/n$. We will assume that f is continuous and that the equally spaced subdivision points are $a, x_1, x_2, \ldots, x_{n-1}, b$. We then have the *trapezoidal rule:*

$$\int_a^b f(x)\, dx \approx [f(a) + 2f(x_1) + 2f(x_2) + \ldots + 2f(x_{n-1}) + f(b)] \frac{\Delta x}{2}$$

The error with the trapezoidal rule is much less than for the rectangular rules, and it is easy to use for numerical work. It turns out, however, that our line of reasoning can be pushed just one more step to come up with another method that often gives a dramatic increase in accuracy.

In Figure 4.3 we connected the tops of the vertical strips with straight lines to form two trapezoids. Instead let's fit a parabola to the three points

$$(a, f(a)) \quad (x_1, f(x_1)) \quad (b, f(b))$$

on the curve $y = f(x)$. We then approximate the area beneath the curve from a to b by the area under this single parabola. (Notice that *one* parabola is associated with the *two* vertical strips in the figure.) The area beneath the parabola turns out to be

$$[f(a) + 4f(x_1) + f(b)] \frac{\Delta x}{3}$$

Next suppose we use four vertical strips associated with the equally spaced subdivision points a, x_1, x_2, x_3, b. We fit one parabola to the set of three points

$$(a, f(a)) \quad (x_1, f(x_1)) \quad (x_2, f(x_2))$$

forming the first double strip, and another parabola to the three points

$$(x_2, f(x_2)) \quad (x_3, f(x_3)) \quad (b, f(b))$$

forming the second double strip to the right. The area beneath the first parabola is

$$[f(a) + 4f(x_1) + f(x_2)] \frac{\Delta x}{3}$$

and beneath the second parabola is

$$[f(x_2) + 4f(x_3) + f(b)] \frac{\Delta x}{3}$$

Thus the total area associated with the two parabolas is obtained by summing these last two expressions, giving the result

$$[f(a) + 4f(x_1) + 2f(x_2) + 4f(x_3) + f(b)] \frac{\Delta x}{3}$$

This last result then approximates the area beneath the original curve.

Now let's generalize the situation to an arbitrary number of strips. Since each parabola requires a *double* strip, the number of subintervals must be *even*. So let $y = f(x)$ be continuous over $a \leqslant x \leqslant b$, and divide the interval into an *even* number of pieces n, using the equally spaced points $a, x_1, x_2,$ $\ldots, x_{n-1}, b$. These results then generalize to the parabolic rule, more commonly known as *Simpson's rule:*

$$\int_a^b f(x)\, dx \approx [f(a) + 4f(x_1) + 2f(x_2) + 4f(x_3) + 2f(x_4) + \ldots$$
$$+ 2f(x_{n-2}) + 4f(x_{n-1}) + f(b)] \frac{\Delta x}{3}$$

As usual, $\Delta x = (b - a)/n$ is the width of each subinterval.

Simpson's rule is one of the most commonly used methods for numerically obtaining the value of a definite integral. The error is usually low, even for small values of n, and the method is easy to apply and easy to program on a computer. Other numerical methods improve upon these numerical techniques. One such improvement, which is presented in many numerical analysis texts, is called *Romberg integration,* but we will not discuss that method here.

We have purposely been omitting any discussion of error in the numerical methods we have been using to find definite integrals. Sooner or later we must come to grips with the question of error in order to know how close an approximation is to the true value we seek. There are formal and rigorous methods to put an upper bound on the error of these numerical approximations, and the upper bounds are derived in most of the standard calculus texts. These error bounds are important tools for theoretical considerations, but they are not easily computed on a calculating device like the TI-59. So they're not going to do us much good here, and that's the reason we've omitted the error analysis.

Instead we will take a very pragmatic approach, using our TI-59 program to get a feel for the error involved in a particular problem. We will work the problem for so many strips, and then work it again with the number of strips increased. If the change in the results occurs only after the fourth decimal place, for example, and we are interested in only two-place accuracy, we can be reasonably sure that the error is under control. We now turn to a discussion of the TI-59 program.

The prepared program INTEGRATE calculates the definite integral of a continuous function $y = f(x)$ over a closed interval $a \leqslant x \leqslant b$ by both the trapezoidal and Simpson's rules. The program is executed much like RECTANGLES, and we summarize the procedures below.

Using the Program INTEGRATE

The integrand function f is keyed in as a subroutine to be called by INTEGRATE. The first two steps of the subroutine must be

| Lb1 | C' |

and the last two steps must be

| INV | SBR |

INTEGRATE uses program steps 000 through 094, along with storage locations 01 through 06. Program steps 095 through 479, as well as memory locations 00 and 07 through 59, are available for use while evaluating $f(x)$.

After keying in the subroutine for $f(x)$, perform the following sequence of steps:

Step 1: Enter the number of subintervals n, and press $\boxed{E}$. *Remember:* If Simpson's rule is to give a correct result, the number n *must* be even.

Step 2: Enter the left endpoint a, and press $\boxed{A}$. The program halts with a displayed.

Step 3: Enter the right endpoint b, and press $\boxed{B}$. The program halts with $(b - a)/n$ displayed.

To obtain the definite integral by the *trapezoidal rule:*

Step 4: Press $\boxed{C}$. The program halts with the trapezoidal approximation in the display.

To obtain the definite integral by *Simpson's rule:*

Step 5: Press $\boxed{x \cdot t}$. The program displays Simpson's approximation to the definite integral.

Let's illustrate the procedures with several examples.

EXERCISE 1.
COMPARING THE TRAPEZOIDAL
AND SIMPSON'S RULES

Consider the function

$$f(x) = \sqrt{1 + x^2} \qquad \text{over } 0 \leqslant x \leqslant 10$$

investigated in the previous section. We will make a table of approximations to the definite integral of f over the given interval for various values of n using both the trapezoidal and Simpson's rules.

With INTEGRATE read into your calculator, key in the subroutine for $f(x)$:

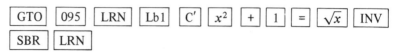

To approximate $\int_0^{10} \sqrt{1 + x^2}\, dx$ by the trapezoidal rule with $n = 10$:

(enter)	10		
(press)		E	Load $n = 10$.
(enter)	0		
(press)		A	Load $a = 0$.
(enter)	10		
(press)		B	Load $b = 10$.
(press)		C	The trapezoidal approximation 51.83109538 is displayed.

To approximate the definite integral by Simpson's rule with $n = 10$ (note that n is *even*):

(press)	$x \blacktriangleright t$	Simpson's approximation 51.75537271 is displayed.

Each time you change the number of subintervals n, you must repeat Steps 1–5 to obtain the approximations. Now verify the following table:

n	Trapezoidal Rule	Simpson's Rule	Running Time (sec)
10	51.83109538	51.75537271	23
20	51.76921935	51.74859400	42
30	51.75770289	51.74849198	63
40	51.75367207	51.74848964	81
100	51.74931878	51.74848958	197
200	51.74869688	51.74848958	394
500	51.74852275	51.74848958	985

Notice the increased accuracy of Simpson's rule over the trapezoidal rule. Such is generally the case when $\Delta x = (b - a)/n$ is small.

If $f(x)$ is a polynomial of degree less than 4, then the approximation by Simpson's rule gives the *exact* value of the definite integral. Yet the program POLYPROBE presented in Chapter 1 gives the exact value of the definite integral for *any* polynomial of degree less than 26. If you are integrating a polynomial, then we suggest you use POLYPROBE. (See Section 1.9 for a review of the procedures.)

Note that both the trapezoidal rule and Simpson's rule are dramatically more accurate than the rectangular rules. (Compare the results of the preceding table, for instance, with the values obtained in Exercises 1 and 3 of the previous section. You can see that we achieved four-decimal place accuracy to the value of the definite integral by Simpson's rule using only 30 subdivisions of the interval, whereas 500 subdivisions were required for the same level of accuracy by the midpoint rule.) Thus the numerical approximations discussed in this section are much faster to obtain on a calculator than are Riemann sums for a satisfactory level of accuracy.

EXERCISE 2.
A SECOND EXAMPLE

We will use INTEGRATE to find

$$\int_0^1 \frac{e^{-x^2/2}}{\sqrt{2\pi}}\, dx$$

This integral is an important one and encountered often in statistics. Key in the subroutine for the integrand:

| GTO | 095 | LRN | Lb1 | C′ | x^2 | ÷ | 2 | = | +/− | INV |

| $\ln x$ | ÷ | (| 2 | × | π |) | $\sqrt{x}$ | = | INV | SBR | LRN |

Verify the following table:

n	Trapezoidal Rule	Simpson's Rule	Running Time (sec)
4	0.3400818445	0.3413554879	12
8	0.3410295157	0.3413454061	22
12	0.3412046843	0.3413448760	30
16	0.3412659693	0.3413447871	38
20	0.3412943313	0.3413447629	46
40	0.3413321432	0.3413447471	90

Inspection of these results reveals that we do get more accuracy with more than sixteen subdivisions, but pay dearly for it in computation time. With sixteen strips we have achieved seven significant digits, which demonstrates that we can usually pick up all the accuracy we need. Most of the time, three or four significant digits is all we really require. The requirement for accuracy must be balanced against the time required to do the computations. Generally if a problem like this is to be run many times (perhaps to generate a table of values) and very little error is permitted, then we would turn to a digital computer rather than to the small programmable calculator.

In each of Problems 1–20, find the value of the definite integral specified by the given integrand over the indicated interval. Use both Simpson's rule and the trapezoidal rule, and give your answer correct to four decimals.

1. $f(x) = 1/x \quad 1 \leqslant x \leqslant 1.5$

2. $f(x) = \dfrac{1}{1 + x^2} \quad -1 \leqslant x \leqslant 1$

3. $f(x) = 6 + x - x^2 \quad -2 \leqslant x \leqslant 3$

4. $f(x) = \dfrac{1}{2}(1 - \cos 4x) \quad 0 \leqslant x \leqslant \pi/2$

5. $f(x) = (1 - x^2)^{-1/2} \quad -0.5 \leqslant x \leqslant 1/\sqrt{2}$

6. $f(x) = (25 - 4x^2)^{-1/2} \quad \dfrac{-5}{4} \leqslant x \leqslant \dfrac{5}{4}$

7. $f(x) = \sqrt{1 + x^4} \quad -1 \leqslant x \leqslant 1$

8. $f(x) = \dfrac{1}{1 + \cos x} \quad -\pi/3 \leqslant x \leqslant \pi/2$

9. $f(x) = \dfrac{x^2 - 2x + 5}{\sqrt{x}} \quad 1 \leqslant x \leqslant 3$

10. $f(x) = \sqrt{1 + \left(\dfrac{1}{x} - \dfrac{x}{4}\right)^2} \quad 1 \leqslant x \leqslant 2$

11. $f(x) = \dfrac{x^3 + 4x^2 + 4x + 1}{(x + 2)^2} \quad \dfrac{3}{2} \leqslant x \leqslant \dfrac{5}{2}$

12. $f(x) = \sec x \quad -\pi/4 \leqslant x \leqslant \pi/3$

13. $f(x) = \sin x \, \cos x \quad 0 \leqslant x \leqslant \pi/2$

14. $f(x) = \dfrac{1}{4 \sin^2 x + 3 \cos^2 x} \quad 0 \leqslant x \leqslant \pi/2$

15. $f(x) = \dfrac{1}{1 + \tan^3 x} \quad 0 \leqslant x \leqslant \pi/2$

16. $f(x) = \dfrac{x}{2 + 3x} \quad 0 \leqslant x \leqslant \dfrac{1}{3}$

17. $f(x) = \dfrac{x}{5 - x^2} \quad -1 \leqslant x \leqslant 2$

18. $f(x) = \dfrac{x}{\pi + x^4} \quad 0 \leqslant x \leqslant 1$

19. $f(x) = \dfrac{1}{3 + x + 2x^2} \quad -1 \leqslant x \leqslant 3$

20. $f(x) = \dfrac{x - 17}{x^2 + x - 12} \quad 4.5 \leqslant x \leqslant 6.5$

The following problems refer to the problems at the end of Section 4.1. Calculate the same definite integrals as you did in those problems, using Simpson's rule instead of the midpoint rule, finding five-place accuracy. By trial and error determine the number of subdivisions required for five-place accuracy, and compare your answer with the midpoint rule for 200 rectangles obtained previously.

21. Problem 13
22. Problem 14
23. Problem 19
24. Problem 17
25. Problem 18
26. Problem 20
27. Problem 16
28. Problem 15

Section 4.3 The Fundamental Theorem and Antidifferentiation

We have taken up the two limiting processes underlying the calculus. The first process is the limit of a certain quotient, yielding the derivative at a point. The second is the limit of a Riemann sum, yielding the definite integral. The derivative can be interpreted as the slope of the tangent line, and the integral can be interpreted as area under a curve (at least for a nonnegative function). There seems to be no apparent connection between these ideas, either in procedure or in interpretation. That is, limits of quotients are not like limits of sums, nor are slopes of lines like areas. One of the remarkable results of the calculus is that the derivative and the integral are, in fact, intimately connected. It turns out that the definite integral is obtained through reversing the process of differentiation. Let's see how this works.

For purposes of discussion it is easier to use a positive continuous function to interpret the integral as area. So we assume that $y = f(t)$ is a positive continuous function over the interval $a \leqslant t \leqslant b$. Pick an arbitrary but fixed point x in the interval, and associate with it the area $A(x)$ lying beneath the graph of f, above the t-axis, and between the vertical lines $t = a$ and $t = x$, just as before. The situation is depicted in Figure 4.4. The varying area A is then a function of the right-hand edge x. We are going to show that

$$A'(x) = f(x)$$

The derivative $A'(x)$ is the limit of $\Delta A/\Delta x$ as $\Delta x \to 0$. Let's look at ΔA geometrically. When x is varied by an increment Δx, we obtain a new area $A(x + \Delta x)$ beneath the graph of $y = f(t)$ from $t = a$ to $t = x + \Delta x$. Thus the area changes by an increment

$$\Delta A = A(x + \Delta x) - A(x)$$

which is the area beneath the graph between the vertical lines $t = x$ and $t = x + \Delta x$ shown in Figure 4.5.

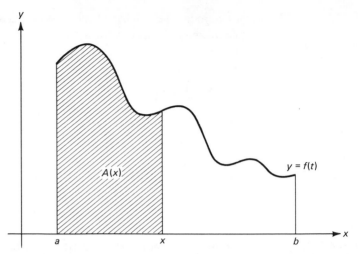

Figure 4.4 The area beneath the curve $y = f(t)$ and above the t-axis from $t = a$ to $t = x$ is symbolized by $A(x)$.

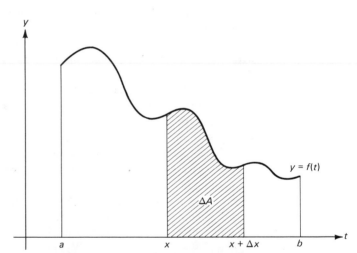

Figure 4.5 When x is incremented by Δx, the area changes by an increment ΔA.

Let $f(m)$ and $f(M)$ denote, respectively, the minimum and maximum values of f assumed over the subinterval $x \leqslant t \leqslant x + \Delta x$. Then in every case

$$f(m) \, \Delta x < \Delta A < f(M) \, \Delta x$$

because the area of the small rectangle with height $f(m)$ and base Δx, as shown in Figure 4.6, is less than the area ΔA beneath the curve, which in turn is less than the area of the larger rectangle with height $f(M)$. For positive Δx this translates to

$f(m) < \dfrac{\Delta A}{\Delta x} < f(M)$

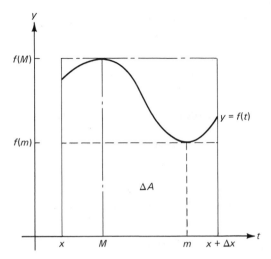

Figure 4.6 The incremental area ΔA lies between the areas of the small rectangle of height $f(m)$ and the large rectangle of height $f(M)$.

Now, as $\Delta x \to 0$, both m and M approach x. The continuity of f then implies that $f(m)$ and $f(M)$ both approach $f(x)$. Therefore

$$\lim_{\Delta x \to 0} \frac{\Delta A}{\Delta x} = f(x)$$

The argument is the same if Δx is negative except that all these inequalities are reversed.

All the preceding discussion can be translated into the language of definite integrals for arbitrary continuous functions. The area $A(x)$ corresponds to the definite integral

$$\int_a^x f(t)\, dt$$

which is now viewed as a function of the upper limit of integration x. (The variable t beneath the integral symbol is just a "dummy variable." It can be any symbol and serves only as a "placeholder." It has no significance to the meaning attached to the definite integral.) The derivative of this integral function with respect to the upper limit of integration x is then the integrand function f evaluated at x. This is the content of the following result.

The Fundamental Theorem of Calculus, Part I

Let f be a continuous function over the interval $a \leqslant x \leqslant b$. Then the function defined by

$$F(x) = \int_a^x f(t)\, dt$$

is differentiable for every x satisfying $a < x < b$, and

$$F'(x) = f(x).$$

219

In other words, the process of differentiation "undoes" the process of integration:

$$\frac{d}{dx}\left(\int_a^x f(t)\, dt\right) = f(x)$$

Let's formalize this idea of "antidifferentiation."

> **Definition.** If $y = F(x)$ is a differentiable function over the domain $a < x < b$ such that
>
> $$F'(x) = f(x)$$
>
> then $F(x)$ is said to be an *antiderivative* of $f(x)$.

In this terminology, the integral function

$$\int_a^x f(t)\, dt$$

is an antiderivative of the function $f(x)$. Let's consider some specific examples.
The function $F(x) = x^2 + 5$ is an antiderivative of $f(x) = 2x$ because

$$\frac{d}{dx}(x^2 + 5) = 2x$$

The function $F(x) = \sin^2 x$ is an antiderivative of $f(x) = 2 \sin x \cos x$ because

$$\frac{d}{dx}(\sin^2 x) = 2 \sin x \cos x$$

The function $F(x) = x^2 - 7\pi$ is an antiderivative of $f(x) = 2x$. Indeed,

$$y = x^2 + C$$

is an antiderivative of $f(x) = 2x$ if C is any constant.

Notice that $F(x) = x^{n+1}/(n + 1) + C$ is an antiderivative of $f(x) = x^n$ for every constant C, because $F'(x) = f(x)$. This is a useful rule to remember.

The next result specifies how the definite integral is obtained through antidifferentiation.

The Fundamental Theorem of Calculus, Part II

> Let f be a continuous function over $a \leqslant x \leqslant b$. If $G(x)$ is any antiderivative of $f(x)$ over $a < x < b$, then
>
> $$\int_a^b f(x)\, dx = G(b) - G(a)$$

While the proof of this last theorem is not difficult, it is found in most standard calculus texts, and so we are going to omit the proof here. Let's look at several illustrations of the theorem. We use the notation

$$G(x)\Big|_a^b = G(b) - G(a).$$

EXERCISE 1.
EVALUATING A DEFINITE INTEGRAL

Let's evaluate

$$\int_1^2 x^3 \, dx$$

using the Fundamental Theorem. Now $F(x) = x^4/4$ is an antiderivative of $f(x) = x^3$ because $F'(x) = f(x)$. Thus

$$\int_1^2 x^3 \, dx = \frac{x^4}{4}\Big|_1^2 = \frac{1}{4}(2)^4 - \frac{1}{4}(1)^4 = 4 - \frac{1}{4} = 3.75$$

Compare this result with that found in Problem 1 in the problem set for Section 4.1.

EXERCISE 2.
A SECOND EXAMPLE

Evaluate

$$\int_{-\pi/2}^{\pi/2} \cos x \, dx$$

Solution. The function $F(x) = \sin x$ is an antiderivative of $F(x) = \cos x$ because $F'(x) = f(x)$. Thus by the Fundamental Theorem,

$$\int_{-\pi/2}^{\pi/2} \cos x \, dx = \sin x\Big|_{-\pi/2}^{\pi/2} = \sin\left(\frac{\pi}{2}\right) - \sin\left(-\frac{\pi}{2}\right) = 2$$

Compare this analytic result with that obtained in Exercise 4 of Section 4.1, where we used the midpoint rule.

EXERCISE 3.
DIFFERENTIATING AN INTEGRAL

Suppose for all values of x the function F is given by

$$F(x) = \int_0^x t^2 \sin t \, dt$$

Then, by the first part of the Fundamental Theorem,

$$F'(x) = x^2 \sin x$$

This is obtained by merely evaluating the integrand $f(t) = t^2 \sin t$ at the upper limit x. The value of the lower limit, provided that it is a constant, is immaterial to the differentiation process.

EXERCISE 4.
THE INTEGRAL OF A DERIVATIVE

If $y = G(x)$ is any differentiable function, then by the Fundamental Theorem,

$$\int_a^x G'(t)\, dt = G(t)\Big]_a^x = G(x) - G(a)$$

That is, the result of integrating the derivative is the original function altered by at most a constant. You now see that the two basic processes of calculus, differentiation and integration, are inverses of each other in the sense that each process "undoes" the other one. It is customary to write

$$\int G'(x)\, dx = G(x) + C$$

for this integration process, where C denotes an arbitrary constant. In this notation, for instance,

$$\int x^n\, dx = \frac{x^{n+1}}{n+1} + C$$

EXERCISE 5.
FINDING DISTANCE
FROM ACCELERATION AND SPEED

In previous chapters you have determined by differentiation the velocity and acceleration of a particle from the equation of its distance traveled along a straight line. Let's reverse the process: that is, given the acceleration at any time and the velocity at a particular instant, find the distance traveled at any instant of time. Here's an example.

A projectile is fired upward from the ground with an initial speed of 1,450 ft/sec. Find its height after t seconds.

Solution. The acceleration due to gravity is approximately the constant value 32 ft/sec^2. Since this *retards* the upward motion of the projectile, the acceleration is negative. Hence

$$a = \frac{dv}{dt} = -32$$

Then, for any time t, the velocity is obtained by integrating the acceleration with respect to time:

$$v = \int a \, dt = -32t + A$$

where A is a constant. Since $v = 1,450$ ft/sec when $t = 0$, we obtain $A = 1,450$ from the previous equation. Thus

$$v = \frac{ds}{dt} = -32t + 1,450$$

Integration of this last expression gives

$$s = -16t^2 + 1,450t + B$$

where B is a constant. Since the projectile is fired from the ground, $s = 0$ when $t = 0$ implying that $B = 0$. Therefore

$$s = -16t^2 + 1,450t$$

is an equation giving the height of the projectile at any time t in seconds after the initial firing.

EXERCISE 6.
DETERMINING TOTAL COST
FROM MARGINAL COST

A manufacturer finds that the marginal cost is $5x^3 - 3x^2 - 50x + 750$ dollars per unit after x units have been produced. The total cost of producing the first 4 units is $3,500. What is the total cost of producing the first 7 units?

Solution. Recall from Exercise 3 of Section 3.1 that marginal cost is the derivative of the total cost function C. Thus

$$C(x) = \int (5x^3 - 3x^2 - 50x + 750) \, dx$$
$$= \frac{5}{4}x^4 - x^3 - 25x^2 + 750x + K$$

for some constant K. Since $C = 3,500$ when $x = 4$, we find that

$$3,500 = \frac{5}{4}(4)^4 - (4)^3 - 25(4)^2 + 750(4) + K$$

or, solving for K, $K = 644$. Thus

$$C(x) = \frac{5}{4}x^4 - x^3 - 25x^2 + 750x + 644$$

The cost of producing the first 7 units is then

$$C(7) = \frac{5}{4}(7)^4 - (7)^3 - 25(7)^2 + 750(7) + 644$$

$$= \$7,327.25$$

A number of important and useful properties are associated with the definite integral, all of which are derived in any standard calculus text. We list them here for reference purposes, but omit any proofs.

Properties of the Definite Integral

Assume f and g are continuous on an interval containing a, b, and c. Then the following properties are true.

1. $\int_a^b k f(x) \, dx = k \int_a^b f(x) \, dx$ for any constant k

2. $\int_a^b [f(x) + g(x)] \, dx = \int_a^b f(x) \, dx + \int_a^b g(x) \, dx$

3. $\int_a^b f(x) \, dx = \int_a^c f(x) \, dx + \int_c^b f(x) \, dx$

4. $\int_b^a f(x) \, dx = - \int_a^b f(x) \, dx$

5. If $f(x) \geqslant 0$ on $a \leqslant x \leqslant b$, then $\int_a^b f(x) \, dx \geqslant 0$

6. $\left| \int_a^b f(x) \, dx \right| \leqslant \int_a^b | f(x) | \, dx$

PROBLEMS 4.3

In each of Problems 1–14, evaluate the integrals and check your results by differentiating the answers. Include an arbitrary constant.

1. $\int 5x^7 \, dx$

2. $\int \left(x + \frac{4}{x^2} \right) dx$

3. $\int (x^{1/3} + x^{-1/2}) \, dx$

4. $\int x(x-1)^2 \, dx$

5. $\int \frac{x^2 - 1}{\sqrt{x}} \, dx$

6. $\int (4 \sin x - 5 \cos x) \, dx$

7. $\int (3e^x - \sec^2 x) \, dx$

8. $\int (2e^{-x} + \sec x \, \tan x) \, dx$

9. $\int \left(\frac{3}{\sin^2 x} - \frac{7}{x^2} \right) dx$

10. $\int \frac{\sin x}{\cos^2 x} \, dx$

11. $\int(\sqrt{\theta} + \sin \theta) \, d\theta$

12. $\int\left(\phi + \dfrac{2}{\cos^2 \phi}\right) \, d\phi$

13. $\int(1 - y^2)^2 \, dy$

14. $\int \dfrac{\cos t}{\sin^2 t} (1 + \cos t) \, dt$

In Problems 15-18, find the areas beneath the specified curves over the given intervals, using the Fundamental Theorem.

15. $y = x^3 + 2x + 1 \qquad 0 \leqslant x \leqslant 2$

16. $y = e^x \qquad -1 \leqslant x \leqslant 3$

17. $y = \sqrt{x} \qquad 2 \leqslant x \leqslant 5$

18. $y = \sin x \qquad 0 \leqslant x \leqslant \pi/2$

19. The speed of a moving particle in feet per second is given by $v = 3.6t^2 - 0.44t^3$. Find the distance traveled from $t = 0$ to $t = 3$.

20. A hockey puck is knocked across smooth ice with an initial speed of 54 ft/sec. If the speed decreases at the rate of 2 ft/sec^2, how far does the puck travel before it comes to rest?

21. A projectile is fired straight upward from a platform 500 ft above the ground with an initial speed of 928 ft/sec.

a. How high does it go?

b. And when does it strike the ground?

22. A particular curve $y = f(x)$ satisfies the property that the slope of the tangent line at any point x is given by $9x^2 - 4x + 2$. Find an equation for the curve if it passes through the point $(-1, 2)$.

23. The marginal cost for producing x items is given by

$$0.25 + \frac{7{,}000}{x^2}$$

If the cost of producing 1,000 items is \$6,000, find the total cost as a function of x.

Section 4.4 Two Analytic Methods of Integration

In the previous section you saw that the process of determining a definite integral can be carried out by first finding an antiderivative of the integrand and then simply taking the difference of the antiderivative values at the limits of integration. We refer to this process as *analytic integration*. To integrate analytically, it is necessary to learn special techniques for finding antiderivatives. Extensive tables of antiderivatives, called *integral tables*, have also been developed to facilitate the finding of antiderivatives. Today we can determine quite easily the value of a definite integral to a high degree of accuracy by numerical methods with the aid of a calculator or computer. For us it is not so necessary to learn an assortment of integration techniques. Yet two techniques are of particular importance, because they can frequently be used, and are based upon specific properties of the integral. The first technique is *integration by substitution,* and the second is *integration by parts.* We will discuss these two methods in this section.

Integration by Substitution

This method is based on the chain rule, that is, on the rule for differentiating a composite function. If $y = f(u)$ and $u = g(x)$, then the chain rule says that

$$\frac{dy}{dx} = \frac{dy}{du} \cdot \frac{du}{dx}$$

where it is assumed that f is a differentiable function of u and that g is a differentiable function of x. Consequently, if it is required to find an antiderivative

$$\int h[g(x)] \, g'(x) \, dx$$

you can find the antiderivative

$$\int h(u) \, du$$

and in the result replace u by $g(x)$.

In applying the substitution rule you first have to decide on the substitution you wish to make. That is, to find the integral

$$\int h[g(x)] \, g'(x) \, dx$$

you must decide on the expression $g(x)$ for which you will substitute the variable u. The factor $g'(x)$ must already be present in the integrand so that du can be substituted for $g'(x) \, dx$, thereby converting the original integral to

$$\int h(u) \, du$$

Next you perform the integration for this last integral in terms of u, and finally substitute the expression $g(x)$ for u in the result. Let's consider several examples.

EXERCISE 1.

Evaluate $\int 2x \sin(x^2) \, dx$.

Solution. Let $u = x^2$ so that $du = 2x \, dx$. Notice that the factor $2x$, which is the derivative of u with respect to x, is part of the integrand. By substitution,

$$\int 2x \sin(x^2) \, dx = \int \sin u \, du = -\cos u + C = -\cos(x^2) + C$$

EXERCISE 2.
ADJUSTMENT BY A CONSTANT MULTIPLE

Frequently you have to multiply by a constant to get the factor $g'(x)\,dx$ exactly. For instance, to find

$$\int xe^{-x^2}\,dx$$

try setting $u = -x^2$ so that $du = -2x\,dx$. The factor $-2x\,dx$ does not quite appear in the integrand, but

$$x\,dx = -\frac{1}{2}\,du$$

does appear. Then the constant $-1/2$ can be factored out from the integrand after the substitution, as follows:

$$\int xe^{-x^2}\,dx = \int e^{-x^2}\,(x\,dx) = \int e^u\,\left(-\frac{1}{2}\,du\right) = -\frac{1}{2}\int e^u\,du$$

$$= -\frac{1}{2}e^u + C = -\frac{1}{2}e^{-x^2} + C$$

EXERCISE 3.

Evaluate $\displaystyle\int \frac{x\,dx}{(5x^2 - 1)^3}$.

Solution. Let $u = 5x^2 - 1$ so that $du = 10x\,dx$. Then,

$$\int \frac{x\,dx}{(5x^2 - 1)^3} = \int \frac{(du/10)}{u^3} = \frac{1}{10}\int u^{-3}\,du = \left(\frac{1}{10}\right)\left(-\frac{1}{2}\right)u^{-2} + C$$

$$= -\frac{1}{20}(5x^2 - 1)^{-2} + C$$

Integration by Parts

This method is based on the product rule. If $u = f(x)$ and $v = g(x)$ are both differentiable functions of x, then

$$\frac{d(uv)}{dx} = u\frac{dv}{dx} + v\frac{du}{dx}$$

or

$$u\frac{dv}{dx} = \frac{d(uv)}{dx} - v\frac{du}{dx}$$

The corresponding integration formula is

$$\int u \, dv = uv - \int v \, du + C$$

The idea behind using the integration by parts formula is the conversion of one integral, $\int u \, dv$, into a second integral, $\int v \, du$, which is easier to obtain. The following examples illustrate the technique.

EXERCISE 4.

Evaluate $\int xe^x \, dx$.

     Solution. In applying integration by parts to an integral, you must first decide which part of the integrand to call u and which to call dv, so that the integral takes the form $\int u \, dv$. As a general rule, pick dv to be the most complicated part of the integrand from which v is still readily obtainable. In this example, pick $dv = e^x \, dx$, in which case $u = x$. Then, $v = e^x$ and $du = dx$, and the integral becomes

$$\int xe^x \, dx = xe^x - \int e^x \, dx + C = xe^x - e^x + C$$

EXERCISE 5.
A REPEATED APPLICATION
OF INTEGRATION BY PARTS

To evaluate

$$\int x^2 \cos x \, dx$$

let $dv = \cos x \, dx$ and $u = x^2$. Then $v = \sin x$ and $du = 2x \, dx$ so the integral becomes

$$\int x^2 \cos x \, dx = x^2 \sin x - \int \sin x \, (2x \, dx) + C$$
$$= x^2 \sin x - 2 \int x \sin x \, dx + C$$

By applying integration by parts to the integral on the right using $dV = \sin x \, dx$, $U = x$, $V = -\cos x$, and $dU = dx$, we obtain

$$\int x^2 \cos x \, dx = x^2 \sin x - 2 [x(-\cos x) - \int(-\cos x) \, dx] + C$$
$$= x^2 \sin x + 2x \cos x - 2 \sin x + C$$

EXERCISE 6.

Evaluate $\int e^x \sin x \, dx$.

     Solution. Let $dv = \sin x \, dx$ and $u = e^x$. Then $v = -\cos x$ and $du = e^x \, dx$ so the integral becomes

$$\int e^x \sin x \, dx = e^x (-\cos x) - \int (-\cos x)(e^x \, dx) + C$$

$$= -e^x \cos x + \int e^x \cos x \, dx + C$$

At first sight it appears that we have accomplished nothing, for the integral on the right is just as complicated as the original one. But now we apply integration by parts again to that new integral: Let $dV = \cos x \, dx$ and $U = e^x$. Then $V = \sin x$ and $dU = e^x \, dx$, which gives

$$\int e^x \cos x \, dx = e^x \sin x - \int e^x \sin x \, dx$$

(We omit introducing another arbitrary constant here because it will be subsumed by C.) Putting this last result together with our previous integration, we have

$$\int e^x \sin x \, dx = -e^x \cos x + e^x \sin x - \int e^x \sin x \, dx + C$$

In this last equation we collect the two terms involving the unknown integral to obtain

$$2 \int e^x \sin x \, dx = e^x (\sin x - \cos x) + C$$

or

$$\int e^x \sin x \, dx = \frac{e^x}{2} (\sin x - \cos x) + K$$

where the arbitrary constant K is just the old arbitrary constant C divided by 2.

PROBLEMS 4.4

In each of Problems 1-12, evaluate the integrals by the method of substitution. Check your results by differentiating the answers.

1. $\int \cos 2x \, dx$

2. $\int e^{-x} \, dx$

3. $\int x \sqrt{x^2 - 3} \, dx$

4. $\int w \sqrt{w - 2} \, dw$

5. $\int x^3 (x^4 - 2)^{2/3} dx$

6. $\int \dfrac{3x^2 - 1}{(x^3 - x)^2} \, dx$

7. $\int \dfrac{\sqrt{x}}{\sqrt{1 + x^{3/2}}} \, dx$

8. $\int \dfrac{\sin \sqrt{x}}{\sqrt{x}} \, dx$

9. $\int \sin x \sec^2 x \, dx$

10. $\int \dfrac{1 + \sin x}{\cos^2 x}\, dx$

11. $\int \sin y\; e^{\cos y}\, dy$

12. $\int \sec^3 x \tan x\, dx$

In problems 13–22, evaluate the integrals by the method of integration by parts. Check your results by differentiating the answers. Be sure to include an arbitrary constant.

13. $\int x \cos x\, dx$

14. $\int x^2 \sin x\, dx$

15. $\int \sin^2 x\, dx$

16. $\int e^{2x} \cos 5x\, dx$

17. $\int e^{-t} \sin 2t\, dt$

18. $\int x^2\, e^{-x}\, dx$

19. $\int \cos^2 \theta\, d\theta$

20. $\int x \sin(2x + 1)\, dx$

21. $\int \sin^4 y\, dy$ (Hint: $u = \sin^3 y$)

22. $\int e^{ax} \cos(bx)\, dx$

In Problems 23–30, evaluate the integrals.

23. $\int \dfrac{x}{\sqrt{1 - x}}\, dx$ (Hint: $u = \sqrt{1 - x}$)

24. $\int \dfrac{y^3}{\sqrt{1 + y^2}}\, dy$

25. $\int e^{2t} \sin(e^t)\, dt$

26. $\int \cos^3 \theta\, d\theta$

27. $\int \cos^3 x \sqrt{\sin x}\, dx$

28. $\int x \sqrt{x + 1}\, dx$

29. $\int x \sin^2 x \cos x\, dx$

30. $\int \tan^2 z\, dz$

Section 4.5 The Natural Logarithm Function

Consider the reciprocal function $y = 1/t$, $t > 0$. For every number $x > 1$, this function is continuous over the interval $1 \leqslant t \leqslant x$. Thus, by Part I of the Fundamental Theorem, the integral

$$\int_1^x \frac{1}{t}\, dt$$

specifies a function of x: It gives the area under the curve $y = 1/t$ from $t = 1$ to $t = x$. If $0 < x < 1$, then

$$\int_1^x \frac{1}{t}\, dt = -\int_x^1 \frac{1}{t}\, dt \qquad\qquad (4.1)$$

so that the integral function is defined for all positive values of x. This function, called the *natural logarithm*, is denoted by $\ln x$ (the symbol "ln" is read "ell-en"). Thus

$$\ln x = \int_1^x \frac{1}{t}\,dt \qquad x > 0 \tag{4.2}$$

From the Fundamental Theorem the natural logarithm function is differentiable, and therefore continuous, at every point $x > 0$. Moreover, the derivative is given by

$$\frac{d}{dx}(\ln x) = \frac{1}{x} \tag{4.3}$$

Since $1/x$ is positive for $x > 0$, the logarithm is everywhere an increasing function of x. The second derivative of the logarithm function is

$$\frac{d^2}{dx^2}(\ln x) = -\frac{1}{x^2} \tag{4.4}$$

so the second derivative is always negative. Thus the natural logarithm is everywhere concave downward.

If $x > 1$, then the definite integral in Equation 4.2 is positive because $1/t$ is positive. If $0 < x < 1$, the integral is negative from 4.1. So $\ln x > 0$ if $x > 1$ and $\ln x < 0$ if $0 < x < 1$. Finally, $\ln 1 = 0$ because

$$\int_1^1 \frac{1}{t}\,dt = 0$$

Using Simpson's rule in the program INTEGRATE, you can verify the following values of the natural logarithm (using $n = 100$):

$$\ln 0.25 = \int_1^{0.25} \frac{dt}{t} \approx -1.386294388$$

and

$$\ln 2 = \int_1^2 \frac{dt}{t} \approx 0.6931471809$$

Both values are accurate to at least seven decimals.

Your TI–59 calculator has the natural logarithm function built into its hardware. The key $\boxed{\ln x}$ calculates the natural logarithm of whatever number is in the display at the time. The number in the display must be positive, or the calculator produces a flashing result to signal an error. Using the key $\boxed{\ln x}$, verify the following table:

x	ln x	x	ln x
0.0001	−9.210340372	2.0	0.6931471809
0.01	−4.605170186	2.5	0.9162907319
0.10	−2.302585093	3.0	1.098612289
0.25	−1.386294361	5.0	1.609437912
0.50	−0.6931471806	100	4.605170186
0.75	−0.2876820725	1000	6.907755279
1.00	0.	10^6	13.81551056
1.5	0.4054651081	10^{20}	46.05170186

It can be verified that $\ln x \to -\infty$ as $x \to 0^+$: Thus the y-axis is a vertical asymptote. Figure 4.7 presents the graph of the natural logarithm function.

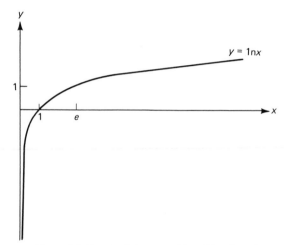

Figure 4.7 Graph of the natural logarithm function.

EXERCISE 1.
AREA UNDER THE GRAPH OF $y = 1/t$.

From the defining equation

$$\ln N = \int_1^N \frac{dt}{t}$$

you see that when $N > 1$, the number $\ln N$ gives the area trapped beneath the curve of $y = 1/t$ and above the t-axis, between the vertical lines $t = 1$ and $t = N$. Thus the area under the curve $y = 1/t$ between $t = 1$ and $t = 2$ is $\ln 2$; between $t = 1$ and $t = 5$, it is $\ln 5$; and so forth. In Exercise 3 of Section 2.4 the irrational number e, which is approximately equal to 2.718281828459045, is that number for which the area under the curve equals exactly one square unit. That is, the number e is defined by the equation

232

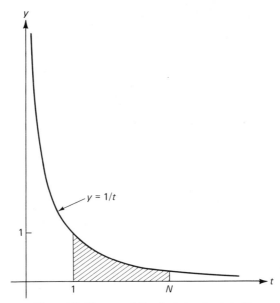

Figure 4.8 The area of the shaded region is ln N.

$$\int_1^e \frac{dt}{t} = 1$$

So ln e = 1. You have also seen (see Exercise 2, Section 2.6) that:

$$e = \lim_{x \to 0} (1 + x)^{1/x}$$

Relationship Between the Natural Logarithm and Exponential Functions

The natural logarithm and exponential functions are related by the basic equations

$$y = e^x \quad \text{if and only if} \quad \ln y = x \tag{4.5}$$

Mathematically, we say that the two functions are *inverses* of each other because each function "undoes" the other one. Symbolically, in terms of composition of functions, this relationship means that

$$\ln (e^x) = x \quad \text{for } every \text{ number } x \tag{4.6}$$

and

$$e^{\ln y} = y \quad \text{for every } positive \text{ number } y \tag{4.7}$$

Because the values of the exponential e^x are always positive (never zero or negative), both of the Equations 4.6 and 4.7 make sense.

233

For all positive numbers a and b, the following are true:

1. $\ln(ab) = \ln a + \ln b$
2. $\ln(1/a) = -\ln a$
3. $\ln(a/b) = \ln a - \ln b$
4. $\ln a^p = p \ln a$ for *every* real number p

The logarithm was developed originally by John Napier in 1614. It was especially useful in astronomical calculations because it reduced the task of complicated multiplications to essentially an addition problem via property 1 above. Today we can complete complicated arithmetic tasks on an electronic calculator like the TI-59, or on a computer, so that particular application of the logarithm is not so important to us. Nevertheless, the natural logarithm function has many other useful applications in various branches of science and mathematics. Let's consider several problems involving the use of the logarithm.

EXERCISE 2.
DIFFERENTIATING A LOGARITHM

Let us find dy/dx if $y = \ln(2x - 3x^5)$. From the chain rule,

$$\frac{dy}{dx} = \frac{dy}{du} \cdot \frac{du}{dx}$$

we find that

$$\frac{d}{dx} \ln(2x - 3x^5) = \frac{1}{2x - 3x^5} \cdot \frac{d(2x - 3x^5)}{dx} = \frac{2 - 15x^4}{2x - 3x^5}$$

EXERCISE 3.

Evaluate $\int \tan x \, dx$.

Solution. Since $\tan x = \sin x / \cos x$, we use the substitution rule with $u = \cos x$ and $du = -\sin x \, dx$. Thus

$$\int \tan x \, dx = \int \frac{\sin x}{\cos x} \, dx = \int \frac{-du}{u} = -\ln|u| + C$$

$$= -\ln|\cos x| + C = \ln|\sec x| + C$$

Notice that we employ the absolute value symbol $|u|$ to ensure that the logarithm is applied to a positive quantity.

EXERCISE 4.
A TROUBLESOME NUMERICAL INTEGRATION

There are situations when numerical integration works, but nevertheless encounters difficulties.* We will consider an example here. The problem is to evaluate the integral

$$\int_{0.01}^{1} \frac{dx}{e^x - 1}$$

This problem may look innocent enough at first glance, but notice that the integrand tends to $+\infty$ as x approaches 0. Thus we can guess that the function is increasing very rapidly at $x = 0.01$, which may prove to be a problem for numerical methods. Suppose we decide to try Simpson's rule anyway. Key in the integrand as a subroutine to INTEGRATE and verify the following table:

n	Simpson's Rule	Running Time (sec)
4	9.925645004	8
8	6.423119546	16
16	4.923714076	30
32	4.362347662	58
64	4.193951775	115

The answer, correct to ten significant digits, is 4.151490874. With 64 subintervals we have succeeded in generating only two correct digits in the answer, and it turns out that 8,192 subintervals are required to obtain ten significant digits (which would take about four hours to compute).

The difficulty hinges on the fact that

$$f(x) = \frac{1}{e^x - 1}$$

"blows up" at $x = 0$. Now it happens that for small values of x, e^x behaves much like $(1 + x)$. You should verify this by evaluating both functions on your calculator for a few small numbers:

x	e^x	$1 + x$
0.25	1.284025417	1.25
0.10	1.105170918	1.10
0.05	1.051271096	1.05
0.02	1.020201340	1.02
0.01	1.010050167	1.01

*This example appeared in Herbert D. Peckham and the author, *Calculator Calculus* (Naval Postgraduate School publication), p. 2-27.

235

Thus for small values of x,

$$\frac{1}{e^x - 1} \approx \frac{1}{(1 + x) - 1} = \frac{1}{x}$$

This arrangement suggests a possible solution to the numerical integration problem. We can use the function $1/x$ to convert the original function into an equivalent one:

$$f(x) = \frac{1}{e^x - 1} = \left(\frac{1}{e^x - 1} - \frac{1}{x}\right) + \frac{1}{x}$$

Thus, using the additive property of the definite integral,

$$\int_{0.01}^{1} \frac{dx}{e^x - 1} = \int_{0.01}^{1} \left(\frac{1}{e^x - 1} - \frac{1}{x}\right) dx + \int_{0.01}^{1} \frac{dx}{x}$$

First, we determine the value of the second integral analytically.

$$\int_{0.01}^{1} \frac{dx}{x} = -\int_{1}^{0.01} \frac{dx}{x} = - \ln 0.01 = 4.605170186$$

correct to ten significant digits. So the original problem is converted to

$$\int_{0.01}^{1} \frac{dx}{e^x - 1} = \int_{0.01}^{1} \left(\frac{1}{e^x - 1} - \frac{1}{x}\right) dx + 4.605170186$$

It may seem that we have made the problem more complicated than before. Yet there is a dramatic improvement in the value of the integral via numerical integration because the new integrand function is better behaved at $x = 0$. As a matter of fact,

$$\lim_{x \to 0} \left(\frac{1}{e^x - 1} - \frac{1}{x}\right) = -\frac{1}{2}$$

which can be verified using LIMIT (you should perform this verification now). The result is that the numerical calculations in Simpson's rule are much more effective. To see this, read INTEGRATE into your TI-59 and key in the subroutine for the new integrand:

GTO	095	LRN	Lbl	C′	STO	00	INV	ln x	−	1
=	1/x	−	RCL	00	1/x	=	INV	SBR	LRN	

With the lower limit $a = 0.01$ and the upper limit $b = 1$, verify the following table for the integral:

n	Simpson's Rule	Running Time (sec)
4	−0.4536792729	10
8	−0.4536793092	21
16	−0.4536793116	41
32	−0.4536793119	80

Therefore

$$\int_{0.01}^{1} \frac{dx}{e^x - 1} = -0.4536793119 + 4.605170186 = 4.151490874$$

By splitting the original problem into one that is part numerical and part analytical, the answer has been nailed down to ten significant digits with only 32 strips and 80 seconds calculating time. This certainly compares favorably with 8,192 strips and four hours running time using a straight application of Simpson's rule. This same strategy will not work for every problem of this kind, but it does illustrate how some numerical problems can be resolved when they are combined with analytic methods. Such strategies are considered in many numerical analysis texts.

EXERCISE 5.
GROWTH OF BACTERIA

The number of bacteria in a yeast culture grows at a rate proportional to the number present. If the population of a colony of yeast bacteria doubles in 50 min, how many bacteria will be present at the end of 3.5 hrs?

Solution. Let $x = x(t)$ denote the number of bacteria present at any time t. Then, for some constant k of proportionality, we are given that

$$\frac{dx}{dt} = kx$$

or

$$\frac{dx}{x} = k \, dt$$

We integrate both sides of this last equation to obtain

$$\ln x = kt + C \tag{4.9}$$

If x_0 denotes the original number of bacteria present, then this last equation implies that

$$\ln x_0 = k \cdot 0 + C \quad \text{or} \quad C = \ln x_0$$

Substitution into Equation 4.9 gives

$$\ln x = kt + \ln x_0$$

or

$$\ln x - \ln x_0 = kt$$

which implies that

$$\ln\left(\frac{x}{x_0}\right) = kt \tag{4.10}$$

When $t = 50$, $x = 2x_0$ so that

$$k \cdot 50 = \ln (2x_0/x_0) = \ln 2$$

Substitution of this value of k into Equation 4.10 then gives

$$\ln\left(\frac{x}{x_0}\right) = \frac{\ln 2}{50}t$$

Finally, when $t = 3.5$ hrs $= 210$ min,

$$\ln\left(\frac{x}{x_0}\right) = \frac{\ln 2}{50} \cdot 210$$

or, upon taking the exponential of both sides,

$$\frac{x}{x_0} = e^{(210)(\ln 2)/50}$$

or

$$x = x_0 \, e^{(210)(\ln 2)/50}$$
$$\approx (18.38)x_0$$

So, at the end of 3.5 hrs, approximately 18.38 times the original number of bacteria will be present.

PROBLEMS 4.5

In each of Problems 1-6, find dy/dx.

1. $y = \ln \sqrt{x^2 - 3}$

2. $y = (\ln x)^2$

3. $y = x^3 \ln x$

4. $y = \ln (e^{2x})$

5. $y = \ln \left(\dfrac{x}{x+1} \right)$

6. $y = \ln (\sec x + \tan x)$

In Problems 7–12, evaluate the integrals.

7. $\int \dfrac{x}{x^2 + 1}\, dx$

8. $\int \dfrac{\cos x}{1 + \sin x}\, dx$

9. $\int \dfrac{dx}{x \ln x}$

10. $\int \dfrac{e^{2y}}{1 + e^{2y}}\, dy$

11. $\int \dfrac{1}{t} \sin (\ln t)\, dt$

12. $\int \dfrac{dt}{\sin t \cos t}$

In Problems 13–16, integrate by parts.

13. $\int \ln x\, dx$ (Hint: let $u = \ln x$)

14. $\int \sin (\ln x)\, dx$

15. $\int x (\ln x)\, dx$

16. $\int (\ln x)^2\, dx$

17. Determine the value of the integral

$$\int_0^1 e^{-\sqrt{x}}\, dx$$

accurate to seven significant digits.

18. Determine the value of the integral

$$\int_{0.01}^1 \dfrac{dx}{e^{x^2} - 1}$$

accurate to eight significant digits.

19. Using the fact that $\cos x$ behaves much like $1 - \dfrac{x^2}{2}$ for small values of x, find

$$\int_\epsilon^{\pi/4} \dfrac{dx}{1 - \cos x}$$

accurate to eight significant digits when:

a. $\epsilon = 0.05$

b. $\epsilon = 0.01$

20. The barometric pressure P in inches of mercury is approximately expressed by the formula $P = P_0 e^{-kh}$ where h is the altitude in miles above sea level, and P_0 and k are constants. At sea level the pressure is about 30 in, and at 3 mi above sea level, it is about 15 in.

a. Find the values of P_0 and k.

b. Find the pressure at 35,000 ft above sea level.

c. Find the rate of change of the pressure P with respect to h at 35,000 ft.

21. *Carbon-14 dating.* In a living organism the ratio between ordinary carbon and radioactive carbon, carbon-14, remains about constant, being about one carbon-14 atom per 10^{12} atoms of regular carbon as in the atmosphere. After a plant or animal dies, however, no new carbon is consumed, and the proportion of carbon-14 experiences radioactive decay. It is known that the *half-life* (that is, the time it takes for half of a sample to decay away) of carbon-14 is about 5,700 years. What percentage of carbon-14 is present in the charcoal from a tree killed by a volcanic eruption 1,927 years ago?

22. a. Show that if $Q = Ce^{kt}$, where C and k are positive constants, represents an exponential growth curve for which t is interpreted as a time variable, then the amount of time required for Q to double is given by $T = \dfrac{1}{k}\ln 2$. The time T is called the *doubling period.*

b. Show that for any time $t = T_1$,

$$\int_0^{T_1} Ce^{kt}\, dt = \int_{T_1}^{T_1 + T} Ce^{kt}\, dt - \frac{C}{k}$$

Thus, the area under the exponential growth curve from time $t = 0$ to time $t = T_1$ is equal to the area under the curve over the next doubling period adjusted by the constant amount C/k. (See Exercise 4 in Section 2.4 for the discussion of the exponential growth curve.)

Section 4.6 Applications of the Definite Integral

The notion of the definite integral arose from the problem of computing the area between the x-axis and the graph of a nonnegative curve $y = f(x)$ over an interval $a \leqslant x \leqslant b$. In this section we will present applications of the definite integral to computing the area between two curves, the volume of a solid of revolution, the length of a plane curve, the area of a surface of revolution, and the average value of a continuous function. Each of these applications can be thought of as the measure of some geometric construct. For that reason we have given the name MEASURES to the TI-59 program that computes those various values.

The program MEASURES uses program steps 000 through 213, and memory locations 01 through 07. The balance of the program steps (214 through 479) and memory locations (00 and 08 through 59) are available for your use while evaluating the functions called for by the various subparts of the program. These functions will be explained as each application is presented. All the integrations in MEASURES are accomplished by Simpson's rule.

All the applications presented in this section are found in the standard calculus texts. Thus we will not derive the formulas that are used, but only state what they are and how they are interpreted in order to put the various calculations into a coherent context.

EXERCISE 1.
AREA BETWEEN TWO CURVES

If $y = f(x)$ and $y = g(x)$ are two continuous curves over the interval $a \leqslant x \leqslant b$, and, furthermore, if $f(x) \geqslant g(x)$ for every x in the interval, then the area bounded above by f, below by g, and on the sides by the vertical lines $x = a$ and $x = b$ is given by

$$A = \int_a^b [f(x) - g(x)] \, dx \tag{4.11}$$

Calculating the Area Between Two Curves

With MEASURES read into your TI-59, perform

Step 1: Key in the subroutine for the function $f(x)$. This subroutine must be labeled with the keystrokes

$\boxed{\text{Lb1}}$ $\boxed{\text{C}'}$

and the last two steps in the subroutine must be

$\boxed{\text{INV}}$ $\boxed{\text{SBR}}$

The subroutine can be located in the program memory 214 through 479.

Step 2: Key in the subroutine for $g(x)$ labeled with the keystrokes

$\boxed{\text{Lb1}}$ $\boxed{\text{D}'}$

and ending the subroutine with

$\boxed{\text{INV}}$ $\boxed{\text{SBR}}$

The keystrokes for $g(x)$ can immediately follow those for $f(x)$ in program memory.

Step 3: Initialize the numerical integration via Simpson's rule:

Enter the number n of subdivisions (an *even* number) and press $\boxed{\text{E}'}$.

When the program halts, enter the left endpoint value, a, and press $\boxed{\text{R/S}}$.

After the program halts, enter the right endpoint value b, and press $\boxed{\text{R/S}}$. The program halts with $(b - a)/n$ in the display.

Step 4: Press $\boxed{\text{C}}$. The program stops with the value of the area between the two curves in the display.

If greater accuracy is required, increase the number n of subdivisions used in Simpson's rule, and repeat Steps 3 and 4 above.

Illustrations   **1.** Let's find the area between the curves

$$f(x) = e^x \quad \text{and} \quad g(x) = \sin^2 x$$

from $x = 0$ to $x = \pi/2$. With MEASURES read into your calculator, key in the subroutines for $f(x)$ and $g(x)$:

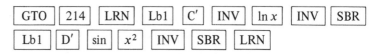

Be sure your calculator is in radians mode: Press $\boxed{\text{Rad}}$. Next initialize the numerical integration and calculate the area:

(enter)	32		
(press)		$\boxed{\text{E}'}$	Load $n = 32$ subdivisions for Simpson's rule.
(enter)	0		
(press)		$\boxed{\text{R/S}}$	Load $a = 0$.
(enter)	$\pi/2$		
(press)		$\boxed{\text{R/S}}$	Load $b = \pi/2$.
(press)		$\boxed{\text{C}}$	Calculate the area between the two curves.

The program stops with the area $A = 3.02507934$ square units in the display. The result is accurate to seven significant digits.

2. Find the area of the plane region bounded by the curves $y = x^3 + 1$ and $y = x^2 + x$.

> *Solution.* The region is shown in Figure 4.9. The two curves intersect when

$$x^3 + 1 = x^2 + x$$

or

$$x^3 - x^2 - x + 1 = 0$$

The roots are $x = -1$ and $x = 1$.
   Key in $f(x) = x^3 + 1$ as the upper curve, and $g(x) = x^2 + x$ as the lower curve:

242

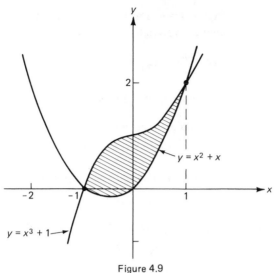

Figure 4.9

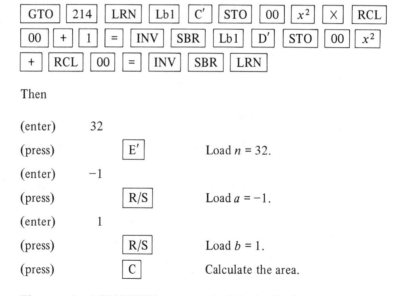

Then

(enter)	32		
(press)		$\boxed{E'}$	Load $n = 32$.
(enter)	−1		
(press)		$\boxed{R/S}$	Load $a = -1$.
(enter)	1		
(press)		$\boxed{R/S}$	Load $b = 1$.
(press)		$\boxed{C}$	Calculate the area.

The area $A = 1.333333333$ square units is in the display.

EXERCISE 2.
VOLUMES BY THE METHOD OF DISKS

243   If $y = f(x)$ is a nonnegative continuous function over $a \leqslant x \leqslant b$, and if the region beneath the graph of f, above the x-axis, and between the vertical lines

$x = a$, $x = b$ is revolved about the x-axis, then the volume of the solid so generated is given by

$$V = \int_a^b \pi [f(x)]^2 \, dx \tag{4.12}$$

The application of Equation 4.12 is called the *method of disks*.

Calculating the Volume of Revolution About the x-axis

With MEASURES read into your TI-59, perform

Step 1: Key in the subroutine for $f(x)$ labeled with the keystrokes

| Lbl | C′ |

and ending the subroutine with

| INV | SBR |

The keystrokes for $f(x)$ can be located in program memory 214 through 479.

Step 2: Initialize the numerical integration:

Enter n, press | E′ | ; enter a, press | R/S | ; and enter b, press | R/S |
The program halts with $(b - a)/n$ in the display.

Step 3: Press | B |. The program stops with the volume of the solid of revolution about the x-axis in the display.

For greater accuracy, increase the number n of subdivisions used in Simpson's rule, and repeat Steps 2 and 3.

Illustration Find the volume of the solid that results when the ellipse $2x^2 + 5y^2 = 10$ is revolved about the x-axis.

> *Solution.* The solid of revolution is obtained by revolving

$$y = 5^{-1/2} \sqrt{10 - 2x^2} \qquad -\sqrt{5} \leqslant x \leqslant \sqrt{5}$$

about the x-axis. So key the subroutine for $y = f(x)$ into MEASURES:

| GTO | 214 | LRN | Lbl | C′ | x^2 | × | 2 | +/− | + | 10 | = |
| $\sqrt{x}$ | ÷ | 5 | $\sqrt{x}$ | = | INV | SBR | LRN |

Then

(enter)	32		
(press)		E′	Load $n = 32$.
(enter)	$-\sqrt{5}$		

(press) | R/S | Load $a = -\sqrt{5}$.

(enter) $\sqrt{5}$

(press) | R/S | Load $b = \sqrt{5}$.

(press) | B | Calculate the volume.

The program stops with the volume $V = 18.73283928$ cubic units in the display.

EXERCISE 3.
VOLUMES BY THE METHOD OF SHELLS

If $y = f(x)$ is a nonnegative continuous function over $0 \leqslant a \leqslant x \leqslant b$, and if the region beneath the graph of f, above the x-axis, and between the vertical lines $x = a$, $x = b$ is revolved around the y-axis, then the volume of the solid so generated is given by

$$V = \int_a^b 2\pi x \, f(x) \, dx \qquad (4.13)$$

The application of Equation 4.13 is called the *method of shells.*

Calculating the Volume of Revolution About the y-axis

With MEASURES read into your TI–59, perform

Step 1: Key in the subroutine for $f(x)$ (using the label C'), just as in Step 1 of Exercise 2.

Step 2: Initialize the numerical integration exactly as in Step 2 of Exercise 2.

Step 3: Press | B' | . The program stops with the volume of the solid of revolution about the y-axis in the display. You can upgrade the accuracy by increasing the number of subdivisions used in the numerical integration.

Illustration   Find the volume of the solid that results when the region bounded by the curve $y = 16/(4 + x^2)$, the x-axis, and the lines $x = 0$, $x = 2$, is revolved about the y=axis.

Solution. Key in the subroutine for $y = f(x)$ into MEASURES:

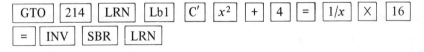

| GTO | 214 | LRN | Lb1 | C' | x² | + | 4 | = | 1/x | X | 16 |

| = | INV | SBR | LRN |

Then

(enter) 48

(press) | E' | Load $n = 48$.

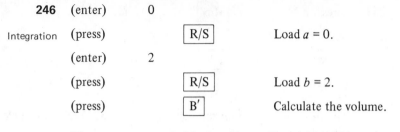

246

Integration

(enter)	0	
(press)	R/S	Load $a = 0$.
(enter)	2	
(press)	R/S	Load $b = 2$.
(press)	B'	Calculate the volume.

The program stops with the volume $V = 34.84137823$ cubic units in the display. The answer is correct to five decimal places.

EXERCISE 4.
LENGTH OF A PLANE CURVE

If $y = f(x)$ is a function with continuous derivative f' over the interval $a \leqslant x \leqslant b$, then the *arc length* L of the curve $y = f(x)$ from $x = a$ to $x = b$ is given by

$$L = \int_a^b \sqrt{1 + [f'(x)]^2}\ dx \qquad (4.14)$$

Calculating the Length of a Curve

With MEASURES read into your TI-59, perform

Step 1: Using the rules of differentiation, calculate analytically the derivative

$$\frac{dy}{dx} = f'(x)$$

Step 2: Key in the subroutine for $\dfrac{dy}{dx} = f'(x)$ labeled with the keystrokes

Lb1	D'

and ending the subroutine with

INV	SBR

The keystrokes for $f'(x)$ can be located in program memory 214 through 479.

Step 3: Initialize the numerical integration:
Enter n, press E' ; enter a, press R/S ; and enter b, press R/S .

Step 4: Press A . The program stops with the length of the plane curve in the display.

Illustration

Find the length of the arc of the parabola $y = x^2$ from the point $(-1, 1)$ to the point $(2, 4)$.

Solution. The derivative is $dy/dx = 2x$. We key this into MEASURES:

GTO	214	LRN	Lb1	D'	×	2	=	INV	SBR	LRN

(enter)	32		
(press)		E′	Load n = 32.
(enter)	−1		
(press)		R/S	Load a = −1.
(enter)	2		
(press)		R/S	Load b = 2.
(press)		A	Calculate the arc length.

The program stops with L = 6.125726221 units in the display. The answer is correct to six decimal places.

EXERCISE 5.
LENGTH OF A CURVE
REPRESENTED PARAMETRICALLY

Suppose you think of a curve C in the plane as the path traced out by a moving particle. At a particular time t, the particle is located at the point $P(x,y)$ on the curve. The coordinates of P depend on t, so we write

$$x = f(t) \quad \text{and} \quad y = g(t) \tag{4.15}$$

to describe the motion of the particle. Equations 4.15 are called *parametric equations* representing the curve C, and the independent variable t is called the *parameter.*

There is a particularly useful formula for calculating the length of a curve that is given parametrically. If $x = f(t)$ and $y = g(t)$ are functions with continuous derivatives $dx/dt = f'(t)$ and $dy/dt = g'(t)$ over the time interval $a \leqslant t \leqslant b$, then the length of the curve traced out by $P(x,y)$, as t varies from $t = a$ to $t = b$, is given by

$$L = \int_a^b \sqrt{[f'(t)]^2 + [g'(t)]^2}\ dt \tag{4.16}$$

Calculating the Length of a Curve Represented Parametrically

With MEASURES read into your TI-59, perform

Step 1: Calculate analytically the derivatives

$$\frac{dx}{dt} = f'(t) \quad \text{and} \quad \frac{dy}{dt} = g'(t)$$

Step 2: Key in the subroutine for $dx/dt = f'(t)$ labeled with the keystrokes

Lbl	C′

and ending the subroutine with

| INV | SBR |

The keystrokes for $f'(t)$ can be located in program memory begin
ning at location 214.

Step 3: Key in the subroutine for $dy/dt = g'(t)$ labeled with the keystrokes

| Lb1 | D' |

and ending with

| INV | SBR |

The keystrokes for $g'(t)$ can immediately follow those for $f'(t)$ in
program memory.

Step 4: Initialize the numerical integration:

Enter n, press | E' | ; enter a, press | R/S | ; and enter b, press | R/S | .

Step 5: Press | A' | . The program stops with the length of the curve repre
sented parametrically in the display.

Illustration   Find the length of the curve given by

$$x = \frac{1}{2} \ln (t^2 - 1) \quad \text{and} \quad y = \sqrt{t^2 - 1}$$

from $t = 3$ to $t = 7$.

Solution. The derivatives of the parametric equations are

$$\frac{dx}{dt} = \frac{t}{t^2 - 1} \quad \text{and} \quad \frac{dy}{dt} = \frac{t}{\sqrt{t^2 - 1}}$$

Now key these subroutines into MEASURES as follows:

| GTO | 214 | LRN | Lb1 | C' | STO | 00 | ÷ | (| RCL | 00 |

| x^2 | − | 1 |) | = | INV | SBR | Lb1 | D' | STO | 00 | ÷ | (|

| RCL | 00 | x^2 | − | 1 |) | $\sqrt{x}$ | = | INV | SBR | LRN |

Then

(enter)   32

(press) | E' | Load $n = 32$.

(enter)   3

(press) | R/S | Load $a = 3$.

(enter)   7

(press)　　　　　　　$\boxed{\text{R/S}}$　　　　Load $b = 7$.

(press)　　　　　　　$\boxed{\text{A}'}$　　　　Calculate the arc length.

The program stops with $L = 4.202732788$ units in the display. The answer is correct to six decimal places.

EXERCISE 6.
AREA OF A SURFACE OF REVOLUTION

If $y = f(x)$ is a nonnegative function with continuous derivative f' over the interval $a \leqslant x \leqslant b$, then the *surface area* S generated by revolving the curve $y = f(x)$ from $x = a$ to $x = b$ about the x-axis is given by

$$S = \int_a^b 2\pi f(x) \sqrt{1 + [f'(x)]^2} \; dx \tag{4.17}$$

Calculating the Surface Area

With MEASURES read into your TI–59, perform

Step 1: Calculate analytically the derivative

$$\frac{dy}{dx} = f'(x)$$

using the formal rules of differentiation.

Step 2: Key in the subroutine for $y = f(x)$ labeled with the keystrokes

$\boxed{\text{Lb1}}$ $\boxed{\text{C}'}$

and ending the subroutine with

$\boxed{\text{INV}}$ $\boxed{\text{SBR}}$

The keystrokes for $f(x)$ can be located in program memory beginning at location 214.

Step 3: Key in the subroutine for $dy/dx = f'(x)$ labeled with the keystrokes

$\boxed{\text{Lb1}}$ $\boxed{\text{D}'}$

and ending with

$\boxed{\text{INV}}$ $\boxed{\text{SBR}}$

The keystrokes for $f'(x)$ can immediately follow those for $f(x)$ in program memory.

Step 4: Initialize the numerical integration:
Enter n, press $\boxed{\text{E}'}$; enter a, press $\boxed{\text{R/S}}$; enter b, press $\boxed{\text{R/S}}$.

Step 5: Press $\boxed{\text{D}}$. The program stops with the area of the surface of revolution about the x-axis in the display.

Illustration   Find the surface area generated when the arc of the curve

$$y = \frac{1}{2}(e^x + e^{-x}) \quad \text{from } x = -1 \text{ to } x = 1$$

is revolved about the x-axis.

Solution. First calculate the derivative

$$\frac{dy}{dx} = \frac{1}{2}(e^x - e^{-x})$$

Next key in the subroutines for $y = f(x)$ and $dy/dx = f'(x)$ into MEASURES as follows:

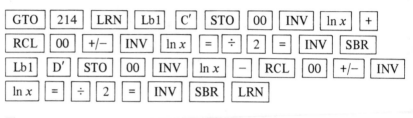

GTO	214	LRN	Lb1	C′	STO	00	INV	ln x	+
RCL	00	+/−	INV	ln x	=	÷	2	=	INV	SBR
Lb1	D′	STO	00	INV	ln x	−	RCL	00	+/−	INV
ln x	=	÷	2	=	INV	SBR	LRN

Then

(enter)	64		
(press)		E′	Load $n = 64$.
(enter)	−1		
(press)		R/S	Load $a = -1$.
(enter)	1		
(press)		R/S	Load $b = 1$.
(press)		D	Calculate the surface area.

The program stops with $S = 17.67730429$ square units in the display, accurate to five decimal places.

Applications of the definite integral abound, and we have only touched on a few of the geometric applications that occur in most standard calculus texts. We will end this section with a few additional examples not specifically programmed into MEASURES. Finally, we will summarize the special labels that give access to the various subprograms in MEASURES.

EXERCISE 7.
AVERAGE VALUE OF A FUNCTION

If $y = f(x)$ is continuous over the interval $a \leqslant x \leqslant b$, then the *average value* of
250   f over the interval is defined to be

Average value $= \dfrac{1}{b-a} \displaystyle\int_a^b f(x)\,dx$ (4.18)

The label $\boxed{\text{E}}$ in MEASURES gives access to the numerical integration via Simpson's rule, so we can use it to determine the average value of a function. For instance, suppose it is known that x days after the beginning of the year, the temperature in degrees Fahrenheit at a northern weather station at 8 AM each day is given according to the formula

$$f(x) = 37 \sin\left[\dfrac{2\pi}{365}\,(x - 101)\right] + 25$$

What is the mean temperature from January 23 to February 14?

Solution. The date February 14 is 45 days from the beginning of the year. The average temperature is given by

$$\dfrac{1}{45 - 23} \int_{23}^{45} \left\{ 37 \sin\left[\dfrac{2\pi}{365}(x - 101)\right] + 25 \right\} dx$$

Key the integrand function into MEASURES with the label C':

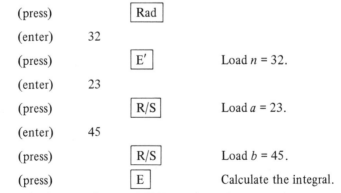

$\boxed{\text{GTO}}$ $\boxed{214}$ $\boxed{\text{LRN}}$ $\boxed{\text{Lb1}}$ $\boxed{C'}$ $\boxed{-}$ $\boxed{101}$ $\boxed{=}$ $\boxed{\times}$ $\boxed{2}$ $\boxed{\times}$ $\boxed{\pi}$
$\boxed{\div}$ $\boxed{365}$ $\boxed{=}$ $\boxed{\sin}$ $\boxed{\times}$ $\boxed{37}$ $\boxed{+}$ $\boxed{25}$ $\boxed{=}$ $\boxed{\text{INV}}$ $\boxed{\text{SBR}}$ $\boxed{\text{LRN}}$

Then set your calculator to radians mode and execute the numerical integration:

(press)		$\boxed{\text{Rad}}$	
(enter)	32		
(press)		$\boxed{E'}$	Load $n = 32$.
(enter)	23		
(press)		$\boxed{\text{R/S}}$	Load $a = 23$.
(enter)	45		
(press)		$\boxed{\text{R/S}}$	Load $b = 45$.
(press)		$\boxed{E}$	Calculate the integral.

Finally, dividing the result in the display by $45 - 23 = 22$ days gives the average temperature value of $-8.62°$ Fahrenheit, rounded to two decimals.

EXERCISE 8.
A VOLUME BY SLICING

Find the volume of the solid generated when the region bounded on the left by the parabola $y^2 = x - 1$, and on the right by the line $y - 1 = 2(x - 2)$, is rotated about the y-axis.

Solution. The region is sketched in Figure 4.10. The parabola and line intersect when

$$x - 1 = [2(x - 2) + 1]^2$$

or

$$4x^2 - 13x + 10 = 0$$

The roots are $x = \frac{5}{4}$ and $x = 2$, yielding the two points of intersection $A\left(\frac{5}{4}, -\frac{1}{2}\right)$ and $B(2, 1)$.

Imagine the solid, obtained by rotating this region about the y-axis, to be cut into thin slices by planes perpendicular to the y-axis. Each slice is like a thin washer of thickness Δy, with an inner radius $r_1 = x = 1 + y^2$ and an outer radius $r_2 = x = (y + 3)/2$. The area of the face of such a washer is

$$\pi r_2^2 - \pi r_1^2 = \pi \left[\tfrac{1}{4}(y + 3)^2 - (1 + y^2)^2\right]$$

So the volume ΔV of the thin washer is

$$\Delta V = \pi \left[\tfrac{1}{4}(y + 3)^2 - (1 + y^2)^2\right] \Delta y$$

If we sum together all these incremental volume elements, and take the limit of the sum as the thickness $\Delta y \to 0$, we obtain the exact volume of the solid as the integral

$$V = \int_{-1/2}^{1} \pi \left[\tfrac{1}{4}(y + 3)^2 - (1 + y^2)^2\right] \, dy$$

Figure 4.10

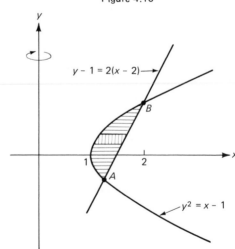

Using MEASURES, we execute this integration numerically:

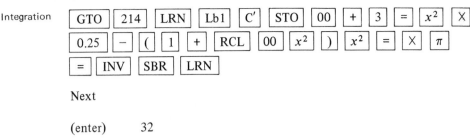

Integration

GTO 214 LRN Lb1 C' STO 00 + 3 = x^2 X
0.25 − (1 + RCL 00 x^2) x^2 = X π
= INV SBR LRN

Next

(enter)	32		
(press)		E'	Load $n = 32$.
(enter)	−0.5		
(press)		R/S	Load $a = -\dfrac{1}{2}$.
(enter)	1		
(press)		R/S	Load $b = 1$.
(press)		E	Calculate the volume.

The program stops with the volume $V = 4.948005396$ cubic units in the display. The answer is correct to five decimal places.

Here is a summary of the labels used in MEASURES for easy reference. The functions keyed in as subroutines depend on the desired output as discussed in each exercise of the text.

LABELS USED IN MEASURES

C'   Subroutine for $f(x)$ or dx/dt

D'   Subroutine for $g(x)$ or $f'(x)$ or dy/dt

E'   Initialization of the numerical integration

A   Calculate the arc length of a plane curve

A'   Calculate arc length for a parametric curve

B   Calculate volume for rotation about x-axis: disk method

B'   Calculate volume for rotation about y-axis: shell method

C   Calculate the area between two curves

D   Calculate surface area of rotation about x-axis

E   Calculate the definite integral $\int_a^b f(x)\,dx$ by Simpson's rule

In each of Problems 1-6, calculate the area of the region between the given curves. Answers are in square units.

1. $y = x^3, y = x$
2. $y = \sin x, y = \cos x \qquad 0 \leqslant x \leqslant \pi/4$
3. $y = 8/x, x + y = 6$
4. $y = 9 - x^2, y = x^2$
5. $y = \tan x, y = e^x \qquad 0 \leqslant x \leqslant 3/2$
6. Use PROBE to find the two roots of $e^{x/5} - x^2 = 0$. Then find the area between the two curves $y = e^{x/5}$ and $y = x^2$.

In Problems 7-11, find the volume of the solid generated by revolving the region beneath the graph of the given curve, above the x-axis, over the specified interval, about the x-axis. Answers are in cubic units.

7. $y = (1 - \sqrt{x})^2 \qquad 0 \leqslant x \leqslant 1$
8. $y = x^{2/3} \quad 0 \leqslant x \leqslant 2$
9. $y = \ln x \qquad 1 \leqslant x \leqslant e$
10. $y = 12/\sqrt{4x^2 + 9} \qquad 0 \leqslant x \leqslant 2$
11. $y = 3 \sec x \qquad -\pi/4 \leqslant x \leqslant \pi/3$

In Problems 12-16, find the volume of the solid generated by revolving the region beneath the graph of the given curve, above the x-axis, over the specified interval, about the y-axis. Answers are in cubic units.

12. $y = x^3 \qquad 0 \leqslant x \leqslant 1$
13. $y = \ln x \qquad 1 \leqslant x \leqslant 3$
14. $y = \sqrt{4x - x^2 - 3} \qquad 1 \leqslant x \leqslant 3$
15. $y = \cos (x^2) \qquad 0 \leqslant x \leqslant \sqrt{\pi}/2$
16. $y = (4 - x^2)^{1/3} \quad 0 \leqslant x \leqslant 4$

In Problems 17-24, find the length of the plane curve.

17. $f(x) = x^2 - \frac{1}{8} \ln x \qquad 2 \leqslant x \leqslant 3$
18. $x = \cos t + t \sin t, y = \sin t - t \cos t \qquad 0 \leqslant t \leqslant \pi/4$
19. $f(x) = \frac{2}{3} x^{3/2} - \frac{1}{2} x^{1/2} \quad 1 \leqslant x \leqslant 2$
20. $f(x) = \ln (1 + x^2) - \frac{1}{8}(\frac{x^2}{2} + \ln x) \qquad 1 \leqslant x \leqslant 2$
21. $x = t^2 \cos t, y = t^2 \sin t \qquad 0 \leqslant t \leqslant 1$
22. $x = e^t \cos t, y = e^t \sin t \qquad 1 \leqslant t \leqslant 3$
23. $y = e^x$ from $A(0, 1)$ to $B(1, e)$
24. $x = \sqrt{5 - t^2}, y = \sqrt{5} \ln \left(\dfrac{\sqrt{5} + t}{\sqrt{5 - t^2}} \right) - t \qquad 0 \leqslant t \leqslant \sqrt{3}$

In Problems 25-29, find the surface area generated when the indicated curve is revolved about the x-axis. Answers are in square units.

25. $y = x^3$ $0 \leqslant x \leqslant 1$

26. $x^2 + 4y^2 = 4$ $0 \leqslant x \leqslant 1.98$

27. $y^2 = 3x$ $0.25 \leqslant x \leqslant 0.95$

28. $y = \sin x$ $0 \leqslant x \leqslant \pi$

29. $y = (1 - x^{2/3})^{3/2}$ $0.04 \leqslant x \leqslant 0.15$

30. Find the average value of $f(x) = \sin^2 x$ over $0 \leqslant x \leqslant \pi$. (This average is used in the study of alternating current.)

31. Find the average temperature at the weather station in Exercise 7 of the text, from June 6 to September 30.

32. Find the average vertical width across the ellipse $7x^2 + 5y^2 = 4$.

33. Find the volume generated when the region between the curves $y = x^2$ and $y = x^{1/2}$ is revolved about the y-axis.

34. Find the surface area generated by revolving about the y-axis the curve $y = x^2$ between $(1,1)$ and $(2,4)$.

35. Find the integral

$$\int_{-1}^{\pi/2} f(x)\, dx$$

where

$$f(x) = \begin{cases} x^3 - e^x & \text{for } -1 \leqslant x \leqslant 0 \\ \sin(e^x) & \text{for } x > 0 \end{cases}$$

Give your answer correct to six decimal places.

Section 4.7 The Inverse Trigonometric Functions

The idea behind the inverse of an operation implies its "undoing" or reversal. That is, if the operation performed is followed by its inverse, the result is a return to the original state. You are already familiar with many inverse operations. For instance, in arithmetic, subtraction is the inverse of addition: If you begin with the number x and add 3, you obtain $x + 3$; subtracting 3 from $x + 3$ then results in the original number x again. Some operations are their own inverses, such as reciprocation: If you begin with a nonzero number x and take its reciprocal, you obtain $1/x$; then the reciprocal of $1/x$ results in the original number x. Another example of an inverse operation is that of taking the cube root of a number as the inverse of cubing.

    Sometimes you have to be careful about the domain of an operation if it is to have an inverse. For instance, the square root operation is the inverse of squaring numbers. However, since the square root of a number is always nonnegative, it is impossible to start with a negative number, say -3, square it (obtaining 9), and then take the square root to get back to the original negative number -3: instead you obtain $\sqrt{9} = +3$. So the square root and squaring operations are inverses, provided that *both* operations are restricted to the nonnegative numbers. Likewise, the natural logarithm function, when applied to positive numbers, is the inverse of the exponential function. Even some limiting operations have inverses: Finding an indefinite integral "undoes" the differentiation operation, resulting in the original function up to an arbitrary constant.

The purpose of this section is to acquaint you with the idea of an inverse to a function and to present the inverse trigonometric functions. These functions are important because their derivatives are familiar algebraic functions, which lead to useful integration formulas.

> *Definition.* The function g, whose domain is the range of the function f, is said to be the *inverse* of f, provided that
>
> $$f(x) = y \quad \text{if and only if} \quad g(y) = x \tag{4.19}$$
>
> for every x in the domain of f and every y in the range of f.

In other words, whenever two functions f and g are inverses of each other, the composite either of f with g or of g with f produces the *identity* function $i(z) = z$. From Equation 4.19,

$$(g \circ f)(x) = g[f(x)] = g(y) = x$$

and

$$(f \circ g)(y) = f[g(y)] = f(x) = y$$

For example, the square root function is the inverse of the squaring function restricted to the nonnegative numbers because

$$\sqrt{x^2} = |x| = x \quad \text{and} \quad (\sqrt{x})^2 = x$$

both hold whenever $x \geq 0$. Likewise, the natural logarithm and exponential functions are inverses of each other by the definition

$$y = \ln x \quad \text{if and only if} \quad e^y = x$$

Equivalently,

$$y = \ln(e^y) \quad \text{and} \quad x = e^{\ln x}$$

are both true whenever $x > 0$ and y is any number.

Every function does not have an inverse. For instance, the entire parabola $y = x^2$ does not have an inverse: We have to impose a restriction like $x \geq 0$ to obtain the inverse $y = \sqrt{x}$. In general, it can be established that *every strictly increasing and every strictly decreasing function has an inverse.* We will not prove that result; nor do we intend to delve deeply into the theory and properties of inverse functions. Nevertheless there is one very important result concerning the derivative of a function and its inverse, which we now state without proof.

If f and g are inverse functions on suitably restricted domains, and if $f(a) = b$ and $g(b) = a$, then

$$g'(b) = \frac{1}{f'(a)} \tag{4.20}$$

provided that the derivatives exist and are nonzero.

For example, if $f(x) = x^2$ for $x \geq 0$, and $g(y) = \sqrt{y}$ is the inverse function, then since $f(3) = 9$,

$$g'(9) = \frac{1}{f'(3)} = \frac{1}{2 \cdot 3} = \frac{1}{6}$$

This agrees with the power rule,

$$\frac{d}{dy}(\sqrt{y}) \bigg|_{y=9} = \frac{1}{2}y^{-1/2}\bigg|_{y=9} = \frac{1}{2}(9)^{-1/2} = \frac{1}{6}$$

The rule expressed in Equation 4.20 is very powerful because it tells you how to obtain the derivative of the inverse function g when you don't know a simple formula for g, but only the expression for the original function f. Usually the case is that it is impossible to find a simple formula for g even though f is known. Equation 4.20 allows you to bypass any formula for g, yet calculate its derivative values by determining the associated derivative values from the known formula for f.

All the basic trigonometric functions have inverses when their domains are suitably restricted. Let's begin our investigation with the sine function and its inverse.

The function $f(y) = \sin y$ is strictly increasing, continuous, and differentiable over the interval $-\pi/2 \leq y \leq \pi/2$. Thus it has an inverse function, called the *arcsine* function and denoted by the symbol $\sin^{-1}$. Symbolically,

$$\sin^{-1} x = y \quad \text{if and only if} \quad x = \sin y \tag{4.21}$$

for all y satisfying $-\pi/2 \leq y \leq \pi/2$ and for all x satisfying $-1 \leq x \leq 1$. In words, the arcsin x, or $\sin^{-1} x$, is the angle y in the interval $-\pi/2 \leq y \leq \pi/2$ for which $\sin y = x$. Thus for instance, $\sin^{-1}\left(\frac{1}{2}\right) = \pi/6$ because the sine of $\pi/6$ rad equals $\frac{1}{2}$. Likewise, $\sin^{-1}(0) = (0)$ and $\sin^{-1}(1) = \pi/2$. The particular range $-\pi/2 \leq y \leq \pi/2$ is called the *principal value* of $y = \sin^{-1} x$. Notice that the minus one in Equation 4.21 does *not* mean the reciprocal $(\sin x)^{-1} = 1/\sin x = \csc x$. Rather, the symbol $\sin^{-1}$ is used to denote the inverse of the sine function; that is, to denote the arcsine function.

Your TI-59 calculator automatically produces the arcsine of any suitable number. Specifically, if x is any number satisfying $-1 \leq x \leq 1$, then the keys $\boxed{\text{INV}}$ $\boxed{\text{sin}}$ give the angle $y = \sin^{-1} x$ in the angular mode active in your calculator at the time: radians if it is in the radians mode or degrees if it is in the degrees mode. (Ordinarily your calculator should be in the radians mode when solving calculus problems involving the trigonometric and inverse trigonometric functions.) If the display contains a number x whose absolute value is larger than 1, pressing the keys $\boxed{\text{INV}}$ $\boxed{\text{sin}}$ results in a flashing display to signal an illegal operation.

If you calculate a few values of $y = \sin^{-1} x$, you can quickly produce the graph presented in Figure 4.11. If the point (x,y) lies on the graph of the arcsine, then $y = \sin^{-1} x$ so that $x = \sin y$. Thus the point (y,x) is on the graph of the sine. Likewise, if (y,x) is on the graph of the sine, the point (x,y) is on the graph of its inverse, the arcsine. In other words, each curve is the reflection of the other across the line $y = x$, as shown in Figure 4.12. This same relationship holds between the graphs of any function and its inverse. That is, *if $y = f(x)$ and $x = g(y)$ are inverse functions, then the point (x,y) lies on the graph of f if and only if the point (y,x), obtained by interchanging the coordinates, lies on the graph of the inverse g.*

The inverse cosine function is defined in a similar manner. The function $f(y) = \cos y$ is strictly decreasing, continuous, and differentiable over the interval $0 \leqslant y \leqslant \pi$. So it has an inverse function, the *arccosine*, denoted by $\cos^{-1}$. Symbolically,

$$\cos^{-1} x = y \quad \text{if and only if} \quad x = \cos y \tag{4.22}$$

for all y satisfying $0 \leqslant y \leqslant \pi$ and for all x satisfying $-1 \leqslant x \leqslant 1$. Thus the range $0 \leqslant y \leqslant \pi$ is the principal value of the arccosine.

The TI-59 keys $\boxed{\text{INV}}$ $\boxed{\text{cos}}$ give the angle $y = \cos^{-1} x$ of whatever number x is in the display. The answer is provided in the angular mode active in your calculator at the time, and x must be in the interval $-1 \leqslant x \leqslant 1$ for the operation to be legal. For example, $\cos^{-1}\left(\frac{1}{2}\right) = \pi/3$, $\cos^{-1}(0) = \pi/2$, and $\cos^{-1}(1) = 0$. The graph of the arccosine function is shown in Figure 4.13.

Figure 4.11 Sin^{-1} x for $|x| \leqslant 1$ is the angle y for which sin $y = x$ and $-\pi/2 \leqslant y \leqslant \pi/2$.

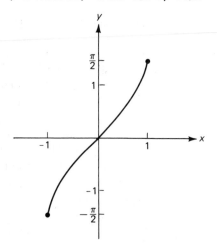

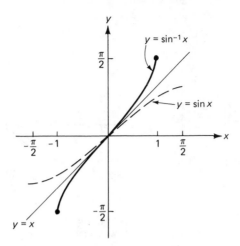

Figure 4.12 The graph of $y = \sin^{-1} x$ is the mirror image of the sine function across the 45° line $y = x$.

The *arctangent* function, denoted by $y = \tan^{-1} x$, is the inverse of the tangent function. It is defined by

$$\tan^{-1} x = y \quad \text{if and only if} \quad x = \tan y \tag{4.23}$$

for all y in the principal range $-\pi/2 < y < \pi/2$, and for all real values of x. The keys $\boxed{\text{INV}}$ $\boxed{\text{tan}}$ give the values of the arctangent function, and its graph is presented in Figure 4.14.

The *arccotangent* function is defined to be

$$y = \cot^{-1} x = \frac{\pi}{2} - \tan^{-1} x \tag{4.24}$$

Figure 4.13 $\text{Cos}^{-1} x$ for $|x| \le 1$ is the angle y for which $\cos y = x$ and $0 \le y \le \pi$.

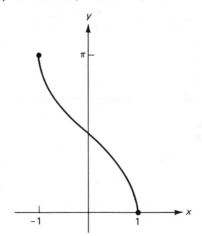

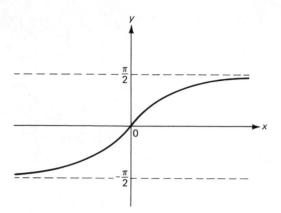

Figure 4.14 Tan^{-1} x for any x is the angle y for which tan $y = x$ and $-\pi/2 < y < \pi/2$.

for all y in the principal value range $0 < y < \pi$ and for all values of x. The graph of the arccotangent is presented in Figure 4.15.

The remaining trigonometric functions also have inverses. The *arcsecant* is defined by

$$y = \sec^{-1} x \quad \text{if and only if} \quad x = \sec y \tag{4.25}$$

for all $y \neq \pi/2$ in the principal value range $0 \leqslant y \leqslant \pi$ and for all x satisfying $|x| \geqslant 1$. Moreover, since

$$x = \sec y \quad \text{if and only if} \quad \frac{1}{x} = \cos y$$

it follows that

$$y = \sec^{-1} x \quad \text{if and only if} \quad y = \cos^{-1}\left(\frac{1}{x}\right) \tag{4.26}$$

Figure 4.15 Cot^{-1} x =$(\pi/2)-$ tan^{-1} x for any x and for $0 < y < \pi$.

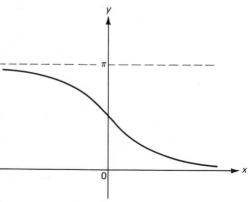

Thus the keys $\boxed{1/x}$ $\boxed{\text{INV}}$ $\boxed{\cos}$ give the values of the arcsecant on your calculator. Likewise, the *arccosecant* is defined by

$$\csc^{-1} x = \sin^{-1}\left(\frac{1}{x}\right) \tag{4.27}$$

so the keys $\boxed{1/x}$ $\boxed{\text{INV}}$ $\boxed{\sin}$ give the arccosecant. The graphs of these inverse trigonometric functions are sketched in Figures 4.16 and 4.17.

Derivatives of the Inverse Trigonometric Functions

There are several ways to obtain the derivatives of the inverse trigonometric functions. We will illustrate one method, which uses Equation 4.20, to calculate the derivative of the arctangent.

If $y = g(x) = \tan^{-1} x$, then $x = f(y) = \tan y$ is its inverse. Then, by Equation 4.20,

$$\frac{dy}{dx} = g'(x) = \frac{1}{f'(y)} = \frac{1}{\sec^2 y} = \frac{1}{1 + \tan^2 y}$$

$$= \frac{1}{1 + [\tan(\tan^{-1} x)]^2} = \frac{1}{1 + x^2}$$

Thus

$$\frac{d}{dx}(\tan^{-1} x) = \frac{1}{1 + x^2} \tag{4.28}$$

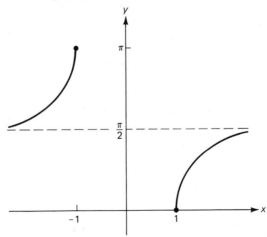

Figure 4.16 $\text{Sec}^{-1} x = \cos^{-1}(1/x)$ for all x satisfying $|x| \geqslant 1$ and for the principal value range $0 \leqslant y \leqslant \pi$ and $y \neq \pi/2$.

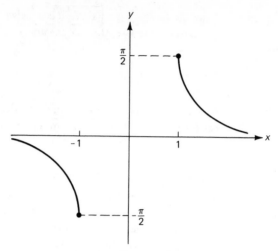

Figure 4.17 $\operatorname{Csc}^{-1} x = \sin^{-1}(1/x)$ for all x satisfying $|x| \geqslant 1$ and for the principal value range $-\pi/2 \leqslant y \leqslant \pi/2$ and $y \neq 0$.

The following formulas may also be derived.

$$\frac{d}{dx}(\sin^{-1} x) = \frac{1}{\sqrt{1-x^2}} \qquad (4.29)$$

$$\frac{d}{dx}(\cos^{-1} x) = \frac{-1}{\sqrt{1-x^2}} \qquad (4.30)$$

$$\frac{d}{dx}(\cot^{-1} x) = \frac{-1}{1+x^2} \qquad (4.31)$$

$$\frac{d}{dx}(\sec^{-1} x) = \frac{1}{|x|\sqrt{x^2-1}} \qquad (4.32)$$

$$\frac{d}{dx}(\csc^{-1} x) = \frac{-1}{|x|\sqrt{x^2-1}} \qquad (4.33)$$

Integrals of the Inverse Trigonometric Functions

$$\int \frac{dx}{1+x^2} = \tan^{-1} x + C \qquad (4.34)$$

$$\int \frac{dx}{\sqrt{1-x^2}} = \sin^{-1} x + C \qquad (4.35)$$

$$\int -\frac{dx}{\sqrt{1-x^2}} = \cos^{-1} x + C \qquad (4.36)$$

$$\int -\frac{dx}{1+x^2} = \cot^{-1} x + C \qquad (4.37)$$

$$\int \frac{dx}{x\sqrt{x^2-1}} = \sec^{-1} |x| + C \qquad (4.38)$$

In each of Problems 1–10, find the derivative dy/dx.

1. $y = \tan^{-1}(x^2)$

2. $y = \sin^{-1} \sqrt{x}$

3. $y = e^x \cos^{-1} x$

4. $y = \sec^{-1}\left(\dfrac{1}{x}\right)$

5. $y = x \sin^{-1} x + \sqrt{1 - x^2}$

6. $y = (\tan^{-1} x)^3$

7. $y = x \tan^{-1} x - \dfrac{1}{2} \ln(1 + x^2)$

8. $y = \tan^{-1}\left(\dfrac{e^x - e^{-x}}{2}\right)$

9. $y = \tan^{-1}(\ln x)$

10. $y = \ln(\cot^{-1} x)$

In Problems 11–20, find the indicated integrals.

11. $\displaystyle\int \dfrac{x\, dx}{\sqrt{1 - x^4}}$

12. $\displaystyle\int \dfrac{dx}{\sqrt{16 - x^2}}$

13. $\displaystyle\int \dfrac{dx}{4 + x^2}$

14. $\displaystyle\int \dfrac{e^{-x}\, dx}{\sqrt{1 - e^{-2x}}}$

15. $\displaystyle\int \dfrac{dx}{1 + 3x^2}$

16. $\displaystyle\int \dfrac{dx}{x\sqrt{x - 1}}$ (Hint: Let $u = \sqrt{x}$)

17. $\displaystyle\int \dfrac{\cos x}{1 + \sin^2 x}\, dx$

18. $\displaystyle\int \dfrac{dx}{x \ln^2 x - x}$

19. $\displaystyle\int \dfrac{dx}{x\sqrt{1 - (\ln x)^2}}$

20. $\displaystyle\int \dfrac{dx}{\sqrt{x - x^2}}$ (Hint: Let $u = \sqrt{x}$)

5
Differential Equations

The physical universe is a complex network in which everything is interrelated and constantly undergoing dynamic change. The positions of the planets in our solar system change with time as they orbit the sun. The speed at which a body falls through the atmosphere changes with the distance it has fallen. Heat in a warm house in winter tends to flow to the colder outside walls. The pressure in a column of sea water changes with its depth below sea level. The populations of two interacting species increase and decrease cyclically as one feeds upon the other. And a pendulum displaced from its vertical equilibrium position oscillates back and forth across its equilibrium. The relationships in all these examples can be expressed by equations involving the various variables and their derivatives, or differentials. Such equations are called *differential equations*.

From a given differential equation, another equation or expression involving the variables is sought. This latter expression "solves" the original differential equation by revealing how only the variables themselves are related, without reference to any derivatives. This solution can then be used to predict what happens to one variable as the others change. For example, a differential equation that expresses the number of bacteria in a certain population changing at a rate proportional to the number present can be solved to determine from the known population the number of bacteria that will be alive at some future time. Later, experiments can be set up to test the prediction and hence the assumptions underlying the differential equation. In such ways science seeks to understand and predict the nature of the physical world.

In this chapter you will study several techniques for solving differential equations involving variables and their first derivatives. We concentrate on numerical solution methods that are easily implemented on your TI-59 calculator.

Before you begin your study, record the program DIFFEQ 1 on a magnetic card. The program is listed in Appendix A and uses standard 479.59 partitioning.

Section 5.1 First-Order Differential Equations

A *first-order differential equation* is an equation involving an independent variable x, a dependent variable y, and its derivative y'. Symbolically, a first-order differential equation can be written as

$$\Phi(x,y,y') = 0 \tag{5.1}$$

where $\Phi(x,y,y')$ can be thought of as an expression in the three variables x, y, and y'. For instance,

$$y' - xy = 0 \qquad e^{x^2}y' + y^2x = 0 \qquad x(y')^2 - y = 0$$

are all examples of first-order differential equations. Equation 5.1 is called *first-order* because y' is the highest order derivative that occurs in the equation.

Our study of first-order differential equations considers those equations that can be solved for y' and written in *normal form* as

$$y' = f(x,y) \tag{5.2}$$

We assume the function f is *continuous* throughout some region in the xy-plane, which means that

$$f(x,y) \to f(x_0,y_0) \quad \text{as} \quad (x,y) \to (x_0,y_0) \tag{5.3}$$

for each point (x_0,y_0) in the region. In other words, Equation 5.3 expresses the property that the value $f(x,y)$ can be made arbitrarily close to the number $f(x_0,y_0)$ by choosing the point (x,y) sufficiently near (x_0,y_0).

The fundamental problem associated with a differential equation is to solve it; that is, to find a differentiable function that satisfies the differential equation. So we define a differentiable function $y = y(x)$ to be a *solution* to Equation 5.2 if

$$\frac{dy}{dx} = f(x,y(x))$$

for all x in the interval over which $y(x)$ is defined.

Let's consider an example. The function

$$y = xe^x + 2$$

solves the differential equation

$$y' = y + e^x - 2 \tag{5.4}$$

because

$$\frac{d}{dx}(xe^x + 2) = xe^x + e^x = (y - 2) + e^x$$

holds for all values of x. More generally, for any constant C the function

$$y = (x + C)e^x + 2 \tag{5.5}$$

solves Equation 5.4 because

$$\frac{d}{dx}[(x + C)e^x + 2] = (x + C)e^x + e^x$$

$$= (y - 2) + e^x$$

Thus the solutions of the differential Equation 5.4 form a one-parameter family of curves in the xy-plane, the parameter being the constant C in 5.5. This family, called the *general solution* of the differential equation, includes infinitely many distinct solutions. The graph of each curve is the geometric representation of the corresponding solution of the differential equation. Selecting a particular curve from the general solution is equivalent to specifying a *particular solution*. You may do so by choosing a point (x_0, y_0) through which the solution curve must pass; that is, by finding a solution $y = y(x)$ to the differential equation

$$y' = f(x,y)$$

subject to the *initial condition*

$$y(x_0) = y_0 \tag{5.6}$$

A first-order differential equation, together with an initial condition, forms an *initial value problem*. A familiar type of initial value problem is illustrated by

$$y' = 3x^2$$

subject to $y(1) = 7$. The solution is obtained by integration and evaluation of the arbitrary constant:

$$y = \int 3x^2 \, dx = x^3 + C$$

and $y(1) = 7$ implies $C = 6$. Thus $y(x) = x^3 + 6$ is the particular solution we seek.

More generally, the Fundamental Theorem of Calculus asserts that the function

$$y(x) = y_0 + \int_{x_0}^{x} f(t) \, dt \tag{5.7}$$

is the particular solution to the initial value problem

$$y' = f(x) \qquad y(x_0) = y_0 \tag{5.8}$$

In other words, you know how to solve initial value problems when the derivative y' is a function of the independent variable x alone, as expressed in Equation 5.8: All you need to do is integrate. But what do you do when y' is a function of *both* variables x and y, as in Equation 5.2? How do you go about solving a more general initial value problem?

Most differential equations do not have solutions that can be expressed simply in terms of known functions, although special classes of initial value problems can be solved by fairly routine procedures. We will investigate two such classes and their associated solution techniques further on in the chapter. However, even when a solution in equation form is found, it may be too complicated to use for computational purposes.

Another approach is to employ a numerical method that is easily implemented on a programmable calculator or computer. Think of a *numerical solution* to an initial value problem as a *table of values* approximating the exact solution function $y = y(x)$, computed for specified values of the independent variable x. If you have such a table of values, you can construct a graph approximating the actual solution curve and revealing its essential qualities. We will consider several numerical methods in this chapter. In this section we will investigate a very simple numerical technique, known as the *Euler method*.

Suppose, then, you wish a table of values from x_0 to x_N giving a numerical solution to the initial value problem

$$y' = f(x,y) \qquad y(x_0) = y_0 \tag{5.9}$$

You already know the first entry in the table of solution values: y_0 goes with x_0. We seek approximations $y_1, y_2, \ldots, y_N$ to the values of the solution $y(x)$ to Equation 5.9 at the specified points

$$x_1, x_2, \ldots, x_N$$

Since the x values are not equally spaced, set

$$x_1 = x_0 + h_1 \qquad x_2 = x_1 + h_2, \ldots, \qquad x_N = x_{N-1} + h_N$$

That is

$$y_k \approx y(x_k)$$

and

$$h_k = x_k - x_{k-1}$$

The increment h_k is called the *step size*. Often the x points are equally spaced so each h_k is of constant value, denoted simply h.

To obtain y_1, proceed as follows. The exact or actual solution curve $y = y(x)$ passes through the point (x_0, y_0), and you saw in Section 3.5 that the tangent line

$$L(x) = y(x_0) + y'(x_0)(x - x_0) \tag{5.10}$$

is a good approximation to $y(x)$ when x is close to x_0. That is, if h_1 is small, then $L(x_1) \approx y(x_1)$. Hence, when $x = x_1 = x_0 + h_1$ you obtain the approximation

$$y_1 = y_0 + h_1 f(x_0, y_0)$$

to the exact value $y(x_1)$ of the solution.

To obtain the next value y_2, repeat this procedure. Start at the point (x_1, y_1) and use the tangent line to obtain the approximation

$$y_2 = y_1 + h_2 f(x_1, y_1)$$

to the exact value $y(x_2)$ of the solution. Continuing in this way, you obtain the sequence of approximations

$$y_1 = y_0 + h_1 f(x_0, y_0)$$
$$y_2 = y_1 + h_2 f(x_1, y_1)$$
$$y_3 = y_2 + h_3 f(x_2, y_2)$$

$$\vdots$$

$$y_N = y_{N-1} + h_N f(x_{N-1}, y_{N-1})$$

Thus the table of values is built up in a step-by-step fashion. At each step of the process, an error is produced. Since the solution curve $y = y(x)$ does not usually coincide with the tangent line L, the point (x_1, y_1), for instance, does not lie on the solution curve, creating an error at the first step. Likewise, an error occurs at the second step, and so on, with each successive step. As these errors accumulate with more and more steps, the approximations y_k get further away from the exact solution curve. This situation is depicted in Figure 5.1.

In the next section you will see how the Euler method can be modified in an attempt to cut back on the error at each step and thereby improve the accuracy of the approximations. For now, let's consider an example illustrating the method.

The prepared program DIFFEQ 1 calculates the successive values $y_1, y_2,$ $\ldots, y_N$ approximating the exact solution to Equation 5.9 by the Euler method. The program uses program steps 000 through 184, and memory locations 01 through 09. You must write a subroutine for DIFFEQ 1 which specifies the keystrokes for evaluating the function $f(x, y)$. The current value of x must be recalled from memory location 01, and the current value of y from location 02, in the evaluation of $f(x, y)$. Program steps 185 through 479, as well as memory steps 00 and 10 through 59, are available for your use in writing the subroutine for $f(x, y)$.

Calculating a Numerical Solution by the Euler Method

Step 1: With DIFFEQ 1 read into your calculator, go to program step 185 and key in the subroutine for $f(x, y)$. Remember that x is stored in 01 and y is stored in 02 for your use in the evaluation of f. The first two steps of your subroutine must be

| Lb1 | | C' |

Figure 5.1 Errors arise at each step of the Euler method and the approximations y_k get further away from the exact solution.

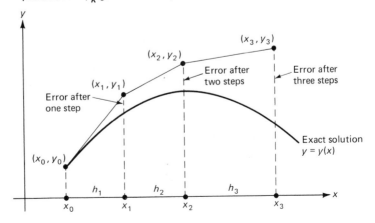

and the last two steps must be

| INV | SBR |

You are free to use the $\boxed{=}$ key in your subroutine.

Step 2: Back in the calculate mode, enter the value x_0 of the independent variable in the initial condition. Press $\boxed{x \rightleftharpoons t}$.

Step 3: Enter the value y_0 of the dependent variable in the initial condition. Press $\boxed{D'}$ to load the initial condition.

Step 4: Enter the step size h_1 of the first step for the Euler method. Press $\boxed{E'}$.

Step 5: Press $\boxed{A}$. The program calculates the first iterate in the Euler method and halts with the value x_1 in the display. Press $\boxed{x \rightleftharpoons t}$, and the approximation y_1 is displayed.

To obtain the next approximation by the Euler method:

Step 6: If the next step size h_{k+1} differs from the preceding one already loaded, enter the new increment h_{k+1} and press $\boxed{E'}$. Then repeat Step 5.

If the next step size h_{k+1} is the same as the preceding one already loaded, simply repeat Step 5.

EXERCISE 1.
A NUMERICAL SOLUTION
BY THE EULER METHOD

In our introductory remarks we verified that the function

$$y = xe^x + 2 \tag{5.11}$$

solves the initial value problem

$$y' = y + e^x - 2 \quad y(0) = 2 \tag{5.12}$$

Let's use DIFFEQ 1 to solve Equation 5.12 by the Euler method and compare the results with the true solution (5.11) for values of $x = 0.0, 0.1, 0.2, 0.3,$ ..., 1.0.

With DIFFEQ 1 read into your TI-59, key in the subroutine for $y' = f(x,y)$, given in Equation 5.12:

| GTO | 185 | LRN | Lb1 | C' | RCL | 02 | + | RCL | 01 |
| INV | ln x | − | 2 | = | INV | SBR | LRN |

Next load the initial value point (0,2) and the step size $h = 0.1$ (we will use the same step size for each approximation because the x values are all equally spaced):

(enter)	0		
(press)		$x \blacktriangleleft t$	Load $x_0 = 0.0$ into the T-register.
(enter)	2		
(press)		D'	Load x_0 and $y_0 = 2$ into storage.
(enter)	0.1		
(press)		E'	Load the step size $h = 0.1$.
(press)		A	The program halts with $x_1 = 0.1$ displayed.
(press)		$x \blacktriangleleft t$	The approximation $y_1 = 2.1$ is displayed.
(press)		A	The program halts with $x_2 = 0.2$ displayed.
(press)		$x \blacktriangleleft t$	The approximation $y_2 = 2.220517092$ is displayed.

By repeatedly pressing the key A followed by $x \blacktriangleleft t$, you obtain the approximations shown in Table 5-1. We have also calculated the exact solution values for purposes of comparison. All values have been rounded to three decimal places. Notice from Table 5-1 that the errors increase at each successive step, and that the error becomes quite substantial after the tenth step: $0.310/4.718 \approx 6.6$ percent. Therefore, the Euler approximations are too crude to be of any practical use for computations. In the next section you will see how the Euler method can be improved for greater accuracy.

Table 5-1 Euler approximations to the solution $y(x) = xe^x + 2$ of the initial value problem $y' = y + e^x - 2$, $y(0) = 2$.

x_k	(Euler) y_k	(Exact) $y(x_k)$	(Error) $|y(x_k) - y_k|$
0.0	2.000	2.000	0.000
0.1	2.100	2.111	0.011
0.2	2.221	2.244	0.023
0.3	2.365	2.405	0.040
0.4	2.536	2.597	0.061
0.5	2.739	2.824	0.085
0.6	2.978	3.093	0.115
0.7	3.258	3.410	0.152
0.8	3.585	3.780	0.195
0.9	3.966	4.214	0.248
1.0	4.408	4.718	0.310

EXERCISE 2.
AN EXAMPLE ILLUSTRATING
UNEQUALLY SPACED POINTS

The function

$$y = \frac{\sin x}{1 + \cos x}$$

solves the initial value problem

$$y' = y \cot x + y^2 \qquad y(\pi/2) = 1 \tag{5.13}$$

Find a table of values approximating the exact solution when $x_1 = 1.6$, $x_2 = 1.65$, $x_3 = 1.75$, $x_4 = 1.875$, $x_5 = 1.975$, and $x_6 = 2$. Notice that these values of x are not spaced the same distance apart.

    With DIFFEQ 1 read into your TI-59, key in the subroutine for y' given in Equation 5.13:

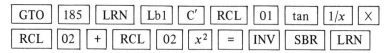

Since y' involves trigonometric functions, set your calculator to the radians mode, and display three decimal places:

(press) | Rad | | Fix | | 3 |

Load the initial data, using the approximation $\pi/2 \approx 1.571$ for x_0:

(enter)   1.571

(press) | $x \leftrightarrow t$ | Load $x_0 = 1.571$.

(enter)   1

(press) | D' | Load x_0 and $y_0 = 1$ into storage.

Load the first step size $h_1 = x_1 - x_0 = 1.6 - 1.571 = 0.029$ and calculate the first approximation y_1:

(enter)   0.029

(press) | E' | Load $h_1 = 0.029$.

(press) | A | The program halts with $x_1 = 1.6$ in the display.

(press) | $x \leftrightarrow t$ | The approximation $y_1 = 1.029$ is displayed.

Next load the second step size $h_2 = x_2 - x_1 = 1.65 - 1.6 = 0.05$ and calculate the approximation y_2:

(enter)   0.05

(press) $\boxed{E'}$ Load $h_2 = 0.05$.

(press) $\boxed{A}$ The program halts with $x_2 = 1.65$ displayed.

(press) $\boxed{x \leftrightarrow t}$ The approximation $y_2 = 1.080$ is displayed.

Now continue in this manner to calculate the next successive step size, load it into the program, and compute the associated successive approximation, thereby obtaining Table 5-2. This table also shows the values of the exact solution, corresponding to each approximation, for comparative purposes.

Table 5-2 Euler approximations to the solution $y(x) = \sin x/(1 + \cos x)$ of the initial value problem $y' = y \cot x + y^2$, $y(\pi/2) = 1$.

h_k	x_k	(Euler) y_k	(Exact) $y(x_k)$
	1.571	1.000	1.000
0.029	1.600	1.029	1.030
0.050	1.650	1.080	1.083
0.100	1.750	1.189	1.197
0.125	1.875	1.338	1.362
0.100	1.975	1.475	1.515
0.025	2.000	1.514	1.557

PROBLEMS 5.1

In each of Problems 1–5, you are given an initial value problem together with its exact solution. Use the Euler method in DIFFEQ 1 with the given value of h for equally spaced points to find a numerical solution over the indicated interval. Determine also the exact solution values corresponding to each calculation. Round all calculations to three decimal places.

1. $y' = 2xe^{x^2}$, $y(0) = 2$ on $0 \leqslant x \leqslant 1$ with $h = 0.1$; $y(x) = e^{x^2} + 1$

2. $y' = 2(2x - y)$, $y(0) = 1$ on $0 \leqslant x \leqslant 1$ with $h = 0.1$;
   $y(x) = 2x - 1 + 2e^{-2x}$

3. $y' = x^3 - 2xy$, $y(1) = 2$ on $1 \leqslant x \leqslant 2$ with $h = 0.1$;
   $y(x) = \frac{1}{2}[x^2 - 1 + 4e^{1-x^2}]$

4. $y' = 2y \cot x + \sin^3 x$, $y(\pi/2) = 1$ on $1.571 \leqslant x \leqslant 2.071$ with
   $h = 0.1$; $y(x) = 2\sin^2 x \sin^2 \frac{x}{2}$

5. $y' = \dfrac{1 + 4y - 3xy}{x(x-2)}$, $y(1) = 2$ on $1 \leqslant x \leqslant 1.9$ with $h = 0.1$;

$y(x) = (x^2 - 5)/2x^2 \, (x - 2)$

In Problems 6-8, use the Euler method in DIFFEQ 1 to find a numerical solution for each initial value problem at the indicated points. Round the calculations to three decimal places.

6. $y' = (x + y)^2$, $y(0) = -1$, $x_1 = 0.1$, $x_2 = 0.15$, $x_3 = 0.30$, $x_4 = 0.37$,
$x_5 = 0.49$, $x_6 = 0.66$, $x_7 = 0.69$, $x_8 = 0.75$, $x_9 = 0.85$, $x_{10} = 1.0$

7. $y' = -\dfrac{x \cos^3 y}{\sin y}$, $y(0) = \pi/4$, $x_1 = 0.05$, $x_2 = 0.15$, $x_3 = 0.25$, $x_4 = 0.37$,
$x_5 = 0.39$, $x_6 = 0.42$, $x_7 = 0.50$

8. $y' = e^{x+y}$, $y(0) = 0$, $x_1 = 0.01$, $x_2 = 0.03$, $x_3 = 0.051$, $x_4 = 0.1$, $x_5 = 0.19$,
$x_6 = 0.25$, $x_7 = 0.35$, $x_8 = 0.5$

Section 5.2 Modified Euler and Runge-Kutta Methods

There are several ways to improve on the Euler method for approximating the initial value problem

$$y' = f(x,y) \qquad y(x_0) = y_0 \tag{5.14}$$

We will consider one improvement for finding a table of approximations associated with *equally spaced* points $x_1 = x_0 + h$, $x_2 = x_1 + h, \ldots, x_N = x_{N-1} + h$. First, observe from the Fundamental Theorem of calculus that the function $y = y(x)$ solves the initial value problem in Equation 5.14, if and only if it solves the integral equation

$$y(x) = y_0 + \int_{x_0}^{x} f[t, y(t)] \, dt \tag{5.15}$$

Without going into the details here, it follows from Equation 5.15 that the approximations $y_1, y_2, \ldots, y_N$ then satisfy the equation

$$y_{k+1} = y_{k-1} + \int_{x_{k-1}}^{x_{k+1}} f[t, y(t)] \, dt \tag{5.16}$$

for each $k = 1, 2, \ldots, N-1$. So if you know y_0 *and* y_1, then $y_2, y_3, \ldots, y_N$ can be obtained successively from 5.16. If you find y_1 by the Euler method, and then employ the midpoint rule to approximate the integrals in Equation 5.16 by setting $f[t, y(t)]$ equal to $f(x_k, y_k)$, you will obtain the following sequence of approximations:

$$y_1 = y_0 + hf(x_0, y_0)$$
$$y_2 = y_0 + 2hf(x_1, y_1)$$
$$y_3 = y_1 + 2hf(x_2, y_2)$$
$$\vdots$$
$$y_N = y_{N-2} + 2hf(x_{N-1}, y_{N-1})$$

Obtaining the table of approximate values in this fashion is known as the *modified Euler method,* and, when *h* is small, the modified Euler method yields significantly better approximations than the Euler method. Next we give an example comparing both methods and illustrating the improved accuracy.

EXERCISE 1.
A NUMERICAL SOLUTION
BY THE MODIFIED EULER METHOD

The program DIFFEQ 1 calculates the successive values $y_1, y_2, \ldots, y_N$, approximating the exact solution to the initial value problem in Equation 5.14, by the modified Euler method. The procedures for determining the approximations are identical to those for the Euler method except that Step 5 is replaced by

Step 5': Press $\boxed{\text{B}}$. The program calculates the first approximation y_1 by the modified Euler method and halts with the value x_1 in the display. Press $\boxed{x \leftrightarrows t}$ for the approximation y_1.

Successive approximations are obtained by repeatedly pressing the key $\boxed{\text{B}}$ followed by $\boxed{x \leftrightarrows t}$.

For instance, consider again the initial value problem

$$y' = y + e^x - 2 \qquad y(0) = 2$$

presented in Exercise 1 of the preceding section. Key into DIFFEQ 1 the subroutine for $y' = f(x,y)$, and load the initial point $(0,2)$ and the step size $h = 0.1$ just as before. Then,

(press)	$\boxed{\text{B}}$	The program halts with $x_1 = 0.1$ displayed.
(press)	$\boxed{x \leftrightarrows t}$	The approximation $y_1 = 2.1$ is displayed.
(press)	$\boxed{\text{B}}$	The program halts with $x_2 = 0.2$ displayed.
(press)	$\boxed{x \leftrightarrows t}$	The approximation $y_2 = 2.241034184$ is displayed.

By repeatedly pressing the key $\boxed{\text{B}}$ followed by $\boxed{x \leftrightarrows t}$, you obtain the approximations shown in Table 5-3 showing the values rounded to three decimal places. You can see from the table that the error associated with the modified Euler method is substantially less than that for the Euler method itself. After the tenth step there is less than 1 percent error in the approximation 4.691 to the actual value 4.718 as compared to the 6.6 percent error found for the Euler approximation 4.408. It should be pointed out that there is a numerical instability in the modified Euler method so that under certain conditions it does not correctly "track" the solution to the differential equation.

Table 5-3 Modified Euler approximations compared to the Euler approximations and exact solution values of the initial value problem $y' = y + e^x - 2, y(0) = 2$.

x_k	(Modified Euler) y_k	(Euler) y_k	(Exact) $y(x_k)$
0.0	2.000	2.000	2.000
0.1	2.100	2.100	2.111
0.2	2.241	2.221	2.244
0.3	2.392	2.365	2.405
0.4	2.590	2.536	2.597
0.5	2.809	2.739	2.824
0.6	3.081	2.978	3.093
0.7	3.389	3.258	3.410
0.8	3.762	3.585	3.780
0.9	4.187	3.966	4.214
1.0	4.691	4.408	4.718

Let's consider another numerical method that yields much more accurate results than either the Euler or modified Euler method. The basic problem with those previous methods is that they assume the slope of the unknown solution function remains constant over the interval associated with the iteration. Generally the slope of the unknown function does not remain constant. If we knew what the slope was at the point $x_{k+1} = x_k + h_{k+1}$, we could average this with the slope at x_k to obtain a better estimate for the change in y over the interval from x_k to x_{k+1}. This averaging technique yields the approximation

$$y_{k+1} = y_k + \frac{1}{2}h_{k+1}\left\{f[x_k, y(x_k)] + f[x_{k+1}, y(x_{k+1})]\right\}$$

To use this formula, we need approximations to both $y(x_k)$ and $y(x_{k+1})$. For $y(x_k)$, we can use the approximation y_k already obtained by the previous iteration. To approximate $y(x_{k+1})$, we use an estimate z_{k+1} derived from the Euler method:

$$z_{k+1} = y_k + h_{k+1} f(x_k, y_k) \tag{5.17}$$

Then, using this estimate, we obtain the approximation

$$y_{k+1} = y_k + \frac{1}{2}h_{k+1} [f(x_k, y_k) + f(x_{k+1}, z_{k+1})] \tag{5.18}$$

The two-step method expressed by Equations 5.17 and 5.18 uses the Euler method to *predict* the value of the next approximation by z_{k+1}, and then *corrects* that prediction for the more accurate y_{k+1} computed by 5.18. This is an example of a *predictor-corrector* method of approximation and often goes by the name *2nd-order Runge-Kutta method.*

The Euler method can be modified to achieve even greater accuracy using a *4th-order Runge-Kutta method.* This improvement is based on four estimates to the value of f over the interval from x_k to x_{k+1}, and we give the method without derivation.

4th-Order Runge-Kutta Solution to $y' = f(x,y), y(x_0) = y_0$

For simplicity in notation, let $h_{k+1} = \Delta x$. Then calculate the four estimates:

$$m_1 = f(x_k, y_k)$$

$$m_2 = f(x_k + \frac{\Delta x}{2}, y_k + \frac{\Delta x}{2} m_1)$$

$$m_3 = f(x_k + \frac{\Delta x}{2}, y_k + \frac{\Delta x}{2} m_2)$$

$$m_4 = f(x_k + \Delta x, y_k + (\Delta x) m_3)$$

The approximation y_{k+1} is then obtained according to the formula

$$y_{k+1} = y_k + \frac{\Delta x}{6} (m_1 + 2m_2 + 2m_3 + m_4) \tag{5.19}$$

The 4th-order approximation (5.19) is very accurate, as you will see in the next example. Programmed in DIFFEQ 1, the method does take greater calculation time than the Euler or modified Euler methods. Keep in mind, however, that more accurate methods permit a larger step size to be used while simultaneously holding the error to acceptable levels. The procedures for determining the 4th-order Runge-Kutta approximation are identical to those of the previous two methods except that the key $\boxed{C}$ is pressed in Step 5 to obtain the approximation. The next example illustrates the performance of the method.

EXERCISE 2.
A NUMERICAL SOLUTION
BY THE 4TH-ORDER RUNGE-KUTTA METHOD

For purposes of comparison we will solve the same initial value problem

$$y' = y + e^x - 2 \qquad y(0) = 2$$

considered before, using the Runge-Kutta method. Once again, key into

DIFFEQ 1 the subroutine for $y' = f(x,y)$, and load the initial value point $(0, 2)$ and the step size $h = 0.1$:

| GTO | 185 | LRN | Lb1 | C' | RCL | 02 | + | RCL | 01 | INV |

| ln x | − | 2 | = | INV | SBR | LRN |

(enter)	0	
(press)	$x \blacktriangleleft t$	
(enter)	2	
(press)	D'	
(enter)	0.1	
(press)	E'	
(press)	C	Calculate the first approximation y_1 by the 4th-order Runge-Kutta method. The program halts with $x_1 = 0.1$ in the display.
(press)	$x \blacktriangleleft t$	The approximation $y_1 = 2.110516931$ is displayed.
(press)	C	The program halts with $x_2 = 0.2$ displayed.
(press)	$x \blacktriangleleft t$	The approximation $y_2 = 2.244280188$ is displayed.

By repeatedly pressing the key $\boxed{C}$ followed by $\boxed{x \blacktriangleleft t}$, you obtain the approximations in Table 5-4. From the table you see that the 4th-order Runge-Kutta approximations coincide perfectly with the exact solution values to three decimal places.

Table 5-4 4th order Runge-Kutta approximations compared to the modified Euler and exact solution values of the initial value problem $y' = y + e^x - 2$, $y(0) = 2$.

x_k	(4th-Order Runge-Kutta) y_k	(Modified Euler) y_k	(Exact) $y(x_k)$
0.0	2.000	2.000	2.000
0.1	2.111	2.100	2.111
0.2	2.244	2.241	2.244
0.3	2.405	2.392	2.405
0.4	2.597	2.590	2.597
0.5	2.824	2.809	2.824
0.6	3.093	3.081	3.093
0.7	3.410	3.389	3.410
0.8	3.780	3.762	3.780
0.9	4.214	4.187	4.214
1.0	4.718	4.691	4.718

The Runge-Kutta method programmed in DIFFEQ 1 does not require that the points $x_1, x_2, \ldots, x_N$ be equally spaced. This is illustrated in the next example.

EXERCISE 3.
RUNGE-KUTTA APPROXIMATIONS
FOR UNEQUALLY SPACED POINTS

Consider the initial value problem

$$y' = y \cot x + y^2 \qquad y(\pi/2) = 1$$

investigated in Exercise 2 of Section 5.1. Let's solve this same problem by the 4th-order Runge-Kutta method using DIFFEQ 1 with the points $x_1 = 1.6, x_2 = 1.65, x_3 = 1.75, x_4 = 1.875, x_5 = 1.975$, and $x_6 = 2$. As before, key in the subroutine for y', set your calculator to the radians mode, and load the initial value point (1.571, 1). Then load each step size with the key $\boxed{E'}$ followed by the keys $\boxed{C}$ and $\boxed{x \blacklozenge t}$, to obtain the successive approximations as follows:

(enter)	0.029		
(press)		$\boxed{E'}$	Load $h_1 = x_1 - x_0$
(press)		$\boxed{C}$	The program halts with $x_1 = 1.6$ in the display.
(press)		$\boxed{x \blacklozenge t}$	The 4th-order Runge-Kutta approximation $y_1 = 1.029422606$ is displayed.
(enter)	0.05		
(press)		$\boxed{E'}$	Load $h_2 = x_2 - x_1$.
(press)		$\boxed{C}$	The program halts with $x_2 = 1.65$ in the display.
(press)		$\boxed{x \blacklozenge t}$	The 4th-order Runge-Kutta approximation $y_2 = 1.082275179$ is displayed.

Continuing in this manner you obtain the values shown in Table 5-5.

Table 5-5 4th-order Runga-Kutta approximations compared with the exact solution values of the initial value problem $y' = y \cot x + y^2$, $y(\pi/2) = 1$. Note the unequally spaced values of x.

h_k	x_k	(4th-Order Runge-Kutta) y_k	(Exact) $y(x_k)$
	1.571	1.00020	1.00020
0.029	1.600	1.02942	1.02964
0.050	1.650	1.08228	1.08251
0.100	1.750	1.19712	1.19742
0.125	1.875	1.36167	1.36207
0.100	1.975	1.51489	1.51540
0.025	2.000	1.55686	1.55741

In each of Problems 1–5, you are given an initial value problem together with its exact solution. Use the modified Euler and 4th-order Runge-Kutta methods in DIFFEQ 1 with the given value of h for equally spaced points to find numerical solutions over the indicated interval. Round all calculations to three decimal places.

1. $y' = 2xe^{x^2}$, $y(0) = 2$ on $0 \leqslant x \leqslant 1$ with $h = 0.1$; $y(x) = e^{x^2} + 1$

2. $y' = 2(2x - y)$, $y(0) = 1$ on $0 \leqslant x \leqslant 1$ with $h = 0.1$; $y(x) = 2x - 1 + 2e^{-2x}$

3. $y' = x^3 - 2xy$, $y(1) = 2$ on $1 \leqslant x \leqslant 2$ with $h = 0.1$;

$$y(x) = \frac{1}{2}[x^2 - 1 + 4e^{1-x^2}]$$

4. $y' = 2y \cot x + \sin^3 x$, $y(\pi/2) = 1$ on $1.571 \leqslant x \leqslant 2.071$ with $h = 0.1$; $y(x) = 2 \sin^2 x \sin^2 (x/2)$

5. $y' = \dfrac{1 + 4y - 3xy}{x(x - 2)}$, $y(1) = 2$ on $1 \leqslant x \leqslant 1.9$ with $h = 0.1$;

$$y(x) = (x^2 - 5)/2x^2 \ (x - 2)$$

In Problems 6–8, use the 4th-order Runge-Kutta method in DIFFEQ 1 to find a numerical solution for each initial value problem at the indicated points. Round the calculations to three decimal places.

6. $y' = (x + y)^2$, $y(0) = -1$, $x_1 = 0.1$, $x_2 = 0.15$, $x_3 = 0.30$, $x_4 = 0.37$, $x_5 = 0.49$, $x_6 = 0.66$, $x_7 = 0.69$, $x_8 = 0.75$, $x_9 = 0.85$, $x_{10} = 1.0$

7. $y' = -\dfrac{x \cos^3 y}{\sin y}$, $y(0) = \pi/4$, $x_1 = 0.05$, $x_2 = 0.15$, $x_3 = 0.25$, $x_4 = 0.37$, $x_5 = 0.39$, $x_6 = 0.42$, $x_7 = 0.50$

8. $y' = e^{x+y}$, $y(0) = 0$, $x_1 = 0.01$, $x_2 = 0.03$, $x_3 = 0.051$, $x_4 = 0.1$, $x_5 = 0.19$, $x_6 = 0.25$, $x_7 = 0.35$, $x_8 = 0.5$

Section 5.3 First Order: Analytic Methods

In this section we present two methods for solving special types of first-order differential equations. Both methods involve analytic integration as studied in the previous chapter. The two methods discussed are of particular importance, and we include them for completeness.

Separable Variables

Consider the differential equation

$$y' = f(x,y)$$

If it is possible to rewrite the equation so that all y terms occur on one side with the differential dy and all x terms occur on the other with dx, then we say that the differential equation has *separable variables*. Thus the equation can be written in the form

$$g(y)\, dy = h(x)\, dx \qquad (5.20)$$

The general solution is then obtained by simply integrating both sides:

$$\int g(y)\, dy = \int h(x)\, dx + C \qquad (5.21)$$

where C is an arbitrary constant.

EXERCISE 1.

Solve the separable variables equation

$$\frac{dy}{dx} = \frac{1}{y} e^{-y} (x \cos x^2)$$

Solution. The equation can be written in differential form with the variables separated:

$$y e^y\, dy = (x \cos x^2)\, dx$$

Now we integrate the left side by parts and the right side by substitution:

$$\int y e^y\, dy = \int (x \cos x^2)\, dx + C$$

$$y e^y - e^y = \frac{1}{2} \sin x^2 + C$$

Linear Equations

If a first-order differential equation can be written in the form

$$\frac{dy}{dx} + Py = Q \qquad (5.22)$$

where P and Q are functions of the variable x only, then the differential equation is said to be *linear*.

Without going through the details of the derivation, it turns out that if you multiply Equation 5.22 through by the integrating factor ρ, defined by

$$\rho = e^{\int P\, dx} \qquad (5.23)$$

then the left side of the resulting equation becomes the derivative of the product ρy. So the solution $y = y(x)$ is obtained by integrating both sides of the resultant equation, giving

$$\rho y = \int \rho Q(x)\, dx + C \qquad (5.24)$$

where ρ is defined by Equation 5.23.

EXERCISE 2.

Solve the linear equation

$$y' - \frac{2y}{x} = x \ln x$$

Solution. The equation is linear with $P(x) = -2/x$ and $Q(x) = x \ln x$ First we determine the integrating factor according to Equation 5.23:

$$\rho = e^{\int(-2/x)\, dx} = e^{-2 \ln x}$$

$$= e^{\ln (x^{-2})} = x^{-2}$$

Next, using Equation 5.24, we find the solution $y = y(x)$ by integration:

$$x^{-2}y = \int x^{-2} \cdot x \ln x\, dx + C$$

$$= \int \frac{1}{x} \ln x\, dx + C$$

$$= \int u\, du + C \qquad \text{where } u = \ln x$$

$$= \frac{1}{2} u^2 + C$$

$$= \frac{1}{2} (\ln x)^2 + C$$

Thus

$$y = \frac{x^2}{2} (\ln x)^2 + Cx^2$$

is the general solution.

EXERCISE 3.

Convert to and solve the linear equation

$$(x + 2)^2\, y' + 2(2xy + 4y - 3) = 0$$

Solution. Writing the equation in the form in 5.22 gives

$$y' + \frac{2(2x + 4)}{(x + 2)^2} y = \frac{6}{(x + 2)^2}$$

or

$$y' + \frac{4}{(x + 2)} y = \frac{6}{(x + 2)^2}$$

The integrating factor is

$$\rho = e^{\int 4\, dx/(x+2)} = e^{4 \ln |x+2|} = (x + 2)^4$$

We then find the solution by Equation 5.24:

$$(x + 2)^4 y = \int (x + 2)^4\, 6(x + 2)^{-2}\, dx + C$$
$$= 2(x + 2)^3 + C$$

Therefore

$$y = 2(x + 2)^{-1} + C(x + 2)^{-4}$$

is the general solution.

PROBLEMS 5.3

In each of Problems 1–12, find the general solution.

1. $xy' = y^3$
2. $y' = xy^2$
3. $yy' = \sec^2 x \csc y^2$
4. $(y + 1)y' = 3x^2 y^2$
5. $xy' + 2y = 4x^2$
6. $y' = x - 2y$
7. $y' = x - 2xy$
8. $y' = e^{-2x} - 3y$
9. $(y^2 + 1)\, dy - xye^x\, dx = 0$
10. $y' = e^{2x-y}$
11. $(\cos^2 x)y' = 1 - y$
12. $(y \cot x)\, dx - dy + (\csc x)\, dx = 0$

Section 5.4 Applications of First-Order Differential Equations

In this section we present a number of examples illustrating how first-order differential equations arise in the physical sciences and economics.

EXERCISE 1.
INTEREST COMPOUNDED CONTINUOUSLY

Suppose a principal amount P_0 in dollars is invested at a *continuous interest rate r* per annum, given as a decimal. In such a case, the rate of change of the amount $A(t)$ accumulated at time t is rA; that is,

$$\frac{dA}{dt} = rA \qquad (5.25)$$

This is a separable differential equation that can be solved by integration:

$$\frac{dA}{A} = \int r\, dt + C$$

$$\ln A = rt + C$$

When $t = 0, A = P_0$ so that $C = \ln P_0$. Thus

$$\ln A = rt + \ln P_0$$

or

$$A = P_0 e^{rt} \qquad (5.26)$$

For instance, if \$1,000 is invested at 13 percent per annum, then after 5 years the amount accumulated will be

$$A = 1{,}000 e^{(0.13)(5)} = 1{,}000 e^{0.65}$$

$$= \$1{,}915.54$$

rounded to the nearest penny.

Let's calculate how many years it takes for the amount P_0 to double itself if it is compounded continuously at 6.25 percent per annum.

$$2P_0 = P_0 e^{0.0625\, t}$$

or

$$2 = e^{0.0625\, t}$$

Taking the logarithm of both sides,

$$0.0625\, t = \ln 2$$

or

284 $\quad t = \ln 2/0.0625 = 11.09$ yrs, approximately

EXERCISE 2.
A MODEL OF BIOLOGICAL
POPULATION GROWTH

Equation 5.26 is an example of exponential growth. You see that such growth derives from the condition that the rate of change in the amount of a substance is proportional to the amount present, as expressed in Equation 5.25. A simple model for population growth expresses the same relationship; that is, if P represents the population of some biological species, then

$$\frac{dP}{dt} = \alpha P$$

where α is some factor of proportionality and P is a function of t. Now if the population model is to be more realistic, it must take into account the effect of limited food supply and living space. In such a model the rate parameter α diminishes as the population P approaches some limiting population P_∞. Thus

$$\alpha = k(P_\infty - P)$$

for some constant k. Substitution yields *Verhulst's Law*

$$\frac{dP}{dt} = \alpha P = k(P_\infty - P)P \tag{5.27}$$

or

$$\frac{dP}{(P_\infty - P)P} = k\,dt \tag{5.28}$$

It follows from elementary algebra that

$$\frac{1}{(P_\infty - P)P} = \frac{1}{P_\infty}\left(\frac{1}{P} + \frac{1}{P_\infty - P}\right)$$

Thus the separable Equation 5.28 can be rewritten as

$$\frac{dP}{P} + \frac{dP}{P_\infty - P} = kP_\infty\,dt$$

which integrates to

$$\ln P - \ln(P_\infty - P) = kP_\infty t + C \tag{5.29}$$

285   If the population is P_0 at time $t = 0$, we find

$$C = \ln \frac{P_0}{P_\infty - P_0}$$

Thus

$$-kP_\infty t = C - \ln \frac{P}{P_\infty - P} = \ln \left(\frac{P_0}{P_\infty - P_0} \cdot \frac{P_\infty - P}{P} \right)$$

or

$$e^{-kP_\infty t} = \frac{P_0 P_\infty}{P_\infty - P_0} \cdot \frac{P_\infty - P}{P P_\infty}$$

Algebraic simplification of this last result gives

$$\left(\frac{1}{P} - \frac{1}{P_\infty} \right) = \left(\frac{1}{P_0} - \frac{1}{P_\infty} \right) e^{-kP_\infty t} \tag{5.30}$$

A plot of the population P versus time t for a great variety of values of P_∞ and k shows a general stable pattern as revealed in Figure 5.2. The point Q on the graph is a point of inflection and occurs when

$$\frac{d^2 P}{dt^2} = 0$$

By direct calculation from the differential Equation 5.27,

$$\frac{d^2 P}{dt^2} = -kP'P + k(P_\infty - P)P'$$
$$= kP'(P_\infty - 2P)$$

and since $k \neq 0$ and $P' \neq 0$ at the point Q, it follows that

$$P_\infty - 2P = 0$$

Figure 5.2 Graph of the limited growth model.

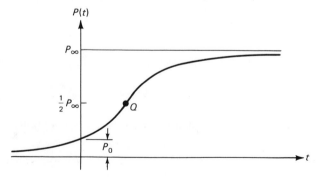

$$P = \frac{1}{2} P_\infty$$

at the point of inflection Q. In words, when the population P reaches half the limiting population P_∞, the growth dP/dt is most rapid and then starts to diminish toward zero.

The equation for P can be written in a different form. Returning to Equation 5.29, write

$$\ln \frac{P}{P_\infty - P} = kP_\infty t + C$$

$$\frac{P}{P_\infty - P} = e^C e^{kP_\infty t}$$

$$P = P_\infty e^C e^{kP_\infty t} - P e^C e^{kP_\infty t}$$

$$P + P e^C e^{kP_\infty t} = P_\infty e^C e^{kP_\infty t}$$

$$P = \frac{P_\infty e^C e^{kP_\infty t}}{1 + e^C e^{kP_\infty t}}$$

If we divide numerator and denominator for this last formula by $e^C e^{kP_\infty t}$, and denote the constant e^{-C} by A, we get

$$P = \frac{P_\infty}{1 + A e^{-kP_\infty t}} \tag{5.31}$$

A curve of this form (5.31) is often called a *logistic curve.*

EXERCISE 3.
A MIXING PROBLEM

In this type of problem, a substance is in solution and the amount of the substance is changing instantaneously with time. For instance, a tank contains 500 gal of brine containing 200 lbs of dissolved salt. If brine containing 0.1 lbs of salt per gal runs into the tank at the rate of 10 gal/min and the thoroughly mixed brine flows out of the tank at the same rate, determine how much salt remains in the tank at the end of 1 hr.

Solution. In this type of problem you always have

Rate of change = Rate of input − Rate of output

Because the brine flowing in contains 0.1 lb of salt per gal, the

Rate of input = (0.1)(10) = 1 lb of salt per min

Let $y(t)$ denote the amount of salt in pounds in the tank after t minutes. Then the concentration of the salt, which is the amount of salt per gallon, is $y/500$ because the tank always contains 500 gal of brine. So the

$$\text{Rate of output} = \frac{y}{500} \cdot 10 = \frac{y}{50} \text{ lb of salt per min}$$

This calculation leads to the following initial value problem, giving the rate of change of the amount of salt in solution:

$$\frac{dy}{dt} = 1 - \frac{y}{50} \quad y(0) = 200 \tag{5.32}$$

Let's solve the separable Equation 5.32 using the Runge-Kutta method in DIFFEQ 1 with a step size of $\Delta t = 10$ to find $y(60)$, the amount of salt remaining after 60 min. With DIFFEQ 1 read into your calculator, enter the keystrokes for the derivative function:

GTO	185	LRN	Lb1	C′	1	−	RCL	02	÷	50	=

INV	SBR	LRN

Then

(enter)	0		
(press)		$x \leftrightarrows t$	Load initial $t = 0$.
(enter)	200		
(press)		D′	Load initial $y = 200$ lb.
(enter)	10		
(press)		E′	Load $\Delta t = 10$ min.

By repeatedly pressing $\boxed{C}$ until the display reads 60, and then pressing $\boxed{x \leftrightarrows t}$, you obtain $y(60) = 95.18$ lbs of salt remaining after 1 hr. This answer agrees with the actual result obtained by integrating the separable Equation 5.32.

EXERCISE 4.
A FALLING BODY
ENCOUNTERING AIR RESISTANCE

In the real world, any object falling through the atmosphere encounters air resistance, the amount of which depends on the speed of the object and the density of the air (as well as other variables). The factor of air resistance in a real problem is a very complicated one, but we will illustrate how it might enter into a simple model.

Suppose that a body with a mass of m slugs is dropped from a height of 4,250 ft. Assume that the air resistance equals $(0.1m)v$, where $v = v(t)$ is the velocity of the object at any time t. What is the velocity of the object after 5 sec?

Solution. Let's take the positive y direction to be downward. Then $v = dy/dt$ and the force of the air resistance acts in the negative direction because it opposes the motion. Newton's Second Law states that

Force = Mass $\times$ Acceleration

The downward force is mg, the weight of the falling object, and this is opposed by an upward force equal to the resistance $(0.1m)v$. Thus an application of Newton's Second Law leads to the differential equation

$$m \frac{dv}{dt} = mg - (0.1m)v$$

or

$$\frac{dv}{dt} + \frac{1}{10}v = g \tag{5.33}$$

where $g = 32$ is (approximately) the acceleration due to gravity, taken as positive since it acts in the selected positive direction. So we obtain the initial value problem

$$\frac{dv}{dt} = 32 - \frac{v}{10} \qquad v(0) = 0$$

We can use DIFFEQ 1 to find $v(5)$ numerically, obtaining $v(5) = 125.9$ ft/sec. However, it will be instructive to solve the linear Equation 5.33 analytically, to obtain the velocity and distance that the object falls in any time t.

The integrating factor for Equation 5.33 is $e^{t/10}$. The general solution to the differential equation is therefore

$$ve^{t/10} = \int 32 \, e^{t/10} \, dt + C_1$$

or

$$v = 320 + C_1 e^{-t/10}$$

When $t = 0$, $v = 0$ so that $C_1 = -320$. Thus

$$v = 320(1 - e^{-t/10}) \tag{5.34}$$

gives the velocity at any time. Integration of 5.34 yields

$$y = 320(t + 10e^{-t/10}) + C_2$$

When $t = 0$, $y = 0$ so that $C_2 = -3,200$. Thus

$$y = 320(t + 10e^{-t/10} - 10) \tag{5.35}$$

is the distance fallen after t seconds.

Notice from 5.34 that as $t \to \infty$, the velocity approaches the limiting value 320 ft/sec. This limiting velocity is called the *terminal velocity* of the falling body.

EXERCISE 5.
A TEMPERATURE PROBLEM

Newton's *law of cooling* asserts that the rate of change in the temperature of a body is proportional to the difference between its temperature and that of the surrounding medium. For example, suppose a body in air at $65°$ F cools from $175°$ F to $130°$ F in 5 min. Let's determine how long it takes for the temperature to reach $95°$ F.

If $T = T(t)$ represents the temperature of the body at any time t, then by the Law of Cooling,

$$\frac{dT}{dt} = -k(T - 65)$$

or

$$\frac{dT}{T - 65} = -k\,dt$$

where the negative sign is indicative of the fact that T is decreasing with time. Integration of this separable differential equation gives

$$\ln(T - 65) = -kt + C$$

When $t = 0$, $T = 175$ so that $C = \ln 110$. Thus

$$\ln\frac{T - 65}{110} = -kt \tag{5.36}$$

Next when $t = 5$, $T = 130$ yielding

$$\ln\frac{65}{110} = -5k$$

or

$$-k = \frac{1}{5}\ln\frac{65}{110} \tag{5.37}$$

Substitution of Equation 5.37 into 5.36 when $T = 95°$ F gives

$$t = -\frac{1}{k} \ln \frac{30}{110} = \frac{5 \ln (30/110)}{\ln (65/110)}$$

$$= 12.35 \text{ min, approximately}$$

which is the required time for the temperature of the body to reach $95°$ F.

PROBLEMS 5.4

1. In a certain town the population at any time changes at a rate proportional to the population. If the population in 1970 was 34,100 and in 1980 it was 41,400, find the expected population in the year 2000.

2. Assuming exponential growth, if a given population doubles in 25 years, in how many years will it triple?

3. A drop of liquid evaporates at a rate proportional to its surface area. Find the radius of the drop as a function of time.

4. A full tank contains 500 gal of brine whose salt concentration is 3 lb/gal. Fresh water flows into the tank at the rate of 2 gal per minute and the mixture, kept uniform by stirring, flows out of the tank at the rate of 5 gal per minute. Find the concentration of the salt when the tank is half empty.

5. At noon a thermometer reading $68°$ F is taken outside where the air temperature is $23°$ F. Five minutes later, the thermometer reading is $49°$ F. At 12:10 PM the thermometer is taken back indoors where the temperature is fixed at $68°$ F. Find the reading of the thermometer at 12:20 PM, to the nearest tenth of a degree.

6. A raindrop falls from a motionless cloud encountering a resisting force proportional to the square of its velocity at each instant.

   a. Determine the velocity as a function of the distance it falls.

   b. Find the terminal velocity.

7. Consider a large number $a + b$ of two types of molecules a and b per unit volume. These molecules react to form a new molecule. If $y(t)$ denotes the number of new molecules per unit volume at each instant of time t, then the *Law of Mass Action* asserts that

$$\frac{dy}{dt} = (a - y)(b - y) > 0$$

Find an analytic expression for y, observing that

$$\frac{1}{(a - y)(b - y)} = \frac{1}{b - a} \left(\frac{1}{a - y} - \frac{1}{b - y} \right)$$

8. A boat is being towed at the rate of 18 ft/sec. At the instant when the towing line is cast off, a man takes up the oars and begins to row with a force of 20 lbs in the direction of the moving boat. If man and boat together weigh 480 lbs, and the resistance (due to friction) is $\frac{7}{4}v$, find the speed of the boat at the end of 30 sec.

9. Radium decomposes at a rate proportional to the amount present. If half the original quantity disappears in 1600 years, find the amount lost in 100 years.

10. At $8\frac{1}{4}$ percent interest compounded continuously, what sum of money would be needed to provide an income of $15/day for 25 years, the principal being exhausted at the end of the time?

11. Oxygen flows through one tube into a liter flask filled with air, and the mixture of oxygen and air (considered well stirred) escapes through another such tube. Assuming that air contains 21 percent oxygen, what percentage of oxygen will the flask contain after 5 liters have passed through the intake tube.

12. If the average person breathes 20 times per minute, exhaling each time 100 in^3 of air containing 4 percent carbon dioxide, find the percentage of carbon dioxide in the air of a 10,000 ft^3 closed room 1 hr after a class of 30 students enters. Assume the air is fresh at the start and that the ventilators admit 1,000 ft^3 of fresh air per minute, and assume that the fresh air contains 0.04 percent carbon dioxide.

13. A body of mass m is dropped from a great height. Assume that the air resistance is $12v$, and find analytic expressions for the velocity and distance that the body falls as a function of time.

6

Infinite Series

The idea of summing together infinitely many numbers is not new. For instance, when you studied decimals in elementary school you learned how to convert a fraction to its decimal representation through the long division process. By that process

$$\frac{9}{7} = 1.285714\overline{285714}\ldots$$

is an infinite repeating decimal; it is an abbreviation for the formal infinite sum

$$1 + \frac{2}{10} + \frac{8}{10^2} + \frac{5}{10^3} + \frac{7}{10^4} + \frac{1}{10^5} + \frac{4}{10^6} + \ldots$$

The question is, what do we really mean by adding together infinitely many numbers? If we are not careful to make the meaning precise, we are likely to encounter some absurdities or "paradoxes," as the following discussion will demonstrate.

For example, apply the long division process to the algebraic fraction $1/(1-x)$:

$$
\begin{array}{r}
1 + x + x^2 + \ldots \\
1-x \overline{\smash{\big)}\, 1 } \\
\underline{1 - x} \\
x \\
\underline{x - x^2} \\
x^2 \\
\underline{x^2 - x^3} \\
x^3 \\
\vdots
\end{array}
$$

That is,

$$
\frac{1}{1-x} = 1 + x + x^2 + x^3 + \ldots
$$

This infinite sum is an example of a *geometric series,* and if we are naive about its meaning we might be tempted to substitute $x = -1$ and thereby obtain

$$
\frac{1}{2} = 1 - 1 + 1 - 1 + 1 - \ldots
$$

But what does this last equation mean? That $\frac{1}{2}$ is the same as 1, or 0, or what? It seems to be nonsensical. When the eighteenth-century mathematician Leonhard Euler substituted $x = 2$ into the same geometric series, he obtained

$$
-1 = 1 + 2 + 4 + 8 \ldots
$$

The infinite sum on the right is clearly larger than any positive number, so it sums to $+\infty$. Since this evidently implied that -1 is greater than ∞, Euler reasoned that, like 0, ∞ must separate the positive and negative numbers. Of course, from a modern point of view Euler's conclusion is absurd. These examples illustrate the kind of difficulties one might encounter in the absence of a precise definition for the concept of an infinite series.

The purpose of this chapter is to introduce the ideas of infinite series and sequences, and to investigate both ideas through the use of your programmable calculator. Certainly the subject of infinite series occupies a very prominent place in applied mathematics.

Before you begin your study of this chapter, record the three programs SERIES, PARTSUM, and POWER on separate magnetic cards. Each program is listed in Appendix A and uses standard 479.59 partitioning.

Imagine a small ball dropped from a height of, say, 2 m. When it hits the flat ground below it, the ball bounces halfway back up to its previous height, to reach a height of 1 m. Then it falls back to the ground and bounces halfway back to its former height again, this time reaching a height of $\frac{1}{2}$ m. As the ball continues to bounce indefinitely in this fashion, it yields the sequential listing of numbers

$$2, 1, \frac{1}{2}, \frac{1}{4}, \frac{1}{8}, \ldots, \frac{4}{2^n}, \ldots$$

representing the ball's height after each successive bounce. This listing is an *ordered* listing because the numbers are read from left to right, just as they are written, to find the correct height of the ball after each bounce. Such a listing is an example of a sequence.

> *Definition.* A *sequence* is a function whose domain is the set of positive integers. The numbers in the range of a sequence are called its *terms*, and the subscripted symbol a_n denotes the *nth term* of the sequence. The positive integer n is called the *index* of the nth term a_n.

In our example of the bouncing ball sequence, the number 2 is the first term, 1 is the second term, $\frac{1}{2}$ is the third term, and so forth. In general,

$$a_n = \frac{4}{2^n}$$

gives a rule for calculating the nth term of that sequence, for $n = 1, 2, 3, \ldots$. It is customary to refer to a sequence by enclosing its nth term in braces, thus

$$\left\{ \frac{4}{2^n} \right\}_{n=1}^{\infty}$$

or simply

$$\left\{ \frac{4}{2^n} \right\}$$

denotes the bouncing ball sequence. More generally, $\{a_n\}$ denotes the sequence whose nth term is a_n.

Sometimes a sequence is identified, but there is no rule or formula that explicitly gives the nth term. For instance, the infinite decimal expansion of the number π gives a sequence of digits that begins as

$$3, 1, 4, 1, 5, 9, 2, 6, 5, 4 \ldots$$

and so forth, but there is no known formula that specifies the nth digit in terms of n.

A sequence may be defined *recursively*. That is, one or more terms of the sequence may be specified, and then each successive term defined by means of the preceding terms. To illustrate a recursive definition, two rules—

1. $a_n = 1$ for $n = 1$ and $n = 2$

2. $a_{n+2} = a_n + a_{n+1}$ for $n \geqslant 1$

define the sequence whose first few terms are

$$1, 1, 2, 3, 5, 8, 13, 21, 34, 55, \ldots$$

Observe that there are always infinitely many *terms* to any sequence. That does not mean, however, that the sequence has infinitely many *values*. For example, the sequence $1, 1, 1, \ldots, 1, \ldots$ has infinitely many terms a_n, but a_n is equal to 1 for every index n. So it is very important that you do not confuse a sequence itself (which is a function or mapping) with the set of values that it assumes (the range of the function).

Consider the sequence $\{4/2^n\}$ for the bouncing ball. As n gets larger and larger, the nth term $4/2^n$ gets closer and closer to the limiting value 0. The sequence $\{1\}$ is already at its limiting value 1 from the first. On the other hand, the terms of the sequence

$$\frac{1}{2}, -\frac{3}{4}, \frac{7}{8}, -\frac{15}{16}, \frac{31}{32}, \ldots, (-1)^{n+1}\left(1 - \frac{1}{2^n}\right), \ldots$$

seem to cluster near the two values -1 and 1. Finally, the terms of the sequence $\{n^2\}$ get larger and larger, failing to cluster anywhere.

The preceding examples illustrate that some sequences approach a unique limiting value and others do not. This suggests the following definition.

The number L is said to be the *limit* of the sequence $\{a_n\}$ if given any $\epsilon > 0$ there is a positive integer N such that

$$|a_n - L| < \epsilon \quad \text{whenever } n > N$$

If L is the limit of the sequence $\{a_n\}$ we say that the sequence *converges* to L and write

$$\lim_{n \to \infty} a_n = L \quad \text{or} \quad a_n \to L \quad \text{as } n \to \infty$$

If no such limit exists, the sequence is said to *diverge*.

In other words, the sequence $\{a_n\}$ converges to L if its terms get closer and closer to L as n gets larger and larger.

The program SERIES calculates the terms of a specified sequence $\{a_n\}$ in order to facilitate investigation of its behavior. The program uses steps 000 through 161, as well as memory locations 01 through 09. You must key in a subroutine for SERIES that specifies the nth term of the sequence, either as a formula in the variable n or recursively. This subroutine will be explained and illustrated. Program steps 162 through 479, as well as memory steps 00 and 10 through 59, are available for your use in writing that subroutine.

Calculating the Limit of a Sequence

Step 1: Read side 1 of the magnetic card SERIES into your TI-59, with standard partitioning.

Step 2: GTO program step 162 and key in the subroutine for the nth term a_n. The first two steps of your subroutine must be

$$\boxed{\text{Lb1}}\quad\boxed{\text{C}'}$$

and the last two steps must be

$$\boxed{\text{INV}}\quad\boxed{\text{SBR}}$$

If a_n is defined by a formula involving only the index n: Simply key in the keystrokes for the formula, assuming that the current index n is in the display upon entry into the subroutine. Then proceed to Step 3.

If a_n is defined recursively in terms of the preceding term a_{n-1} and its index n-1: Key in the keystrokes for a_n, assuming that a_{n-1} is in the display upon entry into the subroutine. The index value $n-1$ is stored in memory location 02. Then proceed to Step 3′.

Step 3: Press $\boxed{\text{E}}$ to initialize the program, and then press $\boxed{\text{A}}$ repeatedly to see the successive terms $a_1, a_2, a_3, \ldots$, and so forth. To see the current index n at any stage, simply press $\boxed{x \leftrightarrows t}$.

Step 3′: Press $\boxed{\text{E}}$ to initialize the program, and then enter the starting value a_1 for the recursion formula and store this value in memory register 03. By repeatedly pressing the key $\boxed{\text{B}}$ you display the successive terms $a_2, a_3, a_4, \ldots$, and so forth. At any stage you may see the current index n by pressing $\boxed{x \leftrightarrows t}$.

The program SERIES allows you control of the index n through the use of the following keys:

A′   Replace the current step size Δn by $10\Delta n$. Initially, $\Delta n = 1$.

B′   Replace the current step size Δn by $\Delta n/10$. Initially, $\Delta n = 1$.

These keys can be used to investigate the limit of a_n as $n \to \infty$ when a_n is defined by a formula. But they *cannot* be used when a_n is defined recursively because each term must be obtained from the immediately preceding one, which is not the case when a_n is defined by formula. The following examples illustrate the use of the program SERIES to investigate the behavior of a sequence.

EXERCISE 1.
A SEQUENCE DEFINED BY FORMULA

Consider the sequence whose nth term is given by

$$a_n = \frac{(3n-1)(2n+5)}{9n^2 + 20}$$

Read the program SERIES into your TI-59, and then enter the subroutine for a_n as follows:

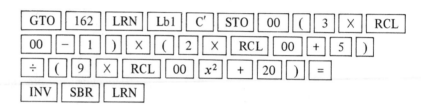

Then

(press)	Fix 5	Display five decimal places.
(press)	E	Initialize the program, setting $\Delta n = 1$.
(press)	A	The program halts with $a_1 = 0.48276$ displayed.
(press)	$x \rightleftharpoons t$	The index $n = 1$ is displayed.
(press)	A	The program halts with $a_2 = 0.80357$ displayed.
(press)	A	The program halts with $a_3 = 0.87129$ displayed.

Continue to press A repeatedly to obtain the following table. Remember, whenever you want to see the current index n, press $x \rightleftharpoons t$ after the program halts with a_n displayed.

n	a_n	n	a_n
1	0.48276	11	0.77908
2	0.80357	12	0.77128
3	0.87129	13	0.76444
4	0.87195	14	0.75841
5	0.85714	15	0.75306
6	0.84012	16	0.74828
7	0.82430	17	0.74399
8	0.81040	18	0.74012
9	0.79840	19	0.73662
10	0.78804	20	0.73343

To investigate the limit of a_n as $n \to \infty$, we need to increase the step size Δn.

(press) $\boxed{A'}$ The display shows $\Delta n = 10$.

(press) $\boxed{A}$ The program halts with $a_{30} = 0.71244$ displayed.

(press) $\boxed{x \blacktriangleright t}$ The index $n = 30$ is displayed.

(press) $\boxed{A}$ The program halts with $a_{40} = 0.70146$ displayed.

Continue pressing the keys $\boxed{A}$ and $\boxed{x \blacktriangleright t}$, sometimes changing the step size Δn of the index with the key $\boxed{A'}$, to obtain the following table:

n	a_n	n	a_n
30	0.71244	400	0.67026
40	0.70146	500	0.66955
50	0.69472	1,500	0.66763
60	0.69016	2,500	0.66724
70	0.68688	3,500	0.66708
80	0.68440	13,500	0.66677
90	0.68246	23,500	0.66673
100	0.68090	123,500	0.66668
200	0.67384	223,500	0.66667
300	0.67146	323,500	0.66667

Thus from the table we see that

$$\frac{(3n - 1)(2n + 5)}{9n^2 + 20} \to \frac{2}{3} \quad \text{as } n \to \infty$$

299

EXERCISE 2.
A SEQUENCE DEFINED RECURSIVELY

Consider the sequence defined by

$$a_1 = 5 \quad \text{and} \quad a_n = \sqrt{a_{n-1}} \quad \text{for } n > 1$$

with SERIES read into your calculator, key in the subroutine for a_n as follows:

| GTO | 162 | LRN | Lb1 | C' | $\sqrt{x}$ | INV | SBR | LRN |

Then

(press)	E	Initialize the program, setting $\Delta n = 1$.
(enter)	5	
(press)	STO 03	Store $a_1 = 5$ in memory register 03.
(press)	B	The program halts with $a_2 = 2.23607$ displayed.
(press)	$x \blacktriangleleft t$	The index $n = 2$ is displayed.
(press)	B	The program halts with $a_3 = 1.49535$ displayed.
(press)	B	The program halts with $a_4 = 1.22284$ displayed.

Continue to press B repeatedly to obtain the following table (whenever you press $x \blacktriangleleft t$, the current index n is displayed):

n	a_n	n	a_n
1	5.00000	11	1.00157
2	2.23607	12	1.00079
3	1.49535	13	1.00039
4	1.22284	14	1.00020
5	1.10582	15	1.00010
6	1.05158	16	1.00005
7	1.02547	17	1.00002
8	1.01265	18	1.00001
9	1.00631	19	1.00001
10	1.00315	20	1.00000

300 From the table we see that $a_n \to 1$ as $n \to \infty$.

EXERCISE 3.
A FORMULA CHANGED
TO A RECURSIVE RULE

Consider the sequence

$$a_n = \frac{4^n}{n!}$$

Because factorials cannot be computed for large values of n on your TI-59, the formula for a_n is not very useful computationally. Yet note that

$$a_n = \frac{4^{n-1}}{(n-1)!} \cdot \frac{4}{n} = a_{n-1} \cdot \frac{4}{n}$$

Thus we can calculate a_n recursively, beginning with $a_1 = 4$. Key the subroutine for a_n into SERIES, remembering that the index value $n-1$ is stored in 02:

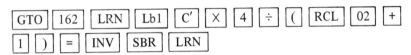

Then

(press)	E	Initialize the program.
(enter)	4	
(press)	STO 03	Store $a_1 = 4$ in memory register 03.
(press)	B	The program halts with $a_2 = 8.0000$ displayed.
(press)	B	The program halts with $a_3 = 10.66667$ displayed.

Continuing, you obtain the following table:

n	a_n	n	a_n
1	4.00000	11	0.10508
2	8.00000	12	0.03503
3	10.66667	13	0.01078
4	10.66667	14	0.00308
5	8.53333	15	0.00082
6	5.68889	16	0.00021
7	3.25079	17	0.00005
8	1.62540	18	0.00001
9	0.72240	19	0.00000
10	0.28896	20	0.00000

301 We conclude from the table that $4n/n! \to 0$ as $n \to \infty$.

EXERCISE 4.
A DIVERGENT SEQUENCE

Consider the sequence

$$a_n = \frac{3^n}{n^3}$$

To avoid overflow for large values of n, we can calculate a_n recursively:

$$a_n = 3\,\frac{3^{n-1}}{(n-1)^3} \cdot \frac{(n-1)^3}{n^3}$$

$$= 3\,a_{n-1}\left(1-\frac{1}{n}\right)^3 \qquad n>1$$

beginning with $a_1 = 3$. With SERIES loaded into your TI-59, key in the subroutine for a_n:

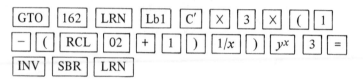

Next

(press)   E

(enter)   3

(press)   STO   03

Now repeatedly press B to obtain the following table:

n	a_n	n	a_n
1	3.00000	11	133.09316
2	1.12500	12	307.54687
3	1.00000	13	725.68184
4	1.26562	14	1,743.06450
5	1.94400	15	4,251.52800
6	3.37500	16	10,509.45337
7	6.37609	17	26,285.39853
8	12.81445	18	66,430.12500
9	27.00000	19	169,450.5711
10	59.04900	20	435,848.0501

302 The table reveals that $\dfrac{3^n}{n^3} \to \infty$ as $n \to \infty$ so the sequence diverges.

Some Fundamental Limit Laws

The following basic laws hold for limits of sequences, and we give them without proof.

Rule 1: If $a_n \to L$ and $b_n \to M$ as $n \to \infty$, then

a. $a_n + b_n \to L + M$ as $n \to \infty$,

b. $a_n b_n \to LM$ as $n \to \infty$, and

c. $\dfrac{1}{a_n} \to \dfrac{1}{L}$ as $n \to \infty$, provided that $L \neq 0$ and a_n is never zero.

Rule 2: If $a_n \to L$ and $b_n \to L$ as $n \to \infty$, and if $a_n \leq c_n \leq b_n$ for all n beyond some index N, then $c_n \to L$ as $n \to \infty$.

Rule 3: If $a_n \to L$ and if f is any function that is defined for each term a_n and is continuous at L, then $f(a_n) \to f(L)$ as $n \to \infty$.

As an illustration of Rule 3, since $(1 + 1/n) \to 1$ as $n \to \infty$, and $f(x) = e^x$ is a continuous function at $x = 1$, we conclude that

$$e^{1 + (1/n)} \to e^1 \qquad \text{as } n \to \infty$$

PROBLEMS 6.1

Determine which of the following sequences $\{a_n\}$ converge and which diverge. Find the limit of each convergent sequence.

1. $a_n = \dfrac{n}{n + 1}$

2. $a_n = \dfrac{3n^2 + 4n - 2}{2n^2 + 1}$

3. $a_n = \dfrac{n}{n + 1} - \dfrac{n + 1}{n}$

4. $a_n = \dfrac{n^3 + 5}{n^2 - 1}$

5. $a_n = (-1)^n(1 + 2^{-n})$

6. $a_n = \ln n / n$

7. $a_n = n^4 / e^n$

8. $a_n = n \sin \dfrac{1}{n}$

9. $a_n = \sin^2 \dfrac{3}{n} + 2 \cos^2 \dfrac{1}{n}$

10. $a_n = \dfrac{(n + 2)!}{n!}$

11. $a_n = \dfrac{n + 1}{n!}$

12. $a_n = \sqrt{2n+1} - \sqrt{n}$

13. $a_n = \ln(2n+1) - \ln n$

14. $a_n = n \sin^{-1} \dfrac{1}{n}$

15. $a_n = n \left[e^{1/n} - \ln\left(1 + \dfrac{1}{n}\right) \right]$

16. $a_n = \dfrac{(-5)^n + 4^n}{5^n}$

17. $a_n = \left(1 - \dfrac{1}{n}\right)^n$

18. $a_n = \sqrt[n]{7} \left(\dfrac{n-1}{n+1}\right)$

19. $a_n = \dfrac{\sqrt{n^2+1}}{3n}$

20. $a_n = \sqrt[n]{n} \left(\dfrac{2n-1}{n+1}\right)$

21. Define $a_n = \dfrac{n!}{n^n}$ recursively, and find the limit as $n \to \infty$.

22. Find the limit of $\{a_n\}$ given by

$$a_n = a_{n-1}\left(1 - \dfrac{1}{n^2}\right) \qquad n > 1$$

$$a_1 = 1$$

23. Find the limit of $\{a_n\}$ given by

$$a_n = \sqrt{2 + a_{n-1}} \qquad n > 1$$

$$a_1 = \sqrt{2}$$

24. Determine if the sequence defined by

$$a_n = \dfrac{a_{n-1}^2}{3a_{n-1}} \qquad \text{for } n > 1$$

$$a_1 = 2$$

converges or diverges. If it converges, find the limit.

25. A solution to the equation

$$f(x) = x$$

is called a *fixed point* of the function f; geometrically, such a solution corresponds to a value of x where the graph of $y = f(x)$ crosses the line $y = x$. Define recursively the sequence

$$x_n = f(x_{n-1}) \qquad n > 1$$

and

$$x_1 = \text{any value in the domain of } f$$

Under certain conditions it can be proved that $\lim_{n\to\infty} x_n$ is a fixed point of f. Apply this algorithm to find the fixed point of $\cos x$, accurate to five decimal places.

26. Solve the equation $\frac{1}{3} e^x = x$ for $0 \leqslant x \leqslant 1$ using the method of Problem 25. Obtain your answer to five-place accuracy.

Section 6.2 The Geometric Series

Let $\{a_n\}$ be a sequence of real numbers, and form the new sequence $\{s_n\}$ whose terms are defined as follows:

$s_1 = a_1$

$s_2 = a_1 + a_2$

$s_3 = a_1 + a_2 + a_3$

$s_4 = a_1 + a_2 + a_3 + a_4$

.

.

.

$s_n = a_1 + a_2 + a_3 + \ldots + a_n \qquad$ for every n

Then the formal sum

$$a_1 + a_2 + a_3 + \ldots + a_n + \ldots = \sum_{n=1}^{\infty} a_n$$

is called an *infinite series;* the numbers a_n are its *terms,* and the numbers s_n its *partial sums.*

If the sequence $\{s_n\}$ of partial sums converges to a limit S, then S is called the *sum* of the infinite series, and it is said that the infinite series *converges.* We write

$$S = \sum_{n=1}^{\infty} a_n$$

If the sequence $\{s_n\}$ does not have a limit, then the series is said to *diverge.*

A series may begin with the first, second, or other terms so that you could write

$$\sum_{n=1}^{\infty} a_n \qquad \sum_{n=2}^{\infty} a_n \qquad \sum_{n=k}^{\infty} a_n$$

and so forth, for an infinite series. If there is no danger of ambiguity, it is permissible to write simply

$$\sum a_n$$

Notice that we defined an infinite series as a "formal" sum, because you cannot add together infinitely many real numbers in any arithmetic sense. The notion of a series makes sense only because we can discuss it within the context of its sequence of partial sums.

An important sequence is known as a *geometric progression* and it is of the form

$$a, ar, ar^2, ar^3, \ldots, ar^n, \ldots$$

in which each term beyond the first is obtained by multiplying the term immediately preceding it by the same number r. The infinite series

$$\sum_{n=0}^{\infty} ar^n \tag{6.1}$$

obtained by summing the terms of a geometric progression is called a *geometric series*. Let's investigate the behavior of the geometric series.

The nth partial sum s_n of the geometric series (6.1) is given by

$$s_n = a + ar + ar^2 + \ldots + ar^{n-1} \tag{6.2}$$

Now observe that multiplication of s_n by the expression $(1-r)$ gives the following result:

$$(1-r)s_n = (1-r)(a + ar + ar^2 + \ldots + ar^{n-1})$$
$$= (a + ar + ar^2 + \ldots + ar^{n-1}) - (ar + ar^2 + \ldots + ar^n)$$
$$= a - ar^n$$

Solving this last equation for s_n, we find that

$$s_n = \frac{a(1-r^n)}{1-r} \qquad r \neq 1 \tag{6.3}$$

If $|r| < 1$, then $r^n \to 0$. Applying that result to Equation 6.3 gives

$$\lim_{n \to \infty} s_n = \frac{a}{1-r} \qquad \text{when } |r| < 1$$

On the other hand, if $|r| > 1$, then $r^n \to \pm\infty$ so that the sequence $\{s_n\}$ diverges. If $r = 1$, then from Equation 6.2

$$s_n = a + a + a + \ldots + a = na$$

and the sequence $\{s_n\}$ diverges. Likewise, if $r = -1$, then

$$s_n = a - a + a - a + \ldots \pm a$$

so that each term s_n is alternately a or 0; again $\{s_n\}$ diverges. These facts are summarized in the following result.

Theorem. If $|r| < 1$, then the geometric series $\sum\limits_{n=0}^{\infty} ar^n$ converges to the number $\dfrac{a}{1-r}$. If $|r| \geqslant 1$, then the geometric series diverges.

The program SERIES calculates any partial sum and its error in approximating the limit of a convergent geometric series.

Calculating the Partial Sum $\sum\limits_{n=0}^{k} ar^n$
and Its Error E_k

Step 1: Read side 1 of the magnetic card SERIES into your TI–59.

Step 2: Enter the number a in the geometric series and press $\boxed{x \blacktriangleleft t}$.

Step 3: Enter the number r, where $|r| < 1$, in the geometric series, and press $\boxed{E'}$. The program halts with the sum of the geometric series displayed.

Step 4: Enter the terminal index k into the display and press $\boxed{C}$. The program halts with the partial sum

$$\sum_{n=0}^{k} ar^n$$

displayed.

Step 5: To see the error $E_k = \sum\limits_{n=k+1}^{\infty} ar^n$ between the partial sum $\sum\limits_{n=0}^{k} ar^n$

and the actual sum $\sum\limits_{n=0}^{\infty} ar^n$ of the geometric series, press $\boxed{x \blacktriangleleft t}$.

The next several examples illustrate the use of SERIES to sum the terms of a geometric series.

EXERCISE 1.
SUMMING THE TERMS
OF A GEOMETRIC SERIES

Consider the series

$$\sum_{n=0}^{\infty} \frac{3}{5^n}$$

This is a geometric series with $a = 3$ and $r = \dfrac{1}{5}$, and so it converges. Let's determine the sum of the terms through $n = 10$. With SERIES read into your TI-59,

(enter)	3	
(press)	$\boxed{x \leftrightarrow t}$	Load $a = 3$.
(enter)	$\dfrac{1}{5}$	
(press)	$\boxed{E'}$	Load $r = \dfrac{1}{5}$. The program halts with the sum 3.75 of the geometric series displayed.
(enter)	10	
(press)	$\boxed{C}$	Load the terminal index $k = 10$. The program halts with the partial sum 3.749999923 displayed.
(press)	$\boxed{x \leftrightarrow t}$	The error $E_{10} = 0.0000000768$ is displayed.

Therefore

$$\sum_{n=0}^{10} \frac{3}{5^n} = 3.749999923 \quad \text{and} \quad \sum_{n=11}^{\infty} \frac{3}{5^n} = 0.0000000768$$

EXERCISE 2.
THE DECIMAL REPRESENTATION
OF ONE-THIRD

The infinite repeating decimal $0.33333\ldots$ can be expressed as a geometric series:

$$0.33333\ldots = \frac{3}{10} + \frac{3}{100} + \frac{3}{1,000} + \frac{3}{10,000} + \ldots$$

$$= \sum_{n=1}^{\infty} \frac{3}{10^n} = \sum_{n=0}^{\infty} \frac{3}{10^n} - 3$$

Now $\displaystyle\sum_{n=0}^{\infty} \frac{3}{10^n}$ is a geometric series with $a = 3$ and $r = \dfrac{1}{10}$; it converges to

$3/(1 - \dfrac{1}{10}) = 10/3$. Thus

$$0.33333\ldots = \sum_{n=0}^{\infty} \frac{3}{10^n} - 3 = \frac{10}{3} - \frac{9}{3} = \frac{1}{3}$$

So the infinite repeating decimal $0.33333\ldots$ is *exactly* equal to the rational number $1/3$.

Calculating $\sum\limits_{n=L}^{U} ar^n$ *for Arbitrary L and U, $0 < L \leqslant U$*

The program SERIES also calculates the sum of the terms of a geometric series between two arbitrary indices L and U. Perform Steps 1-3 for the geometric series, just as before. If these have been performed previously for a specific series, then it is not necessary to repeat them for this finite sum. Then:

Step 4: Enter the lower index $n = L$ and press $\boxed{x \blacktriangleleft t}$.

Step 5: Enter the upper index $n = U$ and press $\boxed{D}$. The program halts with the finite sum

$$\sum_{n=L}^{U} ar^n$$

displayed.

EXERCISE 3.
SUMMING FINITELY MANY TERMS
IN GEOMETRIC PROGRESSION

Let's determine the finite sum

$$\frac{11}{3^5} + \frac{11}{3^6} + \frac{11}{3^7} + \ldots + \frac{11}{3^{17}} = \sum_{n=5}^{17} \frac{11}{3^n}$$

With SERIES read into your TI-59,

(enter)	11		$a = 11$
(press)		$\boxed{x \blacktriangleleft t}$	
(enter)	$\dfrac{1}{3}$		$r = \dfrac{1}{3}$
(press)		$\boxed{E'}$	The program halts with the entire sum 16.5 of the geometric series displayed.
(enter)	5		
(press)		$\boxed{x \blacktriangleleft t}$	The lower index $L = 5$.
(enter)	17		
(press)		$\boxed{D}$	The upper index $U = 17$ is entered, and the finite sum 0.067901192 is displayed.

Thus

$$\sum_{n=5}^{17} \frac{11}{3^n} = 0.067901192$$

EXERCISE 4.
A BOUNCING BALL

Consider again the bouncing ball sequence presented in the introductory re-marks in Section 6.1:

$$2, 1, \frac{1}{2}, \frac{1}{4}, \frac{1}{8}, \ldots, \frac{1}{2^n}, \ldots$$

This is a geometric progression with $a = 2$ and $r = \frac{1}{2}$. The total distance the ball travels up and down is given by the geometric series

1st bounce   5th bounce

$$S = 2 + 2 \cdot 1 + 2 \cdot \frac{1}{2} + 2 \cdot \frac{1}{4} + 2 \cdot \frac{1}{8} + \ldots$$

$$= 2 + 2 \sum_{n=0}^{\infty} \frac{1}{2^n} \qquad\qquad (6.4)$$

$$= 2 + 2 \left(\frac{1}{1 - \frac{1}{2}} \right) = 6 \text{ m}$$

To determine the distance the ball has traveled up and down when it strikes the ground at the 5th bounce, we want

$$2 + 2 \sum_{n=0}^{3} \frac{1}{2^n}$$

because the kth bounce occurs when the index n equals $k-2$ in the geometric series (6.4). Using SERIES,

(enter)	1		$a = 1$
(press)		$\boxed{x \updownarrow t}$	
(enter)	$\frac{1}{2}$		$r = \frac{1}{2}$
(press)		$\boxed{E'}$	
(enter)	3		$k = 3$
(press)		$\boxed{C}$	

The program halts with 1.875 displayed. Thus the ball has traveled a distance $2 + 2(1.875) = 5.75$ m when it strikes the ground at the 5th bounce.

PROBLEMS 6.2

In each of Problems 1-4, determine the given partial sum and its error in approximating the sum of the associated geometric series. Give your answers to five-place accuracy.

1. $\displaystyle\sum_{n=0}^{6} 5\left(\frac{4}{7}\right)^n$

2. $\displaystyle\sum_{n=0}^{7} 3\left(\frac{1}{4}\right)^n$

3. $\displaystyle\sum_{n=0}^{13} (-1)^n(0.7)^n$

4. $\displaystyle\sum_{n=0}^{11} \frac{231}{17}(0.123)^n$

In Problems 5-10, determine the infinite sums to five-place accuracy.

5. $\displaystyle\sum_{n=3}^{\infty} \frac{5^n}{9^{n+1}}$

6. $\displaystyle\sum_{n=4}^{\infty} \frac{7^n}{8^{n-1}}$

7. $\displaystyle\sum_{n=1}^{\infty} (-3)\frac{2^n}{5^{n+2}}$

8. $\displaystyle\sum_{n=2}^{\infty} \left(-\frac{1}{5}\right)\left(\frac{3}{4}\right)^{2n}$

9. $\displaystyle\sum_{n=5}^{\infty} \frac{3}{7}(0.1392)^n$

10. $\displaystyle\sum_{n=8}^{\infty} \left(-\frac{127}{15}\right)e^{1-n}$

Express the repeating decimals in Problems 11-14 as fractions.

11. $0.99999\overline{9}\ldots$

12. $0.6363636\overline{3}\ldots$

13. $1.2727272\overline{7}\ldots$

14. $0.35172172\overline{172}\ldots$

Determine the finite sums in Problems 15-20 to five-place accuracy.

15. $\displaystyle\sum_{n=4}^{8} \frac{5}{3}\left(\frac{1}{6}\right)^n$

16. $\displaystyle\sum_{n=5}^{17} \frac{1}{4}(-0.18)^n$

17. $\displaystyle\sum_{n=7}^{23} (-1)^n(2^{-n} + 3^{-n})$

18. $\displaystyle\sum_{n=6}^{19} 8\left(\dfrac{9^{n-1}}{13^{n+2}}\right)$

19. $\displaystyle\sum_{n=3}^{42} 17(-0.9299)^n$

20. $\displaystyle\sum_{n=18}^{27} \dfrac{1{,}501}{3}(0.9994)^{n-4}$

21. A ball is dropped from a height of 5 m onto a smooth surface. On each bounce the ball rises 70 percent of the height it reached on the previous bounce.

   a. Find the total distance the ball has traveled up and down when it strikes the ground on the 7th bounce.

   b. What is the total distance the ball travels up and down, assuming it bounces indefinitely?

22. Figure 6.1 shows the first five of an infinite series of equilateral triangles. The outermost triangle has side length equal to 1 unit, and each of the other triangles is obtained by joining the midpoints of the sides of the triangle before it.

   a. Find the sum of the areas of all the triangles.

   b. Find the sum of the areas of the first five triangles.

23. In an electronic videogame, a "ball" is bouncing back and forth along a horizontal straight line from one side of the screen to the other side, the two sides acting as "backstops" in the game. As the game begins, the ball leaves one backstop, moving toward the other one. Just at the instant the ball leaves, the two backstops commence moving toward each other. In-itially, the two backstops are apart by the width w of the screen. Each

Figure 6.1

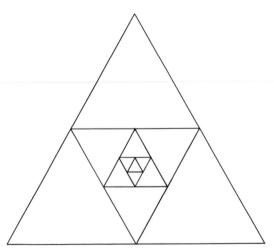

backstop moves toward the other at a rate equal to half the rate the ball is bouncing back and forth between them.

    a. Find a geometric series expressing the distance the ball travels before the backstops come together.

    b. Find the sum of this series.

Section 6.3 Infinite Series

In the preceding section an infinite series

$$\sum_{n=0}^{\infty} a_n$$

was identified with its sequence $\{s_n\}$ of partial sums, where the partial sum s_k is defined by

$$s_k = \sum_{n=0}^{k} a_n \tag{6.5}$$

To know whether or not an infinite series converges, we must find out if the sequence $\{s_n\}$ converges; if $\{s_n\}$ diverges, the series diverges.

    Various standard tests are presented in most elementary calculus texts to aid in determining the convergence or divergence of an infinite series. We are not going to give all those tests here, but rather take a numeric approach to the question of convergence. That is, we will try to settle that question for a specific series through direct examination of the values of its partial sums. In certain cases the partial sums can be misleading, and we will consider an example illustrating such cases. In other instances, the partial sums show very clearly whether the series converges or diverges.

    The program PARTSUM calculates the partial sum (6.5) for a given series and specified nonnegative integer k. The program requires that you key in a subroutine for the general term a_n of the series, either according to a formula or recursively. This subroutine will be explained and illustrated below. The program uses steps 000 through 057, and memory locations 01 through 04. Program steps 058 through 479, as well as memory steps 00 and 05 through 59, are available for your use in the subroutine for a_n.

Calculating Partial Sums of a Series

Step 1: Read side 1 of the magnetic card PARTSUM into your TI–59, with standard partitioning.

Step 2: GTO program step 058 and key in the subroutine for a_n. The first two steps of your subroutine must be

| Lb1 | C' |

and the last two steps must be

| INV | SBR |

If a_n is defined by a formula involving only the index n: Key in the keystrokes for the formula, assuming that the current index n is in the display upon entry into the subroutine. Then proceed to Step 3.

If a_n is defined recursively in terms of the preceding term a_{n-1} and its index $n-1$: Key in the keystrokes for a_n, assuming that a_{n-1} is in the display upon entry into the subroutine. The index value $n-1$ is stored in memory location 02. Then proceed to Step 3'.

Step 3: Enter the terminal index k, and press $\boxed{C}$. The program halts with the partial sum

$$s_k = \sum_{n=0}^{k} a_n$$

displayed. If you wish to calculate another partial sum, enter the new index k and press $\boxed{C}$ again. Repeat as often as desired.

Step 3': Enter the terminal index k, and press $\boxed{x \updownarrow t}$. Then enter the starting value a_0 for the recursion formula, and press $\boxed{B}$. The program halts with the partial sum s_k displayed. If you wish another partial sum, enter the new index k and the starting a_0 just as before, and press $\boxed{B}$ again. Repeat this step as often as desired.

The following examples illustrate the use of the program PARTSUM to investigate the behavior of an infinite series.

EXERCISE 1.
A CONVERGENT SERIES
DEFINED BY FORMULA

Consider the infinite series

$$\sum_{n=0}^{\infty} \frac{1}{(n+1)^4}$$

Let's investigate the sequence of partial sums

$$s_k = \sum_{n=0}^{k} \frac{1}{(n+1)^4}$$

for selected values of k. With PARTSUM read into your TI-59, key in the subroutine for a_n as follows:

$$\boxed{\text{GTO}}\ \boxed{058}\ \boxed{\text{LRN}}\ \boxed{\text{Lb1}}\ \boxed{\text{C}'}\ \boxed{+}\ \boxed{1}\ \boxed{=}\ \boxed{x^2}\ \boxed{x^2}\ \boxed{1/x}$$
$$\boxed{\text{INV}}\ \boxed{\text{SBR}}\ \boxed{\text{LRN}}$$

Next

(press)		$\boxed{\text{Fix}}\ \boxed{5}$	Display five decimal digits.
(enter)	1		$k = 1.$
(press)		$\boxed{\text{C}}$	The program halts with the partial sum $s_1 = 1.06250$ displayed.
(enter)	2		$k = 2.$
(press)		$\boxed{\text{C}}$	The program halts with the partial sum $s_2 = 1.07485$ displayed.
(enter)	3		$k = 3.$
(press)		$\boxed{\text{C}}$	The program halts with the partial sum $s_3 = 1.07875$ displayed.

Continuing in this fashion, you obtain the following table of partial sums:

k	s_k	k	s_k
1	1.06250	8	1.08194
2	1.07485	9	1.08204
3	1.07875	10	1.08210
4	1.08035	20	1.08229
5	1.08112	30	1.08231
6	1.08154	40	1.08232
7	1.08178	50	1.08232

From the table of partial sums we conclude that the series converges. It can
be shown from analytic methods that

$$\sum_{n=0}^{\infty} \frac{1}{(n+1)^4} = \frac{\pi^4}{90} \approx 1.082323234$$

so the partial sum s_{50} is accurate to five decimal places. If you continue
calculating partial sums, you will find s_{500} is accurate to eight decimal places.

A CONVERGENT SERIES
DEFINED RECURSIVELY

Let's investigate the sequence of partial sums for the infinite series

$$\sum_{n=0}^{\infty} \frac{1}{n!}$$

(Remember that $0! = 1$ by definition.) The terms of this series can be defined recursively by

$$a_n = \frac{1}{n!} = \frac{1}{(n-1)!} \cdot \frac{1}{n} = a_{n-1}\left(\frac{1}{n}\right) \qquad n > 0$$

and

$$a_0 = 1$$

With PARTSUM read into your calculator, key in the subroutine for a_n as follows, keeping in mind that the index $n-1$ is stored in memory register 02:

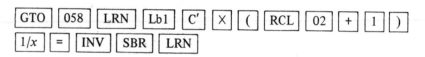

$$\boxed{\text{GTO}}\ \boxed{058}\ \boxed{\text{LRN}}\ \boxed{\text{Lb1}}\ \boxed{\text{C'}}\ \boxed{\times}\ \boxed{(}\ \boxed{\text{RCL}}\ \boxed{02}\ \boxed{+}\ \boxed{1}\ \boxed{)}$$
$$\boxed{1/x}\ \boxed{=}\ \boxed{\text{INV}}\ \boxed{\text{SBR}}\ \boxed{\text{LRN}}$$

Then

(enter)	1		
(press)		$x\!\leftrightarrow\!t$	$k = 1.$
(enter)	1		$a_0 = 1.0.$
(press)		B	The program halts with the partial sum $s_1 = 2$ displayed.
(enter)	2		
(press)		$x\!\leftrightarrow\!t$	$k = 2.$
(enter)	1		$a_0 = 1.0.$
(press)		B	The program halts with the partial sum $s_2 = 2.5$ displayed.

It is not necessary to calculate all the partial sums in order, even though a_n is defined recursively. To calculate s_5:

(enter)	5		
316 (press)		$x\!\leftrightarrow\!t$	$k = 5.$

(enter)   1 $a_0 = 1.0$.

(press) $\boxed{\text{B}}$ The program halts with the partial sum $s_5 = 2.716666667$ displayed.

Continuing in this manner, you obtain the following table of partial sums.

k	s_k	k	s_k
1	2.	15	2.718281828
2	2.5	20	2.718281828
5	2.716666667	25	2.718281828
8	2.71827877	30	2.718281828
10	2.718281801	50	2.718281828

So we conclude that

$$\sum_{n=0}^{\infty} \frac{1}{n!} = e$$

Note the rapid convergence of the sequence of partial sums in this example.

Now suppose that the series $\Sigma\, a_n$ converges, so that the sequence of partial sums $\{s_k\}$ converges, say to S. Observe that

$$a_n = (a_0 + a_1 + \ldots + a_{n-1} + a_n) - (a_0 + a_1 + \ldots + a_{n-1})$$

$$= s_n - s_{n-1}$$

Thus for a convergent series,

$$\lim a_n = \lim s_n - \lim s_{n-1} = S - S = 0$$

That is, *if the series $\Sigma\, a_n$ converges, then the limit of the nth term a_n must equal* 0. This necessary condition is customarily referred to as *the nth term test*.

For example, consider the series

$$\sum_{n=1}^{\infty} \frac{n^n}{n!}$$

Since for each index n,

$$a_n = \frac{n^n}{n!} = \frac{n \cdot n \cdot n \ldots n}{1 \cdot 2 \cdot 3 \ldots n} \geq 1$$

it is impossible for the limit of a_n (if it exists) to be 0. So the series diverges.

Note that the limit of a_n may fail to equal 0 either because the limit fails to exist, or because the limit exists and has a value other than 0. In either case the series diverges.

It may happen that the limit of the nth term is zero, but nevertheless the series diverges. This effect is illustrated in the next example.

EXERCISE 3.
THE HARMONIC SERIES

The infinite series

$$\sum_{n=0}^{\infty} \frac{1}{n+1} \quad \text{or equivalently} \quad \sum_{n=1}^{\infty} \frac{1}{n}$$

is known as the *harmonic series*, because its terms form a harmonic sequence (that is, the reciprocals of the terms are in arithmetic progression). The harmonic series diverges even though the limit of its terms is zero. We will now demonstrate this point analytically.

Look at the partial sums of the harmonic series that are indexed by powers of 2. That is, consider

$$s_{2^1} = s_2 = 1 + \frac{1}{2}$$

$$s_{2^2} = s_4 = 1 + \frac{1}{2} + \overbrace{\left(\frac{1}{3} + \frac{1}{4}\right)}^{\frac{1}{2}} \geq 1 + \frac{1}{2} + \left(\frac{1}{4} + \frac{1}{4}\right) = 1 + 2\left(\frac{1}{2}\right)$$

$$s_{2^3} = s_8 = 1 + \frac{1}{2} + \left(\frac{1}{3} + \frac{1}{4}\right) + \left(\frac{1}{5} + \frac{1}{6} + \frac{1}{7} + \frac{1}{8}\right)$$

$$\geq 1 + \frac{1}{2} + \underbrace{\left(\frac{1}{4} + \frac{1}{4}\right)}_{\frac{1}{2}} + \underbrace{\left(\frac{1}{8} + \frac{1}{8} + \frac{1}{8} + \frac{1}{8}\right)}_{\frac{1}{2}} = 1 + 3\left(\frac{1}{2}\right)$$

In general you can arrange the terms of s_{2^k} in several groups so that each group has sum $\frac{1}{2}$ after substituting smaller values for its terms. When you do so, you can establish that

$$s_{2^k} \geq 1 + k\left(\frac{1}{2}\right) \to +\infty \qquad \text{as } k \to \infty$$

Thus the sequence of partial sums for the harmonic series cannot converge.

Let's examine the harmonic series using PARTSUM. Key in the subroutine for the terms of the series:

| GTO | 058 | LRN | Lb1 | C' | + | 1 | = | 1/x | INV |

| SBR | LRN |

Next determine the following table:

k	s_k	k	s_k
1	1.5	300	6.285986139
10	3.019877345	400	6.572423457
20	3.645358705	500	6.794819438
30	4.027245195	1,000	7.486469861
40	4.302933283	1,500	7.891435571
50	4.518813181	2,000	8.178867853
100	5.197278508	2,500	8.401861502
150	5.597803105	5,000	9.094708812
200	5.883006072		

You can see from the table that the partial sums of the harmonic series grow very slowly. If you had examined only the sequence of partial sums using PARTSUM, you might have concluded that the harmonic series would converge. This example emphasizes that you must interpret the results of PARTSUM with extreme care. In particular, the results of PARTSUM may give the impression that a series converges when in fact it does not. That happens when the sequence of partial sums grows very slowly, for instance. Computer calculations have shown that it takes over 250 million terms to be summed in the harmonic series before the partial sums even reach the value 20; yet the partial sums diverge to $+\infty$! You can see that any intuitive idea resulting from our experience of the finite world may not serve us well when it comes to questions concerning the infinite.

In Exercise 1 it was shown that the series $\Sigma\, 1/n^4$ converges, whereas the harmonic series $\Sigma\, 1/n$ diverges. In general, *the p-series*

$$\sum_{n=0}^{\infty} \frac{1}{n^p} \tag{6.6}$$

converges whenever p is a real number bigger than 1; it diverges if $p \leqslant 1$.

EXERCISE 4.
CHANGING THE INDEX OF SUMMATION

In the previous exercise we indicated that the harmonic series could be expressed in the form

$$\sum_{n=1}^{\infty} \frac{1}{n}$$

where the index of summation begins with $n=1$. Yet the program PARTSUM assumes that the index begins with 0, so we keyed in the expression

$$\sum_{n=0}^{\infty} \frac{1}{n+1}$$

for the harmonic series as a subroutine for PARTSUM. Furthermore,

$$\sum_{n=1}^{5} \frac{1}{n} = \sum_{n=0}^{4} \frac{1}{n+1}$$

are the corresponding equivalent expressions for a partial sum.

In general, the following equation gives a formula for changing the index in the partial sum of a series so that the index begins with 0 (as required by PARTSUM):

$$\sum_{n=j}^{k} a_n = \sum_{n=0}^{k-j} a_{n+j} \tag{6.7}$$

For example,

$$\sum_{n=2}^{9} \frac{3n}{n-1} = \sum_{n=0}^{7} \frac{3n+2}{n+1}$$

and

$$\sum_{n=4}^{21} \frac{\sin n}{n! \ln (n-2)} = \sum_{n=0}^{17} \frac{\sin (n+4)}{(n+4)! \ln (n+2)}$$

EXERCISE 5.
AN ALTERNATING SERIES

If each a_n is a positive number, then a series of the form

$$\sum_{n=0}^{\infty} (-1)^n a_n = a_0 - a_1 + a_2 - a_3 + \ldots \tag{6.8}$$

is called an *alternating series* because every term alternates in sign. It can be established that whenever $\{a_n\}$ is a decreasing sequence such that $a_n \to 0$, then the alternating series (6.8) converges. Moreover, if S is the sum of a convergent alternating series, then the difference between the kth partial sum s_k and the true sum S satisfies

$$|S - s_k| < a_{k+1}$$

In other words, the partial sum s_k approximates the sum S with an error that is less than the numerical value of the first unused term. Furthermore, the sign of the error is always the same as the sign of the first unused term. So if the first unused term is negative, the partial sum approximation s_k is too high; if it is positive, s_k is too low.

For instance, consider the alternating harmonic series

$$\sum_{n=0}^{\infty} \frac{(-1)^n}{n+1}$$

This series converges because $\left\{\frac{1}{n+1}\right\}$ is a decreasing sequence of positive terms that converges to 0. The terms b_n of the alternating harmonic series can be defined recursively:

$$b_n = \frac{(-1)^n}{n+1} = \frac{(-1)^{n-1}}{n} \cdot \frac{-n}{n+1} = b_{n-1}\left(\frac{-n}{n+1}\right) \qquad n > 0$$

and

$$b_0 = 1$$

We can investigate the series using PARTSUM:

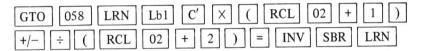

To calculate the partial sum

$$\sum_{n=0}^{16} \frac{(-1)^n}{n+1}$$

and its potential error in approximating the true sum,

(enter)	16		$k = 16$.
(press)		$x{\blacktriangleright}t$	
(enter)	1		$b_0 = 1.0$.
(press)		B	The program halts with the partial sum $s_{16} = 0.7216953798$ displayed.
(press)		E	The possible error -0.0555555556 is displayed.

Because the possible error has a negative sign, the partial sum s_{16} overestimates the true sum S, but by an amount no larger than 0.0555555556.

Now try $k = 100$. You will obtain $s_{100} = 0.6980731694$ with the possible error -0.0098039216. The alternating harmonic series is known to converge to $\ln 2 = 0.6931471806$.

EXERCISE 6.
ANOTHER ALTERNATING SERIES

The series

$$\sum_{n=0}^{\infty} \frac{(-1)^n}{(2n)!}$$

converges to cos 1. The terms of this alternating series can be defined recursively:

$$b_n = \frac{(-1)^n}{(2n)!} = \frac{(-1)^{n-1}}{[2(n-1)]!} \cdot \frac{(-1)}{(2n-1)(2n)} = b_{n-1}\left[\frac{-1}{(2n-1)(2n)}\right]$$

and

$$b_0 = 1$$

Key in the nth term as a subroutine to be called by PARTSUM:

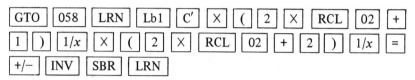

For $k = 2$ we obtain $s_2 = 0.5416666667$ with a possible error of -0.0013888889; for $k = 6$, $s_6 = 0.5403023059$ with possible error $-1.1470746 \times 10^{-11}$. Hence $s_6 = \cos 1$ is accurate to ten decimal places, and you can see that the series converges very rapidly.

PROBLEMS 6.3

In each of Problems 1–10, use PARTSUM to determine the given partial sum. Give your answer to five decimal places.

1. $\displaystyle\sum_{n=0}^{6} \frac{1}{(n+1)^2}$

2. $\displaystyle\sum_{n=0}^{9} \frac{1}{4^n}$

3. $\displaystyle\sum_{n=1}^{15} \frac{1}{n\sqrt{n}}$

4. $\displaystyle\sum_{n=1}^{50} \frac{n^3}{2^n}$

5. $\displaystyle\sum_{n=0}^{25} \frac{3^n}{4^n}$

6. $\displaystyle\sum_{n=0}^{10} \frac{(n+1)(n+2)}{n!}$

7. $\displaystyle\sum_{n=0}^{8} \frac{\cos n}{(n+1)^2}$

8. $\displaystyle\sum_{n=2}^{20} \frac{1}{n(\ln n)^2}$

9. $\sum\limits_{n=0}^{17} \left(-\dfrac{1}{6}\right)^n$

10. $\sum\limits_{n=1}^{12} \dfrac{-n}{3^n}$

In Problems 11–16, find the partial sum

$$s_k = \sum_{n=0}^{k} (-1)^n a_n$$

and the possible error $E = (-1)^{k+1} a_{k+1}$, for the given alternating series and specified value of k. Give your answers to five decimal places.

11. $\sum\limits_{n=0}^{10} (-1)^n \dfrac{1}{n!}$

12. $\sum\limits_{n=2}^{25} (-1)^{n+1} \dfrac{1}{\ln n}$

13. $\sum\limits_{n=1}^{37} (-1)^{n+1} \dfrac{1}{\sqrt{n}}$

14. $\sum\limits_{n=1}^{49} (-1)^n \dfrac{\sin n}{n^2}$

15. $\sum\limits_{n=2}^{100} (-1)^n \dfrac{\ln n}{n}$

16. $\sum\limits_{n=2}^{14} (-1)^n \dfrac{n}{(n+1)!}$

In Problems 17–30, use PARTSUM or results from this section to find out which of the following series converge and which diverge.

17. $\sum\limits_{n=1}^{\infty} \dfrac{(-1)^n}{n^2}$

18. $\sum\limits_{n=1}^{\infty} (-1)^n \dfrac{n}{2n+1}$

19. $\sum\limits_{n=0}^{\infty} \dfrac{\sin(n\pi/2)}{n+1}$

20. $\sum\limits_{n=1}^{\infty} \dfrac{\ln n}{n^2}$

21. $\sum\limits_{n=2}^{\infty} \dfrac{1}{n \ln n}$

22. $\sum\limits_{n=0}^{\infty} \dfrac{2^n}{n!}$

23. $\sum\limits_{n=1}^{\infty} \dfrac{n^4}{4^n}$

24. $\displaystyle\sum_{n=0}^{\infty} (-1)^n\, 7^n 6^{-n}$

25. $\displaystyle\sum_{n=1}^{\infty} \left(\frac{1}{3^n} - 1\right)$

26. $\displaystyle\sum_{n=1}^{\infty} n^2 \left(-\frac{3}{7}\right)^n$

27. $\displaystyle\sum_{n=1}^{\infty} \frac{2^n}{n^2}$

28. $\displaystyle\sum_{n=1}^{\infty} \frac{\cos^n (1.5)}{n!}$

29. $\displaystyle\sum_{n=1}^{\infty} (-1)^{n+1} \frac{(0.02)^n}{n}$

30. $\displaystyle\sum_{n=1}^{\infty} \frac{(0.1)^n}{n}$

Section 6.4 Power Series

In the first chapter you studied the algebra and calculus associated with polynomial functions. We began our study with polynomial functions because algebraically they are of the simplest type: Only the arithmetic operations of addition and multiplication are required in the evaluation of any polynomial. Furthermore, the polynomials are elementary from an analytic point of view: They are easy both to differentiate and to integrate.

On the other hand, you have studied many functions that transcend arithmetic or algebraic processes, such as, for instance, $\sin x$, $\cos x$, $\ln x$, and e^x. It turns out, however, that these transcendental functions can be *approximated* by polynomial functions. The approximating polynomials are the partial sums of a special type of series involving powers of a single variable. This special type of series is known as a *power series,* and it is defined as follows:

Definition. A series of the form

$$\sum_{n=0}^{\infty} a_n x^n = a_0 + a_1 x + a_2 x^2 + \ldots$$

is called a *power series in x.* A series of the form

$$\sum_{n=0}^{\infty} a_n (x - x_0)^n = a_0 + a_1 (x - x_0) + a_2 (x - x_0)^2 + \ldots$$

is called a *power series in $x - x_0$.*

One way in which a power series arises comes from seeking to approximate some function $y = f(x)$ by a polynomial in powers of x. Without going into the details, which can be found in most elementary calculus texts, a sequence of polynomials of the following form can be produced, each approximating the function f:

$$f_k(x) = f(0) + f'(0)x + \frac{f''(0)}{2} x^2 + \ldots + \frac{f^{(k)}(0)}{k!} x^k \tag{6.9}$$

The polynomial $f_k(x)$ is called the *kth-degree Taylor polynomial of f at x = 0*. It has the property that its graph passes through the point $(0, f(0))$, and its first k derivatives equal the first k derivatives of $y = f(x)$ at $x = 0$. Of course all the derivatives of f, up to and including the kth derivative, must exist at $x = 0$ if f is to have a kth-degree Taylor polynomial there. If f has derivatives of all orders at the origin, then the approximating polynomials (6.9) are the partial sums of the following *Maclaurin series* for f:

$$f(0) + f'(0)x + \frac{f''(0)}{2!} x^2 + \ldots + \frac{f^{(n)}(0)}{n!} x^n + \ldots \tag{6.10}$$

For example, it is easy to find that the Maclaurin series for $y = e^x$ is

$$\sum_{n=0}^{\infty} \frac{x^n}{n!} = 1 + x + \frac{1}{2}x^2 + \frac{1}{6}x^3 + \ldots + \frac{1}{n!}x^n + \ldots$$

and for $y = \cos x$ it is

$$\sum_{n=0}^{\infty} (-1)^n \frac{x^{2n}}{(2n)!} = 1 - \frac{x^2}{2!} + \frac{x^4}{4!} - \frac{x^6}{6!} + \ldots$$

Another way in which power series commonly arise is as solutions to differential equations. For example, one solution of the second-order differential equation

$$x^2 y'' + xy' + x^2 y = 0 \quad x > 0$$

is the power series

$$J_0(x) = 1 + \sum_{n=1}^{\infty} (-1)^n \frac{x^{2n}}{2^{2n}(n!)^2}$$

The function $J_0(x)$ is known as the *Bessel function* of the first kind of order zero. The Bessel functions play an important role in many areas of applied mathematics.

Two points are important to realize here. The first is that many of the functions with which you are already familiar, such as the trigonometric, logarithmic, and exponential functions, can be represented by a power series. The second point is that many new and unfamiliar functions are available to

you as power series, such as the Bessel function. These new functions are very
useful in many areas of applied mathematics and science, and they cannot be
formulated in terms of finite expressions involving elementary functions.

A power series

$$\sum_{n=0}^{\infty} a_n (x - x_0)^n \tag{6.11}$$

converges to the sum $S(x)$ for a particular value of x if the sequence of partial
sums

$$S_k(x) = \sum_{n=0}^{k} a_n (x - x_0)^n \tag{6.12}$$

converges to $S(x)$. Clearly the power series (6.11) converges to a_0 when
$x = x_0$; that is, it converges for at least one value of x. It may happen that a
particular power series of the form in 6.11 converges only when $x = x_0$, but it
is also possible that it might converge for all values of x, or even converge for
some values of x and diverge for others. In general, it turns out that any
power series converges for all x within an interval of the form

$$-R < x - x_0 < R \tag{6.13}$$

and diverges whenever $|x - x_0| > R$. The number R is called the *radius of
convergence*, and $R = 0$ is taken to mean that the power series converges only
at $x = x_0$. If the limit

$$\lim_{n \to \infty} \left| \frac{a_{n+1}}{a_n} \right| = q$$

exists, then the radius of convergence is given by

$$R = \frac{1}{q} \quad \text{provided that } q \neq 0 \tag{6.14}$$

If $q = 0$, then the power series converges for all values of x, and we write
$R = +\infty$. If $q = +\infty$, then $R = 0$, and the power series converges only for
$x = x_0$.

Our previous discussion asserts that the power series (6.11) converges
whenever $|x - x_0| < R$, and diverges whenever $|x - x_0| > R$. No information
concerning convergence or divergence is provided when $|x - x_0| = R$. So the
investigation of the behavior of a power series at the endpoints of the interval
of convergence must always be taken up as a separate matter.

For example, consider the power series

$$\sum_{n=1}^{\infty} \frac{x^n}{n}$$

Since

$$\lim_{n \to \infty} \frac{a_{n+1}}{a_n} = \lim_{n \to \infty} \frac{1/(n+1)}{1/n} = 1 = q$$

the radius of convergence is $R = 1/q = 1$. Thus the series converges if $|x| < 1$ and diverges if $|x| > 1$. At the endpoint $x = -1$, the series is the alternating harmonic series

$$\sum_{n=1}^{\infty} \frac{(-1)^n}{n}$$

which converges; at the endpoint $x = 1$, it is the divergent harmonic series $\Sigma \, 1/n$. So the series converges at all values of x satisfying $-1 \leqslant x < 1$.

Our goal is not to present the theory of power series here; the interested reader can refer to any good calculus text for that information. Instead we want to consider power series via the calculator. Specifically, for a given power series of the form in 6.11, we want to evaluate any of its partial sums (6.12) at a designated value of x. The program POWER is designed to do just that.

The program POWER calculates the partial sum (6.12) for a given power series and specified nonnegative integer k at a designated value of x. The program requires that you key in a subroutine for the general coefficient a_n of the power series, either according to formula or recursively. This subroutine will be explained and illustrated. The program uses steps 000 through 104, and memory locations 01 through 07. Program steps 105 through 479, as well as memory steps 00 and 08 through 59, are available for your use in the subroutine to evaluate a_n.

Calculating Partial Sums of a Power Series

Step 1: Read side 1 of the magnetic card POWER into your TI-59, with standard partitioning.

Step 2: GTO program step 105 and key in the subroutine for a_n. Do so in exactly the same manner used for the program PARTSUM in the previous section. As in that program, the first two steps of your subroutine must be

$$\boxed{\text{Lbl}} \quad \boxed{\text{C}'}$$

and the last two steps must be

$$\boxed{\text{INV}} \quad \boxed{\text{SBR}}$$

Step 3: Enter the value x_0, and press $\boxed{x \blacktriangle t}$. Then enter the value x in the display, and press $\boxed{E}$.

If the subroutine for a_n is given by a formula involving only the index n, proceed to Step 4.

If the subroutine assumes a_n is given recursively in terms of the preceding term a_{n-1} and its index $n - 1$, proceed to Step 4'.

Step 4: Enter the terminal index k of the partial sum, and press $\boxed{C}$. The program halts with the value

$$S_k(x) = \sum_{n=0}^{k} a_n(x - x_0)^n$$

displayed. If you want to calculate another partial sum for this same value of x, enter the new index k and press $\boxed{C}$ again. Repeat as often as desired.

Step 4': Enter the terminal index k and press $\boxed{x \blacktriangle t}$. Then enter the starting value a_0 for the recursion formula and press $\boxed{B}$. The program halts with the partial sum $S_k(x)$ displayed. If you want another partial sum for this same value of x, enter the new index k and the starting value a_0 just as before, and press $\boxed{B}$ again. Repeat as often as desired.

Step 5: If you want to calculate the partial sum for a different value of x, go back to Step 3.

The following examples illustrate the use of the program POWER to investigate the behavior of a power series.

EXERCISE 1.
A POWER SERIES DEFINED BY FORMULA

The power series

$$\sum_{n=0}^{\infty} \frac{x^n}{n + 1}$$

converges for $-1 \leqslant x < 1$. Let's examine the partial sums for $x = 0.25$. First key in the subroutine for $a_n = 1/(n + 1)$ after loading POWER into your TI-59:

$\boxed{GTO}$ $\boxed{105}$ $\boxed{LRN}$ $\boxed{Lb1}$ $\boxed{C'}$ $\boxed{+}$ $\boxed{1}$ $\boxed{=}$ $\boxed{1/x}$ $\boxed{INV}$ $\boxed{SBR}$
$\boxed{LRN}$

Next enter the values $x_0 = 0$ and $x = 0.25$:

(enter)   0

(press) $\boxed{x \blacktriangle t}$ $x_0 = 0.0$.

(enter)	0.25		
(press)		E	$x = 0.25$.

To calculate the partial sum $S_2(0.25)$:

(enter)	2		$k = 2$.
(press)		C	The program halts with 1.145833333 displayed.

To calculate $S_5(0.25)$:

(enter)	5		$k = 5$.
(press)		C	The program halts with 1.150683594 displayed.

Continuing in this manner, you obtain the following table, rounded to five decimal places.

k	$S_k(0.25)$	k	$S_k(0.25)$
2	1.14583	12	1.15073
5	1.15068	15	1.15073
10	1.15073	100	1.15073

We conclude that the power series

$$\sum_{n=0}^{\infty} \frac{x^n}{n+1}$$

converges to (approximately) 1.15073 at $x = 0.25$.

To calculate the partial sums at another value of x, say $x = -0.37$, you must return to Step 3. Thus

(enter)	0		
(press)		$x \blacktriangledown t$	$x_0 = 0.0$.
(enter)	−0.37		
(press)		E	$x = -0.37$.
(enter)	5		$k = 5$.
(press)		C	The program halts with $S_5(-0.37) = 0.8505626727$ displayed.

EXERCISE 2.
THE POWER SERIES
FOR THE EXPONENTIAL

The power series

$$\sum_{n=0}^{\infty} \frac{x^n}{n!}$$

converges to the exponential function $y = e^x$ for all values of x. The general coefficient can be defined recursively by

$$a_n = \frac{1}{n!} = \frac{1}{(n-1)!} \cdot \frac{1}{n} = a_{n-1} \left(\frac{1}{n} \right) \qquad n \geqslant 1$$

and

$$a_0 = 1$$

Key the subroutine for a_n into POWER, keeping in mind that the index $n-1$ is stored in memory register 02:

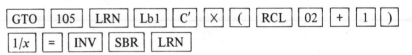

| GTO | 105 | LRN | Lb1 | C' | × | (| RCL | 02 | + | 1 |) |

| 1/x | = | INV | SBR | LRN |

Next enter the values $x_0 = 0$ and $x = -1$:

(enter)	0		
(press)		$x \blacktriangledown t$	$x_0 = 0.0$.
(enter)	−1		
(press)		E	$x = -1.0$.

To calculate the partial sum $S_3(-1.0)$:

(enter)	3		
(press)		$x \blacktriangledown t$	$k = 3$.
(enter)	1		$a_0 = 1.0$.
(press)		B	The program halts with 0.3333333333 displayed.

To calculate $S_5(-1.0)$:

| (enter) | 5 | | |
| **330** (press) | | $x \blacktriangledown t$ | $k = 5$. |

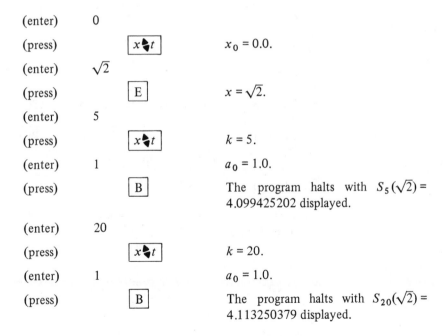

(enter)	1	$a_0 = 1.0.$
(press)	B	The program halts with 0.3666666667 displayed.

Continuing in this manner you can obtain the following table, rounded to five decimal places:

k	$S_k(-1.0)$	k	$S_k(-1.0)$
3	0.33333	10	0.36788
5	0.36667	15	0.36788

Thus the power series

$$\sum_{n=0}^{\infty} \frac{x^n}{n!} = e^x$$

converges to 0.36788 at $x = -1.0$.

To calculate the partial sums at another value of x, say $x = \sqrt{2}$, you must return to Step 3. Thus

(enter)	0	
(press)	$x \blacktriangleleft t$	$x_0 = 0.0.$
(enter)	$\sqrt{2}$	
(press)	E	$x = \sqrt{2}.$
(enter)	5	
(press)	$x \blacktriangleleft t$	$k = 5.$
(enter)	1	$a_0 = 1.0.$
(press)	B	The program halts with $S_5(\sqrt{2}) = $ 4.099425202 displayed.
(enter)	20	
(press)	$x \blacktriangleleft t$	$k = 20.$
(enter)	1	$a_0 = 1.0.$
(press)	B	The program halts with $S_{20}(\sqrt{2}) = $ 4.113250379 displayed.

The program POWER assumes that the partial sum $S_k(x)$ begins with $n = 0$ and that the power series has all integer powers of $(x - x_0)$. If this is not the case, you must make appropriate adjustments in the indices when using POWER. This need is illustrated in the next example.

EXERCISE 3.
A POWER SERIES
WITH MISSING EVEN POWERS

The power series

$$\sum_{n=0}^{\infty} (-1)^n \frac{x^{2n+1}}{2n+1} = x - \frac{x^3}{3} + \frac{x^5}{5} - \frac{x^7}{7} + \dots$$

converges to $\tan^{-1}x$ for $-1 \leqslant x \leqslant 1$. Since the series contains only odd positive powers of x, we rewrite the series as

$$\sum_{n=0}^{\infty} (-1)^n \frac{x^{2n+1}}{2n+1} = x \sum_{n=0}^{\infty} (-1)^n \frac{x^{2n}}{2n+1}$$

$$= x \sum_{n=0}^{\infty} (-1)^n \frac{(x^2)^n}{2n+1}$$

(6.15)

Let's find the value of the series when $x = \frac{1}{2}$. First we define the coefficients in the series recursively:

$$a_n = \frac{(-1)^n}{2n+1} = \frac{(-1)^{n-1}}{2n-1} \left[\frac{(-1)(2n-1)}{2n+1} \right] = a_{n-1} \left[\frac{-(2n-1)}{2n+1} \right] \quad n \geqslant 1$$

and

$$a_0 = 1$$

Next we key in the subroutine for a_n into POWER:

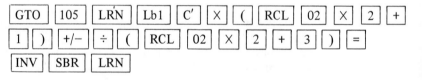

To find $S_2(0.5)$, for instance, we note that $x = 0.5$ but the series (6.15) evaluates powers of $x^2 = 0.25$. Thus

(enter)	0		
(press)		$x \rightleftharpoons t$	$x_0 = 0.0$.
(enter)	0.25		
(press)		E	$x^2 = 0.25$.
(enter)	2		
(press)		$x \rightleftharpoons t$	$k = 2$.

(enter)	1		$a_0 = 1.0$.
(press)		B	The program halts with 0.9291666667 displayed.

Finally, according to Equation 6.15, you must multiply the displayed result by $x = 0.5$ to obtain the partial sum:

$$S_2(0.5) = (0.5)(0.9291666667) = 0.4645833333$$

Now obtain the partial sum $S_{15}(0.5)$:

(enter)	15		
(press)		$x \updownarrow t$	$k = 15$.
(enter)	1		$a_0 = 1.0$.
(press)		B	
(press)		$\times$ $\boxed{0.5}$ $=$	$S_{15}(0.5) = 0.463647609$.

If you calculate $\tan^{-1}(0.5)$ in radians mode, you see that $S_{15}(0.5)$ is correct in all ten decimal places.

Retain the subroutine for a_n in your calculator for the next example.

EXERCISE 4.
RATE OF CONVERGENCE
OF A POWER SERIES

Generally speaking, as the value x gets further away from the point x_0 within the interval of convergence, convergence of the sequence of partial sums $S_k(x)$ becomes slower. To illustrate this phenomenon, let's calculate a table of partial sums for $\tan^{-1}(1.0)$ using the power series in the previous exercise. Thus

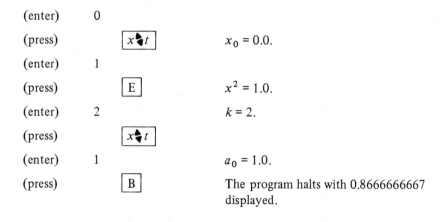

(enter)	0		
(press)		$x \updownarrow t$	$x_0 = 0.0$.
(enter)	1		
(press)		E	$x^2 = 1.0$.
(enter)	2		$k = 2$.
(press)		$x \updownarrow t$	
(enter)	1		$a_0 = 1.0$.
(press)		B	The program halts with 0.8666666667 displayed.

Since $x = 1.0$, we obtain $S_2(1.0) = 0.8666666667$ from Equation 6.15. Continuing in this manner, the following table is obtained, rounded to five decimal places:

k	$S_k(1.0)$	k	$S_k(1.0)$
2	0.86667	30	0.79346
4	0.83492	55	0.78093
6	0.82093	100	0.78787
10	0.80808	500	0.78590
15	0.76979		

The exact value of $\tan^{-1} 1$ is 0.7853981634 rad. Notice that 500 terms give only three-decimal place accuracy at $x = 1.$, whereas fifteen terms provided ten-place accuracy at $x = 0.5$. The value $x = 1$ is an endpoint of the interval of convergence for the power series representing $\tan^{-1} x$, and the convergence of the partial sums is least rapid there.

EXERCISE 5.
THE BINOMIAL SERIES

The power series

$$1 + mx + \frac{m(m-1)}{2!} x^2 + \ldots + \frac{m(m-1)(m-2) \ldots (m-n+1)}{n!} x^n + \ldots$$

is called the *binomial series* because it is the Maclaurin series for the function $f(x) = (1 + x)^m$. The binomial series is known to converge to $(1 + x)^m$ when $|x| < 1$. Let's use the series to determine the value $\left(\frac{4}{3}\right)^{-1/5}$. Thus $m = -\frac{1}{5}$ and $x = \frac{1}{3}$. The general coefficient in the binomial series can be defined recursively as follows:

$$a_n = \frac{m(m-1)(m-2) \ldots (m-n+1)}{n!} = a_{n-1} \left(\frac{m-n+1}{n}\right) \qquad n \geq 1$$

and

$$a_0 = 1$$

Assuming that $m = -\frac{1}{5}$ is stored in memory register 10, key in the following subroutine for a_n to be called by POWER:

GTO	105	LRN	Lb1	C'	×	(	RCL	10	−	RCL

02	)	÷	(	RCL	02	+	1	)	=	INV	SBR	LRN

Next initialize POWER and store the values for $x_0 = 0$ and $x = \frac{1}{3}$. We cannot store $m = -\frac{1}{5}$ as yet because this initialization process zeros all the memory registers prior to the storage of x_0 and x.

(enter)   0

(press) $\boxed{x \leftrightarrow t}$

(enter) $\frac{1}{3}$

(press) $\boxed{E}$

Now store m in register 10:

(enter) $-\frac{1}{5}$

(press) $\boxed{STO}$ $\boxed{10}$

Finally, calculate the partial sum $S_{20}\left(\frac{1}{3}\right)$:

(enter)   20

(press) $\boxed{x \leftrightarrow t}$ $k = 20$.

(enter)   1 $a_0 = 1.0$.

(press) $\boxed{B}$ The program halts with 0.9440875113 displayed.

The value of $\left(\frac{4}{3}\right)^{-1/5}$ using the $\boxed{y^x}$ key on your TI-59 is 0.9440875113 so the convergence of the sequence of partial sums is quite rapid at $x = \frac{1}{3}$.

PROBLEMS 6.4

In each of Problems 1–10, use POWER to determine the partial sum at the given value of x. Give your answer to five decimal places.

1. $\sum\limits_{n=0}^{12} x^n$ $x = -0.5$

2. $\sum\limits_{n=0}^{15} (-x)^n$ $x = 0.13$

3. $\sum\limits_{n=1}^{27} \frac{x^n}{n}$ $x = 0.89$

4. $\sum\limits_{n=0}^{10} \frac{2^n x^n}{n!}$ $x = -1$

5. $\sum\limits_{n=1}^{11} \frac{nx^n}{3^n}$ $x = 1.95$

6. $\displaystyle\sum_{n=1}^{11} (-1)^{n+1} \frac{x^n}{n}$ $x = 0.5$

7. $\displaystyle\sum_{n=1}^{11} (-1)^{n+1} \frac{(x-1)^n}{n}$ $x = 0.5$

8. $\displaystyle\sum_{n=0}^{12} \frac{(x+1)^n}{en!}$ $x = 1$

9. $\displaystyle\sum_{n=0}^{9} \frac{(-1)^n}{(2n+1)!} x^{2n+1}$ $x = \pi/4$

10. $\displaystyle\sum_{n=0}^{14} \frac{(2x+4)^n}{n!}$ $x = -1$

In Problems 11–18, find the radius of convergence of the specified power series.

11. $\displaystyle\sum_{n=0}^{\infty} 2x^n$

12. $\displaystyle\sum_{n=1}^{\infty} \frac{3(x-1)^n}{n}$

13. $\displaystyle\sum_{n=0}^{\infty} \frac{(x+1)^n}{2n!}$

14. $\displaystyle\sum_{n=0}^{\infty} \frac{3^n x^n}{n!}$

15. $\displaystyle\sum_{n=0}^{\infty} \frac{x^n}{4^n}$

16. $\displaystyle\sum_{n=0}^{\infty} (-1)^{n+1} \frac{(x-3)^n}{2^n}$

17. $\displaystyle\sum_{n=1}^{\infty} \frac{nx^n}{3^n}$

18. $\displaystyle\sum_{n=1}^{\infty} \frac{2^n x^n}{n^3}$

19. The Maclaurin series for the sine function is given by

$$\sin x = x - \frac{x^3}{3!} + \frac{x^5}{5!} - \frac{x^7}{7!} + \dots$$

and it converges for all values of x. Use POWER with several values of x in the range $-4\pi \leqslant x \leqslant 4\pi$ to investigate the rate of convergence of the partial sums of the series as x gets further away from $x_0 = 0$.

20. Repeat Problem 19 for the Maclaurin series

$$\ln(1+x) = \sum_{n=1}^{\infty} (-1)^{n+1} \frac{x^n}{n}$$

over the interval $-1 < x < 1$.

Appendix A:
TI-59 Program Listings

Chapter 1

LINES

000	76	Lbl	021	02	02	042	02	2	063	35	1/x
001	11	A	022	33	x^2	043	95	=	064	43	RCL
002	42	STO	023	95	=	044	91	R/S	065	02	02
003	02	02	024	34	$\sqrt{x}$	045	76	Lbl	066	55	÷
004	32	x⬤t	025	91	R/S	046	15	E	067	43	RCL
005	42	STO	026	76	Lbl	047	22	INV	068	01	01
006	01	01	027	13	C	048	44	SUM	069	95	=
007	91	R/S	028	44	SUM	049	02	02	070	42	STO
008	76	Lbl	029	02	02	050	42	STO	071	05	05
009	14	D	030	32	x⬤t	051	04	04	072	49	Prd
010	22	INV	031	44	SUM	052	32	x⬤t	073	03	03
011	44	SUM	032	01	01	053	22	INV	074	43	RCL
012	02	02	033	43	RCL	054	44	SUM	075	04	04
013	32	x⬤t	034	02	02	055	01	01	076	75	−
014	75	−	035	55	÷	056	42	STO	077	43	RCL
015	43	RCL	036	02	2	057	03	03	078	03	03
016	01	01	037	95	=	058	00	0	079	95	=
017	95	=	038	32	x⬤t	059	32	x⬤t	080	42	STO
018	33	x^2	039	43	RCL	060	43	RCL	081	06	06
019	85	+	040	01	01	061	01	01	082	32	x⬤t
020	43	RCL	041	55	÷	062	67	x=t	083	43	RCL

LINES (Cont.)

084	05	05	116	91	R/S	147	18	C′	178	91	R/S
085	91	R/S	117	76	Lb1	148	75	−	179	76	Lb1
086	76	Lb1	118	19	D′	149	43	RCL	180	16	A′
087	35	1/x	119	42	STO	150	02	02	181	36	Pgm
088	00	0	120	07	07	151	95	=	182	01	01
089	35	1/x	121	32	x⇄t	152	94	+/−	183	71	SBR
090	24	CE	122	65	×	153	42	STO	184	25	CLR
091	91	R/S	123	43	RCL	154	03	03	185	91	R/S
092	76	Lb1	124	05	05	155	00	0	186	76	Lb1
093	10	E′	125	85	+	156	32	x⇄t	187	33	x^2
094	65	×	126	43	RCL	157	75	−	188	78	Σ+
095	43	RCL	127	06	06	158	43	RCL	189	91	R/S
096	05	05	128	95	=	159	01	01	190	61	GTO
097	85	+	129	94	+/−	160	95	=	191	33	x^2
098	43	RCL	130	44	SUM	161	67	x=t	192	76	Lb1
099	06	06	131	07	07	162	35	1/x	193	23	ln x
100	95	=	132	43	RCL	163	22	INV	194	22	INV
101	91	R/S	133	05	05	164	49	Prd	195	78	Σ+
102	76	Lb1	134	33	x^2	165	03	03	196	91	R/S
103	12	B	135	85	+	166	43	RCL	197	61	GTO
104	42	STO	136	01	1	167	01	01	198	33	x^2
105	05	05	137	95	=	168	65	×	199	76	Lb1
106	65	×	138	34	√x	169	43	RCL	200	17	B′
107	43	RCL	139	35	1/x	170	03	03	201	69	OP
108	01	01	140	65	×	171	85	+	202	12	12
109	75	−	141	43	RCL	172	43	RCL	203	42	STO
110	43	RCL	142	07	07	173	02	02	204	06	06
111	02	02	143	50	|x|	174	95	=	205	32	x⇄t
112	95	=	144	95	=	175	32	x⇄t	206	42	STO
113	94	+/−	145	91	R/S	176	43	RCL	207	05	05
114	42	STO	146	76	Lb1	177	03	03	208	91	R/S
115	06	06									

QUADS

000	76	Lb1	024	43	RCL	048	22	INV	072	76	Lb1
001	11	A	025	03	03	049	77	x ≥ t	073	35	1/x
002	42	STO	026	95	=	050	34	√x	074	00	0
003	01	01	027	22	INV	051	01	1	075	35	1/x
004	91	R/S	028	77	x ≥ t	052	94	+/−	076	24	CE
005	42	STO	029	35	1/x	053	49	Prd	077	91	R/S
006	02	02	030	34	√x	054	04	04	078	76	Lb1
007	91	R/S	031	85	+	055	76	Lb1	079	12	B
008	42	STO	032	43	RCL	056	34	√x	080	42	STO
009	03	03	033	02	02	057	43	RCL	081	05	05
010	91	R/S	034	50	|x|	058	03	03	082	43	RCL
011	76	Lb1	035	95	=	059	55	÷	083	01	01
012	14	D	036	55	÷	060	53	(	084	65	×
013	00	0	037	53	(	061	43	RCL	085	43	RCL
014	32	x⇄t	038	02	2	062	01	01	086	05	05
015	43	RCL	039	65	×	063	65	×	087	85	+
016	02	02	040	43	RCL	064	43	RCL	088	43	RCL
017	33	x^2	041	01	01	065	04	04	089	02	02
018	75	−	042	54	)	066	54	)	090	95	=
019	04	4	043	95	=	067	95	=	091	65	×
020	65	×	044	42	STO	068	32	x⇄t	092	43	RCL
021	43	RCL	045	04	04	069	43	RCL	093	05	05
022	01	01	046	43	RCL	070	04	04	094	85	+
023	65	×	047	02	02	071	91	R/S	095	43	RCL

096	03	03	155	10	10	214	43	RCL	273	10	10
097	95	=	156	33	x^2	215	10	10	274	65	×
098	92	INV SBR	157	65	×	216	65	×	275	43	RCL
099	76	Lb1	158	43	RCL	217	43	RCL	276	14	14
100	13	C	159	11	11	218	01	01	277	85	+
101	43	RCL	160	95	=	219	85	+	278	43	RCL
102	01	01	161	44	SUM	220	43	RCL	279	16	16
103	65	×	162	09	09	221	06	06	280	95	=
104	02	2	163	43	RCL	222	95	=	281	42	STO
105	65	×	164	10	10	223	42	STO	282	18	18
106	43	RCL	165	33	x^2	224	14	14	283	55	÷
107	05	05	166	65	×	225	43	RCL	284	43	RCL
108	85	+	167	43	RCL	226	05	05	285	17	17
109	43	RCL	168	10	10	227	55	÷	286	95	=
110	02	02	169	95	=	228	43	RCL	287	42	STO
111	95	=	170	44	SUM	229	03	03	288	10	10
112	92	INV SBR	171	07	07	230	95	=	289	91	R/S
113	76	Lb1	172	65	×	231	94	+/−	290	43	RCL
114	15	E	173	43	RCL	232	42	STO	291	14	14
115	12	B	174	10	10	233	10	10	292	75	−
116	42	STO	175	95	=	234	65	×	293	53	(
117	06	06	176	44	SUM	235	43	RCL	294	43	RCL
118	13	C	177	08	08	236	05	05	295	13	13
119	42	STO	178	43	RCL	237	85	+	296	65	×
120	07	07	179	03	03	238	43	RCL	297	43	RCL
121	65	×	180	91	R/S	239	08	08	298	10	10
122	43	RCL	181	61	GTO	240	95	=	299	54	)
123	05	05	182	16	A′	241	42	STO	300	95	=
124	94	+/−	183	76	Lb1	242	15	15	301	55	÷
125	85	+	184	17	B′	243	43	RCL	302	43	RCL
126	43	RCL	185	43	RCL	244	10	10	303	12	12
127	06	06	186	04	04	245	65	×	304	95	=
128	95	=	187	55	÷	246	43	RCL	305	42	STO
129	42	STO	188	43	RCL	247	01	01	306	11	11
130	08	08	189	03	03	248	85	+	307	91	R/S
131	32	$x \blacktriangleleft t$	190	95	=	249	43	RCL	308	43	RCL
132	43	RCL	191	94	+/−	250	09	09	309	01	01
133	07	07	192	42	STO	251	95	=	310	75	−
134	91	R/S	193	10	10	252	42	STO	311	53	(
135	76	Lb1	194	65	×	253	16	16	312	43	RCL
136	10	E′	195	43	RCL	254	43	RCL	313	05	05
137	65	×	196	04	04	255	13	13	314	65	×
138	43	RCL	197	85	+	256	55	÷	315	43	RCL
139	07	07	198	43	RCL	257	43	RCL	316	10	10
140	85	+	199	05	05	258	12	12	317	54	)
141	43	RCL	200	95	=	259	95	=	318	75	−
142	08	08	201	42	STO	260	94	+/−	319	53	(
143	95	=	202	12	12	261	42	STO	320	43	RCL
144	91	R/S	203	43	RCL	262	10	10	321	04	04
145	76	Lb1	204	10	10	263	65	×	322	65	×
146	16	A′	205	65	×	264	43	RCL	323	43	RCL
147	42	STO	206	43	RCL	265	13	13	324	11	11
148	11	11	207	05	05	266	85	+	325	54	)
149	32	$x \blacktriangleleft t$	208	85	+	267	43	RCL	326	95	=
150	42	STO	209	43	RCL	268	15	15	327	55	÷
151	10	10	210	07	07	269	95	=	328	43	RCL
152	32	$x \blacktriangleleft t$	211	95	=	270	42	STO	329	03	03
153	78	Σ+	212	42	STO	271	17	17	330	95	=
154	43	RCL	213	13	13	272	43	RCL	331	32	$x \blacktriangleleft t$

QUADS (Cont.)

332	43	RCL		335	01	01		338	42	STO		341	42	STO
333	10	10		336	43	RCL		339	02	02		342	03	03
334	42	STO		337	11	11		340	32	$x \leftrightarrows t$		343	91	R/S

POLYPROBE

000	76	Lbl		052	76	Lbl		104	15	E		156	00	0
001	19	D'		053	12	B		105	43	RCL		157	38	sin
002	42	STO		054	43	RCL		106	02	02		158	43	RCL
003	02	02		055	02	02		107	91	R/S		159	03	03
004	91	R/S		056	75	−		108	76	Lbl		160	75	−
005	76	Lbl		057	43	RCL		109	16	A'		161	01	1
006	10	E'		058	04	04		110	43	RCL		162	95	=
007	42	STO		059	95	=		111	04	04		163	42	STO
008	04	04		060	42	STO		112	55	÷		164	00	00
009	91	R/S		061	02	02		113	01	1		165	03	3
010	76	Lbl		062	71	SBR		114	00	0		166	05	5
011	18	C'		063	39	cos		115	95	=		167	42	STO
012	47	CMs		064	91	R/S		116	42	STO		168	01	01
013	85	+		065	76	Lbl		117	04	04		169	76	Lbl
014	01	1		066	13	C		118	91	R/S		170	33	x^2
015	95	=		067	43	RCL		119	76	Lbl		171	73	RCL Ind
016	42	STO		068	03	03		120	17	B'		172	01	01
017	00	00		069	75	−		121	43	RCL		173	65	×
018	42	STO		070	02	2		122	04	04		174	43	RCL
019	03	03		071	95	=		123	65	×		175	02	02
020	01	1		072	42	STO		124	01	1		176	95	=
021	00	0		073	00	00		125	00	0		177	32	$x \leftrightarrows t$
022	42	STO		074	03	3		126	95	=		178	01	1
023	01	01		075	05	5		127	42	STO		179	44	SUM
024	76	Lbl		076	42	STO		128	04	04		180	01	01
025	42	STO		077	01	01		129	91	R/S		181	00	0
026	91	R/S		078	71	SBR		130	76	Lbl		182	32	$x \leftrightarrows t$
027	72	STO Ind		079	33	x^2		131	39	cos		183	85	+
028	01	01		080	91	R/S		132	43	RCL		184	73	RCL Ind
029	01	1		081	76	Lbl		133	03	03		185	01	01
030	44	SUM		082	14	D		134	42	STO		186	95	=
031	01	01		083	22	INV		135	00	00		187	72	STO Ind
032	97	Dsz		084	97	Dsz		136	01	1		188	01	01
033	00	0		085	03	3		137	00	0		189	97	Dsz
034	42	STO		086	70	Rad		138	42	STO		190	00	0
035	91	R/S		087	43	RCL		139	01	01		191	33	x^2
036	76	Lbl		088	03	03		140	03	3		192	92	INV
037	11	A		089	42	STO		141	05	5		193	76	Lbl
038	43	RCL		090	00	00		142	42	STO		194	59	Int
039	02	02		091	01	1		143	05	05		195	42	STO
040	85	+		092	00	0		144	76	Lbl		196	07	07
041	43	RCL		093	42	STO		145	38	sin		197	32	$x \leftrightarrows t$
042	04	04		094	01	01		146	73	RCL Ind		198	42	STO
043	95	=		095	71	SBR		147	01	01		199	08	08
044	42	STO		096	33	x^2		148	72	STO Ind		200	43	RCL
045	02	02		097	91	R/S		149	05	05		201	03	03
046	71	SBR		098	76	Lbl		150	01	1		202	42	STO
047	39	cos		099	70	Rad		151	44	SUM		203	00	00
048	87	If flg		100	43	RCL		152	01	01		204	42	STO
049	01	1		101	10	10		153	44	SUM		205	06	06
050	90	List		102	91	R/S		154	05	05		206	01	1
051	91	R/S		103	76	Lbl		155	97	Dsz		207	00	0

208	42	STO	230	08	08	252	55	÷	274	03	3
209	01	01	231	42	STO	253	42	STO	275	05	5
210	76	Lbl	232	02	02	254	02	02	276	42	STO
211	30	tan	233	01	1	255	00	0	277	01	01
212	73	RCL Ind	234	44	SUM	256	42	STO	278	73	RCL Ind
213	01	01	235	03	03	257	04	04	279	01	01
214	55	÷	236	71	SBR	258	86	St flg	280	91	R/S
215	43	RCL	237	39	cos	259	01	1	281	01	1
216	06	06	238	42	STO	260	61	GTO	282	44	SUM
217	95	=	239	09	09	261	11	A	283	01	01
218	72	STO Ind	240	43	RCL	262	76	Lbl	284	97	Dsz
219	01	01	241	07	07	263	90	List	285	00	0
220	01	1	242	42	STO	264	22	INV	286	02	2
221	44	SUM	243	02	02	265	86	St flg	287	78	78
222	01	01	244	71	SBR	266	01	1	288	00	0
223	22	INV	245	39	cos	267	43	RCL	289	35	1/x
224	44	SUM	246	75	−	268	03	03	290	24	CE
225	06	06	247	43	RCL	269	75	−	291	91	R/S
226	97	Dsz	248	09	09	270	01	1	292	25	CLR
227	00	0	249	95	=	271	95	=	293	73	RCL Ind
228	30	tan	250	91	R/S	272	42	STO	294	01	01
229	43	RCL	251	76	Lbl	273	00	00	295	91	R/S

Chapter 2

PROBE

000	76	Lbl	029	43	RCL	058	54	)	087	43	RCL
001	19	D′	030	02	02	059	18	C′	088	01	01
002	42	STO	031	54	)	060	42	STO	089	18	C′
003	01	01	032	42	STO	061	04	04	090	42	STO
004	91	R/S	033	01	01	062	53	(	091	04	04
005	76	Lbl	034	18	C′	063	53	(	092	53	(
006	10	E′	035	91	R/S	064	43	RCL	093	53	(
007	42	STO	036	76	Lbl	065	03	03	094	43	RCL
008	02	02	037	13	C	066	75	−	095	03	03
009	91	R/S	038	53	(	067	43	RCL	096	75	−
010	76	Lbl	039	43	RCL	068	04	04	097	43	RCL
011	11	A	040	01	01	069	54	)	098	04	04
012	53	(	041	85	+	070	55	÷	099	54	)
013	43	RCL	042	43	RCL	071	43	RCL	100	55	÷
014	01	01	043	02	02	072	02	02	101	43	RCL
015	85	+	044	55	÷	073	54	)	102	02	02
016	43	RCL	045	02	2	074	91	R/S	103	54	)
017	02	02	046	54	)	075	76	Lbl	104	91	R/S
018	54	)	047	18	C′	076	14	D	105	76	Lbl
019	42	STO	048	42	STO	077	53	(	106	15	E
020	01	01	049	03	03	078	43	RCL	107	43	RCL
021	18	C′	050	53	(	079	01	01	108	01	01
022	91	R/S	051	43	RCL	080	85	+	109	91	R/S
023	76	Lbl	052	01	01	081	43	RCL	110	76	Lbl
024	12	B	053	75	−	082	02	02	111	16	A′
025	53	(	054	43	RCL	083	54	)	112	53	(
026	43	RCL	055	02	02	084	18	C′	113	43	RCL
027	01	01	056	55	÷	085	42	STO	114	02	02
028	75	−	057	02	2	086	03	03	115	55	÷

PROBE (Cont.)

116	01	1	121	91	R/S	126	02	02	130	54	)
117	00	0	122	76	Lb1	127	65	×	131	42	STO
118	54	)	123	17	B′	128	01	1	132	02	02
119	42	STO	124	53	(	129	00	0	133	91	R/S
120	02	02	125	43	RCL						

LIMIT

000	76	Lb1	022	43	RCL	044	01	01	066	42	STO
001	19	D′	023	03	03	045	75	−	067	01	01
002	42	STO	024	75	−	046	43	RCL	068	18	C′
003	01	01	025	43	RCL	047	03	03	069	91	R/S
004	91	R/S	026	01	01	048	54	)	070	76	Lb1
005	76	Lb1	027	54	)	049	55	÷	071	14	D
006	10	E′	028	55	÷	050	43	RCL	072	53	(
007	42	STO	029	43	RCL	051	02	02	073	43	RCL
008	02	02	030	02	02	052	54	)	074	01	01
009	91	R/S	031	54	)	053	42	STO	075	65	×
010	76	Lb1	032	42	STO	054	01	01	076	43	RCL
011	16	A′	033	01	01	055	18	C′	077	02	02
012	42	STO	034	18	C′	056	91	R/S	078	54	)
013	03	03	035	91	R/S	057	76	Lb1	079	42	STO
014	91	R/S	036	76	Lb1	058	13	C	080	01	01
015	76	Lb1	037	12	B	059	53	(	081	18	C′
016	11	A	038	53	(	060	43	RCL	082	91	R/S
017	53	(	039	43	RCL	061	01	01	083	76	Lb1
018	43	RCL	040	01	01	062	55	÷	084	15	E
019	01	01	041	75	−	063	43	RCL	085	43	RCL
020	85	+	042	53	(	064	02	02	086	01	01
021	53	(	043	43	RCL	065	54	)	087	91	R/S

Chapter 3

DERIVE

000	76	Lb1	020	02	02	040	11	A	060	03	03
001	19	D′	021	91	R/S	041	43	RCL	061	18	C′
002	42	STO	022	76	Lb1	042	01	01	062	44	SUM
003	01	01	023	17	B′	043	42	STO	063	04	04
004	91	R/S	024	53	(	044	03	03	064	53	(
005	76	Lb1	025	43	RCL	045	18	C′	065	43	RCL
006	10	E′	026	02	02	046	91	R/S	066	01	01
007	42	STO	027	65	×	047	76	Lb1	067	75	−
008	02	02	028	01	1	048	12	B	068	43	RCL
009	91	R/S	029	00	0	049	00	0	069	02	02
010	76	Lb1	030	54	)	050	42	STO	070	54	)
011	16	A′	031	42	STO	051	04	04	071	42	STO
012	53	(	032	02	02	052	53	(	072	03	03
013	43	RCL	033	91	R/S	053	43	RCL	073	18	C′
014	02	02	034	76	Lb1	054	01	01	074	22	INV
015	55	÷	035	15	E	055	85	+	075	44	SUM
016	01	1	036	43	RCL	056	43	RCL	076	04	04
017	00	0	037	01	01	057	02	02	077	53	(
018	54	)	038	91	R/S	058	54	)	078	02	2
342 019	42	STO	039	76	Lb1	059	42	STO	079	65	×

DERIVE (Cont.)

080	43	RCL	100	65	×	120	01	01	140	14	D
081	02	02	101	02	2	121	85	+	141	12	B
082	54	)	102	54	)	122	43	RCL	142	42	STO
083	22	INV	103	22	INV	123	02	02	143	05	05
084	49	Prd	104	44	SUM	124	54	)	144	13	C
085	04	04	105	04	04	125	42	STO	145	50	$|x|$
086	43	RCL	106	53	(	126	03	03	146	55	÷
087	04	04	107	43	RCL	127	18	C′	147	53	(
088	92	INV SBR	108	01	01	128	44	SUM	148	01	1
089	76	Lb1	109	75	−	129	04	04	149	85	+
090	13	C	110	43	RCL	130	43	RCL	150	43	RCL
091	00	0	111	02	02	131	02	02	151	05	05
092	42	STO	112	54	)	132	33	x^2	152	33	x^2
093	04	04	113	42	STO	133	22	INV	153	54	)
094	43	RCL	114	03	03	134	49	Prd	154	45	y^x
095	01	01	115	18	C′	135	04	04	155	01	1
096	42	STO	116	44	SUM	136	43	RCL	156	93	.
097	03	03	117	04	04	137	04	04	157	05	5
098	53	(	118	53	(	138	92	INV SBR	158	95	=
099	18	C′	119	43	RCL	139	76	Lb1	159	91	R/S

TANGENT

000	76	Lb1	033	07	07	066	18	C′	099	13	C
001	19	D′	034	95	=	067	42	STO	100	65	×
002	42	STO	035	91	R/S	068	04	04	101	43	RCL
003	01	01	036	76	Lb1	069	53	(	102	02	02
004	91	R/S	037	13	C	070	53	(	103	95	=
005	76	Lb1	038	93	.	071	43	RCL	104	91	R/S
006	10	E′	039	00	0	072	03	03	105	76	Lb1
007	42	STO	040	00	0	073	75	−	106	15	E
008	02	02	041	00	0	074	43	RCL	107	43	RCL
009	91	R/S	042	01	1	075	04	04	108	01	01
010	76	Lb1	043	42	STO	076	54	)	109	91	R/S
011	11	A	044	05	05	077	55	÷	110	76	Lb1
012	43	RCL	045	53	(	078	43	RCL	111	17	B′
013	01	01	046	43	RCL	079	05	05	112	42	STO
014	18	C′	047	01	01	080	54	)	113	06	06
015	92	INV SBR	048	85	+	081	42	STO	114	75	−
016	76	Lb1	049	43	RCL	082	03	03	115	43	RCL
017	12	B	050	05	05	083	43	RCL	116	01	01
018	43	RCL	051	55	÷	084	01	01	117	95	=
019	01	01	052	02	2	085	18	C′	118	42	STO
020	18	C′	053	54	)	086	75	−	119	02	02
021	42	STO	054	18	C′	087	43	RCL	120	91	R/S
022	07	07	055	42	STO	088	01	01	121	76	Lb1
023	53	(	056	03	03	089	65	×	122	16	A′
024	43	RCL	057	53	(	090	43	RCL	123	43	RCL
025	01	01	058	43	RCL	091	03	03	124	01	01
026	85	+	059	01	01	092	95	=	125	85	+
027	43	RCL	060	75	−	093	32	$x \rightleftharpoons t$	126	43	RCL
028	02	02	061	43	RCL	094	43	RCL	127	02	02
029	54	)	062	05	05	095	03	03	128	95	=
030	18	C′	063	55	÷	096	92	INV SBR	129	42	STO
031	75	−	064	02	2	097	76	Lb1	130	01	01
032	43	RCL	065	54	)	098	14	D	131	91	R/S

343

CHAIN

000	76	Lb1	026	04	04	052	42	STO	078	04	04
001	19	D'	027	43	RCL	053	03	03	079	42	STO
002	42	STO	028	01	01	054	53	(	080	07	07
003	01	01	029	71	SBR	055	24	CE	081	53	(
004	93	.	030	30	tan	056	85	+	082	53	(
005	00	0	031	42	STO	057	43	RCL	083	43	RCL
006	00	0	032	05	05	058	02	02	084	06	06
007	00	0	033	91	R/S	059	55	÷	085	75	−
008	01	1	034	76	Lb1	060	02	2	086	43	RCL
009	42	STO	035	13	C	061	54	)	087	07	07
010	02	02	036	01	1	062	71	SBR	088	54	)
011	91	R/S	037	00	0	063	40	Ind	089	55	÷
012	76	Lb1	038	04	4	064	04	04	090	43	RCL
013	11	A	039	42	STO	065	42	STO	091	02	02
014	43	RCL	040	04	04	066	06	06	092	54	)
015	01	01	041	43	RCL	067	53	(	093	92	INV SBR
016	17	B'	042	08	08	068	43	RCL	094	76	Lb1
017	42	STO	043	71	SBR	069	03	03	095	16	A'
018	08	08	044	30	tan	070	75	−	096	42	STO
019	91	R/S	045	65	×	071	43	RCL	097	08	08
020	76	Lb1	046	43	RCL	072	02	02	098	91	R/S
021	12	B	047	05	05	073	55	÷	099	76	Lb1
022	03	3	048	95	=	074	02	2	100	10	E'
023	00	0	049	91	R/S	075	54	)	101	42	STO
024	00	0	050	76	Lb1	076	71	SBR	102	05	05
025	42	STO	051	30	tan	077	40	Ind	103	91	R/S

Chapter 4

RECTANGLES

000	76	Lb1	022	54	)	044	97	Dsz	066	43	RCL
001	15	E	023	55	÷	045	01	1	067	04	04
002	47	CMs	024	43	RCL	046	39	cos	068	95	=
003	42	STO	025	01	01	047	76	Lb1	069	32	x ⬥ t
004	01	01	026	95	=	048	38	sin	070	43	RCL
005	86	St flg	027	42	STO	049	22	INV	071	58	58
006	03	3	028	04	04	050	86	St flg	072	65	×
007	91	R/S	029	91	R/S	051	03	3	073	43	RCL
008	76	Lb1	030	76	Lb1	052	43	RCL	074	04	04
009	11	A	031	13	C	053	04	04	075	95	=
010	42	STO	032	43	RCL	054	44	SUM	076	91	R/S
011	02	02	033	02	02	055	02	02	077	76	Lb1
012	91	R/S	034	71	SBR	056	61	GTO	078	14	D
013	76	Lb1	035	18	C'	057	13	C	079	43	RCL
014	12	B	036	44	SUM	058	76	Lb1	080	04	04
015	42	STO	037	58	58	059	39	cos	081	55	÷
016	03	03	038	87	If flg	060	22	INV	082	02	2
017	53	(	039	03	3	061	44	SUM	083	95	=
018	24	CE	040	38	sin	062	58	58	084	44	SUM
019	75	−	041	44	SUM	063	43	RCL	085	02	02
020	43	RCL	042	59	59	064	59	59	086	61	GTO
021	02	02	043	22	INV	065	65	×	087	13	C

344

INTEGRATE

#	code	key		#	code	key		#	code	key		#	code	key
000	76	Lbl		024	95	=		048	65	×		072	04	04
001	15	E		025	42	STO		049	02	2		073	55	÷
002	47	CMs		026	04	04		050	95	=		074	03	3
003	42	STO		027	91	R/S		051	87	If flg		075	95	=
004	01	01		028	76	Lbl		052	03	3		076	32	$x \rightleftharpoons t$
005	91	R/S		029	13	C		053	38	sin		077	43	RCL
006	76	Lbl		030	86	St flg		054	86	St flg		078	05	05
007	11	A		031	03	3		055	03	3		079	65	×
008	42	STO		032	43	RCL		056	76	Lbl		080	43	RCL
009	02	02		033	02	02		057	39	cos		081	04	04
010	91	R/S		034	18	C'		058	97	Dsz		082	55	÷
011	76	Lbl		035	76	Lbl		059	01	1		083	02	2
012	12	B		036	44	SUM		060	44	SUM		084	95	=
013	42	STO		037	44	SUM		061	55	÷		085	91	R/S
014	03	03		038	05	05		062	02	2		086	76	Lbl
015	53	(		039	44	SUM		063	95	=		087	38	sin
016	24	CE		040	06	06		064	44	SUM		088	44	SUM
017	75	−		041	43	RCL		065	05	05		089	06	06
018	43	RCL		042	04	04		066	44	SUM		090	22	INV
019	02	02		043	44	SUM		067	06	06		091	86	St flg
020	54	)		044	02	02		068	43	RCL		092	03	3
021	55	÷		045	43	RCL		069	06	06		093	61	GTO
022	43	RCL		046	02	02		070	65	×		094	39	cos
023	01	01		047	18	C'		071	43	RCL				

MEASURES

#	code	key		#	code	key		#	code	key		#	code	key
000	76	Lbl		031	40	Ind		062	44	SUM		093	01	1
001	10	E'		032	06	06		063	05	05		094	95	=
002	47	CMs		033	76	Lbl		064	43	RCL		095	34	$\sqrt{x}$
003	42	STO		034	44	SUM		065	05	05		096	92	INV SBR
004	01	01		035	44	SUM		066	65	×		097	76	Lbl
005	91	R/S		036	05	05		067	43	RCL		098	12	B
006	42	STO		037	43	RCL		068	04	04		099	01	1
007	02	02		038	04	04		069	55	÷		100	00	0
008	91	R/S		039	44	SUM		070	03	3		101	06	6
009	42	STO		040	02	02		071	95	=		102	42	STO
010	03	03		041	43	RCL		072	91	R/S		103	06	06
011	53	(		042	02	02		073	76	Lbl		104	61	GTO
012	24	CE		043	71	SBR		074	38	sin		105	59	Int
013	75	−		044	40	Ind		075	44	SUM		106	18	C'
014	43	RCL		045	06	06		076	05	05		107	33	x^2
015	02	02		046	65	×		077	22	INV		108	65	×
016	54	)		047	02	2		078	86	St flg		109	89	π
017	55	÷		048	95	=		079	03	3		110	95	=
018	43	RCL		049	87	If flg		080	61	GTO		111	92	INV SBR
019	01	01		050	03	3		081	39	cos		112	76	Lbl
020	95	=		051	38	sin		082	76	Lbl		113	13	C
021	42	STO		052	86	St flg		083	11	A		114	01	1
022	04	04		053	03	3		084	09	9		115	02	2
023	91	R/S		054	76	Lbl		085	00	0		116	01	1
024	76	Lbl		055	39	cos		086	42	STO		117	42	STO
025	59	Int		056	97	Dsz		087	06	06		118	06	06
026	86	St flg		057	01	1		088	61	GTO		119	61	GTO
027	03	3		058	44	SUM		089	59	Int		120	59	Int
028	43	RCL		059	55	÷		090	19	D'		121	19	D'
029	02	02		060	02	2		091	33	x^2		122	42	STO
030	71	SBR		061	95	=		092	85	+		123	07	07

MEASURES (Cont.)

#	code	op	#	code	op	#	code	op	#	code	op
124	43	RCL	147	42	STO	170	18	C'	192	95	=
125	02	02	148	07	07	171	92	INV SBR	193	34	$\sqrt{x}$
126	18	C'	149	43	RCL	172	76	Lb1	194	92	INV SBR
127	75	–	150	02	02	173	16	A'	195	76	Lb1
128	43	RCL	151	18	C'	174	01	1	196	17	B'
129	07	07	152	65	×	175	08	8	197	02	2
130	95	=	153	02	2	176	01	1	198	00	0
131	92	INV SBR	154	65	×	177	42	STO	199	04	4
132	76	Lb1	155	89	π	178	06	06	200	42	STO
133	14	D	156	65	×	179	61	GTO	201	06	06
134	01	1	157	43	RCL	180	59	Int	202	61	GTO
135	04	4	158	07	07	181	18	C'	203	59	Int
136	01	1	159	95	=	182	33	x^2	204	18	C'
137	42	STO	160	92	INV SBR	183	42	STO	205	65	×
138	06	06	161	76	Lb1	184	07	07	206	02	2
139	61	GTO	162	15	E	185	43	RCL	207	65	×
140	59	Int	163	01	1	186	02	02	208	89	π
141	19	D'	164	07	7	187	19	D'	209	65	×
142	33	x^2	165	00	0	188	33	x^2	210	43	RCL
143	85	+	166	42	STO	189	85	+	211	02	02
144	01	1	167	06	06	190	43	RCL	212	95	=
145	95	=	168	61	GTO	191	07	07	213	92	INV SBR
146	34	$\sqrt{x}$	169	59	Int						

Chapter 5

DIFFEQ 1

#	code	op	#	code	op	#	code	op	#	code	op
000	76	Lb1	028	95	=	056	43	RCL	084	18	C'
001	19	D'	029	42	STO	057	03	03	085	42	STO
002	22	INV	030	02	02	058	65	×	086	06	06
003	86	St flg	031	86	St flg	059	02	2	087	43	RCL
004	01	1	032	01	1	060	85	+	088	04	04
005	47	CMs	033	76	Lb1	061	43	RCL	089	85	+
006	42	STO	034	50	$|x|$	062	04	04	090	43	RCL
007	02	02	035	43	RCL	063	95	=	091	03	03
008	42	STO	036	03	03	064	32	$x \rightleftharpoons t$	092	55	÷
009	04	04	037	44	SUM	065	43	RCL	093	02	2
010	32	$x \rightleftharpoons t$	038	01	01	066	02	02	094	95	=
011	42	STO	039	43	RCL	067	42	STO	095	42	STO
012	01	01	040	02	02	068	04	04	096	01	01
013	91	R/S	041	32	$x \rightleftharpoons t$	069	32	$x \rightleftharpoons t$	097	43	RCL
014	76	Lb1	042	43	RCL	070	42	STO	098	05	05
015	10	E'	043	01	01	071	02	02	099	85	+
016	42	STO	044	91	R/S	072	61	GTO	100	43	RCL
017	03	03	045	76	Lb1	073	50	$|x|$	101	03	03
018	91	R/S	046	12	B	074	76	Lb1	102	65	×
019	76	Lb1	047	87	If flg	075	13	C	103	43	RCL
020	11	A	048	01	1	076	43	RCL	104	06	06
021	18	C'	049	59	Int	077	01	01	105	55	÷
022	65	×	050	61	GTO	078	42	STO	106	02	2
023	43	RCL	051	11	A	079	04	04	107	95	=
024	03	03	052	76	Lb1	080	43	RCL	108	42	STO
025	85	+	053	59	Int	081	02	02	109	02	02
026	43	RCL	054	18	C'	082	42	STO	110	18	C'
027	02	02	055	65	×	083	05	05	111	42	STO

112	07	07	131	85	+	149	42	STO	167	85	+
113	43	RCL	132	43	RCL	150	09	09	168	43	RCL
114	05	05	133	03	03	151	43	RCL	169	09	09
115	85	+	134	95	=	152	03	03	170	54	)
116	43	RCL	135	42	STO	153	65	×	171	55	÷
117	03	03	136	01	01	154	53	(	172	06	6
118	65	×	137	43	RCL	155	43	RCL	173	85	+
119	43	RCL	138	05	05	156	06	06	174	43	RCL
120	07	07	139	85	+	157	85	+	175	05	05
121	55	÷	140	43	RCL	158	02	2	176	95	=
122	02	2	141	03	03	159	65	×	177	42	STO
123	95	=	142	65	×	160	43	RCL	178	02	02
124	42	STO	143	43	RCL	161	07	07	179	43	RCL
125	02	02	144	08	08	162	85	+	180	04	04
126	18	C'	145	95	=	163	02	2	181	42	STO
127	42	STO	146	42	STO	164	65	×	182	01	01
128	08	08	147	02	02	165	43	RCL	183	61	GTO
129	43	RCL	148	18	C'	166	08	08	184	50	|x|
130	04	04									

Chapter 6

SERIES

000	76	Lbl	033	01	1	066	07	07	099	05	05
001	23	ln x	034	44	SUM	067	92	INV SBR	100	71	SBR
002	43	RCL	035	07	07	068	76	Lbl	101	23	ln x
003	05	05	036	43	RCL	069	14	D	102	91	R/S
004	55	÷	037	06	06	070	42	STO	103	76	Lbl
005	53	(	038	49	Prd	071	04	04	104	15	E
006	01	1	039	07	07	072	32	x⇄t	105	47	CMs
007	75	−	040	61	GTO	073	75	−	106	01	1
008	43	RCL	041	39	cos	074	01	1	107	42	STO
009	06	06	042	76	Lbl	075	95	=	108	01	01
010	54	)	043	30	tan	076	42	STO	109	91	R/S
011	95	=	044	85	+	077	08	08	110	76	Lbl
012	92	INV SBR	045	01	1	078	43	RCL	111	11	A
013	76	Lbl	046	95	=	079	04	04	112	43	RCL
014	38	sin	047	92	INV SBR	080	13	C	113	01	01
015	42	STO	048	76	Lbl	081	32	x⇄t	114	44	SUM
016	04	04	049	13	C	082	42	STO	115	02	02
017	32	x⇄t	050	71	SBR	083	09	09	116	43	RCL
018	00	0	051	38	sin	084	43	RCL	117	02	02
019	67	x=t	052	65	×	085	08	08	118	18	C'
020	30	tan	053	43	RCL	086	13	C	119	32	x⇄t
021	43	RCL	054	05	05	087	32	x⇄t	120	43	RCL
022	06	06	055	95	=	088	75	−	121	02	02
023	42	STO	056	42	STO	089	43	RCL	122	32	x⇄t
024	07	07	057	07	07	090	09	09	123	91	R/S
025	76	Lbl	058	71	SBR	091	95	=	124	76	Lbl
026	39	cos	059	23	ln x	092	91	R/S	125	16	A'
027	43	RCL	060	75	−	093	76	Lbl	126	01	1
028	07	07	061	43	RCL	094	10	E'	127	00	0
029	22	INV	062	07	07	095	42	STO	128	49	Prd
030	97	Dsz	063	95	=	096	06	06	129	01	01
031	04	4	064	32	x⇄t	097	32	x⇄t	130	43	RCL
032	30	tan	065	43	RCL	098	42	STO	131	01	01

SERIES (Cont.)

132	91	R/S	140	43	RCL	148	02	02	155	43	RCL
133	76	Lb1	141	01	01	149	43	RCL	156	02	02
134	17	B'	142	91	R/S	150	03	03	157	85	+
135	01	1	143	76	Lb1	151	18	C'	158	01	1
136	00	0	144	12	B	152	42	STO	159	95	=
137	22	INV	145	43	RCL	153	03	03	160	32	$x \gtrless t$
138	49	Prd	146	01	01	154	32	$x \gtrless t$	161	91	R/S
139	01	01	147	44	SUM						

PARTSUM

000	76	Lb1	015	43	RCL	030	43	RCL	044	39	cos
001	13	C	016	01	01	031	03	03	045	43	RCL
002	47	CMs	017	18	C'	032	44	SUM	046	03	03
003	42	STO	018	85	+	033	04	04	047	85	+
004	01	01	019	43	RCL	034	18	C'	048	43	RCL
005	76	Lb1	020	04	04	035	42	STO	049	04	04
006	38	sin	021	95	=	036	03	03	050	95	=
007	43	RCL	022	91	R/S	037	01	1	051	91	R/S
008	01	01	023	76	Lb1	038	44	SUM	052	76	Lb1
009	18	C'	024	12	B	039	02	02	053	15	E
010	44	SUM	025	47	CMs	040	43	RCL	054	43	RCL
011	04	04	026	42	STO	041	02	02	055	03	03
012	97	Dsz	027	03	03	042	22	INV	056	18	C'
013	01	1	028	76	Lb1	043	77	$x \geqslant t$	057	91	R/S
014	38	sin	029	39	cos						

POWER

000	76	Lb1	027	76	Lb1	053	43	RCL	079	03	03
001	15	E	028	38	sin	054	04	04	080	18	C'
002	47	CMs	029	43	RCL	055	91	R/S	081	42	STO
003	42	STO	030	02	02	056	76	Lb1	082	03	03
004	06	06	031	18	C'	057	12	B	083	01	1
005	32	$x \gtrless t$	032	65	×	058	42	STO	084	44	SUM
006	42	STO	033	43	RCL	059	03	03	085	02	02
007	05	05	034	07	07	060	01	1	086	43	RCL
008	22	INV	035	95	=	061	42	STO	087	06	06
009	44	SUM	036	44	SUM	062	07	07	088	49	Prd
010	06	06	037	04	04	063	00	0	089	07	07
011	91	R/S	038	22	INV	064	42	STO	090	43	RCL
012	76	Lb1	039	97	Dsz	065	04	04	091	02	02
013	13	C	040	01	1	066	42	STO	092	22	INV
014	85	+	041	30	tan	067	02	02	093	77	$x \geqslant t$
015	01	1	042	43	RCL	068	76	Lb1	094	39	cos
016	95	=	043	06	06	069	39	cos	095	43	RCL
017	42	STO	044	49	Prd	070	43	RCL	096	03	03
018	01	01	045	07	07	071	03	03	097	65	×
019	01	1	046	01	1	072	65	×	098	43	RCL
020	42	STO	047	44	SUM	073	43	RCL	099	07	07
021	07	07	048	02	02	074	07	07	100	85	+
022	00	0	049	61	GTO	075	95	=	101	43	RCL
023	42	STO	050	38	sin	076	44	SUM	102	04	04
024	04	04	051	76	Lb1	077	04	04	103	95	=
025	42	STO	052	30	tan	078	43	RCL	104	91	R/S
026	02	02									

348

Appendix B:
Answers to Problems

Chapter 1

SECTION 1.1

1. a. $(1.7, 1.7)$ b. $(-4, 1.6)$ c. $(1.5, -1.4)$ d. $(-0.3, -2.8)$ e. $(-8.9, 1.5)$
 f. $(7.1, -3.7)$
2. a. 8.322 b. 12.491 c. 8.023 d. 5.960 e. 5.854 f. 10.161
4. a. $(0.5, -2.75)$ b. $(-2.13, 4.96)$ c. $(1.14, 5.00)$ d. $(2.30, -1.10)$
 e. $(0.64, -0.23)$ f. $(-1.98, 4.18)$
5. a. 1 b. -1.082 c. -0.775 d. 60.158 e. -21.608 f. 0.766
6. Yes, common slope is approximately -0.318.
7. a. $45°$ b. $71°33'54''$ c. $92°38'59''$

SECTION 1.2

1. $y = -0.75x - 0.5$
2. $y = 0.33x - 2.33$
3. $y = -4.61x + 30.82$
4. $y = -0.64x + 0.61$

5. $y = -49.18x + 17.78$

6. $y = -0.39x + 1.26$

7. $y = 60.16x + 12.33$

8. $y = -0.49x + 3.28$

9. $y = 0.51x + 8.41$

10. $y = 1.94x - 3.76$

11. 7

12. 4.56

13. -0.16

14. 1.90

15. $m = 0.6, \quad b = 3$

16. $m = -0.12, \quad b = 1.5$

17. $m = 0.56, \quad b = 0.81$

18. $m = -0.45, \quad b = 0.14$

19. $y = 2x - 5.5$

20. $y = 0.57x + 3.86$

21. $y = -x + 7.24$

22. a. 1.67 b. -1.20 c. 0.87 d. 6.69
e. 0 f. 0

23. Slope AB = slope $CD \approx 0.42$;
slope AD = slope $BC \approx 1.33$

SECTION 1.3

1. a. $(1.3, -2.41)$ b. $(-0.79, 41.37)$
c. $(-3, -2)$ d. $(-3.54, -1.31)$

2. $y = -x + 1$

3. $y = -0.8125x + 0.6875$

4. $y = -0.57x + 2.66$

5. $(4.69, 2.54)$

6. a. 0.4 b. 2.3 c. 8.21 d. 6.72
e. 3

7. 5.13

8. 3.88

9. $d = 4.8, \quad Q(3.84, 2.88)$

10. $y = 5.89x + 9.37$

11. $y = 0.56x + 2.21, \quad 4.84$

12. $y = 5.31x - 10{,}352.23, \quad 127.54$
index in 1972

13. 498

14. 3.56

15. $T = 35.73r - 361.698, 71.55°$ C

16. 0.2114 μamps

17. 0.00241 in/in

SECTION 1.4

(Answers are rounded to two decimals.)

1. $r_1 = 4, r_2 = 1$; concave upward

2. $r_1 = -3, r_2 = 1$; concave downward

3. $r_1 = -\dfrac{4}{3}, r_2 = -\dfrac{1}{2}$; concave upward

4. $r_1 = 4, r_2 = -\frac{2}{3}$; concave upward

5. $r_1 = -4.35, r_2 = 0.35$; concave downward

6. Roots are complex; concave upward

7. Roots are complex; concave upward

8. $r_1 = 3.24, r_2 = 0.091$; concave upward

9. $r_1 = -23.26, r_2 = 23.26$; concave upward

10. $r_1 = 1.31, r_2 = 0$; concave downward

SECTION 1.5

1. -1.000

2. 0.117

3. 4.899

4. 2.592

5. 5.894

6. 1.507

7. $y = 8.8x + 0.25$

8. $y = -0.19x - 0.07$

9. $y = 1.34x - 0.53$

10. $y = -0.29x + 2.04$

11. Double root $r = 1.9$, where slope is zero

12. a. $y = -8.2x + 16.61, -7.744$
b. $0.0064, 0.0004, 0.0001$

SECTION 1.6

1. $y = 4x^2 - 3x + 1$

2. $y = -2.7x^2 + 3.8x - 6.12$

3. $y = 4x^2$

4. $y = 0.67x^2 - 0.06x + 3.19$

5. a. $s = 3.2t^2$, $16.2\ m$ b. 14.4 m/sec

6. a.

Day	0	30	60
Length	850	922	932

b. $f(x) = -0.034x^2 + 3.43x + 850$

c. $f(49) = 935.53$, $f(50) = 935.56$, $f(51) = 935.51$, $f(52) = 935.40$
The longest day is 50 days after May 1, or June 20.

7. $s = 0.098v^2 - 0.399v + 4.552$; 185.7 ft

8. $T = 0.012x^2 + 0.854x + 133.236$; $237.78°\ C$

9. $s = 16.57t^2 - 1.14t + 0.486$; $s(3) = 146.2$ ft; 98.29 ft/sec

10. 37.78 lb/ton

11. 0.00018451

12. $58.2°\ F$

13. 2.62 mph

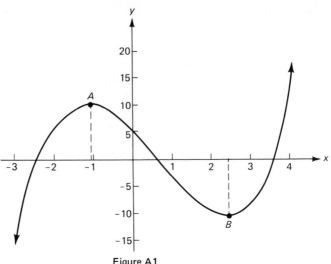

Figure A1

SECTION 1.7

1. The graph is sketched in Figure A.1.

Roots: −2.392, 0.675, 3.718

Relative maximum at A: 11.049 at $x = -1.097$

Relative minimum at B: −10.901 at $x = 2.431$

2. The graph is sketched in Figure A.2.

Roots: −3.147, 0.819, 2.329

Relative maximum at B: 2.709 at $x = 1.633$

Relative minimum at A: −14.709 at $x = -1.633$

Figure A2

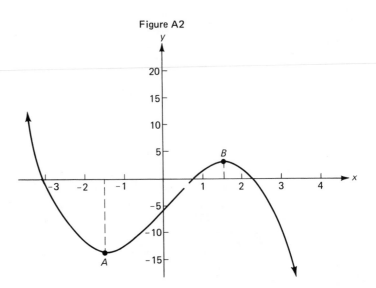

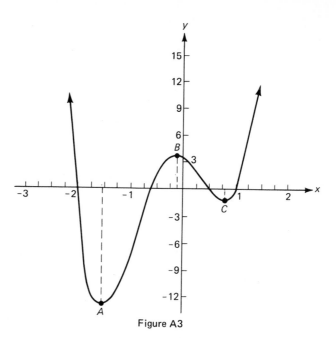

Figure A3

3. The graph is sketched in Figure A.3.
   Roots: -2.000, -0.667, 0.500, 1.000
   Relative maximum at B: 4.288 at $x = -0.140$
   Relative minimum at A: -12.511 at $x = -1.517$
   Relative minimum at C: -1.487 at $x = 0.782$

4. The graph is sketched in Figure A.4.
   Roots: ± 3, ± 1
   Relative maximum at A: 16.000 at $x = -2.236$

Figure A4

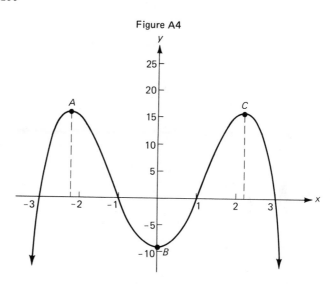

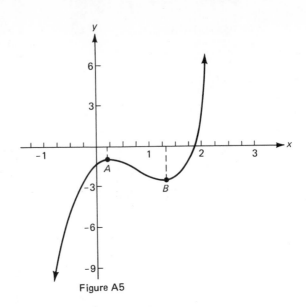

Figure A5

Relative maximum at C: 16.000 at $x = 2.236$

Relative minimum at B: −9.000 at $x = 0.000$

Note the symmetry of the graph about the y-axis.

5. The graph is sketched in Figure A.5.

Root: 1.823

Relative maximum at A: −0.804 at $x = 0.216$

Relative minimum at B: −2.416 at $x = 1.331$

6. 1.912931

7. −1.67513, −0.53919, 2.21432, 3.00000

8. 2.7219

9. 3.82469 cm

10. 0.75023 cm

11. Volume $= \frac{1}{2}(18 - 2h)(8 - 2h)h$, 48 in^2, $h = 2.5359$ in

12. a. 2 m b. 0.5924 m

13. 4.2154 m

14.

x	−2	$-\sqrt{2}$	−1	0	$\sqrt{3}$	π
$f(x)$	1,046,529.	5,601.1	100	1	7,846.1	511,273,655.8
$f'(x)$	−8,382,462	−54,722.4	−900	−2	85,229.5	3,008,006,817.

1. $q(x) = 6x^3 + 10x^2 - 8x - 8$ $R = 0$
2. $q(x) = x^2 - 0.7x + 2.39$ $R = -0.503$
3. $q(x) = x^3 - 6.8x^2 + 21.84x - 72.992$
   $R = 283.3696$
4. $q(x) = 2x^4 - 0.9x^3 + 4.055x^2$
   $- 1.74225x + 0.1706375$
   $R = -0.820830625$
5. $q(x) = x^3 - 4.1x^2 + 7.81x - 36.021$
   $R = 167.6861$
6. $q(x) = x^9 + x^8 + x^7 + x^6 + x^5 + x^4$
   $+ x^3 + x^2 + x + 1$ $R = 0$
7. $q(x) = 7x^4 - 21x^3 + 57x^2 - 171x$
   $+ 513$ $R = -1{,}537$
8. $q(x) = 1.2x^3 + 1.56x^2 - 3.282x$
   $- 4.2666$ $R = -3.84658$
9. $q(x) = x^5 - 2x^4 + 3x^3 - 4x^2 + 5x - 6$
   $R = 7$
10. $q(x) = 0.2x^4 - 0.217x^3 + 0.297x^2$
    $- 0.45x + 0.925$ $R = -0.846$
    (coefficients and remainder rounded
    to three decimals)
11. $4.3125 - 1.5(x - \frac{1}{2}) - 1.5(x - \frac{1}{2})^2$
    $- 2(x - \frac{1}{2})^3 + (x - \frac{1}{2})^4$
12. $-1 + 5(x + 1) - 10(x + 1)^2$
    $+ 10(x + 1)^3 - 5(x + 1)^4 + (x + 1)^5$
13. $-0.05 + 1.75(x - 1) + 4(x - 1)^2$
    $+ 3(x - 1)^3 + 1.25(x - 1)^4$
    $+ 0.25(x - 1)^5$
14. $7(x - 1) + 21(x - 1)^2 + 35(x - 1)^3$
    $+ 35(x - 1)^4 + 21(x - 1)^5 + 7(x - 1)^6$
    $+ (x - 1)^7$
15. $1849 - 11{,}610(x + 2) + 33{,}619(x + 2)^2$
    $- 59{,}252(x + 2)^3 + 70{,}717(x + 2)^4$
    $- 60{,}182(x + 2)^5 + 37{,}443(x + 2)^6$
    $- 17{,}162(x + 2)^7 + 5{,}753(x + 2)^8$
    $- 1{,}376(x + 2)^9 + 223(x + 2)^{10}$
    $- 22(x + 2)^{11} + (x + 2)^{12}$

SECTION 1.9

1. 93.6
2. 49.066
3. 4.487
4. 498.778
5. 523,192.385
6. 20.833
7. 31.333
8. 11.333
9. 23.667
10. 43.104
11. 38.437
12. 14.028
13. 9.031
14. 65.067
15. 5.196

Chapter 2

1.

x	-3	-2	-1.5	-1.2	-1.1	-1.05	-0.95	-0.9	-0.8	-0.5	-0.2	0.0
$f(x)$	1.3	1.7	2.6	5.5	10.5	20.5	-19.5	-9.5	-4.6	-1.7	-1.1	-1.0

The graph is symmetric about the y-axis; $y = 1$ is a horizontal asymptote; $x = -1$ and $x = 1$ are vertical asymptotes; there are no roots.

2.

x	0.05	0.10	0.20	0.50	1.0	1.5	2.0	2.5	3.0	4.0	5.0
$f(x)$	60.0	30.0	15.0	6.1	4.0	5.4	9.5	16.8	28.0	64.8	125.6

The graph is symmetric about the origin; $x = 0$ is a vertical asymptote; there are no roots.

3.

x	-1.0	0.0	1.0	2.0	3.0	3.5	3.9	3.95	4.05	4.1	4.5	4.9	4.95	5.05
$f(x)$	-0.1	-0.1	-0.1	0.0	0.5	2.0	17.3	37.1	-43.2	-23.3	-10.0	-32.2	-62.1	58.1

x	5.1	5.5	6.0	6.5	7.0	8.0	25.0
$f(x)$	28.2	4.7	2.0	1.2	0.8	0.5	0.1

The graph is not symmetric about the origin or the y-axis; $x = 4$ and $x = 5$ are vertical asymptotes; $y = 0$ is a horizontal asymptote; $x = 2.0000$ is the only root.

4.

x	0	1.0	2.0	2.5	2.75	2.95	2.99	3.01	3.05	3.5	4.0
$f(x)$	-0.4	-0.5	-0.8	-1.5	-2.8	-13.4	-66.8	66.6	13.2	1.2	0.6

The graph is symmetric about the y-axis; $y = 0$ is a horizontal asymptote; $x = -3$ and $x = 3$ are vertical asymptotes; there are no roots.

5.

x	-5.0	-4.0	-3.0	-2.5	-2.25	-2.1	-2.05	-1.95	-1.9	-1.75	-1.5	-1.0	-0.5	0.0
$f(x)$	1.4	1.7	2.4	3.9	6.9	15.9	30.9	-29.1	-14.1	-5.1	-2.1	-0.7	-0.2	0.0

x	0.5	1.0	1.5	1.75	1.95	1.99	2.01	2.05	2.25	2.5	3.0	4.0	5.0	6.0	7.0
$f(x)$	0.1	0.0	-0.4	-1.4	-9.4	-49.4	50.6	10.6	2.6	1.7	1.2	1.0	1.0	0.9	0.9

x	8.0	9.0	10.0
$f(x)$	0.9	0.9	0.9

The graph has no symmetries; $x = -2$ and $x = 2$ are vertical asymptotes; $y = 1$ is a horizontal asymptote; $r_1 = 0.0000$ and $r_2 = 1.0000$ are the roots.

6.

x	-3.0	-2.0	-1.0	0.0	1.0	1.5	2.0	2.1	2.2	2.3	2.32	2.34	2.4	2.5
$f(x)$	-0.3	-0.4	-0.5	-0.7	-1.3	-2.0	-5.0	-7.1	-12.5	-50.0	-125.0	250	25.0	10.0

x	3.0	4.0	5.0	6.0	7.0	10.0	25.0	100
$f(x)$	2.5	1.0	0.6	0.5	0.4	0.2	0.1	0.0

The graph has no symmetries; $x = \dfrac{7}{3}$ is a vertical asymptote; $y = 0$ is a horizontal asymptote; there are no roots.

7.

x	−3.0	−2.5	−2.0	−1.5	−1.45	−1.43	−1.42	−1.41	−1.40	−1.35	−1.2	−1.0	−0.5
f(x)	−0.5	−0.7	−1.2	−7.3	−17.4	−39.3	−106.9	146.5	43.3	9.5	2.7	1.3	0.5

x	0.0	0.2	0.5	1.0	1.2	1.35	1.40	1.41	1.42	1.43	1.45	1.5	2.0	2.5
f(x)	0.2	0.1	−0.1	−0.7	−1.5	−5.7	−26.7	−90.5	66.3	24.4	10.9	4.7	0.8	0.5

x	3.0	5.0	10.0	25.0
f(x)	0.4	0.2	0.1	0.0

The graph has no symmetries; $x = -\sqrt{2}$ and $x = \sqrt{2}$ are vertical asymptotes; $y = 0$ is a horizontal asymptote; $r = 0.3333$ is the only root.

8.

x	−5.0	−4.0	−3.0	−2.0	−1.5	−1.0	−0.75	−0.50	−0.25	0.0
f(x)	0.2	0.3	0.5	0.8	1.0	1.2	1.3	1.3	1.4	1.4

The graph is symmetric about the y-axis; $y = 0$ is a horizontal asymptote; there are no roots.

9.

x	−3.0	−2.0	−1.0	−0.5	−.25	−0.1	−0.05	−0.01	0.01	0.1	0.2	0.5	1.0	1.25
f(x)	0.7	0.6	0.6	0.8	1.3	3.2	6.5	33.1	−33.6	−3.6	−2.1	−1.5	−3.0	−6.6

x	1.45	1.49	1.51	1.52	1.55	2.0	2.5	3.0	4.0	6.0	10.0	50.0
f(x)	−35.9	−182.6	184.1	92.4	37.5	4.5	2.7	2.1	1.7	1.4	1.2	1.0

The graph has no symmetries; $y = 1$ is a horizontal asymptote; $x = 0$ and $x = 1.5$ are vertical asymptotes; there are no roots.

10.

x	−4.0	−3.0	−2.0	−1.5	−1.25	−1.1	−1.05	−1.01	−0.99	−0.95	−0.90	−0.50	0.0	1.0
f(x)	1.0	1.0	1.1	1.4	2.0	4.0	7.3	34.0	−32.7	−6.0	−2.7	−0.1	0.0	0.5

x	1.5	2.0	2.5	3.0	4.0
f(x)	0.8	0.9	0.9	1.0	1.0

The graph has no symmetries; $x = -1$ is a vertical asymptote; $y = 1$ is a horizontal asymptote; $r = 0$ is the only root.

11.

x	−4.0	−3.0	−2.5	−2.25	−2.1	−2.01	−1.99	−1.9	−1.75	−1.5	−1.0	0.0	0.5
f(x)	25.7	20.5	22.9	32.8	66.0	575.5	−557.9	−48.4	−15.1	−4.9	−1.0	−0.5	−0.9

x	0.75	0.95	0.99	1.01	1.05	1.25	1.5	2.0	2.5	3.0	4.0	6.0
f(x)	−1.9	−12.3	−65.6	67.8	14.5	4.2	3.5	4.3	5.9	8.2	14.3	32.4

The graph has no symmetries; $x = -2$ and $x = 1$ are vertical asymptotes; there are no roots.

12.

x	−3.0	−2.0	−1.5	−1.25	−1.1	−1.01	−0.99	−0.95	−0.75	−0.5	0.0	0.5	0.75	0.95
f(x)	−0.3	−0.5	−0.9	−1.7	−4.0	−37.7	37.3	7.3	1.3	0.5	0.0	−0.4	−1.0	−5.0

x	0.99	1.01	1.1	1.25	1.5	2.0	2.5	2.75	2.95	2.99	3.01	3.25	3.5	4.0	5.0
f(x)	−25.0	25.0	2.5	1.0	0.4	0.0	−0.5	−1.3	−7.3	−37.3	37.7	1.7	0.9	0.5	0.3

The graph has no symmetries; $x = -1$, $x = 1$, and $x = 3$ are vertical asymptotes; $y = 0$ is a horizontal asymptote; $r_1 = 0.0000$ and $r_2 = 2.0000$ are the roots.

13.

v	0.01	0.05	1.0	1.5	2.0	2.5	3.0	4.0	5.0	6.0	7.0	8.0	9.0	10.0	20.0
$p \times 10^2$	300	60	30	20	15	12	10	7.5	6.0	5.0	4.3	3.6	3.3	3.0	1.5

v	30.0	40.0	50.0	100.0
$p \times 10^2$	1.0	0.75	0.6	0.3

The line $v = 0$ is a vertical asymptote, and $p = 0$ is a horizontal asymptote.

14.

$x(\%)$	10	20	30	40	50	60	70	80	90	95	99
$C(x)$	0.7	1.7	2.9	4.4	6.7	10.0	15.5	26.6	59.9	126.4	658.4

Thus the cost to remove 99 percent of the pollutant is $658,400 (approximately); $x = 100$ is a vertical asymptote, so it is not possible to remove 100 percent of the pollutant.

15.

x	1	2	3	4	5	6	7	8	9	10	11
$C(x)$	2,370.5	1,214.5	842.2	665.8	567.7	508.8	472.4	449.9	436.7	430.1	428.2

x	12	13	14	15	20	25	30	40	50	100
$C(x)$	429.9	434.3	440.9	449.2	507.6	581.5	663.4	838.8	1,022.0	1,973.5

Thus 11 machines give a minimum cost of $428.20.

16. 15.625 lb
17. $r = -0.7937$
18. $r = 1.4000$
19. $r = 1.7100$
20. $r_1 = -1.0000$
    $r_2 = 3.0000$
21. $r_1 = 2.6180$
    $r_2 = 0.3820$
22. $r_1 = -1.1774$
    $r_2 = 1.3216$
    $r_3 = 3.8558$
23. $r = 1.8231$

SECTION 2.2

1.

x	0.00	0.25	0.50	0.75	1.00	1.50	2.00	2.50	3.00	4.00	5.00	6.00	8.00	10.00	20.00
y	0.00	0.63	0.79	0.91	1.00	1.14	1.26	1.36	1.44	1.59	1.71	1.82	2.00	2.15	2.71

x	40.00	100.00
y	3.42	4.64

The graph is symmetric about the origin.

2. Since $x - x^2 = x(1 - x)$ must be positive, the variable x satisfies $0 \leqslant x \leqslant 1$. There are no symmetries.

x	0.0	0.10	0.20	0.30	0.40	0.50	0.60	0.70	0.80	0.90	1.00
y	0.0	0.30	0.40	0.46	0.49	0.50	0.49	0.46	0.40	0.30	0.00

Note that $y^2 = x - x^2$ or $y^2 = -(x - \frac{1}{2})^2 + \frac{1}{4}$. Thus $(x - \frac{1}{2})^2 + y^2 = \frac{1}{4}$. The graph is a circle with center $C(\frac{1}{2}, 0)$ and radius $r = \frac{1}{2}$.

3.

x	0.0	0.5	1.0	1.5	2.0	2.5	3.0	3.5	4.0	4.5	5.0	10.0	15.0	20.0	25.0
y	3.00	3.04	3.16	3.35	3.61	3.91	4.24	4.61	5.00	5.41	5.83	10.44	15.30	20.2	25.18

x	30.0	35.0	40.0	50.0	100.0
y	30.15	35.13	40.11	50.09	100.04

Note that the value of y approaches the value of x as x gets larger and larger: The line $y = x$ is an *asymptote*. The graph is symmetric about the y-axis.

4.

x	−5.0	−4.0	−3.0	−2.0	−1.0	0.0	0.25	0.50	0.75	1.00	1.25	1.5	2.0	3.0
y	−1.23	−0.44	0.24	0.76	1.00	0.00	1.69	2.89	3.98	5.00	5.98	6.93	8.76	12.24

x	4.0	5.0	10.0
y	15.56	18.77	33.92

5. Notice that x must satisfy $x > -0.5$ for the denominator.

x	−0.4	−0.3	−0.2	−0.1	0.0	0.25	0.50	0.75	1.00	1.25	1.50	1.75	2.00	2.5
y	15.12	10.74	8.83	7.73	7.00	5.97	5.48	5.26	5.20	5.25	5.38	5.57	5.81	6.43

x	3.0	3.5	4.0	5.0
y	7.18	8.04	9.0	11.16

The line $x = -0.5$ is a vertical asymptote.

6. Notice that x must satisfy $x < -1$ or $x \geqslant 0$ in order not to attempt the square root of a negative number.

x	−100	−50	−10	−5.0	−4.0	−3.0	−2.0	−1.5	−1.25	−1.1	−1.01	−1.001
y	1.01	1.01	1.05	1.12	1.15	1.22	1.41	1.73	2.24	3.32	10.05	31.64

x	−1.0001	0.0	1.0	2.0	3.0	4.0	5.0	10	20	40	100
y	100.00	0.0	0.71	0.82	0.87	0.89	0.91	0.95	0.98	0.99	1.00

The line $x = -1$ is a vertical asymptote, and $y = 1$ is a horizontal asymptote. There are no symmetries.

7.

x	0.0	0.10	0.20	0.30	0.40	0.50	0.60	0.70	0.80	0.90	1.00	1.5	2.0	2.5
y	0.0	−0.36	−0.38	−0.37	−0.34	−0.29	−0.24	−0.19	−0.13	−0.07	0.00	0.36	0.74	1.14

x	3.0	4.0	5.0	10.0
y	1.56	2.41	3.29	7.85

The graph is symmetric about the origin.

8. Observe that x must be nonnegative.

x	0.0	0.5	1.0	1.5	2.0	2.5	3.0	3.5	4.0	4.5	5.0	7.0	9.0	11.0	13.0
y	0.0	0.46	0.50	0.47	0.41	0.33	0.23	0.12	0.0	−0.13	−0.26	−0.85	−1.50	−2.18	−2.89

x	15.0	20.0	50.0	100.0
y	−3.63	−5.53	−17.93	−40.00

9.

x	−10.0	−5.0	−4.0	−3.0	−2.0	−1.0	−0.75	−0.50	−0.25	0.0	0.25	0.50	0.75	1.00
y	9.95	7.34	6.69	5.96	5.11	4.00	3.64	3.22	2.66	1.0	0.14	0.04	0.01	0.00

x	1.25	1.50	2.0	2.5	3.0	4.0	5.0	10.0	15.0	20.0	50.0
y	0.01	0.02	0.07	0.13	0.20	0.35	0.50	1.33	2.15	2.94	7.20

10.

x	0.0	0.5	1.0	1.5	2.0	2.5	3.0	3.5	4.0	5.0
y	6.25	4.00	2.25	1.00	0.25	0.00	0.25	1.00	2.25	6.25

The graph is symmetric about the y-axis.

11. $r_1 = 0.0000$
$r_2 = 2.3704$

12. $r_1 = 0.0000$
$r_2 = 3.2796$

13. $r_1 = -3.3750$
$r_2 = 0.0000$

14. $r_1 = 0.6458$
$r_2 = 6.6120$

SECTION 2.3

1. 0.47997
2. 3.80045
3. 5.62431
4. −0.21118
5. 10.10895
6. 3.07986
7. 115.35°
8. 49.53°
9. −96.67°
10. 281.96°
11. 612°
12. −570°
13. −0.75680
14. 0.99719
15. −1.64835
16. −0.32423
17. 1.07029
18. −1.09462
19.

x	0.0	0.5	1.0	1.5	2.0	2.5	3.0	3.5	4.0	4.5	5.0	5.5	6.0	6.5	7.0	7.5	8.0
y	−1.0	−0.4	0.3	0.9	1.3	1.4	1.1	0.6	−0.1	−0.8	−1.2	−1.4	−1.2	−0.8	−0.1	0.6	1.1

20.

x	0.00	0.25	0.50	0.75	1.00	1.25	1.50	1.75	2.00	2.25	2.50	2.75	3.00	3.25	3.50
y	0.00	0.58	0.84	0.96	1.00	0.97	0.88	0.76	0.60	0.43	0.25	0.06	−0.13	−0.30	−0.46

x	3.75	4.00
y	−0.61	−0.73

21.

x	−4.0	−3.5	−3.0	−2.5	−2.0	−1.5	−1.0	−0.5	0.0	0.5	1.0	1.5	2.0	2.5	3.0
y	16.7	13.2	10.0	7.1	4.4	2.2	0.5	−0.6	−1.0	−0.6	0.5	2.2	4.4	7.1	10.0

x	3.5	4.0
y	13.2	16.7

22.

x	0.0	0.4	0.8	1.2	1.6	2.0	2.4	2.7	3.1	3.5	3.9	4.3	4.7	5.1	5.5	5.9	6.3
y	2.0	1.4	−0.1	−1.6	−2.0	−1.1	0.4	1.7	1.9	0.9	−0.7	−1.9	−1.8	−0.6	1.0	1.9	1.7

$\Delta x = \pi/8 \approx 0.4$

23.

x	0.0	0.4	0.8	1.2	1.6	2.0	2.4	2.7	3.1	3.5	3.9	4.3	4.7	5.1	5.5	5.9
y	−4.0	−4.0	−3.9	−3.7	−3.5	−3.2	−2.8	−2.4	−2.0	−1.5	−1.0	−0.5	0.0	0.5	1.0	1.5

x	6.3
y	2.0

$\Delta x = \pi/8 \approx 0.4$

24.

x	0.00	0.25	0.50	0.75	1.00	1.25	1.50	1.75	2.00	2.25	2.50	2.75	3.00	3.25
y	−1.92	−1.79	−0.70	0.76	1.82	1.90	0.96	−0.49	−1.68	−1.97	−1.20	0.22	1.51	2.00

x	3.50	3.75	4.00
y	1.41	0.07	−1.31

25.

x	0.0	0.4	0.8	1.2	1.6	2.0	2.4	2.7	3.1	3.5	3.9	4.3	4.7	5.1	5.5	5.9	6.3
y	0.0	0.4	0.6	0.5	0.0	−0.8	−1.7	−2.5	−3.1	−3.3	−2.8	−1.7	0.0	2.0	3.9	5.4	6.3

$\Delta x = \pi/8 \approx 0.4$

26.

x	−0.9	−0.7	−0.5	−0.3	−0.1	0.1	0.3	0.5	0.7	0.9	1.1	1.3	1.5	1.7	1.9
y	−5.0	−2.4	−1.5	−1.0	−0.7	−0.4	−0.2	0.0	0.2	0.4	0.7	1.0	1.5	2.4	5.0

$\Delta x = \pi/16 \approx 0.2$

The graph has vertical asymptotes at $x = -\pi/3$ and $x = 2\pi/3$.

27.

x	0.0	0.2	0.4	0.6	0.8	0.9	1.1	1.3	1.5	1.7	1.9	2.1	2.3	2.4	2.6	2.8	3.0
y	−4.2	22.5	3.2	2.1	2.1	3.1	18.7	−4.3	−2.3	−2.0	−2.6	−6.7	7.1	2.6	2.0	2.3	4.2

The graph has vertical asymptotes at $x = \dfrac{1}{2\pi}$, $1 + \dfrac{1}{2\pi}$, and $2 + \dfrac{1}{2\pi}$ ($\dfrac{1}{2\pi} \approx 0.1592$).

28.

x	0.0	0.4	0.8	1.2	1.6	2.0	2.4	2.7	3.1	3.5	3.9	4.3	4.7	5.1	5.5	5.9	6.3
y	3.0	2.6	1.4	0.1	−1.0	−1.5	−1.4	−1.1	−1.0	−1.1	−1.4	−1.5	−1.0	0.1	1.4	2.6	3.0

x	6.7	7.1	7.5	7.9	8.2	8.6	9.0	9.4	9.8	10.2	10.6	11.1	11.4	11.8	12.2	12.6
y	2.6	1.4	0.1	−1.0	−1.5	−1.4	−1.1	−1.0	−1.1	−1.4	−1.5	−1.0	0.1	1.4	2.6	3.0

$\Delta x = \pi/8 \approx 0.4$

29.

x	-3.1	-2.4	-1.6	-0.8	0.0	0.8	1.6	2.4	3.1	3.9	4.7	5.5	6.3	7.1	7.9	8.6	9.4
y	0.0	0.3	0.6	0.9	1.0	0.9	0.6	0.3	0.0	-0.2	-0.2	-0.1	0.0	0.1	0.1	0.1	0.0

Note that $\Delta x = \pi/4 \approx 0.8$. The indicated $x = 0$ is actually the value $x = -1.5 \times 10^{-12}$ because of roundoff error. Thus no division by zero is taking place. So if we assign the value $y = 1.0$ when $x = 0.0$ we obtain a connected graph.

34. 18.85

35. 25.28

36. 1.42 rad

37. 1.35 rad

38. 2,171.18959 mi

39. 3°49'11"

42. 43.92 knots

SECTION 2.4

1.

x	-4.0	-3.5	-3.0	-2.5	-2.0	-1.5	-1.0	-0.5	0.0	0.5	1.0	1.5	2.0	2.5	3.0
y	54.6	33.1	20.1	12.3	7.5	4.7	3.1	2.3	2.0	2.3	3.1	4.7	7.5	12.3	20.1

x	3.5	4.0
y	33.1	54.6

Notice that the graph is symmetric about the y-axis.

2.

x	-3.0	-2.0	-1.0	0.0	1.0	2.0	3.0	4.0	5.0
y	27.0	9.0	3.0	1.0	0.3	0.1	0.0	0.0	0.0

The x-axis is a horizontal asymptote.

3.

x	-4.0	-3.0	-2.0	-1.0	0.0	1.0	2.0	3.0	4.0	5.0
y	0.0	0.0	0.1	0.3	0.5	0.7	0.9	1.0	1.0	1.0

The lines $y = 0$ and $y = 1$ are horizontal asymptotes.

4.

x	-2.0	-1.0	0.0	1.0	2.0	3.0	4.0	5.0
y	0.0	0.1	0.3	0.5	0.7	0.9	1.0	1.0

The lines $y = 0$ and $y = 1$ are horizontal asymptotes.

5.

x	-3.5	-3.0	-2.5	-2.0	-1.5	-1.0	-0.5	0.0	0.5	1.0	1.5	2.0
y	-0.1	-0.1	-0.2	-0.3	-0.3	-0.4	-0.3	0.0	0.8	2.7	6.7	14.8

The line $y = 0$ is a horizontal asymptote: $y \to 0$ as $x \to -\infty$.

6.

x	-3.0	-2.5	-2.0	-1.5	-1.0	-0.5	-0.4	-0.3	-0.2	-0.1	0.1	0.2	0.3	0.4	0.5
y	1.1	1.1	1.2	1.3	1.6	2.5	3.0	3.9	5.5	10.5	-9.5	-4.5	-2.9	-2.0	-1.5

x	1.0	1.5	2.0	3.0	4.0	5.0
y	-0.6	-0.3	-0.2	-0.1	0.0	0.0

The lines $y = 1$ and $y = 0$ are horizontal asymptotes; $x = 0$ is a vertical asymptote.

7.

x	−4.0	−3.0	−2.0	−1.0	−0.5	−0.4	−0.3	−0.2	−0.1	0.0
y	0.0	0.0	0.0	0.4	0.8	0.9	0.9	1.0	1.0	1.0

The graph is symmetric about the y-axis; $y = 0$ is a horizontal asymptote.

8.

x	−6.3	−4.7	−3.1	−1.6	0.0	1.6	3.1	4.7	6.3	7.9
y	0.0	0.0	0.0	0.0	1.0	0.0	−23.1	0.0	535.5	0.0

The graph is shown in Figure A.6.

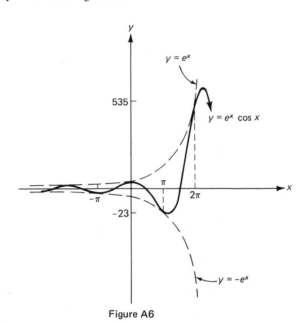

Figure A6

9. $0.55; $11,532 (rounded to the nearest dollar)
10. a. 65 million b. 80.2 million, 98.9 million
11. $(0.5)^{325/1,620} \approx 87$ percent
12. 1.85718386
13. 448 lb
14. 21.91° Celsius
15. 21.2768 in
16. Approximately 0.2419014289 atmospheres
17. Approximately 10.6 percent
18. $66,733.15

SECTION 2.5

1. a. The values of $f(x) - f(1)$ are: −0.32, −0.13, −0.0575, −0.0103, −0.001003, −0.00010003; 0.08, 0.07, 0.0425, 0.0097, 0.000997, 0.00009997
   b. The values of $f(x) - f(2)$ are: −1.52, −0.73, −0.3575, −0.0703, −0.007003, −0.00070003; 1.28, 0.67, 0.3425, 0.0697, 0.006997, 0.00069997

   The differences $f(x) - f(2)$ are larger in part b for the same values of h measuring how near x is to either 1 or 2. For example, when $h = -0.001, f(x) - f(2) = 0.006997$, whereas $f(x) - f(1) = 0.000997$.

2. Continuous everywhere
3. Continuous whenever $x \geqslant 1$
4. Continuous everywhere
5. Discontinuous at $x = -2$ and $x = 2$
6. Discontinuous at $x = 0$
7. Discontinuous at $x = 2$
8. Discontinuous when the denominator is zero: $x = -2.392, x = 0.675, x = 3.718$
9. Discontinuous when $\sin^2 x = 1$, or $x = n\pi/2$ for n an odd integer

SECTION 2.6

1. 14.0
2. −2.5
3. 1.5
4. 0.0
5. −0.5
6. 0.4082
7. 0.2887
8. 0.5
9. 2.7183
10. 7.3891
11. 2.0
12. 1.5
13. −0.5
14. 0.3679
15. −0.1667
16. 0.125
17. 2.7183
18. 0.6931
19. 0.0
20. 2.0
21. 0.3333
22. 0.5
23. −1.0
24. 2.0

25. Yes; define $f(0) = 0$
26. No, because $\lim\limits_{x \to -1^-} f(x) = 3$ and $\lim\limits_{x \to -1^+} f(x) = 2$
27. No, because $\lim\limits_{x \to 4^-} f(x) = -1$ and $\lim\limits_{x \to 4^+} f(x) = 1$
28. No, because $x = 0$ is a vertical asymptote.
29. Yes; define $f(1) = 1$
30. Horizontal asymptote: $y = 2$
    Vertical asymptote: $x = -6$
31. Horizontal asymptote: $y = 1$
    Vertical asymptotes: $x = -1$ and $x = $
32. Horizontal asymptote: $y = 1$
    Vertical asymptotes: $x = -2$ and $x = $
33. Horizontal asymptote: $y = 1$
    Vertical asymptote: $x = -1$
34. $\left[\dfrac{2x^3 - x^2 + 7}{x^2 + 4} - (2x - 1) \right] \to 0$
    as $x \to \infty$
35. 0.4124, 0.0164
36. mg/k   ft/sec
37. $\sqrt{mg/k}$ ft/sec

Chapter 3

SECTION 3.1

1. −5.09, −0.69
2. a. 369.84 ft/sec b. 90.38 ft/sec
3. 39.02
4. 12.13 m/sec
5. a. \$563.40 b. \$570.90
6. a. 52.20 ft/sec b. 8 sec c. 576 ft
7. a. 207,360,000 b. 9.25 lb/in²
   c. −0.15
8. 11.38 items/yr

9. 1,992 persons/yr (rounded)
10. 0.58
11. −2.11
12. 10.79
13. 515.12
14. −0.98
15. 4.33
16. a. 636,112,863 b. 40.585 lb
    c. −0.018677 lb/mi

SECTION 3.2

1. −4,192.75	**12.** 0.71
2. 0.275	**13.** 0.78
3. 0.275	**14.** 0.44
4. −48.31	**15.** 1.23
5. 3.49	**16.** 1.00
6. −0.361	**17.** 1.25
7. 3.97	**18.** 8.66
8. 4.50	**19.** −1.43
9. 16.09	**20.** 0.098
10. −2.72	**21.** 6.77
11. −0.10	**22.** 0.84

23. f is differentiable and $f'(1) = 4$.

24. Left-hand derivative is −1, right-hand derivative is 0, f is not differentiable at $x = 0$.

25. Left- and right-hand derivatives equal 5.437; f is not continuous and therefore not differentiable at $x = 1$.

26. Left-hand derivative is −1, right-hand derivative is +1, f is not differentiable at $x = 0$.

27. f is differentiable and $f'(0) = 0$.

28. $r'(1) = 3$ since r is continuous at $x = 1$.

29. $s'(0.25) = 0.091$, $s'(0.50) = -0.244$

Since the velocity is positive when $t = 0.25$ and negative when $t = 0.50$, the particle has reversed its direction at an instant t between these two times and is returning to the starting position.

30. $P(5) = 460,500$; $P'(5) = 164,000$ bacteria/hr.

SECTION 3.3

1. 7.828, −1.312, −4.500, 1.002, concave downward

2. 0.753, 1.522, −1.424, 0.236, concave downward

3. 1.395, 0.901, −0.481, 0.197, concave downward

4. 3.035, −0.056, 0.090, 0.089, concave upward

5. −1.683, −3.242, 15.146, 0.388, concave upward

6. 0.892, 0.093, −0.112, 0.111, concave downward

7. 3.280, 3.842, 3.280, 0.052, concave upward

8. −0.253, −0.134, −0.015, 0.015, concave downward

9. 6.413, −5.677, 1.175, 0.006, concave upward

10. 1.555, −1.251, 3.107, 0.757, concave upward

11. (−1,2) and (1,2)

12. (3,0)

13. (−0.577, 0.75) and (0.577, 0.75)

14. (2.000, 0.271)

15. (−0.789, 0.028) and (−0.211, 0.028)

16. No points of inflection

17. $v = -2.186$, $a = -0.507$

18. a. $t = 5$ sec   b. 162.5 m/sec   c. 541.67 m

19. a. 50.96839959 sec   b. 12,742.0999 m   c. −9.81 m/sec²

20. a. 44.145 m/sec   b. 99.326 m   c. 5.008 sec

1. Max: $f(-0.333) = 19.852$, min: $f(3) = -32$
2. Max: $f(1.333) = 0.756$, min: $f(0) = 0$
3. Max: $f(1.500) = 1.299$, min: $f(0) = f(2) = 0$
4. No maximum, min: $f(25.502) = 44.167$
5. Max: $f(1.500) = 1.310$, no minimum
6. Max: $f(0.463) = 2.236$, no minimum
7. No maximum, min: $f(-0.524) = 1.732$
8. Max: $f(8.378) = 5.055$, no minimum
9. Max: $f(1) = 1$, min: $f(-0.707) = -1.414$
10. Max: $f(0.262) = f(1.309) = 1.500$, min: $f(2.356) = -3.000$
11. $y = x + 1/x$ has an absolute minimum at $x = 1$
12. Area sum $= \dfrac{x^2}{4\pi} + \dfrac{\sqrt{3}}{36}(5 - x)^2$ has a minimum value at $x = 1.884$ m, where x represents the circumference of the circle. Then $5 - x = 3.116$ m is the length of the part bent into a triangle.
13. $Q = x(19 - x)^3$ is an absolute maximum at $x = 4.75$; $19 - x = 14.25$
14. C is located $x = 1.565$ mi down the beach from P, obtained by minimizing the time
$$T = \frac{1}{3}\sqrt{(1.75)^2 + x^2} + \frac{1}{4.5}(3.2 - x).$$
15. $A = 2xy = 2x\sqrt{(6.31)^2 - x^2}$ is a maximum when $x = 4.462$ and $y = 4.462$ m. The rectangle is 8.924 by 4.462.
16. Maximize $A = xy$ where $2x + \pi y = 225$. Here x is the length of the rectangle, and y its width (and the diameter of each semicircle at the ends). The solution is $x = 56.250$ ft and $y = 35.810$ ft.
17. Minimize total cost $= \dfrac{(785)(1.37)}{29.6}\left(\dfrac{77}{x} + \dfrac{x}{41.5}\right)$ to obtain $x = 56.529$ mph.
18. $P = (11x - 1.5x^2) - \left(\dfrac{x^3}{2.9} - 4.1x^2 + 9x\right)$ is maximized at $x = 5.386$. The maximum profit occurs when 5,386 units are produced.
19. $D = \sqrt{(x - 1.37)^2 + (\sqrt{x} - 2.49)^2}$ is at a minimum when $x = 1.798$ and $y = \sqrt{x} = 1.341$.
20. $D = \sqrt{(35 - 11.2t)^2 + (9.3t)^2}$ has the minimum value of 22.359 ft when $t = 1.850$ sec.
21. $y + 2\sqrt{(16 + (3 - y)^2}$ is an absolute minimum when $y = 0.69060$ cm, the distance of P from C.
22. $C = (27.5)\pi r^2 + (15.5)2\pi rh$ and $\pi r^2 h = 10,000$, where r is the radius of the tank and h is its height. The cost C has the minimum value \$38,268.07 when $r = 12.151$ ft.
23. Minimize $L = 4.5 \csc\theta + 6.2 \sec\theta$ to obtain $L = 15.06805$ ft when $\theta = 0.73209$ rad.

SECTION 3.5

1. $df = 0.0036$, $\Delta f = 0.0037$
2. $df = 1.7277$, $\Delta f = 1.7480$
3. $df = 0.9748$, $\Delta f = 0.9844$
4. $df = -0.0801$, $\Delta f = 0.2015$
5. $df = 0.0045$, $\Delta f = 0.0045$
6. $df = 0.0167$, $\Delta f = 0.0174$
7. $df = -1.3459$, $\Delta f = -1.3252$
8. $df = 73.7661$, $\Delta f = 87.2978$
9. $df = -0.0500$, $\Delta f = -0.0499$
10. $df = 0.0066$, $\Delta f = 0.0065$

11. $L(x) = 10.07x - 5.30$
12. $L(x) = -0.58x + 1.15$
13. $L(x) = -0.15x - 0.07$
14. $L(x) = 1.07x - 0.01$
15. $L(x) = -0.42x + 1.30$.
16. 27.1096 cm^3
17. ± 45.3332 in^3, 45.2389 in^3
18. 0.3555 m^3
19. 45.9653 cm^2, 6.1 percent
20. Within 0.5 percent

1. $51x^2 - 18x + 4$

2. $-10x^{-6} - 26x^{-3} + 4 + 14x$

3. $\frac{4}{7}x^{-6/7} - 6x^2 + 5x^{-8/3}$

4. $4(14x - 3x^2 + 2x^{1/2})^3(14 - 6x + x^{-1/2})$

5. $(2 + x^2)^2(78x - 8x^3 - 10x^5)$

6. $(3x^4 - 3x + 3)(x^4 - 2x + 3)^{-1/2}$

7. $\dfrac{2x(x^2 + x - 1)}{(x + 1)^2}$

8. $\dfrac{2(5x^2 - 4x - 7)}{(3x^2 - 2x + 5)^2}$

9. $-\dfrac{1}{x^2} + \dfrac{1}{2\sqrt{x}}$

10. $\dfrac{-2(x^5 - x^4 + 2x^3 - 4x^2 + 4x + 1)}{[(x - 2)(x^3 + 2)]^2}$

11. $\dfrac{6(x - 1)^2}{(x + 1)^4}$

12. $\dfrac{3}{2}(3\sqrt{x} + 2x - 5)^{1/2}\left(\dfrac{3}{2\sqrt{x}} + 2\right)$

13. $2(4 - 3x^2)^{-1/3}(2 - 5x)^5(55x^2 - 4x - 60)$

14. $2e^{2x}$

15. $\tan x \sec x\,(1 + 2\sec x)$

16. $e^x(\tan x + \sec^2 x)$

17. $-e^{-x}(\sin x + \cos x)$

18. $2(e^{2x} - e^{-2x})$

19. $\dfrac{1}{2}\sin x\,(\sin^2 x + \cos x)^{-1/2}(2\cos x - 1)$

20. $x^2 e^x(x + 3)$

21. $x \cos x$

22. $\tan^2 x$

23. $\dfrac{e^{-x}}{(1 + e^{-x})^2}$

24. $e^{-x}(1 - x)$

25. $-\cot x\,\csc^2 x\,(2 + 3\cot x)$

26. $\dfrac{dy}{dx} = \lim_{\Delta x \to 0}\dfrac{\dfrac{1}{x + \Delta x} - \dfrac{1}{x}}{\Delta x} = \lim_{\Delta x \to 0}\dfrac{-\Delta x}{\Delta x(x + \Delta x)(x)} = -\dfrac{1}{x^2}$

27. $\dfrac{dy}{dx} = \lim_{\Delta x \to 0}\dfrac{\sin(x + \Delta x) - \sin x}{\Delta x}$

$\qquad = \lim_{\Delta x \to 0}\dfrac{\sin x \cos \Delta x + \cos x \sin \Delta x - \sin x}{\Delta x}$

$\qquad = \lim_{\Delta x \to 0}\left[\sin x\left(\dfrac{\cos \Delta x - 1}{\Delta x}\right) + \cos x\left(\dfrac{\sin \Delta x}{\Delta x}\right)\right]$

$\qquad = (\sin x)(0) + (\cos x)(1) = \cos x$

1. 5.143
2. −0.005
3. 2.185
4. 0.953
5. 2.456
6. 0.247
7. $\frac{2}{3}(5x^4 - 3x^3 + 4x - 3)^{-1/3}(20x^3 - 9x^2 + 4)$
8. $\frac{1}{2}\left(x + \frac{1}{x}\right)^{-1/2}\left(1 - \frac{1}{x^2}\right)$
9. $\cos(5x - 2) - 5x \sin(5x - 2)$
10. $\dfrac{\sec 3\sqrt{x}}{2x\sqrt{x}}(3\sqrt{x} \tan 3\sqrt{x} - 1)$
11. $20(3 - e^{-5x})^3 e^{-5x}$
12. $-2xe^{-x^2} \cos(e^{-x^2})$
13. $3x^2 \sec^2 x^3 e^{\tan x^3}$
14. $e^{-2x}(\cos x - 2 \sin x)$
15. $0.150 \text{ cm}^2/\text{sec}$
16. Decreasing at 1.53 ft/sec
17. a. 0.279 ft/min   b. 0.208 ft/min
18. 2.456 ft/sec
19. 0.0865 in/sec
20. a. 62.65 mph b. 62.65 mph
21. 0.4348 ppm/yr
22. 0.0136 ft/min
23. −6.3059 ft/sec
24. −539.33
25. a. 10.969 ft/sec   b. 78 ft/sec
26. Decreasing at $6.341 \text{ cm}^2/\text{sec}$
27. 2.073 sec

Chapter 4

1. a. 3.76751875 b. 3.73251875
   c. 3.749990625
2. a. 5.574103313 b. 5.561775497
   c. 5.56794306
3. a. 0.694398743 b. 0.691898743
   c. 0.6931463993
4. a. 1.00392185 b. 0.9960678687
   c. 1.00000257
5. a. 25.27385108 b. 25.12518116
   c. 25.19967494
6. a. 19.91549131 b. 19.52113816
   c. 19.71732886

7. a. 10.0601 b. 9.9401 c. 9.99995
8. a. 1.493048084 b. 1.486370584
   c. 1.489695543
9. a. 2.491999152 b. 2.469104867
   c. 2.480638021
10. a. 325.5097682 b. 321.3040266
    c. 323.4036267

11.

n	$\underline{S}_n$	$\overline{S}_n$	S_n
100	0.245025	0.255025	0.2499875
200	0.24750625	0.25250625	0.249996875
500	0.249001	0.251001	0.2499995
1000	0.24950025	0.25050025	0.249999875

12.

n	$\underline{S}_n$	$\overline{S}_n$	S_n
100	1.897265236	1.9129732	1.905298426
200	1.901281831	1.909135813	1.905253625
500	1.903663115	1.906804708	1.90524108
1000	1.904452098	1.906022894	1.905239288

13. 54.00045
14. 16
15. 8.417199507
16. 1.0134531×10^{22}
17. 2.198314419
18. 1.000020562
19. 3.141594737
20. 0.5000051405

SECTION 4.2

1. 0.4055
2. 1.5708
3. 20.8333
4. 0.7854
5. 1.3090
6. 0.5236
7. 2.1789
8. 1.5774
9. 7.5610
10. 1.0681
11. 2.0635
12. 2.1983
13. 0.5000
14. 0.4534

15. 0.7854
16. 0.0210
17. 0.6931
18. 0.1449
19. 0.7408
20. -1.0607
21. $54.00000, n = 2$
22. $16.00000, n = 2$
23. $3.14159, n = 6$
24. $2.19833, n = 30$
25. $1.00000, n = 26$
26. $0.50000, n = 14$
27. $1.01620 \times 10^{22}, n = 266$
28. $8.41601, n = 11,500$

SECTION 4.3

1. $\frac{5}{8}x^8 + C$

2. $\frac{x^2}{2} - \frac{4}{x} + C$

3. $\frac{3}{4}x^{4/3} + 2x^{1/2} + C$

4. $\frac{1}{4}x^4 - \frac{2}{3}x^3 + \frac{1}{2}x^2 + C$

5. $\frac{2}{5}x^{5/2} - 2x^{1/2} + C$

6. $-4\cos x - 5\sin x + C$

7. $3e^x - \tan x + C$

8. $-2e^{-x} + \sec x + C$

9. $\dfrac{7}{x} - 3 \cot x + C$

10. $\sec x + C$

11. $\dfrac{2}{3} \theta \sqrt{\theta} + \cos \theta + C$

12. $\dfrac{1}{2} \phi^2 + 2 \tan \phi + C$

13. $\dfrac{1}{5} y^5 - \dfrac{2}{3} y^3 + y + C$

14. $-\cot t - \csc t + C$

15. 10

16. $e^3 - \dfrac{1}{e} \approx 19.718$

17. $\dfrac{1}{3}(10\sqrt{5} - 4\sqrt{2}) \approx 5.568$

18. 1

19. 23.49 ft

20. 729 ft

21. a. 13,956 ft   b. 58.534 sec after initial firing

22. $y = 3x^3 - 2x^2 + 2x + 9$

23. $C(x) = 0.25x - \dfrac{7,000}{x} + 5,757$

SECTION 4.4

1. $\dfrac{1}{2} \sin 2x + C$

2. $-e^{-x} + C$

3. $\dfrac{1}{3}(x^2 - 3)^{3/2} + C$

4. $\dfrac{2}{5}(w - 2)^{5/2} + \dfrac{4}{3}(w - 2)^{3/2} + C$

5. $\dfrac{3}{20}(x^4 - 2)^{5/3} + C$

6. $-(x^3 - x)^{-1} + C$

7. $\dfrac{4}{3} \sqrt{1 + x^{3/2}} + C$

8. $-2 \cos \sqrt{x} + C$

9. $\sec x + C$

10. $\tan x + \sec x + C$

11. $-e^{\cos y} + C$

12. $-\dfrac{1}{3} \sec^3 x + C$

13. $x \sin x + \cos x + C$

14. $(2 - x^2) \cos x + 2x \sin x + C$

15. $\dfrac{1}{2}(x - \sin x \cos x) + C$

16. $\dfrac{e^{2x}}{29}(5 \sin 5x + 2 \cos 5x) + C$

17. $\dfrac{-e^{-t}}{5}(\sin 2t + 2 \cos 2t) + C$

18. $-(x^2 + 2x + 2)e^{-x} + C$

19. $\dfrac{1}{2}(\theta + \sin \theta \cos \theta) + C$

20. $\dfrac{1}{4} \sin (2x + 1) - \dfrac{x}{2} \cos (2x + 1) + C$

21. $-\dfrac{1}{4} \sin^3 y \cos y - \dfrac{3}{8} \sin y \cos y + \dfrac{3}{8} \sin y + C$

22. $\dfrac{e^{ax}}{a^2 + b^2} [a \cos (bx) + b \sin (bx)] + C$

23. $\frac{2}{3}(1-x)^{3/2} - 2(1-x)^{1/2} + C$

24. $\frac{1}{3}(1+y^2)^{3/2} - (1+y^2)^{1/2} + C$

25. $\sin(e^t) - e^t \cos(e^t) + C$

26. $\sin\theta - \frac{1}{3}\sin^3\theta + C$

27. $\frac{2}{3}\sin^{3/2}x - \frac{2}{7}\sin^{7/2}x + C$

28. $\frac{2}{5}(x+1)^{5/2} - \frac{2}{3}(x+1)^{3/2} + C$

29. $\frac{x}{3}\sin^3 x - \frac{1}{9}\cos^3 x + \frac{1}{3}\cos x + C$

30. $\tan z - z + C$

SECTION 4.5

1. $x/(x^2 - 3)$

2. $\dfrac{\ln(x^2)}{x}$

3. $x^2(1 + 3\ln x)$

4. 2

5. $1/x(x+1)$

6. $\sec x$

7. $\ln\sqrt{x^2 + 1} + C$

8. $\ln(1 + \sin x) + C$

9. $\ln(\ln x) + C$

10. $\ln\sqrt{1 + e_{2y}} + C$

11. $-\cos(\ln t) + C$

12. $\ln|\tan t| + C$

13. $x\ln x - x + C$

14. $\frac{x}{2}[\sin(\ln x) - \cos(\ln x)] + C$

15. $\frac{x^2}{4}[\ln(x^2) - 1] + C$

16. $x(\ln x)^2 - 2x\ln x + 2x + C$

17. 0.5284822

18. 98.532582

19. a. 37.5774527   b. 197.5841203

20. a. $P_0 = 30, k = \dfrac{\ln 2}{3} \approx 0.231049$

   b. approximately 6.48585 in

   c. approximately -1.49855 in/mi

21. $e^{-(1,927/5,700)\ln 2} \approx 79.11$ percent

SECTION 4.6

1. 0.5

2. 0.4142135624

3. 0.4548225555

4. 25.45584412

5. 0.832901325 ($n = 200$)

6. Roots are -0.912765 and 1.118326; area is 1.367859124

7. 0.2097998913 ($n = 200$)

8. 6.785414879 ($n = 200$)

9. 2.256548915

10. 69.91641227

11. 77.24691672

12. 1.256637061

13. 18.49616004

14. 19.73847868 ($n = 500$)

15. 2.221441469

16. 79.69 (rounded)

17. 5.050683139

18. 0.3084251375

19. 1.426058198

20. 1.190434129

21. 1.060113296

22. 24.5610077

23. 2.003497112

24. 1.024444233 ($n = 100$)

25. 3.563121852

26. 10.67545559 ($n = 100$)

27. 8.826156781

28. 14.42359969

29. 1.1173422 ($n = 100$)

30. 0.5

31. 53.79°

32. 1.40494458 ($n = 1000$)

33. 0.9424779524 ($n = 200$)

34. 30.8464897

35. -0.240399

1. $2x/(1 + x^4)$

2. $\frac{1}{2}(x - x^2)^{-1/2}$

3. $e^x \left(\cos^{-1} x - \dfrac{1}{\sqrt{1 - x^2}} \right)$

4. $-(1 - x^2)^{-1/2}$

5. $\sin^{-1} x$

6. $3(\tan^{-1} x)^2/(1 + x^2)$

7. $\tan^{-1} x$

8. $2/(e^x + e^{-x})$

9. $1/[x(1 + \ln^2 x)]$

10. $-1/[(1 + x^2) \cot^{-1} x]$

11. $\frac{1}{2} \sin^{-1} x^2 + C$

12. $\sin^{-1} \frac{x}{4} + C$

13. $\frac{1}{2} \tan^{-1} \frac{x}{2} + C$

14. $\cos^{-1} (e^{-x}) + C$

15. $\dfrac{1}{\sqrt{3}} \tan^{-1} (\sqrt{3}\, x) + C$

16. $2 \sec^{-1} \sqrt{x} + C$

17. $\tan^{-1} (\sin x) + C$

18. $\cot^{-1} (\ln x) + C$

19. $\sin^{-1} (\ln x) + C$

20. $2 \sin^{-1} \sqrt{x} + C$

Chapter 5

SECTION 5.1

1.

x_k	y_k	$y(x_k)$
0.0	2.000	2.000
0.1	2.000	2.010
0.2	2.020	2.041
0.3	2.062	2.094
0.4	2.127	2.174
0.5	2.221	2.284
0.6	2.350	2.433
0.7	2.522	2.632
0.8	2.750	2.896
0.9	3.054	3.248
1.0	3.458	3.718

2.

x_k	y_k	$y(x_k)$
0.0	1.000	1.000
0.1	0.800	0.837
0.2	0.680	0.741
0.3	0.624	0.698
0.4	0.619	0.699
0.5	0.655	0.736
0.6	0.724	0.802
0.7	0.819	0.893
0.8	0.936	1.004
0.9	1.068	1.131
1.0	1.215	1.271

3.

x_k	y_k	$y(x_k)$
1.0	2.000	2.000
1.1	1.700	1.726
1.2	1.459	1.508
1.3	1.282	1.348
1.4	1.168	1.246
1.5	1.115	1.198
1.6	1.118	1.200
1.7	1.170	1.247
1.8	1.264	1.333
1.9	1.392	1.452
2.0	1.549	1.600

4.

x_k	y_k	$y(x_k)$
1.571	1.000	1.000
1.671	1.100	1.089
1.771	1.176	1.151
1.871	1.223	1.182
1.971	1.234	1.179
2.071	1.208	1.139

5.

x_k	y_k	$y(x_k)$
1.0	2.000	2.000
1.1	1.700	1.740
1.2	1.479	1.545
1.3	1.313	1.399
1.4	1.189	1.293
1.5	1.098	1.222
1.6	1.038	1.191
1.7	1.011	1.217
1.8	1.033	1.358
1.9	1.157	1.925

6.

h_k	x_k	y_k
	0.00	−1.000
0.10	0.10	−0.900
0.05	0.15	−0.868
0.15	0.30	−0.791
0.07	0.37	−0.774
0.12	0.49	−0.754
0.17	0.66	−0.742
0.03	0.69	−0.742
0.06	0.75	−0.742
0.10	0.85	−0.742
0.15	1.00	−0.740

7.

h_k	x_k	y_k
	0.00	0.785
0.05	0.05	0.785
0.10	0.15	0.782
0.10	0.25	0.775
0.12	0.37	0.759
0.02	0.39	0.755
0.03	0.42	0.749
0.08	0.50	0.729

8.

h_k	x_k	y_k
	0.000	0.000
0.010	0.010	0.010
0.020	0.030	0.030
0.021	0.051	0.053
0.049	0.100	0.107
0.090	0.190	0.218
0.060	0.250	0.308
0.100	0.350	0.483
0.150	0.500	0.828

SECTION 5.2

1.

x_k	(Modified Euler) y_k	(Runge-Kutta) y_k
0.0	2.000	2.000
0.1	2.000	2.010
0.2	2.040	2.041
0.3	2.083	2.094
0.4	2.172	2.174
0.5	2.271	2.284
0.6	2.429	2.433
0.7	2.615	2.632
0.8	2.886	2.896
0.9	3.222	3.248
1.0	3.695	3.718

2.

x_k	(Modified Euler) y_k	(Runge-Kutta) y_k
0.0	1.000	1.000
0.1	0.800	0.837
0.2	0.760	0.741
0.3	0.656	0.698
0.4	0.738	0.699
0.5	0.681	0.736
0.6	0.865	0.802
0.7	0.815	0.893
0.8	1.099	1.004
0.9	1.015	1.131
1.0	1.413	1.271

3.

x_k	(Modified Euler) y_k	(Runge-Kutta) y_k
1.0	2.000	2.000
1.1	1.700	1.726
1.2	1.518	1.508
1.3	1.317	1.348
1.4	1.273	1.246
1.5	1.153	1.198
1.6	1.256	1.200
1.7	1.168	1.247
1.8	1.444	1.333
1.9	1.295	1.452
2.0	1.832	1.600

4.

x_k	(Modified Euler) y_k	(Runge-Kutta) y_k
1.571	1.000	1.000
1.671	1.100	1.089
1.771	1.153	1.151
1.871	1.195	1.182
1.971	1.179	1.178
2.071	1.151	1.139

5.

x_k	(Modified Euler) y_k	(Runge-Kutta) y_k
1.0	2.000	2.000
1.1	1.700	1.740
1.2	1.558	1.545
1.3	1.362	1.399
1.4	1.308	1.293
1.5	1.186	1.222
1.6	1.199	1.191
1.7	1.173	1.217
1.8	1.313	1.358
1.9	1.639	1.926

6.

h_k	x_k	y_k
	0.00	−1.000
0.10	0.10	−0.918
0.05	0.15	−0.887
0.15	0.30	−0.827
0.07	0.37	−0.811
0.12	0.49	−0.794
0.17	0.66	−0.786
0.03	0.69	−0.786
0.06	0.75	−0.785
0.10	0.85	−0.785
0.15	1.00	−0.782

7.

h_k	x_k	y_k
	0.00	0.785
0.05	0.05	0.785
0.10	0.15	0.780
0.10	0.25	0.769
0.12	0.37	0.749
0.02	0.39	0.744
0.03	0.42	0.737
0.08	0.50	0.714

8.

h_k	x_k	y_k
	0.000	0.000
0.010	0.010	0.010
0.020	0.030	0.031
0.021	0.051	0.054
0.049	0.100	0.111
0.090	0.190	0.235
0.060	0.250	0.334
0.100	0.350	0.543
0.150	0.500	1.046

SECTION 5.3

1. $-\frac{1}{2}y^{-2} = \ln x + C$

2. $y(x^2 + C) = 2$

3. $\frac{1}{2}\cos y^2 + \tan x = C$

4. $\ln y - \frac{1}{y} = x^3 + C$

5. $y = x^2 + Cx^{-2}$

6. $4y - 2x + 1 = Ce^{-2x}$

7. $y = \frac{1}{2} + Ce^{-x^2}$

8. $y = e^{-2x} + Ce^{-3x}$

9. $y^2 + \ln y^2 = 2(x - 1)e^x + C$

10. $y = \ln\left(\frac{1}{2}e^{2x} + C\right)$

11. $y = 1 + Ce^{-\tan x}$

12. $y = C \sin x - \cos x$

SECTION 5.4

1. 61,023

2. 39.62 yrs

3. $r = r_0 - kt$

4. 1.7617 lb/gal

5. $61.1°$ F

6. $v^2 = \frac{mg}{k}(1 - e^{-2ky/m}); \sqrt{mg/k}$

7. $y(t) = ab\left[\dfrac{e^{(b-a)t} - 1}{be^{(b-a)t} - a}\right]$

8. 11.6 ft/sec

9. 95.8 percent remains after 100 years

10. $57,926.45

11. 99.468 percent

12. 0.179 percent

13. $v = \frac{mg}{12}(1 - e^{-12t/m}); \quad y = \frac{mgt}{12} + \frac{m^2 g}{144}(e^{-12t/m} - 1)$

Chapter 6

SECTION 6.1

1. Converges to 1
2. Converges to 3/2
3. Converges to 0
4. Diverges
5. Diverges
6. Converges to 0
7. Converges to 0
8. Converges to 1
9. Converges to 2
10. Diverges
11. Converges to 0
12. Diverges
13. Converges to ln 2

14. Converges to 1
15. Converges to 0
16. Diverges
17. Converges to $1/e$
18. Converges to 1
19. Converges to 1/3
20. Converges to 2
21. Converges to 0
22. Converges to 1/2
23. Converges to 2
24. Diverges
25. 0.73909
26. 0.61906

SECTION 6.2

1. $11.43456, E_6 = 0.23210$
2. $3.99994, E_7 = 0.00006$
3. $0.58425, E_{13} = 0.00399$
4. $15.49400, E_{11} = 0.00000$
5. 0.04287
6. 37.51563
7. −0.08000
8. −0.14464
9. 0.00003
10. −0.01221

11. $9/9 = 1$
12. 63/99
13. 126/99
14. 35,137/99,900
15. 0.00154
16. −0.00004
17. −0.00555
18. 0.00187
19. −6.69613
20. 4,948.09429

21. a. 25.58819 m   b. 28.33333 m

22. a. $A = \displaystyle\sum_{n=0}^{\infty} \frac{\sqrt{3}}{4} \left(\frac{1}{2}\right)^{2n} = 0.57735$ square units

   b. 0.57679 square units

23. $\displaystyle\sum_{n=0}^{\infty} \frac{2}{3} \left(\frac{1}{3}\right)^{n} w = w$; the total distance is the original width of the screen

SECTION 6.3

1. 1.51180
2. 1.33333
3. 2.10444
4. 26.00000
5. 3.99774

6. 19.02797
7. 1.03828
8. 1.77868
9. 0.85714
10. −0.74999

11. $0.36788, E = 0.00000$
12. $-0.76993, E = -0.30693$
13. $0.68654, E = -0.16222$
14. $-0.65023, E = -0.00010$
15. $0.18280, E = -0.04569$
16. $0.23576, E = 0.00000$
17. Converges
18. Diverges
19. Converges
20. Converges

21. Diverges
22. Converges
23. Converges
24. Diverges
25. Diverges
26. Converges
27. Diverges
28. Converges
29. Converges
30. Converges

SECTION 6.4

1. 0.66675
2. 0.88496
3. 2.19721
4. 0.52691
5. 5.08092
6. 0.40548
7. -0.69311
8. 2.71828
9. 0.70711

10. 7.38906
11. $R = 1$
12. $R = 1$
13. $R = +\infty$
14. $R = +\infty$
15. $R = 4$
16. $R = 2$
17. $R = 3$
18. $R = 1/2$

Index